PRAISE FOR *SPIRITUAL GUIDANCE ACROSS RELIGIONS*

"A wonderful resource for every professional working with different faith traditions. Whether [you are] organizing spiritual community or counseling an individual, this book and its team of authors opens the door to many historic and traditional paths in a way that makes those practicing each faith accessible and approachable. I recommend this book to everyone I know in ministry and in spiritual counseling and direction."

—**Rev. Tim Miner, OUnI**, executive director,
Council of Interfaith Communities of the United
States; secretary, Order of Universal Interfaith

"Why did no one ever do this before? This is an excellent, trustworthy, and needed resource for spiritual directors today!"

—**Fr. Richard Rohr, OFM**,
Center for Action and Contemplation

"Finally, the go-to textbook that chaplains and spiritual directors, the frontline of the interfaith movement, deserve.... Goes deeper than the traditional who-what-why-when-where approach to world religions by focusing on spiritual care and healing. It is about the lived depths of religion, along with the facts, and that humanizes everything. It's full of gold."

—**Paul Chaffee**, editor, *The Interfaith Observer* (*TIO*)

"The first—possibly *only*—book of its kind! This remarkable gift of a resource brings the revered experts, accessibly and intimately, into the hands of spiritual guides who aspire to serve the people of our world in ever-more aware and relevant ways."

—**Rev. Lauren Van Ham**, interfaith spiritual
director and dean, Chaplaincy Institute:
An Interfaith Seminary and Community

"A wealth of richly detailed information on interfaith spiritual guidance among religious and spiritual traditions from around the world. The contemporary spiritual guide would do well to have this dynamic book as part of their collection and as on-going education in the field."

—Anne Huffman, PhD, director,
MA in Spiritual Guidance, Sofia University

AFRICAN DIASPORA SPIRITUALITY ✢ AMERICAN METAPHYSICS ✢ HINDUISM
SPIRITUAL ECLECTICISM ✢ CONFUCIANISM ✢ DAOISM ✢ HUMANISM
JAINISM EASTERN ORTHODOX NISM
NEW CHRISTIANITY BAHÁ'Í FAITH BUDDHISM
UNITARIAN UNIVERSALISM ✢ ZOROASTRIANISM ✢
ISLAM AFRICAN DIASPORA SPIRITUALITY ✢ AMERICAN METAPHYSICS ✢
SPIRITUAL ECLECTICISM ✢ CONFUCIANISM ✢ DAOISM ✢ HUMANISM
JAINISM ✢ NATIVE AMERICAN RELIGION ✢ NEO-PAGANISM
JUDAISM NEW THOUGHT ✢ SHINTO ✢ SIKHISM ✢ BAHÁ'Í FAITH
UNITARIAN UNIVERSALISM ✢ ZOROASTRIANISM

AFRICAN DIASPORA
SPIRITUALITY
✢ AMERICAN
METAPHYSICS ✢
SPIRITUAL
ECLECTICISM ✢
CONFUCIANISM
✢ DAOISM ✢
HUMANISM
JAINISM ✢
NATIVE AMERICAN
RELIGION ✢ NEO-
PAGANISM
NEW THOUGHT
✢ SHINTO ✢
SIKHISM ✢ BAHA'Í

Spiritual
Guidance
across
Religions

AFRICAN DIASPORA
SPIRITUALITY
✢ AMERICAN
METAPHYSICS ✢
SPIRITUAL
ECLECTICISM ✢
CONFUCIANISM
✢ DAOISM ✢
HUMANISM
JAINISM ✢
NATIVE AMERICAN
RELIGION ✢
NEO-PAGANISM
NEW THOUGHT
✢ SHINTO ✢
SIKHISM ✢ BAHA'Í

ROMAN CATHOLICISM
AFRICAN DIASPORA SPIRITUALITY ✢ AMERICAN METAPHYSICS ✢
SPIRITUAL ECLECTICISM ✢ CONFUCIANISM ✢ DAOISM ✢ HUMANISM
JAINISM ✢ NATIVE AMERICAN RELIGION ✢ NEO-PAGANISM
EVANGELICAL CHRISTIANITY SIKHISM ✢ BAHÁ'Í FAITH
UNITARIAN UNIVERSALISM ✢ ZOROASTRIANISM ✢
AFRICAN DIASPORA SPIRITUALITY ✢ AMERICAN METAPHYSICS ✢
SPIRITUAL ECLECTICISM ✢ CONFUCIANISM ✢ DAOISM ✢ HUMANISM
JAINISM ✢ NATIVE AMERICAN RELIC REFORMED CHRISTIANITY
NEW THOUGHT ✢ SHINTO ✢ SIKHISM ✢ BAHÁ'Í FAITH
UNITARIAN UNIVERSALISM ✢ ZOROASTRIANISM ✢ MORMONISM
AFRICAN DIASPORA SPIRITUALITY ✢ AMERICAN METAPHYSICS ✢

Spiritual Guidance across Religions:
A Sourcebook for Spiritual Directors and Other Professionals Providing Counsel to People of Differing Faith Traditions
2014 Hardcover Edition, First Printing
© 2014 by John R. Mabry

For information regarding permission to reprint material from this book, please mail or fax your request in writing to SkyLight Paths Publishing, Permissions Department, at the address / fax number listed below, or email your request to permissions@skylightpaths.com.

Library of Congress Cataloging-in-Publication Data
Mabry, John R.
 Spiritual guidance across religions : a sourcebook for spiritual directors and other professionals providing counsel to people of differing faith traditions / edited by Rev. John R. Mabry, PhD.
    pages cm
 ISBN 978-1-59473-546-2
1. Spirituality. 2. Spiritual direction. 3. Counseling—Religious aspects. 4. Pastoral counseling. I. Title.
 BL624.M28 2014
 206'.1—dc23
                                2013050749
 ISBN 978-1-59473-565-3 (eBook)
10 9 8 7 6 5 4 3 2 1
Manufactured in the United States of America
Cover Design: Tim Holtz
Interior Design: Michael Myers
Cover art: Cloud image—© Markus Gann/Shutterstock.com; compass—Tim Holtz

SkyLight Paths Publishing is creating a place where people of different spiritual traditions come together for challenge and inspiration, a place where we can help each other understand the mystery that lies at the heart of our existence.

SkyLight Paths sees both believers and seekers as a community that increasingly transcends traditional boundaries of religion and denomination—people wanting to learn from each other, *walking together, finding the way.*

SkyLight Paths, "Walking Together, Finding the Way" and colophon are trademarks of LongHill Partners, Inc., registered in the U.S. Patent and Trademark Office.

Walking Together, Finding the Way
Published by SkyLight Paths Publishing
A Division of LongHill Partners, Inc.
Sunset Farm Offices, Route 4, P.O. Box 237
Woodstock, VT 05091
Tel: (802) 457-4000   Fax: (802) 457-4004
www.skylightpaths.com

Spiritual
Guidance
across
Religions

**A Sourcebook for Spiritual
Directors and Other
Professionals Providing Counsel
to People of Differing Faith
Traditions**

Edited by Rev. John R. Mabry, PhD

Walking Together, Finding the Way®
SKYLIGHT PATHS®
PUBLISHING
Woodstock, Vermont

A NOTE ON THE ORGANIZATION OF THIS BOOK

Religions are grouped by the geographical region of their initial emergence. The only exception to this is Christianity. This book was compiled with a largely North American readership in mind, and as there are so many varieties of Christianity in this culture, it seemed prudent to give it its own section. Religions from each region are listed in order of chronological emergence.

RELIGIONS BY ESTIMATED U.S. POPULATION

Evangelical Christianity

Roman Catholic Christianity

Mormonism

Judaism

Reformed Christianity

Eastern Orthodox Christianity

Islam

Buddhism

Hinduism

Spiritual Eclecticism

Unitarian Universalism

Neo-Paganism

Bahá'í Faith

Sikhism

Shinto

Humanism

New Thought (American Metaphysics)

Zoroastrianism

Native American Religion

African Diaspora Spirituality

Daoism

Jainism

Confucianism

CONTENTS

RELIGIONS ORIGINATING IN THE MIDDLE EAST

CHRISTIAN DENOMINATIONS

INTERFAITH, HUMANIST, AND ECLECTIC TRADITIONS

INTRODUCTION

Rev. John R. Mabry, PhD

When the phone rang, Peggy was delighted to discover that it was a potential client for her spiritual direction practice. The young man on the other end of the phone sounded a little nervous, but pleasant and intelligent. Peggy, being new to the ministry, was a little nervous herself, but as they introduced themselves to each other, they both began to relax. After a few minutes, the caller said, "I'm kind of scared to tell you this ... but I'm Shinto. Can I still come to see you?" Peggy assured him that she was open to people of all faith traditions and would be glad to meet with him. They set a date for their first appointment, said good-bye, and Peggy hung up the phone.

And instantly began to panic. "Oh my God," she said to her cat, "what in the world is Shinto? What do I know about guiding someone who's Shinto?" Peggy had been trained in a Christian spiritual direction program. She was an active Presbyterian, though she prided herself on being very open-minded. She did yoga, went on Buddhist meditation retreats with her friend Jan, and sometimes went to the Jewish Renewal synagogue with another friend.

But her training had not prepared her to direct someone who was Shinto—or from any other faith tradition. What should she do? What should she read? Whom should she call? Her cat licked a paw and did not seem to comprehend the gravity of her questions.

AN INTERFAITH WORLD

These are vital questions for any ministry or profession that involves spiritual guidance. In the spiritual direction certificate program I direct at the Chaplaincy Institute in Berkeley, California, we specifically work to prepare students to provide effective and responsible spiritual guidance to anyone who walks through the door—no matter what faith tradition the client comes from (even if it is no faith at all).

I believe that interfaith training in spiritual direction and other ministry contexts is vital, because the days of segregated communities being tended solely by their proprietary clergy are over; fewer and fewer people are affiliating with spiritual communities, and hospital and hospice settings cannot afford to hire a wide selection of chaplains to serve their patients. As any working spiritual director can tell you, he or she is seeing people from a wide variety of faith traditions in his or her practice. Without a doubt, the era of interfaith ministry is upon us.

The book you are holding grew out of an attempt to address this very great need. It is a resource intended to help spiritual directors and other ministers provide effective spiritual guidance to people outside their own faith tradition—information that most spiritual directors and ministers are not provided in their training.

MEANING AND STRUCTURE

At the school where I teach spiritual direction, the Chaplaincy Institute, we honor two different meanings of the word *interfaith.* One meaning refers to people who practice a particular faith tradition but desire to minister to people of a great variety of faith traditions. The other meaning refers to people who are eclectic in their spiritualities, who draw on a variety of religions, philosophies, and traditions to construct a spirituality that is uniquely theirs. This book is intended for readers of both types of "interfaith" spiritual guides and ministers and also addresses clients from specific traditions as well as those who are eclectic in their spiritualities.

The contributions were all commissioned specifically for this collection. For the most part, religions are grouped by the geographical region of their initial emergence. (The only exception to this is Christianity. This book was compiled with a largely North American readership in mind, and as there are so many varieties of Christianity in this culture, it seemed prudent to give it its own section.) Religions from each region, in turn, are listed in order of chronological emergence.

In structure, the chapters parallel our pedagogy in the Chaplaincy Institute; we bring in spiritual guides from a variety of faith traditions to talk to our students about those traditions and to offer valuable information on how to provide guidance to people from those traditions. We encourage them to include such vital topics as "common spiritual problems encountered by people of such-and-such a tradition," as well as tips, techniques, and practices helpful for people of these faiths.

Just so, the authors of these chapters were asked to give a quick overview of their faith traditions, including basic beliefs, but then to also describe the methods of spiritual guidance honored in their traditions. In most chapters, authors also discuss common spiritual pitfalls and offer helpful tools and methods drawn from their traditions.

I encouraged the authors to be informal and friendly in their tone, even to have some fun with their presentations. Of course, some are more formal than others. I gave them a very simple assignment. I told them about Peggy and proposed that Peggy's client is from whatever religion the writer happened to represent. I told them to imagine that instead of panicking, Peggy simply walks over to her bookshelf and pulls down the book you are holding now. She turns to the chapter on the religion her new client practices ... and she relaxes. Yes, everything she needs is here. She reads the chapter and feels ready to meet with her client.

A LITTLE PEGGY IN EACH OF US

All of us are a little bit Peggy now and then, and whether you are a spiritual director, hospital or hospice chaplain, minister or rabbi or imam, social worker, psychotherapist, or any other sort of helping professional for whom spiritual guidance is sometimes part of your work, I hope that you will find *Spirivual Guidance across Religions* just as helpful in your own practice as Peggy does in hers.

Of course, the chapters in this book are brief and largely introductory in nature. As you work with someone from a specific tradition, you will no doubt want to explore that tradition more deeply. I encourage you to do so. Yet, these contributions are a good place to start, if only because it helps to know what people consider to be the most important aspects of their own traditions and what information will be most helpful in working with clients from those traditions.

NATIVE
TRADITIONS

Chief Luisah Teish is an elder in the Ifa/Orisha tradition of the West African diaspora. She is the author of *Jambalaya: The Natural Woman's Book of Personal Charms and Practical Rituals*, a women's spirituality classic. She is a mixed-media artist, a ritual design consultant, and a global village activist.

As Spirit Walks among Us

Insights into the Spiritual Culture of the African Diaspora

Chief Luisah Teish

I n keeping with the practices of my tradition, I begin by giving praise and thanks to the ancestors of the world, gratitude to the elders who have taught and nurtured me, and blessings to the children and those who are yet to come.

DANCING THE DIASPORA

What do you need to know and understand to effectively serve a client of bio-cultural African descent or a person who is a practicing member of the African diaspora spiritual culture? First, you need to understand that many people of mixed ancestry practice the traditions of the African diaspora.

The term *African diaspora* refers to the spiritual cultures created by the combination of people who survived the West African slave trade, the indigenous Americans who endured the invasions of their lands, and indentured European pagans who were displaced by the church.

The slave trade extended across much of the West Coast of Africa, from Gambia to Angola and into the Congo. The Yorubas, Ibos, Bakongos, and Bantus were thrown together and shipped for sale to ports in the Caribbean Islands, Brazil, and North America. We estimate that as many as twenty million Africans were exported in the slave trade.

Even though their eating habits and manner of dress were different, they nevertheless maintained several important commonalities: they shared a belief in nature worship and ancestor

3

reverence, performed similar magical practices, and spoke dialects of the Kwa and Bantu languages.

They were dispersed throughout the Western Hemisphere. Some areas received a larger number of people from a common kinship group than others. Consequently, we find large concentrations of Yorubas in Brazil and Cuba, Dahomeans and Bakongos in Haiti, and the Ashanti in the English Islands. A significant number of Dahomean, Senegalese, and Congolese people were scattered across North America.

As these people landed, they were confronted with several spiritual contradictions. The first was the hypocrisy of the Catholic Church, which preached a philosophy of "salvation," "brotherhood," and "charity" while making a fortune from the slavery of African people. The idea to import Africans as slaves to the New World was conceived and promoted by a Portuguese priest, Father Bartolomé de las Casas. Further, the church required that the Africans become Christians in order to be "proper" slaves. Black people were branded, baptized, and given Christian names.

The laws regarding the slaves were harsh. They were forbidden in most places to marry, own property, speak their own language, play drums, congregate publicly, and above all else worship their own gods. The penalty for worshipping the African deities was death. The church made worship of the saints imperative. Yet, the African way was and is the way of power. They drew parallels between the saints (deified ancestors) and their own deities in order to worship them with impunity. African people viewed the miracles of Jesus as the acts of a powerful medicine man; he was the human sacrifice, and the drinking of his blood was magic. The slaves saw in Mary, Star of the Sea, their own Ocean Goddess, Yemonja, and they embraced Her. So Mary not only represented Yemonja but was also recognized as a sister-power, another Goddess who could be invoked to work magic on behalf of the slaves.

The Africans also discovered that the peoples of the so-called New World had a religion and culture very similar to their own. The shamanism of the indigenous peoples recognized Mother Earth and Father Sky as the parents of nature. Their ritual practices included the use of the curing herbs of the forests and swamplands, the drum and rattle with music and dance, offerings from the harvest, and kinship with totem animals through sacrifice.

The Africans also encountered European paganism. They interacted with Spanish Moors, the French Gypsies, and English witchcraft. This concoction of traditions created Candomble and Macumba in Brazil, Lucumi and Santeria in Cuba and Puerto Rico, Kumina in Jamaica, Voudou in Haiti, and Hoodoo in New Orleans. These traditions compose the "African diaspora."

Because these traditions recognize the manifestation of ancestral patterns in health and illness, race and culture are important issues to address. This chapter will take you into a world where spirit lives, not merely as a theological notion or a psychological construct, but as an interactive power. I will share with you some of the beliefs that compose reality in my tradition. However, many of the rituals and practices that heal wounds and maintain the health of spirit, body, mind, and community can only be prescribed and fulfilled by initiated priests and elders. Therefore, I will limit this chapter to the presentation of information that will help the spiritual guide to understand those practices from outside the tradition.

Finally, I hope that this chapter will help you to transcend the limitations of an education in Eurocentric psychology and religion!

THE ENCOUNTER

There you are, in your office. You may be male or female, young or old, married or single, American or foreign born. Here I am assuming that your skin is white.

The door opens and a person unknown to you walks in. He or she may be wearing a business suit, casual clothes, or clothes that represent an ethnic group. That person may be male or female, young or old, married or single. He or she may be fair, brown, or deep black skinned. There may be a hint of another language in his or her voice. That other tongue may be Spanish, Portuguese, Creole, or Yoruba. He or she may have come from Africa, Cuba, Haiti, New Orleans, or San Francisco. The person has dressed for the visit to see you, the spiritual guide, in your office, in a reality you have defined.

On another day this CEO, housewife-mother, or art student may be dressed in luminous white clothes, wearing several strings of multicolored beads. I will assume that this client, whom I will name

"Ade," is an African American woman. The name "Ade" implies that she is an initiated member of a spiritual community. She brings with her a long history of surviving oppression that is now encoded in the cells of her body. She lives in a culture that is preserved by an extended family, and they exist easily in a world where ancestors walk with them daily and deities descend to dance with the community.

You should know that she is checking you out and sizing you up. Ade is taking into account your personal carriage, the evidence of your socioeconomic class, and the manner in which you address her. She is listening to your every word, watching every gesture and movement you make. Most importantly, she is receiving information intuitively about you that will determine whether she takes a seat or walks out the door. There are a few things that you should know about her.

LIFE IN THE VILLAGE

Prior to colonization, West Africans lived in primal life cultures. By *primal life*, I mean cultures based on a lifestyle that is spirit and nature directed. There is a regulated kinship among spirits, humans, animals, minerals, and vegetables. These are all regarded as members of an extended family. In such a culture, it is natural and desirable to preserve life by creating rituals and rites of passage and by observing celebrations on a daily basis.

Primal life people recognize that they have been graced with the personal power to hunt, farm, and eat, but they also recognize that they must give back that which is given to them. As a result of this view, the dynamic interaction of energy through the use of work, celebration (in music, song, dance, storytelling), and placation (sacrifice, offering) was the standard mode of worship for early African peoples.

The world is populated by deities who are prehuman entities. They are expressions of the forces of nature. They are called orishas and are perceived as male and female. Whereas the Most High God is more intelligent than humans can comprehend, the component deities are more like us. Their primary function is to act as intermediaries between humans and Olodumare, the Great One. The orishas have incredible powers, sparkling personalities, and *ase*, the ability to prompt or encourage change. Their epic adventures are preserved in the sacred orature of the people. In addition, they speak to us through oracles that provide guidance and direction.

Our personalities associate us with their power in nature. When divination identifies a person's primary deity, that person experiences herself as a child of that aspect of nature. The orishas mingle their intelligence with ours by means of possession.

For example, Oshun presented Herself to the African community as the Goddess of Love. People experienced the voluptuous flow of the river, with its sweet water and beautiful stones, and perceived intuitively that they were in the presence of the Divine Feminine. "*Ore Yeye O!*" they joyfully chant Her name. They enter the waters of the river to heal their wounds, to increase their life force, and to receive inspiration and love.

They further noticed that a certain woman carried the flow of the river in her stride, spoke with a honeyed voice, and took great pleasure in adorning herself, so they called her an *omo Oshun,* "the daughter of Oshun." They knew that the river came before the woman and that the woman's stride was affected by the flow of the river.

Ade's identification with the Goddess for whom she has been initiated grounds her sanity. It reflects her emotional life, directs her behavior, and affects the way her community views her. The *omo Oshun* is destined to be emotionally sensitive, socially charming, generous with her time and resources, and unforgiving. When she is experiencing spiritual imbalance, her energy may manifest as depression, sexual dysfunction, and intestinal difficulties.

THE ANCESTRAL PAST

As Ade enters your office, you see a single person. But she is not alone. She is escorted by an entourage of ancestors. They are there in her cells, in her DNA. They are there in her perceptions of her culture and herself. They are standing behind her on her left and on her right. For her, they are real and present, and their history and experience walk in with her. As I have said in my book *Jambalaya,*

> Africans believe that those who go before us make us
> what we are. Accordingly, ancestor reverence holds an
> important place in the African belief system. Through
> reverence for them we recognize our origins and ensure
> the spiritual and physical continuity of the human race.

> Ancestors influence human life through hereditary physical and personality traits, but in the African view they continue to exist and create in the spirit world. Not only does their energy find a home in the "wood that groans" but at the proper time and under the right circumstances they can be reborn.[1]

Ade's cells remember her history. They remember the routine rape of African women, the castration of men, and the "picnics" where black people were tarred and feathered and then lynched as Sunday entertainment for white families.

Ade's memory of this oppression is cellular, multigenerational, and operative in her daily life. It rises up anew to survive the moment she walks into your office. This will make her cautious about sharing "the whole truth" with you, because she is not sure that you can fully understand her world.

THE FAMILY OF SPIRIT

It is important for the spiritual guide to withhold a judgment of "superstition" and to invest in understanding the concept of *the family of spirit*. People in this tradition, Ade and I, believe that one enters and reenters the world (*ile aiye*) through a specific family line; that is, one's lineage is traced through a biological system, whether it be patrilineal or matrilineal. Within this system we created a culture based on the extended family, with a large and important network of grandparents, aunts and uncles, cross-cousins, nieces and nephews, sons and daughters. This is very different from the property-oriented nuclear family of the West.

We believe that members of the extended family continue to serve as vessels of reincarnation for each other. A newborn child may be bringing important aspects of the spirit of her grandmother, mother, or auntie back into the world with her birth. The possibility exists of bringing both "blessings and curses" on each return.

During the slave period, our lineages were disturbed, and the names of families, clans, and tribes were eradicated. Incest, which was forbidden in tribal life, was enforced under slave rule. The slave woman was forced to mate with her own children and with strangers. We can speak of blood lineage for only a few generations. In our recovery from slavery, we have reconstructed our kinship systems along spiritual as well as biological lines. We believe it is possible that the newborn brings back to *ile aiye* the spirit and intelligence of blood relatives, family friends, national figures, and spiritual leaders. Therefore, Ade may be a "target child" or a "wise old soul," according to her family's spiritual perception of her.

PRACTICAL ANCESTOR REVERENCE

When she rises in the morning, Ade bathes and then addresses her ancestors. She goes to her shrine, which is adorned with images, candles, water, stones, and other natural objects. This shrine will also house personal items that belonged to various ancestors: grandpa's walking cane, a piece of auntie's jewelry, and a rattle made from a gourd. She will perform a *mojuba* by pouring libations, calling the names of her ancestors, asking for personal guidance, and giving thanks. At night she will meditate before this altar. Guidance may come to her in a dream, where the ancestors send visions, evoke emotions, and provide instruction.

Please be clear that her dreams are "real." The characters in her dream are identifiable; she knows their history, talks with them regularly, and receives messages for herself and other members of her family. (However, unfamiliar spirits may be cause for concern.) She may have a system of dream interpretation full of symbolism that is radically different from any systems with which you are familiar.

For example, a snake may have no connection to the garden in Eden, nor Freud's interpretation of it. Rather the snake may represent the Haitian deity Damballah, the rainbow serpent who holds the calabash of the world together. Ade may experience out-of-body travel with ease. She is accustomed to visitations from deceased relatives. Their light bodies may be seen by her and others walking through the house. Sometimes Ade will set out a plate of food and drink for the spirits to consume. This is a relationship of mutual admiration and support.

On a particular night, she sits at a table dressed with a white cloth, candles, and glasses of water, surrounded by her *ile* sisters and brothers, who may or may not be related by blood, but they are members of an extended family based on spiritual kinship. They are under the service of an *iya/madrina/mãe de santo/mambo* (spiritual mother) and a *baba/padrino/pai de santo/houngan* (spiritual father), who provide life guidance on a regular basis. On this night, they recite prayers, cleanse themselves in scented water, and call upon a community of spirits. After a while, an ancestor appears in a cloud of cigar smoke and speaks through a medium, a man or woman in a deep trance. Now the ancestor will share information and give instructions for the entire community. These are designed to cleanse and energize the many layers of the soul.

THE MULTILAYERED SOUL

In the spiritual traditions of the African diaspora, devotees experience a multilayered soul. The most comprehensive delineation of these layers comes to us from the Igbimolosha (Priest Council) of Oyotunji Village in Sheldon, South Carolina. The priests there have studied the beliefs of the entire diaspora and composed a description of the nine layers of the soul. I am indebted to those priests.[2]

The Universal Soul

The first layer is called the universal soul. According to the Priest Council of Oyotunji Village, the universal soul is that connection with "cosmic force," the magnitude of Olodumare, which "unites the human being with every animate and inanimate thing in the universe." For the Western thinker, this layer is born out of the "big bang" that set the creation of the universe in motion. For us, this is the work of the deities who set creation into motion. Through the universal soul, we gaze at the heavens and know that we too are made of stardust like the rocks, the trees, and the animals. We are all animated, interactive, receptive, and responsive.

The Human Soul

The human soul connects us with the manifestation of the cosmic energy in the *Homo sapiens* form. Here the spiritual guide is invited to consider the findings of mitochondrial DNA. DNA reminds us that all of us who call ourselves human come from an original mother (the deity Yemonja), a common source, a beginning in Africa. We chose this form, with its gifts and limitations. That choice determined our destiny. We share "the total human experience" from conception to death. And Ade has survived a political and social system that, at one time, enslaved her people, declared them three-fifths human, and continues to relegate her to second-class citizenship.

The Sexual Soul

The sexual soul represents that part of consciousness (*ori*) that chooses gender. The intelligence that guides the spinning of the child in the womb (the deity Obatala, the maker of all heads) decides, at a specific time in the development of the fetus, to become female or male. In so doing, the soul agrees to address the gifts and limitations of that body choice and to share in the experience of others of the same gender. Now Ade finds herself in the dominant culture where gender issues are political and social. The age-grade groups, rites of passage, and secret societies of her ancestors are missing. She may experience injury to her gender identity (such as rape), genetic modification (hormone-laden foods, medicines, and clinical experimentation), and alienation (abandonment by community due to personal choice).

The Racial Soul

This layer bestows upon people their physical characteristics and the "genius of their race." The racial soul decides what skin color and hair texture will adorn the baby. It also endows a person with the talents common to a particular race: a style of movement, a contemplative nature, a predisposition for art; these aspects of character or being are often guided by the environment in which a group evolved. Although these talents may be inherent in all people, they may be applied differently according to racial temperament. Fear and misunderstanding of the racial soul (governed by the deity Olokun) are the cause of racism in human beings. If Ade is biracial, she may have identity issues that are especially aggravated by a racist society.

The Astral Soul

The astral soul represents an individual's relationship to the forces of nature. The astral soul is expressed through the person's power place in nature and the identification of a person's primary orisha. Here one chooses a personal temperament, which flavors the experience of life in the marketplace of the world. The astral soul "provides individuals with special talents, proclivities, and adversities."

The National Soul

The national soul (governed by the deity Shango) is expressed through cultural and political identity and the quest for social organization. It is this layer that separates itself from humanity and creates war, connects primarily with its own and sustains ethnocentrism, or extends itself beyond the boundaries of land and culture to embrace peaceful coexistence. Our client has come of age in a climate of "democracy" and dictators, classism and exploitation. She may be proud or ashamed of her country, depending on its treatment of herself and others.

The Ancestral Soul

The ancestral soul channels the human and racial characteristics through the gifts and limitations inherent in the genes of a particular family line (*egungun*). This talent or that attitude "runs in the family." This is the place where we find the "family curse." Sometimes the curse is physiological (an inheritable disease or neurological condition), but most often the family curse is psychosocial (e.g., generational incest, alcoholism). When these behaviors are repeated with fear and guilt, they usurp power from the other layers of existence and appear so large as to become a "curse from God."

Perhaps this is the area of concern that has led Ade to your office. And this is where the spiritual guide will need more education. Please see the list of resources at the end of this chapter. Also, know that several healing practices can be applied to this matter, a few of which I will discuss later. With clear commitment and diligent work, these generational curses can be healed.

The Historical Soul

According to the Priest Council of Oyotunji Village, the historical soul "provides individuals with the characteristics of their generation." It is a relative of the national soul and can be connected to astral events. A particular generation can be affected by planetary forces (for instance, the slow movement of Pluto affects entire generations of people) or by the political events of its time (Republican rule) and may respond to and participate in those events under the urgings of astrological influences (Scorpio: sex, death, and transformation). Children of the sixties viewed the world differently (free love) than did children of the eighties (AIDS epidemic). Depending on her age and the quality of her education, Ade may be unaware of the historical forces affecting her life.

The Guardian Soul

The Oyotunji Priest Council describes the guardian soul as that "which controls, counsels, and protects individuals as they seek to integrate themselves with their other souls and the rest of the world. It is the *ori* [consciousness] directing the fulfillment of destiny." (This destiny is guided by *Ifa*—the system of divination that contains the wisdom of the traditions and is consulted to advise seekers on the fulfillment of their destiny.)

THE GODS AMONG US

If Ade surmises that you might be *willing* to try to understand, she may decide to "open up" and discern whether or not you are *able* to understand.

She'll begin to talk to you about the mysteries in her life that go beyond the scope of psychology, science, and Western theology. She'll begin to talk about phenomena such as "possession" by deities who are forces of nature. She will speak of them in very human terms, calling them *iya* and *baba* (mother and father), and talk about the ceremony where the Trickster opened the door and Thunder came down to dance with the Wind. Perhaps she has experienced full possession herself because she is an initiated priestess. She may not be able to tell you what she said and did while in possession. Please be clear that when in possession, she is not psychotic, she is divine. I will attempt to explain the makings of the mystery.

The initiation, known as *kariocha*, is a seven-day process of transformation, during which time the *yawo* (the initiate) experiences a rebirth. We understand that some of the thoughts, feelings, habits, and beliefs acquired through socialization can become a kind of pollution that lingers in the egg of electromagnetic energy surrounding the body.

Like most cosmogenetic traditions, we recognize that every person comes into the world with a series of pre-birth choices. We choose our historical time, our race and gender, our place and time of birth, and (believe it or not) our country, ancestors, and family

members. Most importantly, we choose our spirit's longings and
unique talents (personal power, *ase*). These longings and unique
talents compose the layers of the soul spoken of above.

These pre-birth choices are deposited into the *ori* (consciousness)
at birth, and if remembered, they guide and direct destiny. Children
may leave the land of the ancestors and arrive into this earth plane with
a full understanding of who they are and what they came here to do.
However, in the process of adjusting to society, the *ori* may experience
forgetfulness, because the culture imposes ideas that are confusing
and engenders attitudes that are antithetical to holistic living.

Kariocha can be described as a series of spiritual works,
including ancient prayers and invocations, offerings and sacrifices,
and elaborate baths, designed to strip the initiate of old thoughts,
feelings, and beliefs that impede spiritual growth.

This cleansing is followed by an empowerment process, known
as feeding the *ori*, which enhances the predispositions, talents, and
personal attributes that the *yawo* has inherited from the ancestors.
The *yawo* is kept in incubation for one year and seven days so that
this empowerment will rest firmly in their new energy field. During
this time, the *yawo* dresses in immaculate white clothes, observes
many taboos, and may not be touched by the uninitiated. She may
experience headaches and mood swings that are completely natural.
At times, she may exhibit *fluido*, a shaking that indicates power and
energy are passing through her body. This is akin to "Kundalini
rising" but is additionally associated with tempering the person to
become a living vessel for the deity. (And I advise you, spiritual guide,
that this is the time to contact Ade's spiritual elder, because you
cannot take care of this on your own.)

One of the most important features of *kariocha* is an in-depth
divination session called the *ita*, which gives the *yawo* guidelines for
her priesthood and the rest of her everyday life. It also provides the
initiate with a series of sacred stories (known as *Odu*), whose content
parallels the adventures one may encounter on the road to a new life.

Further, *Odu* then recommends personal and communal rituals
(called *ebbo*) to help guard against distraction, arrogance, bad judgment, accidents, and a host of other conditions that would impede
the manifestation of a good destiny.

The *ita* is the voice of the spirit speaking directly to Ade. The content of the *ita* will be regarded by Ade and her community as more important than anything resulting from a psychological consultation or a spiritual direction session. Any actions you recommend that are contrary to the *ita* will simply be ignored by everyone in the community.

Ade may be suffering from a biochemical imbalance, from the distress of a dysfunctional family, or from cellular memory of centuries of oppression. Perhaps she has been referred to you by a medical doctor, a local or state agency, or her own need for attention. Be clear that she is not crazy, just trained in a different reality.

If you decide to take her on as a client, get ready for an amazing adventure into unfamiliar territory, for she was raised in a different reality that may well challenge many of the assumptions and principles you have learned or that have guided your practice.

NOTES

1. Luisah Teish, *Jambalaya: The Natural Woman's Book of Personal Charms and Practical Rituals* (San Francisco: HarperOne, 1985), 68.
2. See Luisah Teish, *Carnival of the Spirit: Seasonal Celebrations and Rites of Passage* (New York: HarperCollins, 1994).

RESOURCES

Brown, Diane, and Verna Keith. *In and Out of Our Right Minds: The Mental Health of African American Women.* New York: Columbia University Press, 2003.

DeGruy, Joy Leary. *Post Traumatic Slave Syndrome: America's Legacy of Enduring Injury and Healing.* Portland, OR: Uptone Press, 2005.

Myers, Linda James. *Understanding an Afrocentric Worldview: An Introduction to an Optimal Psychology.* Dubuque, IA: Kendall/Hunt, 1993.

Teish, Luisah. *Carnival of the Spirit: Seasonal Celebrations and Rites of Passage.* New York: HarperCollins, 1994. See esp. "The Layers of the Soul" (pp. 175–79) as defined by the Igbimolosha (Priest Council) of Oyotunji Village in Sheldon, South Carolina.

Teish, Luisah. *Jambalaya: The Natural Woman's Book of Personal Charms and Practical Rituals.* San Francisco: HarperOne, 1985.

Fr. Scott McCarthy, DMin, celebrating forty years of pastoral ministry as a Catholic priest in the central California Diocese of Monterey, has experienced a variety of multicultural parochial settings. His travels have taken him to Europe and most of North America, but lately he concentrates his free time visiting tribes in Central and South America, learning their ways and offering spiritual counseling as needed. He is author of *Celebrating the Earth: An Earth-Centered Theology of Worship with Blessings, Prayers, and Rituals; All One: A Handbook of Ecumenical and Interfaith Worship; People of the Circle, People of the Four Directions;* and *Sacraments and Shamans: A Priest Journeys Among Native Peoples.* Many years ago he was also adopted by a family of the Apsaalooke (Crow) Tribe of Montana.

Spiritual Guidance in Native American Religion

Fr. Scott McCarthy, DMin

A BRIEF HISTORY OF NATIVE AMERICAN RELIGIONS

The Native Peoples of the Americas have a history far more ancient than modern historical measurements can properly determine. Most never speak, as traditional anthropologists and archaeologists have usually indicated, of a migration from Mongolia or Siberia. Rather, the Native People insist that from the very beginning they came forth on this part of Mother Earth at the Creator's will and, therefore, have always been here. Non-Native people, however, guided by various scientific explanations, are surprised and often baffled by this belief. Nevertheless, this is an important starting point of understanding for those who would seek to offer spiritual guidance to contemporary descendants of the ancient ones who inhabited this part of the globe called "Turtle Island" in some tribal traditions. Whenever and however the ancestors of any and all the world's peoples rose to human consciousness, their first activity most likely had to do, nonetheless, with relating to the environment with which they were locally surrounded.

Most human beings generally celebrate their spirituality and faith with contextual diversity. Just as we belong or relate to the earth, so do we belong or relate to the Creator (or, as some would say, a Higher Power). We find ourselves living in several dimensions or realities at the same time. As we celebrate the present, we move toward our future, mindful of the heritage of the past, and we do so within a particular spatial environment. The environment, we come to find, differs as we move from one place to another. Native Peoples were and are always conscious of this.

The usual place where we reside most often has the greatest effect on us. We feel attached to our environment and become quite familiar with both the positive and negative effects of what that particular place has to offer throughout the seasons. We might marvel at the golden leaves of fall, but we also dread oncoming cold and snow. We might enjoy the excitement of a large city like Los Angeles, New York, Toronto, Mexico City, or Rio de Janeiro, but disenchantment enters the scene when we experience the problematic situations of super-concentrations of people and buildings, muggings, traffic congestion, and twenty-four-hour noise. Although we might temporarily overcome the less desirable aspects of our physical setting or context, they are nonetheless constantly there before us.

It is important for a spiritual guide to know that from ancient times the Native Peoples of the Americas have lived with habitats that were indeed many and varied. They always recognized and appreciated the diverse gifts that each region provided, blessing both Creator and Mother Earth for what they received. They adapted well to their environments. As generations passed, the Native People living in a specific area could be recognized and known by the way that they lived with the local terrain. Language and dialect, art and handiwork, song and dance, housing and games, myths and spirituality—all these and more expressed their relationship with what was around them.

Some lived a nomadic life; others, more settled, built lasting dwellings and planted a variety of crops, an abundance of which we still enjoy today. Many of the Native Peoples both hunted and gathered while at the same time allowing themselves to come home to permanent or semipermanent villages. They shared and traded and enjoyed hearing stories about what was going on nearby and far away, just as many people do nowadays.

The geology, the fauna and flora, and the weather patterns of their habitat became personally known to the Native Peoples, and they found marvelous ways of not only surviving the elements, but also drawing benefits from everything that surrounded them. Rocks, trees, and animals became tools and shelter material, weapons, clothing, and art. Manufactured items both practical and beautiful became part of the heritage of each Native People's culture, and it is the same today for many of them.

The physical environment and its climate always have some control over those who live within it. We must always work with the materials available to sustain our lives. Sometimes the terrain and weather are harsh, but often they are conducive to leisure and a more relaxed life. We do what we can with what is at our disposal. For many of the Native Peoples, the following saying has been most often true: "Bloom where you are planted." A counselor, a spiritual listener, or advisor needs to be aware of the ambiance surrounding the Native heritage client, whether it is the objective presence of her or his physical surroundings (like mountains, rivers, deserts, or jungle) or how the individual relates to what is all around.

The Native Peoples, from Alaska down to Patagonia, understand themselves as one, and that oneness has within it a great diversity of expression. Ethnologists and those who try to learn the ways of the Native Peoples have for various reasons grouped them into "cultural areas" because of similarity in habitat, language, or customs. We know that scholarly or bureaucratic, or even racist, classifications of human beings have at times caused pain and misunderstanding for many of us. Often this is due to erroneous conclusions drawn from the available, often scanty, data. Still, a spiritual guide must have both a panoramic view of Native Peoples as to origin and placement as well as a more specific "cultural" understanding of the client's tribal and territorial heritage long before an individual's spiritual needs are assessed.

For a Native person, the earth and all within it are never regarded as "objects," but rather as living beings. It would indeed be difficult to be of assistance to a person of Native heritage if the spiritual guide did not possess an understanding of and respect for the client's deeply held reverence for the relationship between

Creator and Mother Earth and their respective relationship to the individual and to the community.

TRADITIONS OF SPIRITUAL GUIDANCE IN NATIVE AMERICAN RELIGIONS

For those of Native heritage, spiritual guidance is an ongoing process, beginning with grandparents and uncles and aunts and soon reaching out to the larger community surrounding the individual. The place lived in with others on Mother Earth, the fauna and flora, the terrain, are also important as related to an individual's spirituality. It is always about relationship (*mitakuye oyasin*, "all my relations," as they say in Lakota).

Types of Spiritual Leaders

Among some tribes the recognized medicine person, the shaman, the healer, the herbalist, the wise person, or the spiritual guide (sometimes all bound together in one individual) was invaluable to a growing person, especially in the preteen and teen years. Known not only for offering times of teaching or direction, such a leader, often with the help of family members, would prepare the young person for her or his time of "vision quest," or fasting alone in the woods or mountains for several days. This was, and still is for many, an important time to learn self-reliance and deeper connection with the spiritual world, and it could be repeated later on during moments of life questioning or before certain important decisions needed to be made. Often the preparation included a sweat lodge ceremony before and after the fasting period. Every tribe had unique rites for puberty initiation, a good many of which have been superseded or forgotten in our own time.

One tradition of guidance involves an uncle (for boys) or an aunt (for girls) who imparts the family, clan, and tribal ways to the young person as the years go by. While these relatives might appear to take on some of the parenting responsibilities, tribal wisdom has shown that it has been helpful for spiritual growth as well. Perhaps the role is similar to responsible "godparents" who take a continual interest in the spiritual and moral development of their charges. Along with showing the young people how to do things according to custom, they would allow time for special teaching on how to live well and responsibly. Traditional mythic storytelling, often with humorous tales, would round out some of this teaching. The well-known and beloved Road Runner cartoon series is perhaps a modern rendering of this kind of storytelling, which explores human vices and virtues. The "Bre'r Rabbit" folk stories, based on Cherokee and Creek Native traditions (often blended with African heritage stories as well), are another example of storytelling and have been told from generation to generation, to the amusement of all the listeners.

Plant specialists, herbologists, and ancient ethnobiologists among the Native Peoples knew how to name and use plants for healing and ceremonies. At an early age, children came to connect with the plant world, learning how to ask permission of the living plant before harvesting it and then giving thanks for it as they made food or medicine from it. Adults constantly made "field trips" with their charges to introduce them to their plant relatives.

SPIRITUAL PRACTICES IN NATIVE AMERICAN RELIGIONS

Many and varied are the spiritual practices of the Native Peoples, depending on tribe and community. Some of the more common ones include the following.

Dance and Song

The tradition of dance is integral to Native spirituality. Dancers follow the sound of the drum, which is imitative of the human heartbeat. The circling of a central object, like a fire or a sacred pole or tree, is ubiquitous among the Native Peoples, and there are even dances where individuals whirl around many times during the dance as they honor life's great circle: conception to birth to childhood to adulthood to old age and death and rebirth. In this way, earthly and mortal seasons are remembered, along with the changing moods of the human heart. The rattle might take up the drumbeat as dance becomes prayer. The modern powwow or indigenous fiesta expresses the perennial need for dance, even sacred dance, among the Native People. For Native People, it could be said that to dance is to live.

Songs not only express feelings, but they also speak melodically of a continuous connection with the "spirit world," the world that exists contemporaneously with our own lived-out world of time and space. Though some songs might seem a bit "composed," as those in our modern dominant culture, Native folks usually understand that they are really gifts given from the realm of the spirit world, and they "belong" to the individual for the benefit of others and are to be sung at the appropriate times. Many times these songs are expressed more in vocal sounds rather than in Western poetic forms so familiar to non-Natives. Often recognized words and phrases are intertwined with sounds like "he-ya" or "na-na." God, Mother Earth, animals, plants, ancestral ways, times of life, feelings, mythic time, history—these aspects and more are expressed in songs, which are usually accompanied by musical instruments like the drum, rattle, flute, or even guitar, violin, or harmonica. Songs, and sometimes dances, may be "gifted" to others as long as proper appreciation is shown by the giver. This type of gift giving is one powerful and sacred way that songs are passed on. Though many chants are sacred for the individual, clan, band, and tribe, others are sung just for the occasion, like a birthday, during a powwow, or at a special gathering. Some songs provoke laughter or, simply, just good feelings.

Tobacco

The proper traditional use of tobacco has been kept among the Native Peoples from generation to generation and is celebrated even today. In earlier times, the sacred tobacco plant was a valued trade item among the tribes and was always carried as part of a non-Native trader's stock of supplies. Sometimes tobacco is prepared for a simple everyday "smoke," much in the same way that many folks smoke a cigarette or a pipe in any culture. At other times, according to local tradition, tobacco is made use of for prayer and rituals of healing. Shredded pieces of this plant, after being offered to the four directions of east, south, west, and north and also to Mother Earth and Creator, are then smoked from a long pipe made of wood and stone. This is an important ritual for most of the tribes. Sometimes tobacco is offered in prayer and then cast into a sacred fire. Among some tribes, especially in the southeastern parts of the United States, tobacco was sometimes used ritually as an internal purgative, to purify an individual before an important ceremony. After appropriate individual or communal purification had taken place, the ceremony could then properly begin. It could be said that this use of tobacco, as with some other sweet-smelling herbs, moves the participant from secular time to sacred time, dispelling any negative energy as it burns and is moved about ceremonially.

Herbs and Plants

As they followed the round of the seasons, the Native Peoples knew when to plant and to harvest, whether it was corn, rice, acorns, cassava, potatoes, or the myriads of other plants available to them where they lived. Many of these items still fill our own dinner plates today. Native Peoples knew quite well the medicinal powers of certain plants. But the specialists, the healers, the *curanderos*, used plants with prayer, ritual, and song to treat specific maladies like fevers, headaches, and wounds. Such spiritual leaders were always well respected and even to this day have a special place of honor and admiration in Native communities.

A number of plant properties helped to produce visions during certain ceremonies and rituals; but, as improper use could signal danger and even death, always they were led by the appropriate medicine people, who safely balanced the ritual through prayer, spiritual recitation, song, music, and guided activities. Tobacco, peyote, datura, San Pedro cactus, ayahuasca, *yopo*—these are some of the special healing plants that are properly tended and used by the medicine leaders, both male and female. Sadly, as a result of historical circumstances and not through their own choosing, some tribes have forgotten these ways, and even now seek to relearn something of this lost heritage. Often medicine people of other tribes come forward to share their medicine ways so that the balance becomes somewhat restored. But, as many tribes have the dauntless task of rescuing some of the old traditions in regard to healing plants, it is not always an easy task.

A spiritual guide should also be aware of the sweet-smelling herbs like sage, cedar, sweetgrass, mugwort, and rosemary that are burned ceremonially by North American Natives and also certain incense-like substances that are more popularly used in ceremonies south of the U.S. border, like copal, *palo santo*, *caraña*, and rosemary. They are really comforting for those who know how to pray with them.

The Circle

It would be difficult to measure the full impact of the circle's meaning for Native Peoples. The importance of a circle is expressed in countless ways—from a simple gathering of a few or many people as they surround an individual or a fire to the shape used to make a dwelling or ceremonial place. A circle expresses unity and inclusivity. As needed, it can be enlarged or diminished without losing its meaning of oneness. Native Peoples have always favored the circle over the common method for other cultures of gathering people in rows, as in a classroom or church. A circle speaks of the seasonal round of living with the environment, the human stages of life that include forms of birth and rebirth, while at the same time reflecting many aspects of the physical shapes that are found within the natural world.

The Directions

The directions of east, south, west, and north (along with the intercardinal directions) have always been important to Native Peoples. They offer a sense of positioning, a recognition of one's place on the land as well as within the movements of life. Though there are many ways to describe the meaning and function of each direction, there are some similarities that the Native Peoples have in common regarding them. East, the direction of the rising sun, can speak of new beginnings, while west, the direction of the setting sun, can speak of completion or even the direction where deceased relatives travel on their way to the spirit world (heaven). South speaks of warm breezes and the goodness of daily life, while north, with its colder winds, might appropriately describe some of life's difficulties. We are able, from any place on Mother Earth, to be cognizant of and to welcome gifts that come from each direction: foods, friends, visitors, rain. Any spot on earth can become a center and from that selfsame center, we are able to extend our consciousness in thankful or petitionary prayer for people and all other aspects of the creation. This is a spiritual practice of having our feet planted firmly on the Creator's earth while contemporaneously knowing also that we are in relationship to all that is around.

Colors

Colors have had a special significance for Native Peoples, as they have for most other world cultures. Red is a dominant color cherished by most Native Peoples throughout the Western Hemisphere. Depending on the particular tribes, colors have most often been associated with the four directions. Nowadays throughout North America and in other European lands, the Lakota (Sioux) tribal colors of red, yellow, black, and white seem to have been picked up by many Native and non-Native individuals to convey spiritual understandings. In the Andes of South America, the rainbow represents the many colors exhibited by Mother Earth, and special flags with colorful stripes are carried about during the fiestas and special ceremonies. Colorful face and body paint is often used by dancers during powwows and during special ceremonies like the sun dance and special feasts. People take time to adorn themselves with paint and they show great pride in their designs. Some of these colorful designs have been passed down in families and in groups since antiquity.

Animals and Birds

Some tribes speak of animal ancestors in the mythic past and have many stories to tell about them. Such stories relate them to these ancestors as well as to now-living animals within their particular ambiance. These tribes respect not just some but all animals and birds, as well as all forms of life, known and not yet known. So intense is their respect for all beings coming from the hands of the Creator, Native Peoples would most likely allow for the possibility of existing life forms on other planets in other galaxies. Some First Nations people continue to respect and honor the tradition of an animal or bird coming forward in a dream or a vision quest to "adopt" the human being concerned, promising to guide him or her throughout life.

Early in life children learned to appreciate the world of animals and birds. Often an adult would bring a bird, young deer, small raccoon, turtle, dog, or other animal to a child to be raised as a pet. They would hear many stories about animals, especially in regard to these essential beings of the surrounding natural world offering themselves as food for the people in times of need. Seeing hunters regularly bring home fish and game affirmed the meaning of these stories. In earlier times, certain animals and birds, like deer, buffalo, hawks, and eagles, had become part of tribal culture. After first contact, it became common in some Native communities for older children to care for horses as well as goats, sheep, and cattle.

Dreams

Dreams or visions, and sometimes trances, are an opening to the spirit world and a way of learning what might need to be done to proper advantage by an individual in the near or distant future.

Those of the First Nations of the land have always trusted their dreams because of their connection with the spirit world. Often a medicine person or other elder would be called on to help interpret what was experienced by the dreamer.

Some dreams would unfold in the night during sleep; others might come during a vision quest or a ceremony. Often animals and birds or ancestors are part of the dream and come to have special meaning for the individual. The tradition of dream interpretation seems not to be as prominent today as in past times. Yet a spiritual guide needs to be aware of its importance and should understand well how dream symbols are to be properly interpreted according to the client's heritage and background, as well as her or his life experiences.

Gift Giving

To give a gift is to offer one's heart and best wishes to another person. Sometimes the giving of gifts followed important events between groups of people, as in the making of a treaty or peacemaking after some kind of provocation. According to Native ways, gifts are always bestowed freely and are never to be given back. Some tribes in North America have the practice of giving gifts to another person in sets of four items at a time. The idea of "fourness" expresses a kind of sacredness to the action and that what has just been done between the individuals concerned should not be taken lightly. That "all life is a gift" is very much a Native concept, as all life and all possibilities are considered to have their origin in the Creator. In imitating the actions of the Creator, who is the prime giver of all gifts, especially mediated through Mother Earth, an individual fulfills her or his life purposes.

Sweat Lodge Ceremony

Some kind of prayerful ceremony where hot rocks give off steam within an enclosed structure has always been practiced by the Native Peoples of Central and North America as a form of cleansing, purification, and healing. The sweat lodge (or as it is often called in Spanish-speaking areas, *temescal* or *temazcal*) has become very popular today as individuals from tribes who have lost the practice now once again are able to learn of its healing value. Even to this day archaeologists discover the remains of such places where people in more ancient times daily or regularly prayed for the renewal of personal and communal life. Especially before or after hunting or battle, Native Peoples collected special rocks, which they heated to red-hot. The rocks were put into a small circular or square structure, and participants entered to receive the effects of very hot healing vapors on their bodies and in their lungs. Toxins and other mental and emotional wastes were allowed to leave the individual by means of customary prayers, songs, and the pouring of water upon the rocks. As weakness humbled all the participants, new strength soon became available to help them in their post-sweat-lodge activities in daily life. Nowadays the sweat lodge is quite often made available to Native inmates in prison and, when properly led, has been found to be most helpful in alcohol and drug rehabilitation among both Native and non-Native participants. The spiritual guide needs to experience this ritual first before suggesting it to a client.

Blended Religious Practices

Since first contact at least five hundred years ago, the Native Peoples of the Americas have experienced, to put it frankly, a painful and continually devastating culture clash with those who came from other continents. The history is bittersweet. As with intermarriage, so also with religious practices, many of the Natives of this part of the world came to express themselves religiously in the symbols of one or several of the sacred ways of the newcomers. However, a certain number of folks have always tried to maintain the more ancient customs of the First Peoples of the land. For them, it has often been a struggle to stay true to the ways of the ancestors as well as to celebrate those ways relevantly for those of this generation. Sometimes this is called "traditional spirituality." Usually such people practicing "traditional" spiritual ways do not use the symbols of Christianity or any other world religion as they worship.

Yet many welcomed the newer ways and were able to "translate" or modify them to suit their own needs. To this day, for example, Native Catholic masses or blessings may include, at special moments, the use of the sacred pipe, smudging with sage or cedar or copal, peyote songs, and danced entries to the place of worship. Also, in indigenous celebrations of Catholic patron saints, it is not uncommon for Native drummers or others to use rattles (maracas) in both the processions and the dances.

Indigenous people have always used symbolic imagery to express their spiritual ways. In many places Native people connected their own symbolism with Catholic ritual and sacramental expressions. A good number of Natives have experienced Protestant forms of worship for many generations and even now possess a treasury of hymns in their own languages. Some of these worship traditions, coming from the time of the Protestant Reformation, are more auditory or verbal and less symbolic or ritualistic in practice. At times Natives who are used to worshipping at their reservation churches in "the Indian way," with songs or smudging with sage, experience tension when they enter into worship in a "white" church where these rituals are neither practiced nor accepted. Often they feel something to be ritually or symbolically missing. Such differing modes of worship are from time to time problematic and frustrating for Native folks.

It would be most helpful for a guide to appreciate that though most Native people have been affected for better or worse by dominant spiritual cultures, quite often they have taken into their own spirituality what they liked in the spiritual traditions and religiosity of the dominant culture surrounding them, and what they felt was not good for them they usually rejected. Most likely this pattern of acceptance and rejection was practiced both before and after contact with Europeans and even later on, with people coming from other parts of the world.

For many Native people, belief is not so much a doctrinal or theological kind of reality; rather, it is a way of life. Wholeness and balance in all dimensions of one's life is to be sought after as it has been experienced and passed on in each generation. The concept of tradition is very important, not only as far as specific cultural items go, like making baskets a particular way or working with beads in certain patterns, but also in regard to one's personal and communal spirituality. Though an individual's specific tribal or personal ways of drawing close to the Creator through ceremonies may be preferred, nonetheless a perennial respect for the importance of other people's religious leanings is also embraced. Perhaps it could be said that for many Native people ecumenism, or respect for interreligious activities and ceremonies, comes easily, because of their recognition of the Creator's presence in every individual throughout the whole world.

HOW SPIRITUAL DEVELOPMENT IS UNDERSTOOD IN NATIVE AMERICAN RELIGIONS

For Native Peoples of this hemisphere, spiritual growth has to do with being fully oneself in body, mind, and spirit as we continue to develop through all the days of our lives, while at the same time being in balance with Mother Earth along with all other beings (including humans). Though this might seem to be impossible for some individuals, a sort of tall order, it nonetheless includes both the means and the goal of all human growth, no matter what one's culture might be.

Being cognizant of the ancestral past of a person's tribe, band, or group is ever so important. This connection with an indigenous past promotes a sense of both pride and possibility. We might say that if our ancestors were successful in their own life times, no matter what the obstacles were for them, then we should be able to continue in that same tradition and seek to be successful. Drawing on the present and available power of the ancestors who reside now in the spirit world (heaven) but are also invariably close to us, we are able to live with a sense of purpose that is greater than ourselves. Continually sensing a connection, not only with the mysterious spirit world, but also with the mineral, plant, and animal worlds, is also of importance in this regard. Whenever possible, we follow the ancient pattern by having a family and, despite life's difficulties, continue to seek balance with all around us.

COMMON SPIRITUAL ISSUES FOR NATIVE AMERICAN RELIGIOUS PEOPLE

In an era of increasing multiculturalism and global exchange, the person of Native heritage is often perplexed. How should such a person "live out" the native experience in a pluricultural setting? What is important? What can be left behind, and what necessarily must be maintained?

Tradition

For some Native Peoples, tradition is understood as repeating, more or less exactly as they have been taught, what was done by the previous generation or generations. Such people would be very conscious of ritually performing sacred actions correctly as precisely as possible in the way that they received it. The special songs, prayers, and rituals surrounding a pipe ceremony, which vary from tribe to tribe, are one example. For others, tradition means bringing forward what they indeed have received from the past, yet adapting it as necessary to serve present circumstances.

Perhaps for a Native person, tradition is not just occasionally wearing an older, handed-down dress or a sacred headdress like the eagle feather warbonnet of one's grandfather, nor is it so much about bringing an item out of an anthropological museum cabinet to "show and tell." Rather, it really about doing an ancient activity, but in a new and fresh way, like ... having a baby! And in so doing, the ancient pattern becomes freshly expressed in a particular moment of revelation. Some accoutrements must necessarily be left behind as an individual or community carries forward into the next generation what is considered to be really important. The question of tradition, the question of receiving or handing on what is truly essential, very often defines the ways that a Native person attempts to live spiritually.

Identity

A spiritual guide must learn just how a directee identifies as a person of Native heritage. Native identity is somewhat of a "mixed bag" for individuals and groups. There are those who are "pure bloods" and experience their culture as more or less intact. They know who their relatives are and can easily identify with their tribal culture. Perhaps they still speak their own language as well as the dominant one and look forward to celebrating their ceremonies at important moments throughout the year. Some other folks, although they may have an indigenous look or certain physical aspects of the First Nations, nevertheless are bereft of their own people's proper culture and spirituality. They have not had the chance really to "live it out" in a setting where the traditions are regularly practiced. Perhaps they are in an urban locale where Native ways are not respected by those around them or are not easily accessible because relatives are distant and the family connections are weak.

Some individuals are "mixed tribe," "mixed blood," "mixed race," *mestizo/a*, *métis*, and have not yet found ways to relate to both sides of their being. This is a common problem of identity in other cultures as well. Occasionally you may meet Native people who apparently choose to be at odds with each other much more than they exhibit working

together in promoting cultural and spiritual harmony, especially in
the context of dealing with the dominant society's often conflicting
value systems. The ones who really suffer in these sad affairs are the
next generations or the young children. Sometimes the difficulties
are about deciding exactly who really belongs in the tribe, the band,
or the local group. Frequently it is about land, property issues, or
even revenues gained from gambling casino enterprises. Every now
and then some names are removed from tribal roles for one reason
or another, usually because some of their ancestors were known to
be of mixed racial parentage. But more often it may concern how
"Indian" someone is now by the blood quantum or the shade of skin
or certain physical features. Very often, those causing such problems
forget a most important intertribal, intercultural value: "The honor
of one is the honor of all."

There are some folks who have heard that they have some Native
ancestry, but the information passed on to them is often vague.
They identify with a particular tribe or ancestor that they have heard
about from family members, and this prompts them to seek Native
spirituality in their lives. Such persons often flock to Native gatherings
like powwows or special ceremonies such as sweat lodges and begin to
display certain indigenous symbols like dream catchers or feathers on
their rearview mirrors as signs of their identity. Invariably they come
to meet others who themselves express their own Native identity well
and help them find what they seek.

There are some individuals of recognizable or verifiable Native
heritage who opt out of celebrating or paying special attention to
their "Indianness" in the public arena. For example, many people
south of the U.S. border have indigenous histories and cultures that
can be historically verified. Yet, they do not necessarily "feel" Native
within themselves and often do not want to be regarded as "indio." For
some, the blame might be imputed to intentional colonial prejudices
and caste systems or even present-day repressive governmental
educational programs; for others, it might be due to many years of
experienced racism or prejudice; for still others, it may be that they
just feel more comfortable being part of the general public and do
not feel the need to give answers all the time to questions of cultural
differentness posed by those of the dominant society in which they
live and of which they are a part. Outsiders invariably seem to regard

such individuals and groups as "generic Mexicans or Latinos," failing to honor their proper ethnicity or tribal group. Sometimes this attitude is later jumped over successfully by their offspring who seek a richer appreciation of their given heritage. Similar problems are experienced by indigenous folks north of the U.S. border.

Many tribal groups continue to practice the ancient custom of "making relatives," of adopting individuals into their life and family, not just as an honorary status. Only individuals within a tribe adopt. A tribe per se does not adopt; however, this is a tradition accepted not only by the tribe of the individual, but also by the larger Native community as well. Often a name is given, which then will seal the person's true place within the tribal community. The tribe hopes then that the adoptee will participate with the Native father or mother in many of the important family and tribal occasions. Adoptions can occur at any age, and individuals can also be laterally adopted as a brother or sister. Adoption in the Native way knows no racial boundaries.

Over the years since first contact with Europeans, new peoples have been created from the multitude of races and cultures that arrived on the continent of the Americas as they gradually came to merge, to coalesce, with First Nations peoples. Nowadays, this new "race of bronze" claims even younger siblings who contain bloodlines and heritages from parents who arrived here even more recently from lands far to the west in the Pacific Ocean and the Orient. For these hundreds of years, Native heritage people have found themselves living in moments of great change and their societies experiencing tremendous flux. Perhaps the wisdom of all their backgrounds and cultures and spiritualities will continue to serve them well in the time to come. Drawing from these spiritual traditions and finding what is useful for their human growth will always be important for such individuals.

Self-Esteem

Some individuals of Native heritage experience low self-esteem and, often being in the minority, find it difficult to assert themselves without feeling out of place to some extent. Many wait a very long time before speaking up in groups, much to the consternation of many non-Native people. Others are bothered by too many rapid-fire questions aimed at them. Being silent and looking away from the questioner often troubles and even baffles the questioner. Yet later, at a time that seems appropriate to the Native person, answers will be given, and these will have plenty of thoughtful substance in them. Also, in the indigenous way, as people sit in a circle, they usually listen, consider, and then offer ideas, going around the circle with their responses. The crisscross method of anyone just "butting in" while someone else is speaking is not usually considered respectful and is never the preferred manner of discussion.

A good many Native heritage folks feel like outsiders, unable to easily penetrate the circle's edge so as to feel comfortable with everyone else inside it. They feel left out. While everyone else seems to be relating well, they themselves often exhibit symptoms of loneliness and depression, along with their ensuing addictions to alcohol, drugs, sex, and gambling. Many folks suffer this kind of pain even when they are surrounded by their own ethnic or tribal communities.

A good knowledge of Native history is important for a spiritual guide in this regard. How the client's people experienced and survived the invaders' onslaughts must necessarily have an effect on how Native communities and individuals perceive themselves. For many, especially those living on reservations (or, in other countries, reserves, territories, *reservas*, or *comarcas*), there is always pain involved in the telling and the hearing of what happened to their people since initial contact with Europeans and others. The oral tradition has many storytellers, and this sad narrative is repeated in countless ways. The hearing of it from generation to generation really does affect individuals quite deeply. For many folks, the whole sad experience of what has been done to tribes and communities over many years has engendered a general distrust of non-Natives, especially white people. However, often this distrust breaks down as individuals gradually experience outsiders as human beings with similar joys, sorrows, and stories. Individual friendships, tested over time, that are made with those of other ethnic communities also help build self-esteem in Native-heritage individuals.

Urban Life and Reservation Life

Indigenous people raised in a city far from their ancestral lands often have difficulties celebrating their Native culture and spirituality. Those living on the reservation (the "rez") or on land that is replete with trees, rivers, birds, animals, and the like seem to be able to operate more from a situation that is somewhat more historically and culturally intact. Often there are spiritual guides or medicine persons who are more easily available to the seeker. Such leaders, who show up for prayer at important moments in life, are also usually available to mentor others or to do counseling. Often the person seeking counsel brings to these individuals a gift (like tobacco wrapped in red cloth) or offers a meal (as a sign that he or she truly appreciates the spiritual leaders' time and the wisdom imparted). On occasion, these people are called to help others in the cities and are habitually present at funerals, memorials, or special events where Native people gather. It would be most helpful for any spiritual guide to be able to refer a client to these people who come from within the indigenous community itself. These Native spiritual leaders are usually quite cooperative with other spiritual guides and clergy. They recognize the common purpose and mission and are really the most appropriate ones to enhance the spiritual guidance by means of their abilities in leading special ceremonies and rituals.

Sense of Time

In the world of the non-Native, time is usually monitored by the clock. At a certain moment—according to the timepiece—an event begins or ends. In the indigenous world, time for a ceremony begins not so much by the clock, but when the people have gathered. Then we move ritually from secular time to sacred time and then back again. When all have gathered, that is the right time to begin. Though the general guides for timing have to do with the seasons, and especially the solstices, and sunrise and sundown, much leeway is given as people gather.

Such a way of ordering and dealing with time often frustrates non-Native folks, who usually plan and do things by the clock. Early and tardy take on different meanings for Natives, depending on which "world" or zone they are operating in: their own or that of the dominant society. Spiritual guides might want to allow for some tardy (or even early) arrivals of their clients. Perhaps smudge with sage in the meantime!

Sacred Sites, Sacred Places

Sacred sites are essential for all Native people. Sometimes they are connected with the physical location where the ancestors emerged or were created or where ceremonies have been celebrated from time immemorial. Some are natural places by rivers, while others are special rock formations in mountains, like Bear Butte in the Black Hills of South Dakota. Others are built up, like the temple complexes of Central America and Machu Picchu in Peru, or other kinds of sacred architecture, like *kivas* (underground worship "chapels") in the American Southwest or the Cahokia Mounds in Illinois.

We know that over the years and over the generations, many Native people have been lured to the cities to look for work and they never really have been able to return home to live a traditional life. As many young people attempt to seek out and maintain the ancient rituals and prayers of their ancestors, they often find themselves living like "strangers in a strange land." In the midst of the larger cities, "friendship houses" attempt to offer a place where Natives can come together and relate to one another. Counseling, even spiritual guidance, is usually made available. Perhaps new additional sacred sites will have to be created in the large metropolises and urban settings where many Native heritage folks reside. Those who are the elders, those who are the leaders, will in the near future most likely need to seek out suitable places like large halls, parks, or places on the edges of the towns that have some natural beauty around them. These places will need to be dedicated for regular sacred use. Perhaps these, too, will become locations where, not only in office rooms but also upon occasion in an outdoor nature setting, a spiritual counselor can do what he or she is so good at: be available to people while they travel on their spiritual paths.

Spiritual Connections

All people have, or should have, the opportunity to learn more and more about their own spiritual traditions and even learn something of their neighbors' spiritual ways. The future of Native Peoples lies in their spirituality, not just in the externals of their culture. Spirituality gives that deeper meaning to what is done in the name of a particular culture's traditions. A truly wise spiritual counselor will always look for those unique spiritual points of connection that unite Native people within themselves as they encounter many others also seeking full human growth and balance as they journey together along the paths of Mother Earth.

Rev. Ann Llewellyn Evans is a Shinto priestess, trained and licensed by Tsubaki Kami Yashiro, one of the oldest Shinto shrines in Japan. She has helped introduce Shinto to North America through her involvement with Tsubaki Shrine of America in Granite Falls, Washington, through the Bright Woods Spiritual Center in Canada, and through publication of *Shinto Norito: A Book of Prayers*, an English translation of traditional Shinto prayers.

Spiritual Guidance in Shinto

The Way of the Kami

Rev. Ann Llewellyn Evans

A BRIEF HISTORY OF SHINTO

Shinto is the ancient, indigenous religion of Japan. Its traditions and teachings are based on thousands of years of tradition, rather than on any founder or sacred text. Predating written history, Shinto's early roots reach back to folk practices as early as 14,000 BCE. In the sixth century CE, the Chinese arrived in Japan, bringing a multitude of cultural influences, including writing and Buddhism. With the introduction of a different religious practice, it was of course necessary for the Japanese to differentiate their practices from the Chinese practices. Thus, they used the terms *Shinto*, or "the Way of the Kami," and *Butsudo*, "the Way of Buddha." Shinto and Buddhism continue to coexist throughout Japan; most Japanese will tell you that they visit the Shinto shrine as well as the Buddhist temple. There is no requirement by either faith for exclusivity.

With the introduction of Buddhism into Japan, the Japanese court felt it was important to document the origins of Japan and the kami, and Empress Gemmei directed that a chronicle be written to record this information. In 712, *Kojiki* (Record of Ancient Matters) was completed, and in 720, *Nihongi* (Chronicles of Japan) was finished. In addition to information on the various emperors of Japan, both texts record the mythology and tales that had been handed down from generation to generation and outline the creation of our world, the many kami that came into being, and various points of cultural reference, such as the history of Japan. These texts are not considered sacred, like the Bible, Torah, or Qur'an. Rather, they record cultural history.

Shinto is unique in that it has no founding father, no sacred book, and no doctrine or commandments. When you ask Shintoists to explain their faith tradition, they may not be able to do so easily. This does not mean they do not understand it but merely that it is difficult for them to explain its meaning. How then, you may ask, does one determine the meaning of Shinto?

Comparative mythology scholar Joseph Campbell recounts a story of a Western man who did not understand Shinto and requested further explanation from a Shinto priest:

> "You know," he said, "I've been now to a good many ceremonies and have seen quite a number of shrines, but I don't get the ideology; I don't get your theology."
>
> The Japanese (you may know) do not like to disappoint visitors, and this gentleman, polite, apparently respecting the foreign scholar's profound question, paused as though in deep thought, and then, biting his lips, slowly shook his head. "I think we don't have ideology," he said. "We don't have theology. We dance."
>
> That, for me, was the lesson of the congress. What it told was that in Japan, in the native Shinto religion of the land, where the rites are extremely stately, musical, and imposing, no attempt has been made to reduce their "affect images" to words. They have been left to speak for themselves—as rites, as works of art—through the eyes to the listening heart. And that, I would say is what we, in our own religious rites, had best be doing too. Ask an artist what his picture "means," and you will not soon ask such a question again. Significant images render insights beyond speech, beyond the kinds of meaning speech defines.[1]

Shinto is experiential. The substance of Shinto is not found through study and philosophy, but through "doing," through action. In this chapter, I will discuss the foundational beliefs, practices, and terms of Shinto, and I will also try to convey the experience of Shinto—for that "dance," as Joseph Campbell called it, is the essence and the core of Shinto spirituality. Shinto is not learned, but experienced. The substance of Shinto is not found through study and philosophy, but through doing, through action. That is, the essence of Shinto is absorbed through the practice of ritual and prayer.

Shinto's scripture, to use a Western term, is nature. Even for us, as modern people, the experience of being in an old-growth forest or by a pristine, pounding waterfall can certainly invoke awareness of the sacred. The original Shinto shrines were sacred groves of trees or mountain peaks. In certain situations, kami were recognized to be extant in sacred sites. In other circumstances, the kami were entreated to descend to a purified site, alighting on the tops of the trees and mountain peaks, creating a connection between heaven and earth, between sacred and temporal.

In Shinto, this awareness of Great Nature, *Dai Shizen*, is central to humankind's understanding of its relationship to the rest of creation. Great Nature goes beyond nature as trees, rivers, and living beings; it encompasses all of creation, including living nature as well as inert matter such as rocks, mountains, and natural formations. According to historian J. W. T. Mason, "In Shinto there is no separation between the universe and divine creative spirit. The universe is divine creative spirit extending itself as matter and as life."[2] Living in harmony with Great Nature is central to Shinto. We are part of this magnificent creation and should live respectfully and harmoniously with all components of Great Nature.

SPIRITUAL TRADITIONS IN SHINTO

Shinto emphasizes each person's sacred nature. Human beings are descendants of the kami, the spiritual beings that have existed since the universe formed. As descendants of the kami, we are innately pure and bright beings. However, from time to time, this luster may be dulled through impurities acquired or encountered either within or outside our selves. Through the rituals of Shinto, we can purify our beings and restore our original brightness and purity and find great joy in our lives.

Simply, Shinto is centered on the following precepts:

- The kami, the spiritual beings throughout all existence, are revered.

- We should live in harmony with Great Nature.

- Humankind is descended from the kami, and thus we have innate brightness within us.

- We can purify ourselves and our surroundings to return to original purity.

Shinto

The word *Shinto* means "the way of the kami." In Japanese, *Shinto* is written as two characters, or kanji. The first kanji can be pronounced either *shin* or *kami* and means "spiritual being." The second character can be pronounced either *tou* or *michi*, meaning "path" or "road." The two characters combined are pronounced either *Shinto* or *Kami no Michi*, both meaning "the path of the kami."

Kami

Kami is a difficult term to translate. Simply, kami are the myriad spiritual beings that are present throughout creation. To someone from the West, the concept of multiple deities sometimes seems confusing. I often explain that the kami are spiritual beings akin to angels. In Christianity, various spiritual beings are identified as angels; and in many Christian traditions, prayers and offerings are made to saints as well.

So, in the West, we actually do recognize multiple spiritual beings, although Jewish, Christian, and Islamic traditions teach that there is only one God. This brings us to the issue of translation. The terms *God* and *kami* are not the same, although you may find that some texts erroneously use these words interchangeably. The Western concept of the term *God* implies omnipotence: unlimited, universal power and authority. Kami do not exert authority, nor are they omniscient guides.

To further understand the concept of kami, let us look at the Shinto creation mythology. *Kojiki* (Record of Ancient Matters), written in the eighth century, records:

> Now when Chaos had begun to condense, but force
> and form were not yet manifest, and there was naught

named, naught done, who could know its shape?
Nevertheless, Heaven and Earth first parted and the
Three Kami performed the commencement of creation.
(Preface of Yasumaro (712 CE) to the *Kojiki*)

J. W. T. Mason discusses this concept of spontaneous creation:

Absolutist omnipotence or mechanism must know in
advance of the use of force or form what the eventual
shape will be. Since there was no such advance knowledge, it is clearly indicated how Shinto tradition, at the
very beginning, moved away from omnipotent mechanism toward the idea of creativeness.[3]

Thus, at the beginning of creation, there was spontaneous creation
of the universe as well as of the kami. In Shinto, there was a rather
formless universe, and then the kami were created, and they
subsequently influenced creation of earthly life; this contrasts with
the biblical tradition of God existing first and then planning and
forming creation. Thus, in Shinto tradition, we move away from the
idea of omnipotence toward creative or spontaneous evolution.

Kami can vary in characteristics. In some situations, kami are
humanlike; in others, kami are animistic, existing in phenomena
of nature (mountains, rivers, rocks, and trees) and in natural forces
(lightning, wind, and waves).

Kami are present throughout the universe; kami spirit is present
not only in living beings, but in nonliving entities or objects as well.
When we see a great work of nature, such as a magnificent waterfall or
majestic mountain, there is spirit or life energy present in that object.
We refer to this as kami, since kami reside in the object. However,
kami and the object are not the same. For example, a special waterfall
may have particular sacred qualities and have kami resident within
the waterfall, yet the waterfall itself is not kami. Motoori Norinaga,
a scholar in the late eighteenth century, wrote, "Whatever seemed
strikingly impressive, possessed the quality of excellence and virtue,
and inspired a feeling of awe was called *kami*." So when we happen
upon an especially spiritual location—which may be marked by a
shrine, a tree, a rock, or ocean waves—we bow in gratitude and offer

prayer in reverence. This action itself is a way to connect to the divine and to brighten our own spirit.

There are too many kami to name, and many kami are associated with specific regions or natural sites. However, there are a few primary kami:

> *Amaterasu O Mikami:* Kami of the sun, she is head of all heavenly kami. The primary place of enshrinement is Ise Grand Shrine in Mie Prefecture, Japan. Reverence to Amaterasu O Mikami is based on the life-giving properties of the sun as the divine solar source of life.

> *Sarutahiko no O Kami:* Head of all *kunitsu kami,* or earthly kami. Sarutahiko guided Amaterasu's grandson, Ninigi, from heaven down to earth. He is the kami known for guidance and protection.

> *Ame no Uzume no Mikoto:* Wife of Sarutahiko no O Kami. Kami of divine movement, entertainment, and marriage. In Shinto mythology, when Amaterasu hid in a cave, casting the world into darkness, Ame no Uzume performed a dance that enticed Amaterasu out of the cave, and once again Amaterasu's light shone throughout the universe.

> *Inari O Kami:* Well-known deity of the rice harvest and the guardian of commerce. The principal Inari shrine, Fushimi Inari Taisha, is located outside Kyoto at the foot of Mount Inari. Inari is closely associated with the fox as its messenger.

> *Ubusuna no kami:* Literally, "kami of one's birthplace." This is one's personal guardian kami.

> *Amatsu kami:* All the kami of heaven.

> *Kunitsu kami:* All the kami of earth.

> *Yao yorozu no O kami:* Eight million kami, often translated as "myriad of kami."

Prayers are often addressed to "*Amatsu kami, kunitsu kami, yao yorozu no kami,*" meaning that one is addressing all kami.

Humankind as Descendants of the Kami

When creation evolved into the forms of heaven and earth, kami were created. Life then was handed down from kami to kami, from kami to human beings, from our ancestors to our grandparents and parents and ultimately to us. A genealogical link connects every human being to generations of ancestors and kami. Let us further explore the depth of this connection.

In Shinto, the spirit or soul is referred to as *mitama. Mitama* is the vital life source that is handed down at conception and at death returns to the unseen world. We use the same word to refer to the *mitama* of humans as well as that of kami. For example, the *mitama* of one kami may be enshrined in many different locations. We refer to this multiple enshrinement as *bunrei,* literally "divided spirit." You may ask, "How can one spirit be divided?" *Mitama* can be divided without lessening the energy of the origin. If you have a fire, the fire can be divided without lessening the intensity of the original flame, since each division will grow again in energy. *Wakemitama,* or "divided *mitama,*" similarly retains its original intensity.

When we consider *mitama,* then, as it is passed from kami to human being and from generation to generation, the original spirit, or *mitama,* has divided and been passed on again and again, so that we, as descendants, not only have received life from kami but have kami spirit within us. This is a central pillar of Shinto, as it provides the basis for our view that we are innately pure, innately good. In Shinto, we believe that people are inherently bright and good. Through various life experiences—situations as well as personal actions—this brightness may be occluded or clouded over. Through prayer and ritual, we seek to remove these impurities and return to our pure state of being, which is inherently good. We will discuss this idea of purification later in detail.

Thus our connection to kami is quite intimate and personal. We often use the term *musubi,* which literally means "to tie or bind" or "bound together." The kanji for *musubi* is a combination of "ancestor" and "good fortune." Our connection to the kami and to our ancestors is "vertical *musubi*"; think of a vertical line from heaven, down through the generations of kami and ancestors, to yourself now living on earth, and on to your children and future descendants. At the same time, we are also fundamentally tied to other human beings through "horizontal *musubi*"; think now of a horizontal line that connects you to your neighbor, your town, your country, and others throughout the world. Since all humans have originated from the same source, we are inextricably tied together. *Musubi* connects us spiritually to the past and the future through the vertical axis and to all other beings through the horizontal axis. The *musubi* that binds us connects us physically through DNA that has been passed on from generation to generation, and it also connects us spiritually, through the *mitama* that has divided and divided.

Purification

The concept of purification is central to all Shinto practices and beliefs. During our daily lives, we are subjected to impurities, either through actions we commit, actions of others, or situations or environments in which we find ourselves. These impurities cloud or deplete our *ki*, our life vitality. Through Shinto practices, through *harai*, we can remove *kegare* (impurities or pollution of oneself or other individuals) and *tsumi* (impurities or impediments between oneself and other people, or between oneself and the environment). Through *harai*, we return to purity and brightness, to cheerfulness of heart and spirit.

We purify our minds and spirits through prayer and ritual, our bodies through ritual washing, and our homes through ritual as well as by constant cleaning. A clean environment provides for a more pure *ki*, or life energy. By contrast, a dirty environment would diminish *ki*, with the subsequent result not only of lower, baser energy, but perhaps attracting misfortune. Thus, we strive to have a clean, orderly environment to support our efforts to live in a more spiritual manner. This cleaning affects not only the *ki*, or life energy of our physical being, but also our relationship to our environment by emphasizing actions with deliberate thought.

Prayer and *Kotodama*

Shinto prayers are chanted in Japanese because there is a sacred sound quality to the chosen words. *Kotodama*, literally "word soul," describes the particular spiritual energy that individual words possess. Thus, the choice of words that are chanted are significant, both for context and for *kotodama*. For Western practitioners, prayers are printed in *romaji*, with the words spelled out phonetically in English letters so that a non-Japanese speaker can pronounce the word. Personal prayers are uttered in one's mind and heart in one's own language.

Kamidama

It is customary to have a *kamidana*, or "kami shelf," in the home. A *kamidana* is a miniature shrine that is placed on a shelf in the home. Inside the *kamidana* is usually an *ofuda*, a paper or wooden plaque with the name of a kami or group of kami written on it. The *ofuda* will have been blessed at a shrine and is a place to which the *mitama* of the kami descends and resides. If space does not allow for a *kamidana*, the *ofuda* may be placed on a high shelf by itself instead.

Each morning one bows and offers prayers to the kami residing in the *kamidana* or *ofuda*. Having a *kamidana* creates a sacred space, bringing positive *ki* to the home and family, and is a reminder to start each day with prayer, to acknowledge with gratitude the blessings of each new day. It also provides a focal point for solitude, meditation, and prayer, a place to nourish the spirit.

SPIRITUAL GUIDANCE IN SHINTO

Spiritual guidance in Shinto centers on helping a person to return to his or her innate brightness handed down from the kami and to live in harmony with Great Nature.

Because we are descendants of the kami, we have the same brightness of spirit. This brightness can become occluded, however, by our own impurities, by negative interactions with others, or by negative events. In Shinto practice, we seek to remove these impurities through purification.

We also strengthen our spiritual foundation by learning to live in harmony with Great Nature, with all of creation. Great Nature, as life itself, is cyclical like the seasons. There are beginnings and endings, soft breezes, and violent storms. In Shinto, we acknowledge the ceaseless movement of the universe, the ever-changing aspects of Great Nature. Our task as human beings is to be present, to be able to ride through all the variations of life with as much spiritual light as possible, to ride the waves of life more buoyantly, cutting through the difficulties rather than feeling frightened or depressed.

Purification through Prayer

Prayer is a powerful tool that affects our life energy. Through prayer, we can return to our innate brightness, our "kami nature." Life challenges all of us with ups and downs, twists and turns. Practicing prayer will not remove all our difficulties. However, if we have a solid foundation, a spiritual light within us, then we experience these challenges in a different way.

How should one approach prayer in Shinto tradition?

• Which prayers should one use? *Misogi no O Harahi* is the

primary prayer used for purification. It is a supplication to the kami of purification, chanted when Izanagi no O Kami performed the first *misogi* ritual, purification by bathing in cold water. *O Harahi no Kotoba* has been chanted for more than one thousand years and entreats purification from all sorts of calamities and impurities of self, that these aspects of life may be cast off and swallowed by the kami of the underworld, returning our spirits and our situations to brightness and purity.

- When praying, still the mind and focus one's energy on the *hara*, the region just below the navel that is the seat of the soul. Focus on the vibration of the words, sending the energy into the *hara*; this invigorates the soul and calms the soul into a condensed energy. It enlivens the kami nature within.

- Traditional prayers should be chanted in Japanese, since the vibratory sound is important. The *kotodama*, or soul of the word, is embodied in its sound as well as in its meaning.

- Always focus on gratitude; gratitude is central in Shinto. When we are able to live with deep-seated gratitude, our view and experience of living changes; it brightens our *ki*, or life energy, which in itself attracts more positive situations and people to us. A dark or subdued *ki* will, in contrast, attract negative events and people.

Purification of Physical Being

Maintaining cleanliness of one's physical body is also important for supporting a strong, bright spirit. So, regular cleanliness and hygiene are essential for purity of the soul as well. Whenever we visit a shrine, we ritually wash our hands and mouth to ready ourselves to receive the spiritual energy of the kami before entering shrine grounds. The shrine grounds themselves are swept, and the buildings are kept clean by daily sweeping and cleaning.

The ancient ascetic practice of *misogi* is a ritual that physically cleanses the body, mind, and spirit through immersion and chanting in cold water such as a waterfall, river, or ocean. The practice originates from the mythology recorded in *Kojiki* where Izanagi no O Kami, after visiting the "bottom country," or place of afterlife, returned to earth and bathed in the Tachibana River to rid himself of defilement and pollution. *Misogi* can have life-changing spiritual effects; however, because of the challenging nature of the practice, it is best taught by a priest who is trained in Shinto ritual methods.

Purification of Environment

The spiritual energy, or *ki,* of our physical environment is extremely important. If it is positive and uplifting, this will affect all living or working there.

In your home, designate a sacred area. It may be a shelf, a table, a corner of a room. You might place there a *kamidana,* an *ofuda* (paper or wooden tablet with the name of a kami), or another sacred object. It might even be a special natural item, such as a stone, into which you invite the spirit of kami to reside. Make this a regular place of prayer.

Also purify your home or work area. First, clean the area to be purified. Remove and put away clutter; wash, sweep, and dust. This prepares the area for purification. Then, perform a ritual purification by performing the following steps:

1. Fill a small bowl two-thirds full with clean water. Add several pinches of salt. Cut a small evergreen branch (about six inches long), and rest it on the rim of the bowl. You will use these items during the ceremony below.

2. Begin the ceremony in the center of the space of home. Recite *Misogi no O Harahi.*

3. Holding the bowl of saltwater in your left hand, with your right hand dip the tips of the branch into the water and gently fling drops of saltwater to the left, to the right, and to the left again. While doing this, chant the following: *Harae tamae, kiyome tamae, rokkonshojo.* Repeat this sequentially in the center, then in the corners of northwest, northeast, southeast, and southwest, and finally at the entrance to the home or space.

Connecting with Nature

Living in harmony with Great Nature is at the core of Shinto. We are part of a much larger creation. Connecting with the natural world lifts our spirits and restores our kami nature.

How can we connect with Great Nature?

• Get out and walk through a natural setting: a park, a beach, a mountain trail. Feel your presence blending with the natural environment around you.

- Bring nature into your home. This could be through a garden, a plant, or a bowl filled with lovely stones from the mountains or the shore.

- The sun provides light, and heat sustains all life on our planet. Sunrise and sunset are powerful energy changes every day. Make yourself aware of the awesome nature of this daily change. Watch the sunrise or sunset, and notice more than the spectacular colors. Feel the subtle changes in the air, in the sounds of the day. Bow, clap, and offer prayers to Amaterasu O Mikami, the kami of the sun, with gratitude for your life and the blessings you have received.

Morihei Ueshiba, the founder of aikido, expressed the importance and benefits of connecting with Great Nature:

> Rise early in the morning to greet the sun. Breathe in and let yourself soar to the ends of the universe; breathe out and let the cosmos back inside. Next breathe up all the fecundity and vibrancy of the earth. Blend the Breath of Earth with that of your own, becoming the Breath of Life itself. Your body and mind will be gladdened, depression and heartache will dissipate, and you will be filled with gratitude.[4]

DEATH IN SHINTO

Shinto practice is focused primarily on life. Death is a transition from the visible world to the unseen world. When a person departs from this world, priests perform a series of rituals that assist the person's *mitama*, or spirit, to leave the body and to reside in a wooden plaque called a *reiji*, or *mitamashiro*. After this transition, the body is an empty shell, is treated respectfully, and is either cremated or buried, according to the family's wishes.

The spirit of the departed is supported in its transition to the unseen world through prayer and ritual over a period of fifty days. The prayer recited daily is *Mitama Shizume no Kotoba*, or "Words to Calm the Spirit." The transition of the spirit from residing in a body in this world to existing as spirit in the unseen world may be difficult and tumultuous. Through prayer, the departed's spirit is calmed and reassured that all will be well for the departed as well as with family and friends remaining in the visible world. In Shinto, we believe the journey of the spirit differs as a result of the spiritual development and acuity of the departed as well as the circumstances surrounding the passing.

The prayer ritual over fifty days sustains the passage of the departed and helps family and friends as they make the transition through their own period of grief and mourning. An enduring relationship with the departed is enhanced through a daily ceremony with their loved one as a spirit, a *mitama*, now abiding in the unseen world.

Earlier we discussed the ancestral relationship with kami. It is this same vertical *musubi* with the kami and with the generations that existed before us that our loved one's spirit joins. Through the support of prayer, we are helping their *mitama* to be calm and settle into the spiritual realm of their ancestors.

It is common to keep the *reiji* in the home. Family events and circumstances are reported to the *mitama* residing in the *reiji*; prayers of reverence and gratitude are offered as well.

THE SHINTO CLIENT

People of Shinto faith share common spiritual questions and challenges with people of other faiths. In Shinto, we find answers and resolution through the practice of purification and in *kansha*, or gratitude. A few frequent concerns follow.

How do I connect with and experience the kami? We are descendants of the kami, and so we have kami within us. By purifying our minds, bodies, and environment, we return our state of being to its innate purity. This changes our *ki*, or life energy, so that we are more receptive to experiencing the sacred nature of kami.

How can I find peace and happiness? Positive *ki*, or life energy, enables us to feel heightened spiritual awareness as well as joy and gladness. Conversely, negative *ki* will make us feel dark, sad, and isolated. Negative *ki* can also attract harmful situations into our lives. To have bright *ki*, practice purification and meditate on the inherent goodness in the life given to us. By putting gratitude at your core, your prayers will have a purity and spiritual strength that will connect you with the kami, giving you brightness and joyfulness.

Can the kami help me deal with conflict or disappointment? We believe in living in harmony with Great Nature; just as Great Nature cycles through the seasons, our lives also cycle through positive and negative experiences. To see this flow rather than to focus on the immediate situation helps us to have a broader perspective. To move forward, we must purify ourselves and pray with heartfelt gratitude for life itself. Through these actions and attitudes, our spirituality will be raised and we will become closer to the kami, receiving inspiration from the divine world and vitality from Great Nature itself.

Someone close to me has died; how do I deal with my sadness? What happens after we die? Since Shinto teaches us that death is a passage from the visible world to the unseen world, we counsel those in grief to understand death as a passage, not as an end. Those who have passed can be supported in this journey through prayer, especially during the fifty days subsequent to passing. Daily recitation of *Mitama Shizume* (a traditional prayer available from a Shinto priest) assists the departed in his or her passage as well as helping the person grieving by giving structure and purpose during this complex time.

These are but a few examples of spiritual questions. In general, counsel followers of Shinto to purify themselves and their homes and to pray to the kami with gratitude and openness.

The way of Shinto is the path of the kami; it is an acknowledgment of divinity throughout our world and a personal commitment to live one's life with the spirituality and brightness of the original kami of creation. Through the ancient traditions of Shinto, we learn that the essence of spirituality is found within oneself, since we are inextricably part of the divine.

NOTES

1. Joseph Campbell, *Myths to Live By* (New York: Penguin Books, 1972), 102.
2. J. W. T. Mason, *The Meaning of Shinto* (Victoria, BC: Trafford, 2002), 38.
3. Ibid., 42.
4. John Stevens, *The Essence of Aikido: Spiritual Teachings of Morihei Ueshiba* (Tokyo: Kodansha International, 1993), 25–26.

RESOURCES

Bocking, Brian. *A Popular Dictionary of Shinto.* Surrey, UK: Curzon Press, 1997.

Evans, Ann Llewellyn. *Shinto Norito: A Book of Prayers.* Victoria, BC: Trafford, 2001.

Nelson, John K. *A Year in the Life of a Shinto Shrine.* Seattle: University of Washington Press, 2000.

Mason, J. W. T. *The Meaning of Shinto.* Victoria, BC: Trafford, 2002.

Picken, Stuart D. B., and Yukitaka Yamamoto. *Shinto Meditations for Revering the Earth.* Berkeley, CA: Stone Bridge Press, 2002.

Yamakage, Motohisa, Paul de Leeuw, and Aidan Rankin. *The Essence of Shinto: Japan's Spiritual Heart.* Tokyo: Kodansha America, 2006.

Yamamoto, Yukitaka. *Kami no Michi—The Way of the Kami: The Life and Thought of a Shinto Priest.* Stockton, CA: Tsubaki America Publications, 1999.

———. *Introduction to Shinto: The Way of the Kami.* Mie, Japan: Tsubaki Grand Shrine, 2010.

James Michael Reeder, LCPC, CPRP, is a Neo-Pagan and a psychotherapist in private practice in Baltimore, Maryland. He holds a master of science in clinical community counseling and a post-graduate certificate in spiritual and existential counseling, both from Johns Hopkins University. He can be reached at michael@hygeiacounseling.com and www.hygeiacounseling.com.

Spiritual Guidance in the Neo-Pagan Traditions

James Michael Reeder, LCPC, CPRP

A BRIEF HISTORY OF NEO-PAGANISM

Paganism and Neo-Paganism (terms used interchangeably) refer to a group of mainly Eurocentric religions that focus on reviving the pre-Christian practices of Europe and/or developing new and borrowed practices compatible with ancient Pagan worldviews. These religions include the many traditions of Wicca (the largest religion in the cluster), British Traditional Witchcraft,[1] Asatru (the worship of ancient Norse and Germanic deities), Hellenismos (the worship of Greek gods), Druidism, and many others.

Aboriginal faiths, African diaspora religions (Regla de Ocha/ Santeria, Voudun, Umbanda, Candomble), major non-Abrahamic faiths from Asia, and other scripture-based religions are not included. Satanism is also not included as it is viewed by most Neo-Pagans as a reaction to Christianity, which has nothing to do with either ancient or contemporary Pagan belief or practice.

The cluster of Neo-Pagan religions are similar enough that they can be discussed together in a broad way. Due in part to the scarce numbers of adherents, these religions often mount joint conferences and semipublic rituals at which they all participate and which tend to be mostly Wiccan in structure by default.

Interest in European Pagan religions began to revive in the mid-twentieth century. These revivals can be seen as either the public reemergence of hidden ancient sects or the modern re-creation of practices from scraps of records and myths that survived destruction during the Christianization of Europe. Regardless, Pagan religions today incorporate both ancient pre-Christian European beliefs as well as newly invented elements. Many followers of these Eurocentric religions borrow practices from around the world, while retaining distinctly Pagan identity and worship patterns. Neo-Pagans are distinct from the New Age movement, although the two share many practices and tools (crystals, astrology).

Some precursor source material to modern Neo-Paganism can be found in the works of Charles Leland, Aleister Crowley, Dr. Margaret Murray, Israel Regardie, Dion Fortune, and Robert Graves.

Gerald Gardner, a retired British civil servant, founded the first Wiccan tradition, a mystery tradition that he billed as a revival of British folk witchcraft traditions. This tradition eventually became known as Gardnerian Wicca. After the British Parliament did away with laws making witchcraft illegal, Gardner published *Witchcraft Today* in 1954. It is contested by Doreen Valiente (1989) and numerous others as to what ancient knowledge Gardner actually revealed versus what he and his associates borrowed or invented. Regardless, Gardner was a colorful founder who generated the excitement and charisma necessary to launch Wicca as a world religion. Along the way, associates such as Doreen Valiente, one of Gardner's high priestesses, and Raymond and Rosemary Buckland, initiates of Gardner, helped to develop the religion further.

A few other strains of Wicca include Alexandrian Wicca (from Alex Sanders), which is highly ceremonial, also initiatory, but more liberal in practices than Gardnerian Wicca; Dianic Wicca (founded by Morgan McFarland and Mark Roberts), which has one branch that is primarily oriented around the Goddess and another that is politically feminist; Blue Star Wicca; various forms of Faery Wicca, which put more emphasis on spirit contacts with fairies or the fey; Correllian Nativist Tradition; Georgian Wicca; Central Valley Wicca; Strega (an Italian witchcraft); Reclaiming Tradition (Starhawk is one of its most famous authors); and countless others.

In the early 1960s, Robert Cochrane, a rival of Gardner, put forth an alternative variation of British Traditional Witchcraft (BTW). Some surviving forms derived in part from his teachings include the 1734 Tradition, The Regency, and the Clan of Tubal Cain. There are notable differences in methodology, ethics, and emphasis of practice between Wicca and BTW. These groups are highly secretive.

The Feri Tradition (not Wicca) was founded in the 1940s and 1950s by Victor and Cora Anderson and carried along by persons such as Gwydion Pendderwen and most recently T. Thorn Coyle. Feri incorporates the use of tools for personal power (like the iron pentacle), the Hawaiian Huna concept of three souls, and sexual mysticism. It has an especially strong emphasis on evolving the spiritual self.

The Order of Bards, Ovates, and Druids, currently the largest Druid organization in the world, was founded by Cambridge academic Ross Nichols in 1964 along with other former members of the Ancient Druid Order—a turn-of-the-century organization with roots traceable to the seventeenth century. Isaac Bonewits was a well-known American Druid who founded Ár nDraíocht Féin in 1983 (the largest Druidic organization in the United States; also known as ADF). Druidism, like all Neo-Paganism, is a combination of invention, scholarship, and ancient practice. ADF attempts to base its teachings on contemporary scholarship. Its beliefs are not tremendously different from Wicca, but its organizations, politics, ritual forms, and traditions all differ from Wicca.

Norse Paganism (you may hear such groups referred to as Heathen, Asatru, Odinist, Theodist, and/or Wotanist) refers primarily to the worship of the Norse gods (like Odin, Thor, and Freya). There is also a revival of elements of Old Norse culture, ethical conduct, and feelings of kinship. Honoring the ancestors and the earth are emphasized. The nineteenth century and Nazi periods saw revivals of romanticized versions of Germanic faith. Many current folklore- and history-based Norse Pagan groups arose in the 1970s, such as the Asatru Association in Iceland and the Odinic Rite in England. Current organizations in the United States include the Troth and the Asatru Alliance. Most contemporary groups go to great pains to distance themselves from any sort of racist doctrine or practice.

Hellenic Polytheistic Reconstructionism concerns itself with the reconstruction of the ancient Greek faiths, such as Hellenismos (primarily the worship of the Olympian gods) and other Greek spiritual practices like the Eleusinian and Dionysian mysteries. Modern reconstruction of these religions and practices has been occurring mainly since the 1990s.

Recently, with increased access to Russia and Eastern European countries, other culture-specific Pagan practices, revivals, and reconstructions have begun emerging in English-language publications.

BASIC TEACHINGS OF NEO-PAGAN TRADITIONS

Beliefs in the Neo-Pagan traditions vary widely but in general include the following.

Immanence of Deity and the Interconnectedness of Life

Neo-Pagans believe that deity is present on and in the earth here with us. Most Neo-Pagans also believe deity to be transcendent as well, to have a concentration of presence somewhere beyond our sphere. In addition to distinct god forms, there is a holy interconnection of spirit flowing through all of us and nature. The immanence of deity and the interconnectedness of life are foundational beliefs for many Pagans.

A Predominant Focus on the Here and Now Rather Than the Afterlife

A curious thing happens when you ask most Neo-Pagans about the afterlife. They will hesitate and then give you a vague memorized answer as though they were instructed in it years ago for about ten minutes and have not thought about it since. There is a rather pervasive belief in reincarnation, although this belief is not central to most forms of Neo-Paganism. What matters is how you live your life now; the afterlife will take care of itself.

The Earth as Sacred, Not a Trial, Punishment, or Exile from the Divine

This belief is very important. It is not sinful or a mistake to focus on your life here and now (rather than the hereafter) and to enjoy physical sensations. "Pleasure is of the Goddess" is an oft-quoted phrase, and many groups have some Dionysian tendencies (an enjoyment of earthly pleasures, emotion, and a bit of excited chaos). Neo-Pagans believe they can be in direct connection with the Divine right now here on earth. There is a strong undercurrent of environmentalism and reconnection with nature.

Many Pagans believe in inherent divinity, that we are perfect and divine, only needing to grow into our full expression. The ideas of reincarnation and the earth as a training school for evolving our souls into this full expression are prevalent in Neo-Paganism.

A Religious Interest in and Rites to Acknowledge the Seasons of the Year and Other Sacred Natural Processes such as Birth, Growth, Dying, and Fertility

A change in season, an equinox, a rainstorm—all are aspects of the Divine. Regardless of the particularities of a given Neo-Pagan religion's holidays, these holidays will convey a belief in the sacredness of the earth, the body, and the processes of life. For example, the Wiccan wheel of the year includes eight major holidays spaced roughly six weeks apart. Dates given are for the Northern Hemisphere:

Samhain: October 31–November 2. The beginning of the new year in most systems, the last harvest festival of the fall, and a time to remember and communicate with the Ancestors.

Yule/Winter Solstice: December 19–23. The rebirth of the God or the Oak King. Wiccan traditions generally have the God growing and dying in accordance with the seasons. Some traditions have two gods battling for control—one more associated with growth (Oak King) and one with decline and renewal (Holly King).

Imbolc/Candlemas: February 1–2. Related to the Irish deity Bridget. This is a time when new plans for the coming spring and year are set after a period of winter reflection and retreat.

Ostara/Vernal Equinox: March 19–23. The Lord and Lady are growing and bonding, and spring is arriving. Painted eggs as symbols of new life are often incorporated into celebrations.

Beltaine: May 1. A fertility holiday with bonfires and maypoles. The Lord and Lady may consummate their love. Actual orgies among Neo-Pagans, while not unheard of, are almost entirely the stuff of urban legend.

Litha/Midsummer (Summer Solstice): June 19–23. The fertility and growing power of the earth reaches its zenith and starts declining into fall and winter. In some traditions, the Oak King and Holly King again fight for control as the cycle turns to the decline and renewal.

Lammas/Lughnasadh: August 1. This is the first of three harvest festivals, which often concentrates on grain and bread.

Mabon/Autumn Equinox: September 20–24. A harvest festival often concerned with fruit.

These holidays are derived from a mixture of Celtic, Germanic, and other European festivals.

A Freedom to Be Creative in Belief and Practice

Newness, creativity, and borrowing are not generally considered negative, and most Neo-Pagans assume they are authorized to improvise. Some Neo-Pagans are reconstructionists, basing their practice more firmly in historical contexts, but most are not.

There is also the curious phenomenon of "Techno-Pagans." While nature is sacred, a large number of Pagans really love computers, libraries, and air-conditioning. The culture of Neo-Paganism has grown to rely on online communications to keep scattered adherents in communication, and there are some who seem to mainly funnel their spiritual activities into online discussions and websites.

Exploration of Ancient Wisdom for Its Relevance to the Modern World

There is no assumption that new is better. Neo-Pagans tend to buy lots of books, and a Neo-Pagan may be as likely to read a history or anthropology textbook as a religious book. There is more than the usual amount of scholarship involved, as bits of lore are actively being discovered, researched, and/or invented. Spiritual directors and other counselors need to understand that for their Neo-Pagan clients, what constitutes spiritual activity is broader than for the general population. So, reading a history text on the ancient Roman Empire is spiritual activity if that person worships Athena, in part because ancient religion has become lost or obscured and so you can't just study books in the religion section in order to reclaim it.

Direct Personal Deity Contact with Little to No Church Hierarchy

Neo-Pagans pray, trance journey, paint, write, sing, and engage in divination, all with the assumption that the Divine is right there waiting for them to figure out how to complete contact. Clergy are not needed for this, although guided trance journeys during rituals are very common (think group hypnosis, as the procedure is similar, but assume that actual spiritual contacts are happening and astral travel occurring). Each Neo-Pagan has the ability to pursue deity contacts that are right for him or her, and individual deities may contact people, too.

Personal Responsibility for Spiritual Growth and Mundane World Affairs

Individuals being responsible for their own spiritual development has meant rather slow growth for spiritual guidance skills among Neo-Pagan clergy. It has also resulted at times in the custom of making would-be group members jump through hoops to find and contact Neo-Pagan organizations (thus proving they are serious enough to be worth attention from the group). This is slowly changing. Many Neo-Pagans consider evangelism an obnoxious tool and make no efforts to be visible to Neo-Pagan seekers looking for them.

Extensive Use of Tools and Props in Religious Ritual

Pagans use techniques and concepts such as the dark night of the soul, meditation, guided journeys, labyrinths, sweats, Reiki, shamanic journeying and healing, chanting, and self-hypnosis. They are also generally interested in divination (like tarot cards and runes), herbalism, auras, Kabbalah, and all manner of occult subjects.

To better focus the will and mind, Pagans use tools like wands, stones, and robes. Successful magic is thought to have energy behind it, and so chanting and dancing may be used to whip up energy. As people themselves are a part of the Divine, magic may be accomplished through their own power as well as by requesting the aid of the gods.

In this context, seemingly outlandish practices make lots of sense. If you believe that robes and candles help set mood and intent to worship, then you will use them. If you believe movement adds energy to the effectiveness of prayer or magic, then you will dance.

Subdivision of the Divine into Components for Easier Understanding and More Personal Relationship (Gods and Goddesses, Nature Spirits, Ancestor Spirits, Elemental Forces)

Neo-Paganism is about relationship. Pagans feel it is very hard to relate to an all-powerful, all-knowing god in the sky. So gods are broken down into functions to make them easier to get to know. Pagans consider this approach more useful to them because individuals know to whom to go with what type of concern.

Spirit is in everything (pantheism), so many Pagans believe there to be a spirit inhabiting just about everything (even rocks and trees) that can be talked with and interacted with. That said, most Pagans will only do this in specific spiritual activities and don't go through life constantly hearing voices coming at them from all the objects around them. An operating assumption is that all gods and spirits are real. This is both to be polite to others and a safe expediency just to be sure. There will be certain spirits and gods that matter to individuals and others to which they never give a second thought.

Neo-Paganism is a spiritual system of interacting with the world; it is not defined by which entities are interacted with. Thus, Wicca has a series of customs, rituals, and beliefs, but which gods and goddesses the system is applied to work with depends on individual covens and traditions.

The subdivision of spiritual powers into multiple gods, goddesses, spirits, and elemental forces can also lead to a sense of balance as one learns to use multiple such contacts for different reasons. In particular, each of the four elements (earth, air, fire, water—and sometimes spirit for a fifth element) has different important qualities that together sum up just about the whole of what is possible in life and provide a life-balancing system.

Wiccan traditions are often duo-theistic, worshipping the Lord and Lady. Some feel that all of the various gods and goddesses are alternative names for the Lord and the Lady, while others are "hard polytheists" who work with a pantheon of discretely separate deities. Some groups place a stronger focus on the Goddess in their workings. For some, referring to the Lord and Lady is merely convenient shorthand for the male and female principles of the Divine and also extremely useful for Pagan gatherings where Neo-Pagans of differing stripes get together and somehow have to worship in concert. So an observer may well encounter a Wiccan who refers to a singular "the Goddess" in one sentence and then in the next launches into a rendition of the many different goddesses she believes in. Another variant on this would be a Wiccan who believes it is possible to pray to and connect with a giant amorphous Goddess but who also believes he can select from within that "Goddess cloud" more concrete specific deities such as Isis, Hecate, or Cerridwen, among others, all of whom are aspects of the Goddess.

A Belief in Magic

The Pagan belief in magic may best be thought of as prayer that is enhanced through the use of tools and rituals. Well-known early-twentieth-century occultist Dion Fortune (otherwise known as psychotherapist Violet Firth) defined magic as "the art of causing changes in consciousness at will."[2] It may be best to leave it ambiguous as to whether or not Pagans are changing their own mental states or the world around them with magic. The overlap between magic, psychotherapeutic techniques, and self-hypnosis is considerable. Not all Pagans use magic, though Wiccans almost always do. Usually the intended effects of magic are similar to the hoped-for effects of prayer: healing, good fortune, guidance requests, and the like. Neo-Pagans and Wiccans generally don't believe they can physically manipulate objects (like flying on broomsticks or turning into toads).

A "Harm None" Philosophy and Strong Ethical Code

Generally Wicca will tend to have a prohibition against harming others. Wicca also allows members to do whatever they want to as long as no one is harmed. Other Neo-Pagan religions may instead emphasize doing what is necessary to protect loved ones. They (such as some forms of British Traditional Witchcraft) will not have a "harm none" approach to ethics but may instead be constrained by the Law of Return—that is, the energy and intent you send out into the universe tends to come back at you in similar form. Therefore, you'd typically better act and intend the best for others unless there is a really strong need to do otherwise, since you can expect to get smacked in return for whatever actions you take against or on behalf of someone. The Asatru (Norse deity worship) system of ethics consists of the nine noble virtues: courage, truth, honor, fidelity, discipline, hospitality, self-reliance, industriousness, and perseverance. Druids have wisdom texts from ancient lore and mythology from which can be gleaned ethics related to honor, balance, and reverence for life. Regardless, a strong emphasis on personal responsibility tends to occur in Neo-Pagan religions.

NEO-PAGAN COMMUNITIES

Many Pagan paths, particularly in British Traditional Witchcraft and some Wicca, are closed and secret. Members undergo a many-year "traditional" training program, which controls quality and conveys power. An initiatory tradition may believe that there is a "power download" conveyed through the lineage to the new initiate upon initiation; that is, the initiate will have greater magical abilities and connection with divinities due to the energy and authority transmitted from generation to generation down through the lineage. Clients from these traditions may not be permitted to tell spiritual guides everything about what they do.

On the other hand, many strains of knowledge have been released into publication and onto the Internet. Today the majority of Neo-Pagans are reading from eclectic sources and talking openly about topics as they find their way well outside of secret paths. They may be more generically Neo-Pagan; that is, they are not members of a particular Pagan religion, like Wicca, but rather are solitary practitioners. The common community that this cluster of religions holds in common makes such solitary practice easy. Pagan festivals and conferences typically invite all Pagans to play, learn, and worship together. This is also in part why it is proper to capitalize Paganism and Neo-Paganism as a religion even as it becomes apparent that there are several religions under the Pagan umbrella.

DEMOGRAPHICS OF NEO-PAGANS

Reliable statistics and demographics regarding Neo-Pagans are hard to determine because of individuals' reluctance to come forward for fear of persecution, solitary followers unaffiliated with known groups, and Pagans identifying themselves as "no religion," Unitarian Universalist, or New Age on surveys.

Estimates in the United States have the Neo-Pagan population placed at between two hundred thousand and one million. A number of surveys show the Wiccan population exploding at astounding rates.

The best survey research data available is from the book *Voices from the Pagan Census*, derived from a nationwide sample of 2,089 people across the United States. It lists the U.S. Pagan population as follows:

90.8 percent white

64.8 percent female

52.9 percent with at least a college degree or better

87.9 percent between the ages of twenty and forty-nine

28.3 percent homosexual or bisexual

There are also high rates of acceptance and/or practice of group marriages, cohabitation, and ritual but not legal marriages (called handfastings). Neo-Pagans are active politically, trend strongly toward liberalism and the Democratic Party (only 6.6 percent are Republicans), and strongly support environmental concerns.[3]

Neo-Pagans generally look like anyone else. They may have a tendency to wear fantasy symbols, like dragons and fairies, on their clothes, and some may sport symbols such as pentacles, goddess symbols, triple moons, and spirals on jewelry or tattoos. Not all people wearing pentacles are Neo-Pagan; some wear them for shock effect or other reasons.

TRADITIONS OF SPIRITUAL GUIDANCE IN NEO-PAGANISM

At first glance there would not seem to be much of a tradition of spiritual guidance in most of Neo-Paganism. Clergy usually lack training in counseling skills and instead are trained to facilitate group rituals, teach knowledge of the tradition to students, and be proficient in specific spiritual tools, like the proper use of incense, candles, herbs, and divinatory methods. Most clergy (certainly of the Wiccan variety) go through a three- to ten-year course of tutorage with veteran clergy, as well as home study and a series of initiations. When they are considered fully trained (third degree in some Wiccan traditions), they are blessed to go form their own group. It is also the case that Neo-Pagan clergy are facilitators of energy rather than the primary performers of religious acts. In Neo-Pagan circles, everyone is trained to be his or her own priest or priestess, and the clergy member (usually known as a high priest or priestess) is more of a clergy instructor and arbiter of disputes within the group. As such, there is much less of an expectation that the clergy member will take care of the members.

For most Neo-Pagans spiritual guidance would usually consist of studying a curriculum (often set out as degrees of initiation) involving learning about the self, the spirits, the gods, the four elements (earth, air, fire, and water), ritual protocol, the major holidays, and the tools of craft such as divination systems, herbs, crystals, and perhaps spell casting. There is a strong expectation of personal responsibility; members learn their own capabilities, and then they care for themselves.

A member having personal troubles in a Wiccan coven might approach the clergy member for permission to have the group engage in spell work at the next appropriate ritual, such as a money spell for poor finances, healing work for health concerns, or construction of a protective amulet against spiritual attacks and negative influences.

Clergy meeting privately with members are likely to use divination to assist with the member's questions—such as a tarot spread or casting runes to help the member make a decision. Most clergy will have rudimentary peer counseling training at best and will be quick to refer complicated counseling and mental health concerns to professional therapists, and medical concerns to licensed doctors or an accomplished lay herbalist.

Most Neo-Pagans are first-generation converts of Caucasian descent from Western industrial cultures. Although they believe in magic and spiritual interventions, they also believe in the scientific method and modern medicine. They will usually seek standard Western medical and counseling help first and resort to their spiritual communities and clergy only in a secondary way. They will, however, often choose not to discuss their spirituality with helping professions, which can lead to shallower therapeutic alliance.

The topic of spiritual guidance in Neo-Paganism is, in fact, currently a hot and contentious topic. There is an increasing cognizance of the lack of spiritual direction and counseling training of clergy and a difference of opinion as to what to do about it. Some clergy are forming alliances with community members who are also licensed helping professionals, and others are going to newly formed professional seminaries like Cherry Hill Seminary. Some are taking crash courses in peer counseling similar to those that crisis hotline or hospital volunteers complete. Still others do not see this as being part of their job description; members are to learn to take care of themselves or seek professional help.

HOW SPIRITUAL DEVELOPMENT IS UNDERSTOOD IN NEO-PAGANISM

Each tradition is likely to have its own model of spiritual development, which the spiritual guide should endeavor to understand. Generally, most Neo-Pagans will view life as a training school, and their religious leaders as the instructors or mentors. It is their job to achieve personal responsibility and efficacy of action on both the mundane and spiritual planes. Most Neo-Pagans will have a vague understanding that they are involved in a series of earthly reincarnations, but the final outcome of such is murky, as Neo-Paganism is more concerned with the here and now.

Some other assumptions underlie spiritual development, although they are rarely stated aloud:

- The members will have a variety and depth of communication with spirits and gods. The members will use these communications in conducting their lives and benefiting the community.

- The members will have a sense of personal mission, quite possibly as a result of alignment with personal gods with which they resonate.

- The members will have a proper balance and relationship with earth, air, water, and fire, which will result in greater balance across all areas of life, including mental and physical health.

- The members will have a good understanding of themselves.

- The members will be effective and decisive in the world.

SPIRITUAL PRACTICES IN NEO-PAGANISM

Neo-Pagan practices include active and energetic methodologies to connect with the Divine (prayer, trance journeys, painting, writing, singing, divination, guided journeys, chanting, dancing) along with an expectation that individual Neo-Pagans have the power to initiate such contacts. Neo-Pagan worship is as much concerned with the movement and facilitation of energies as it is with connection to people, place, spirits, and gods. So, in addition to connecting with a wealth deity, a Neo-Pagan performing magic might conceive of ways to get the energy of wealth flowing toward her.

Neo-Pagans will also use focal points to fix their attention and intent. They will typically have shrines and altars with many images and statues of deities. They may have shrines to dead loved ones at which they may leave offerings. These could be altars inside one's home or offerings left outside at sites deemed holy.

Neo-Pagans will attempt connections with the living land and spirits around them for the purposes of being good neighbors, to solicit assistance, and because felt connection to the earth leads to caring about the earth. The altars and offerings mentioned above are one method of doing this because they direct the Neo-Pagan's energy and attention and strengthen intent to interact with the land and spirits.

Healing and facilitation of energy movement is often accomplished through the mastery and application of herbalism, Reiki, crystals, and other tools. Vast correspondence lists exist of what different herbs do (medicinally and magically), the purposes of different types of crystals, the purposes of different colors of candles, and the specific uses of different incenses. An experienced Neo-Pagan client will have memorized listings of such correspondences, and many seemingly random scents, colors, and objects around them will be purposefully chosen. The stone selected for a necklace likely has a purpose, and your client's color of clothing might be helping him or her with emotional mood. Concrete representations affect mental and spiritual states and sometimes physical reality. So, for example, a green or gold candle set on top of a magnet and a dollar bill might be drawing money to the Neo-Pagan. A ring with a certain type of stone in it might be providing spiritual protection.

Divination systems are popular; some folks will have regular consultations with tarot cards, runes, and the like. Some Neo-Pagans will rely heavily on such tools for important decision making.

COMMON SPIRITUAL ISSUES FOR NEO-PAGANS

The concept of personal responsibility is central in most forms of Paganism. Wiccans handle religious matters personally, pursuing direct contact with the Divine and often acting as their own priest or priestess. This religious stance can be used to empower clients toward taking responsibility for their lives. Believing that life events are under one's own control can lead to significantly better coping skills. In a similar vein, the concept of inherent divinity should be useful with clients suffering low self-esteem or feelings of worthlessness.

Personal connection to the Divine is critical in Paganism. In some cases, the type of gods being worked with can be adjusted to help the client. An artist might look to Bridget (Irish goddess of healing, inspiration, and smith craft) for inspiration. A client with social skills deficits might work with Oghma (Irish god of eloquence) or Aphrodite (Greek love goddess). The nurturing, mothering aspects of goddesses (or the Wiccan Goddess) can be emphasized for clients needing healing and love. These gods' myths can be looked to for inspiration and ideas to emulate.

Spiritual guides could look to Jungian and archetypal psychology for ways that they or individuals might work with gods. Some clients will be amenable to the idea that gods are alive and formational in the makeup of the human unconscious and personality.

Books such as Seena Frost's *SoulCollage: An Intuitive Collage Process for Individuals and Groups* or Judy Harrow's *Devoted to You: Honoring Deity in Wiccan Practice* can also assist spiritual directors in helping Neo-Pagan clients deepen their faith and find meaning in it (see Resources at the end of this chapter). Using Frost's book, clients develop collage pictures representing different pieces of themselves ("adult," "warrior") and do exercises and meditations with these pictures or collages to get to know themselves better. Clients could do very similar work to determine which deities the client thinks she is most similar to or composed of and the nature of the personal relationship with each deity. Harrow's book outlines ways to set up altars, collect myths, run rituals, and generally grow closer to various deities.

Spiritual directors can take meditations, guided imagery, affirmations, and relaxation exercises from Pagan rituals and spiritual practices to facilitate working with Neo-Pagan clients. Pagan clients usually carry with them a well-developed arsenal of practices that most spiritual guides don't know their clients have and that can be reactivated. Spiritual guides who have studied hypnosis will see huge overlaps between many Neo-Pagan spiritual and meditative techniques and their hypnotherapy training.

For example, many Neo-Pagans will have developed astral travel capabilities—similar to guided meditation techniques and self-hypnosis—in which they are able to leave themselves and go in search of spirit guides, deities, or experiences that will answer a problem or question. A spiritual guide might ask a Neo-Pagan client trying to find a career more in touch with her spiritual needs to use known astral travel techniques to look for guidance on this issue. Similarly, the client might develop and conduct a ritual in which guidance is requested from a spiritual source, use a divination technique, or watch for information in dreams and signs in nature.

Many spiritual guides can start sessions with a prayer, deep cleansing breaths, a vowel sound, or some other method to calm and focus the client's mind and mark the time in the session as special. Most Wiccan clients will already know a "ground and center" exercise (a relaxation visualization and breathing technique) that the spiritual guide might use instead of other calming and focusing exercises from their own tradition.

Most active Neo-Pagans will likely go to see a Neo-Pagan spiritual leader for spiritual issues. Neo-Pagans consulting a spiritual guide may be coming because they have doubts about the Neo-Pagan religious path as a whole or have had an especially negative experience with a Neo-Pagan leader or group.

To help address the questions or needs of clients with overall doubts as to their proper spiritual path, spiritual guides might use general toolsets for spiritual seekers. I like to use the "Belief-O-Matic," a questionnaire at www.beliefnet.com named with tongue-in-cheek playfulness but useful in initially matching seekers with the world religious traditions that might best match their views. Seekers can then investigate religions as their hearts dictate. Spiritual guides should notice that there is no general restriction within Neo-Paganism forbidding Neo-Pagans from participating in other religions as well as Neo-Paganism. You may well have a client come to you for spiritual guidance in another religion, only to find out that the client also attends Pagan rituals. Indeed, people who mix other religious traditions with Paganism often refer to themselves playfully with terms such as "Jewitches" or "Episcopagans." Some Pagan groups may limit such participation for persons in specific advanced Pagan clergy training programs.

The varied quality and homegrown nature of some Pagan organizations can result in poor experiences. Therefore spiritual guides may find themselves assisting Neo-Pagans who have fled a disappointing group. Spiritual guides may assist discouraged Pagans to realize that disastrous encounters with specific groups or individuals do not mean that their spiritual paths are entirely unsuitable.

Some Neo-Pagans struggle with the challenge of understanding or discerning which gods and goddesses are calling to them. Spiritual guides may wish to help these clients develop a structure in which the clients read about, meditate on, and participate in rituals for various entities until they feel some affinity and connection with gods as a result. Some clients may have lost their feeling of connection with specific deities with which they once worked. In addition to trying to help clients regain their connections with deities, it is also okay for spiritual guides to advise Neo-Pagans to let connections lapse and to try new deity relationships if this feels right to the client. Sometimes certain gods and spirits will work with a person for a time, only to bow out when they have completed their work or finished the lesson they wanted to teach the person.

There are many common spiritual guidance problems that a non-Pagan spiritual guide is unlikely to be called upon to address with Pagans. These include learning to feel and communicate with the four elements (earth, air, fire, and water), learning to hear Spirit as a channel for successful divination or mediumship, learning to set up and take down the energies of sacred space used for rituals, and learning to submit to entities for divine possession. Spiritual guides who happen to have skillsets with the use of crystals, herbs, and incense should feel encouraged to ask if these might be of benefit to Neo-Pagan clients.

Historian Dr. Ruth Crocker outlines many ways in which a client's Paganism might have an impact on the issues she brings to a psychotherapy session, many of which are also pertinent to spiritual guidance. Pagans who attend only occasional festivals, instead of regular congregational involvement, may be experiencing feelings of isolation. The client might be questioning the reality of shamanic experiences, such as hearing voices or seeing visions, because the larger society around her might question the truth of such experiences. Due to a higher percentage of women, lesbians, and gays participating in Neo-Paganism, spiritual guides may see more conscious, personal grappling with issues of sexuality, gender, and sexual orientation than in other religions with different demographics. Pagans often struggle with the impact of telling others about their religion ("coming out of the broom closet"), and the social implications of being known as Pagan can affect jobs, relationships, and child custody. Symptoms of trauma may be more prevalent among Pagans, owing to the lack of acceptance or the outright hostility shown by family and prior religious institutions. Issues regarding confidentiality may surface in spiritual guidance because many Pagans are forbidden by oath from discussing certain aspects of their training or rituals.

Dr. Crocker also suggests strengths upon which spiritual guides can capitalize, including existing familiarity with Jungian psychology, high educational level, strong social support from small ritual groups, the psychotherapeutic value of Pagan rituals, Pagan leadership training in helping professions, and a generally high sense of personal responsibility.[4]

SPIRITUAL GUIDE ATTITUDES AND SPIRITUALITY VERSUS PSYCHOSIS

Pagan clients often do not tell their helping professionals about their religion for fear of being thought crazy. In my own psychotherapy practice, I had one client quit her former psychiatrist and therapist after he increased her antipsychotic medications without discussion once she made mention of talking with her goddesses. Our dialogue on this topic quickly revealed her deity contacts to be sources of comfort and strength that in no way damaged her abilities to hold a job, maintain friendships, or otherwise engage mundane reality.

Spiritual guides do not generally diagnose or work with clear mental health concerns. Yet spiritual guides have to learn when to handle client concerns spiritually versus referring them to licensed mental health professionals. This may prove especially challenging with Neo-Pagan clients, whose spiritual beliefs and abilities would seem psychotic to some in mainstream Western society.

While it is wise to seek licensed mental health consultation as a precaution, I think that you can apply some commonsense questions when making a preliminary determination if mental health boundaries have been crossed:

- Are the spiritual contacts harming the client or causing him or her to lose connection with mundane reality?
- Are the client's activities, beliefs, and perceptions well outside the Pagan norm?
- Does the situation bother, hurt, or move the client away from health?
- Does the situation interfere with work or everyday living?
- Can the client put the situation aside when needed? Can the client focus on mundane life when needed?
- Will the client listen to trusted people to tell the client when situations are interfering with life and social connections?
- Is the client unduly rigid and inflexible in religious matters?
- Does the situation assist the client's functioning in some way and/or bring peace and joy?

OFFERING GUIDANCE TO NEO-PAGANS

I find Neo-Pagans to be among my most enjoyable clients. There is so much variety among them; one moment you will be discussing ancient practices, and the next moment your Pagan clients will simply invent or modify practices to their liking! These clients tend to be action oriented, so brainstorming plans with them can be very rewarding. Just keep an open mind, be willing to be educated—you may learn some fascinating practices and history—and treat them as empowered and esteemed co-creators in spiritual development. You will enjoy being able to suggest tools you have learned elsewhere (meditations, crystals, incense, Reiki) and see how they can be integrated into your Pagan clients' practices.

NOTES

1. Generally Wicca and British Traditional Witchcraft (BTW) are thought of as separate religions, but there is a bit of overlap. Gardnerian Wicca is thought of as being BTW in part because it is an initiatory secret religion revealed from older British witchcraft practices. Generic Wicca, especially where it lacks initiations and is freely available in published books, is not considered BTW.
2. W. E. Butler, *Magic: Its Ritual, Power and Purpose* [1952] (Wellingborough, England: The Aquarian Press, 1975), 12.
3. Helen A. Berger, Evan A. Leach, and Leigh S. Shaffer, *Voices from the Pagan Census: A National Survey of Witches and Neo-Pagans in the United States* (Columbia, SC: University of South Carolina Press, 2003), 1–35.
4. Ruth Crocker, "Psychotherapy with Pagans: Religiously Sensitive Therapy with Followers of the 'Old Religion'" (lecture, symposium on "Implications for Counseling" at the Third Annual Mid-Year Conference on Religion and Spirituality, sponsored by the American Psychological Association, Division 36 and the Department of Pastoral Counseling at Loyola College, Columbia, MD, April 1–2, 2005).

RESOURCES

Online Resources

Ár nDraíocht Féin: A Druid Fellowship (ADF): www.adf.org/core

Covenant of the Goddess (CoG): www.cog.org

A guide for hospital chaplains and other health care providers: www.washington-baltimore-paganclergy.org/archives/hospital-chaplaincy-education-slideshow

The Order of Bards, Ovates, and Druids: www.druidry.org

Proteus Coven Library: http://proteuscoven.com/library.htm

Raven Kindred (Asatru): www.ravenkindred.com

The Shadow of Olympus (Hellenismos): www.iskios.com

The Witches' Voice: www.witchvox.com/basics/wfaq.html

A Few Good Basic Books

Clifton, Chas S. *Her Hidden Children: The Rise of Wicca and Paganism in America.* Lanham, MD: AltaMira Press, 2006.

Cunningham, Scott. *Wicca: A Guide for the Solitary Practitioner.* St. Paul, MN: Llewellyn, 2001.

Farrar, Janet, and Stewart Farrar. *The Witches' Goddess.* Blaine, WA: Phoenix, 1987.

Frost, Seena B. *SoulCollage: An Intuitive Collage Process for Individuals and Groups.* Santa Cruz, CA: Hanford Mead, 2001.

Harrow, Judy. *Devoted to You: Honoring Deity in Wiccan Practice.* New York: Citadel Press, 2003.

Harrow, Judy. *Spiritual Mentoring: A Pagan Guide.* Toronto, ON: ECW Press, 2002.

Hillman, James. *A Blue Fire: Selected Writings by James Hillman.* Edited by Thomas Moore. New York: Harper & Row, 1989.

K., Amber. *True Magick: A Beginner's Guide.* St. Paul, MN: Llewellyn, 1997.

RELIGIONS ORIGINATING IN CHINA

Joshua Snyder taught English at the Pohang University of Science and Technology in North Gyeongsang Province, in the Confucian heartland of South Korea, where he lived for fourteen years. He is an American Catholic who works at the Rochester Institute of Technology in upstate New York.

Spiritual Guidance in the Confucian Tradition

Joshua Snyder

A BRIEF HISTORY OF CONFUCIANISM

Confucianism can claim to have guided more people over a longer period of time than any of the world's religious or philosophical traditions. It has provided the ethical underpinning for Chinese civilization for close to two and a half millennia. For hundreds of years it has similarly guided the peoples of Vietnam, Korea, and Japan. The millions of Chinese, Vietnamese, Koreans, and Japanese in their countries' diasporas have brought the teachings of Confucianism to host countries throughout the world. Confucian teachings, translated into Latin and brought back to Europe by Catholic missionaries, had a profound influence on European Enlightenment thinkers; the civil service examinations that now exist in all Western countries were a Chinese import.

Thus, it can be rightly said that no human being has had more influence over more people for more time than Confucius (551–479 BCE), although the sage himself might disagree. "I transmit but do not innovate," he said. "I am truthful in what I say, and devoted to antiquity" (Analects VII:1). For Confucius, the ethical system he laid down was not an innovation, but simply an attempt to recover the ancient knowledge that had been lost or forgotten by his contemporaries, living as they were in what he saw as degraded times. Confucius believed that the ancients, understanding as they did the order and hierarchy of heaven and earth, provided the model not only for a rightly ordered society, but for individuals as well.

Confucius (or K'ung Fu-tzu, from which his Latinized name comes) was born in the Chinese state of Lu (present-day Qufu) into the minor nobility in what is known as the "Spring and Autumn Period" of China's history, a time of great social upheaval and uncertainty, which would devolve, after the sage's death, into the "Warring States Period." While this period was characterized by social disruption, violence, and chaos, it also saw the birth of the "Hundred Schools of Thought"—the golden age of Chinese philosophy—of which the school that would be known as Confucianism was to be the most prominent.

K'ung Ch'iu, as Confucius was known in his youth, lost his father at the age of three and was raised in poverty by his mother. He entered what was then a relatively new social class, the *shu*, which was situated between the commoners and the nobility and relied on talent, not accidents of birth, for social mobility. The *shu* might rightly be called the world's oldest meritocracy.

In the second chapter of the Analects, the main record of his teachings, Confucius offers this briefest of intellectual autobiographies: "At fifteen my heart was set on learning; at thirty I stood firm; at forty I had no more doubts; at fifty I knew the mandate of heaven; at sixty my ear was obedient; at seventy I could follow my heart's desire without transgressing the norm" (Analects II:4).

In his youth, Confucius was said to have worked as a farmhand, as a clerk, and as a bookkeeper. He rose to the position of minister of justice in the state of Lu at the age of fifty-three but found the duke under whom he was serving to be corrupt morally. He resigned his service and left the state of Lu and for years wandered throughout the neighboring states teaching his political and moral principles. Legend has it that at some point during his travels, he met Lao Zi, the founder of Daoism, China's main other—and more otherworldly—philosophy. Although he was often received into the courts of the rulers of those states, he did not see his ideas implemented by any of them. Disappointed, he returned home, where he taught his disciples and transmitted the teachings of the ancients through what the Chinese call the "Five Classics."

Confucianism is both a political philosophy and a method for self-cultivation. Indeed, for Confucius and his followers, the two are not separate. The idea that "the personal is political" would not seem strange to Confucius.

In the *Great Learning*, Confucius summarized his teachings as follows:

> The ancients who wished to illustrate illustrious virtue throughout the kingdom first ordered well their own states. Wishing to order well their states, they first regulated their families. Wishing to regulate their families, they first cultivated their persons. Wishing to cultivate their persons, they first rectified their hearts. Wishing to rectify their hearts, they first sought to be sincere in their thoughts. Wishing to be sincere in their thoughts, they first extended to the utmost their knowledge. Such extension of knowledge lay in the investigation of things. (*Great Learning* I:5–8)

A well-ordered society was a reflection of the hierarchies of heaven. Just as only the eldest son was deemed proper to perform familial sacrificial offerings, only the emperor himself could offer sacrifices to heaven. Respect for hierarchy and social duty were not only social obligations; they had a spiritual and even religious dimension as well, and in fulfilling these, one was following the will of heaven.

Thus, Confucians see the state as an extension of the family. The family, in turn, is ordered by filial piety, or respect of children toward elders. This respect extends beyond the grave, and mourning rituals played and play an extensive role in the development of Confucianism. The importance of relationships is central to Confucianism, which has historically determined five reciprocal relationships: ruler to ruled, father to son, husband to wife, elder brother to younger brother, and friend to friend.

For self-cultivation, Confucianism rests on two pillars, *jen* and *li*. *Jen* is often translated as "benevolence" or "humanity." Indeed, one of the oldest expressions of the Golden Rule is found in the Analects: "Do not do unto others what you would not have them do unto you" (Analects XV:24). Confucianism's second most important philosopher, Mencius (385–302 BCE), or Meng Ke, held that people were born naturally good and would argue that a ruler without "humanity" had lost the "mandate of heaven."

Li might be simply translated as "ritual," although not exclusively in the religious sense of the word. For Confucians, propriety and etiquette in everyday life, in relation to persons and even things, are of utmost importance.

The goal of Confucian self-cultivation is to become a gentleman, or "superior man," by cultivating one's filial piety and loyalty as well as humanity and benevolence. By cultivating one's self morally in such a way, one is able to cultivate others by example. Confucian political philosophy extols rule by example, not by force, and this ideal is to be carried out in everyday life as well.

Confucianism met with various successes and failures in the Warring States Period, which came to an end in 221 BCE with Chinese unification under the Qin Empire. Under the first emperor, Confucianism was violently suppressed in favor of the official state ideology of legalism, which held that strong laws and harsh punishments, not moral self-cultivation, were required for a stable and flourishing society. Confucian texts were burned. Confucian scholars were said to have been buried alive.

In 206 BCE, the Qin Dynasty was replaced by the Han, and Confucianism became the state ideology and would remain so until the twentieth century. The greatest development during this long period was the advent of Neo-Confucianism, whose most notable proponent was Chu Hsi (1130–1200 CE). Neo-Confucianism added certain spiritual concepts from Buddhism and Daoism to Confucianism, adding to it perhaps a deeper spiritual dimension. It was this Neo-Confucianism that spread to Korea and Japan and had a profound influence in shaping those countries, to such an extent that Korea is said to be even more Confucian than China.

In China, Confucianism was again repressed following the Communist victory in 1949 in the Cultural Revolution of the 1960s. However, following the country's economic development in the 1980s and 90s, the Chinese government recognized not only the importance of Confucianism in forming Chinese culture and civilization, but also the potential it could play in providing cohesiveness and stability to a rapidly modernizing society. Thus, China is currently experiencing a Confucian renaissance of sorts.

But whatever periodic declines or flourishing that this philosophical traditional may have experienced, Confucianism in its two-millennia tutelage of the people of East Asia has profoundly shaped the cultures of China, Vietnam, Korea, and Japan. The mark it has left is so indelible that a person from any of these countries can be considered Confucian to a certain extent, even if he or she does not identify him- or herself as a Confucian.

This is also true for those who profess adherence to another religion, such as a Vietnamese Buddhist or a Korean Christian, for example. Thus, when approaching spiritual matters with an East Asian person of any religion, or even of no religion, it is helpful to keep Confucianism in mind. What, then, is the Confucian outlook toward spiritual matters?

TRADITIONS OF SPIRITUAL GUIDANCE IN CONFUCIANISM

It might at first seem odd to talk about spiritual guidance in a system of thought that not only emphasizes self-cultivation, but also to a certain extent de-emphasizes the spiritual aspects of life, about which Confucius himself was largely silent. While Neo-Confucianism introduced some more overtly spiritual content from Buddhism and Daoism, this knowledge is largely confined on a practical basis only to those who have studied the doctrines of Confucianism deeply.

Furthermore, as Confucianism is, properly speaking, more of a philosophical system than a religion, there is no full-time priesthood. When Confucian rituals are performed (as they are most markedly in South Korea in ancestral remembrance ceremonies), it is the head of each household, the eldest male, traditionally, who acts as the celebrant. With no clergy to speak of, the Confucian appears to have no one to whom to turn when confronted with difficult spiritual matters.

Yet, since Confucianism emphasizes the practical social aspects of life and is based on harmonious relationships with others, it is in the social realm where the Confucian seeks spiritual guidance. Let us return to the five reciprocal relationships mentioned earlier and analyze them at a deeper level to see how the typical Confucian would go about seeking spiritual guidance:

> *Between parent and child, there must be closeness.*
> *Between ruler and subject, there must be justice.*
> *Between husband and wife, there must be distinction.*
> *Between old and young, there must be order.*
> *Between friends, there must be trust.*

Between parent and child, there must be closeness. A Confucian seeking spiritual guidance on a particularly intimate matter might first go to his or her parents for assistance. While in the West, upon reaching adulthood, children are seen as social equals to their parents, this is not the case in East Asia. Parents in the East still exert a significant influence on their children well into adulthood. Parental counsel in major life decisions, such as marriage, career, and family, are taken seriously by adult Confucians.

Between ruler and subject, there must be justice. Practically speaking, in modern societies, whether Eastern or Western, leaders no longer exert moral or spiritual authority over the citizens of their countries. However, when the people perceive moral or spiritual matters as being egregiously violated by officials, be they elected or not, social disharmony can follow, which can have a negative effect on an individual's spiritual state. The ultimate expression of the social disharmony negatively affecting an individual's spiritual state, practically unknown in the West, is the practice of suicide as social protest.

Between husband and wife, there must be distinction. Just as in Western countries where modernization has had an impact on the traditional roles played by husbands and wives, Eastern counties have recently experienced the dramatic shifts associated with women entering the workforce and families having fewer children. Yet it might be said the changes here have been more gradual and less abrupt. While it may be true that a wife might be more inclined to seek spiritual guidance from her husband, a husband might also be aware of the spiritual gifts of his wife and seek her guidance, perhaps in a less direct way.

Between old and young, there must be order. East Asians sometimes say that in Confucian societies, there is a generation gap even among twins. Elder siblings, particularly eldest brothers, are not only expected to take care of their parents, they also have certain responsibilities toward their younger siblings. In turn, these younger siblings offer certain deference to the opinions of their elder siblings, while also enjoying a bit of freedom from the responsibilities with which these latter are shouldered. Confucian society is familial in nature, and similar relationships exist at schools between upperclassmen and lowerclassmen and in companies between senior and junior employees. Thus, it would not be uncommon for a Confucian to seek advice on spiritual matters from an elder sibling or senior member of an institution.

Between friends, there must be trust. Friendship is highly valued in Confucian societies. The first book in Chinese written by Matteo Ricci, sixteenth-century Catholic missionary to China, was a treatise on friendship, which won him many admirers among the Chinese literati. Thus, on a confidential spiritual matter requiring trust, a Confucian might first turn to a friend for guidance.

Thus, depending on the nature of the spiritual guidance sought, a Confucian might turn to any number of people within his or her social circle for assistance. Another figure playing an important role in Confucian society, to whom anyone might turn for advice in spiritual matters, is the teacher. Irrespective of subject, students might approach a teacher who commands moral authority and respect, even much later in life. There is a saying in Confucian societies, "Once a teacher, always a teacher." It is not uncommon for students who have a fond attachment to a certain teacher or professor to visit him or her several decades after graduation.

Also occupying this position of teacher are others whose roles are similar in life, such as mentors, supervisors, pastors, and community leaders, for example. To any of these, a Confucian might turn for advice on spiritual matters.

SPIRITUAL PRACTICES IN CONFUCIANISM

Confucianism, being a social philosophy more than a religion, presents certain obvious challenges when it comes to any discussion of its spiritual practices. As mentioned earlier, Confuicians place a great deal of emphasis on ritual. Confucians particularly emphasize mourning rituals in their lives, which is why Confucianism has come to be associated with "ancestor worship" by Westerners.

Interestingly, Confucius himself expressed doubt about the presence of ancestral spirits at the ceremonies. For him, the important issue was that people maintain a proper attitude of respect and gratitude toward one's ancestors, especially one's parents. He would agree that funerals are for the living. Perhaps it was Confucius's own ambivalence toward the spiritual dimension of mourning rites that has resulted in a decline in what Westerners would recognize as "ancestor worship" in the East. Indeed, only in South Korea are ancestral offerings still widely practiced, and even there they are limited to certain lunar calendar holidays and death anniversaries.

Chinese and Vietnamese may have home altars on which pictures of parents and grandparents are placed, but although Confucian in origin, the practice is often more associated with Buddhism. Chinese and Koreans have a holiday in the fall sometimes called Grave Sweeping Day in which the final resting places of parents and grandparents are visited and maintained. Of course, a good Confucian will find other times throughout the year to visit the graves of loved ones.

Outside of mourning rites and practices, there is very little that a Westerner would identify as distinctly "spiritual" in Confucian practice. However, for the Confucian, the social world has a spiritual dimension. A Confucian might not see the social and spiritual worlds as separated. The dividing line between heaven and earth is not as distinct as it is in, say, the Abrahamic religions. Thus, what a Westerner might see as an exclusively familial or social issue could very well be seen by a Confucian as having spiritual consequences.

Meditation, while not specifically mentioned by Confucius, was developed by the Neo-Confucians, who, as we have seen, incorporated some practices from Buddhism and Daoism into the philosophy. This meditation, however, can take on myriad forms for Confucians. It could be the contemplation of a text or merely the enjoyment of nature.

HOW SPIRITUAL DEVELOPMENT IS UNDERSTOOD IN CONFUCIANISM

Confucianism is a social philosophy that stresses self-cultivation. The goal of the Confucian is to fulfill his or her social and familial roles to the best of his or her ability and to emulate as well as possible the models put forth in the Confucian canon (and in the many popular tales from ancient days that remain as exemplars to the people of China, Vietnam, Korea, and Japan). An adult child will strive to sacrifice for his or her parents in their old age, providing for them both materially and emotionally, just as a parent will sacrifice for his or her children when they are young.

At what might be considered a more spiritual level, the Confucian will strive to be a moral agent in his or her life, to "do the right thing" in each particular circumstance occasioned by the different social roles one plays. To the outsider, even this may seem an entirely worldly focus and have little to do with spiritual matters, but as mentioned before, the Confucian does not divide these realms as a Westerner might.

The ultimate goal of the Confucian in life is to become what is often translated as a "superior person." This ideal Confucian would be a person of impeccable morality who is esteemed socially. For a modern person, this might well entail a degree of social success, but more importantly it would involve leading a virtuous, harmonious life and fulfilling all of one's social and familial responsibilities.

COMMON SPIRITUAL ISSUES FOR CONFUCIANS

Confucianism is a philosophy that stresses harmonious familial and social relations. Thus, when there is disharmony and discord in one's family or workplace, the individual suffers a spiritual toll. Also, as being esteemed socially is important, the concept of "saving face" (i.e., protecting one's reputation) is considered by Confucians to be of utmost importance when repairing damaged social relationships (especially providing ways for others to save face).

Scholars have often made a distinction between the "shame cultures" of the East and the "guilt cultures" of the West. While this can be a helpful distinction, it often oversimplifies matters. While it is true that for the Confucian, the opinion of others about oneself plays a great role in life, it would be wrong to suggest that Confucians are not also conscious of their own moral failings, even if they are unknown to others.

The social and familial emphasis of Confucianism leads its adherents to suffer spiritually when there is disharmony at work or at home. When an individual believes that he or she is the cause of this disharmony, he or she may feel a profound sense of guilt. This person may be highly reticent to discuss such an issue, as this would result in shame. Anything arousing shame in a Confucian must be carefully avoided by those interacting with the individual.

With the philosophy's stressing of filial piety, failings (real or perceived) toward one's aged parents will particularly be a source of inner strife for the Confucian. Likewise, failings toward one's children, or conversely the failings of these children, no matter what their age, will cause spiritual turmoil for a Confucian.

The Confucian may turn to any of the five reciprocal relationships (ruler to ruled, father to son, husband to wife, elder brother to younger brother, and friend to friend) for spiritual guidance. If these spiritual matters involve discord in one of these relationships, direction must be sought from another person.

Finally, given the importance of relationships, the Confucian might be unwilling to seek advice in spiritual matters from a person he or she perceives to be an outsider. Thus, it is important in giving spiritual guidance to a Confucian first to establish a relationship. In this, age may prove to be a critical factor as to the type of relationship established. An older spiritual guide might approach his or her Confucian client as a caring parent would a child or as a teacher would a student. If the difference in age is closer, the relationship of a trusted friend would be appropriate. Finally, if such a relationship proves impossible, it would be best to guide the Confucian toward the personal resources in his or her own life where guidance can be found.

RESOURCES

Confucius (film). Directed by Mei Hu. 2010.

Fung, Yu-Lan. *A Short History of Chinese Philosophy*. New York: Free Press, 1997.

Lin, Yutang. *The Importance of Living* [1937]. New York: William Morrow, 1998.

Setton, Mark. *Chong Yagyong: Korea's Challenge to Orthodox Neo-Confucianism*. Albany, NY: State University of New York Press, 1997.

He Feng Dao Shi (Thom McCombs, DO) is the Ridgecrest Junction Way Teacher and an osteopathic physician in private practice in Northern California. He was Abbot of the Golden Elixir Temple in Issaquah, Washington, from 1992–2001. His teacher was Share K. Lew (Phoenix Mind Way Teacher) of Yellow Dragon Temple in Guangdong, China. They transmit the Dao Dan Pai (Way of the Elixir) and Tai Ji Chir (Great Pivot Ruler) traditions of Daoist cultivation. Dr. Thom also plays classical guitar and is fond of geology.

Spiritual Guidance in Daoism

He Feng Dao Shi

DAOISM: THE WAY OF THE WAY

Contemporary Daoism has its beginnings in the indigenous religions of East Asia. It begins as a formal religion around the year 150 CE in what is today known as Han Dynasty China, at that time a disintegrating empire previously assembled out of numerous warring states. With each state honoring different indigenous gods, this lack of religious cohesion made unifying these states difficult. People believed that the gods interfered in human destiny and provoked war and dissension, much as the Greek gods did throughout the Trojan War.

Centuries before this time, both Lao Zi and Chuang Zi had written about the Dao (the Way), but Daoism was far from a recognizable religion. Then, about two millennia ago, a wise sage named Zhang Daoling stepped forward to found a formal religion around those teachings—a religion that would eventually unify China. This religion put an end to sacrifice, both human and animal, insisting that incense instead of blood be offered to the gods. All gods would be honored, none worshipped. Instead of worshipping any particular god, the followers of this religion would venerate Dao. The Dao was too large to be contained within any single religion, too vast to exclude anything or any deity, too ineffable to be grasped by any doctrine. To simply "go with the flow" was to follow the Dao—a way of yielding suppleness. This is true in both directions: to follow the Dao is to be one with the Dao. In this new religion, humans would fulfill their own destinies as free beings, not as servants of rival gods. Religious wars were over.[1]

83

When Buddhism entered China (also about two millennia ago), it brought with it a tone of harmony and acceptance that embraced the deities of both faiths, who were often depicted as companions. Many a Daoist venerates Gwan Yin, a Buddhist goddess revered throughout East Asia for the past thousand years and throughout the world today. Chan (Zen) Buddhism is strongly informed by Daoism. The Complete Reality schools of Daoism are strongly inspired by Chan Buddhism.

There is no grand cosmic drama in the Daoist narrative, no contest between good and evil for the souls of humankind. The world was self-condensed out of the Void, not created to stage a morality play. Hells exist, administered by divine wardens that judge souls and administer punishments. Heavens exist, ruled by the Jade Emperor, operating a vast administration similar to that seen in any busy country.

BASIC TERMS AND TEACHINGS OF DAOISM

Dao is "the Way," the context in which all energy flows through the universe. Objects condense out of Dao, are carried along with it through their lives, and then dissolve into it at death, never really separate from it.

De is often translated "virtue" but has a mystical implication that makes "grace" more apt. A follower of the Way lives a life that generates, respects, and is guided by such virtue.

Jing is "seed," the life force of sexual vitality. It naturally transforms into *qi*, a process nurtured and amplified by Daoist practices.

Neidan is "inner elixir," or internal alchemy, deep practices of meditative transformation that fuse sexuality, breath, and spirit into a transcendent Being.

Qi (*chi*) is "energy," the life force of the body and universe, swirling through the Void. Things condense out of the Void around swirls of qi, just as clouds form out of the sky out of swirls of wind. Qi moves into the body through breathing and is generated from *jing*.

Qigong is "energy work," cultivation of the life force through breathing and movement. It amplifies the currents of life and can be mildly aerobic.

Shen is "spirit," the highest level of energy. It is made from qi within the body, and it is also the Divine, the frequency on which the universe operates.

Tai Ji (Tai Chi) is the "Great Pivot" in the yin/yang cycle, where one extreme pivots to become the other, the point where inhale becomes exhale, or when the wave pauses at the top of the beach before receding.

Wu wei is "not doing," an attitude of nonattachment to action. By abandoning force as an approach to life, the follower of the Way "goes with the flow" as things develop.

Yang is like the sunny side of the hill—warm, bright, and outgoing.

Yin is like the shady side of the hill—cool, dark, and withdrawn.

Yin and *Yang* cycle back and forth throughout nature: inhale/exhale, systole/diastole, sunrise/sunset, waxing/waning of the moon, swelling of the tides and seasons of the year—all are expressions of this cycle.

Ziran is "what is so-of-itself," the ultimate authenticity. When things, and practitioners, operate from out of their intrinsic nature, Dao is operating.

Zuowong is "sitting and forgetting": seated, nonconceptual meditation. Quiet observation of one's interior world is conducted without visualization or mantra.

TWO MAJOR SECTS OF DAOISM

The Heavenly Teacher (Tian Shi) lineage is now almost two thousand years old, continuing the legacy of Zhang Daoling in Taiwan. The current Heavenly Teacher is his sixty-fifth generational descendant. Tian Shi priests live in the community, marry and raise families, care for the local spirits, and have a strong practice focused on ritual.

The Complete Reality (Quanzhen) lineage was founded by Lu Dongbin, a Daoist sage born in the year 798 CE. Quanzhen priests live as monks. They are celibate, are vegetarian, and have a strong focus on martial arts and qigong. They are headquartered in the White Cloud Temple in Beijing. There have been about twenty-five generations of monks since the school was founded.

Both schools practice ritual, chanting, healing, meditation, internal alchemy, astrology, divination, geomancy, scholarship, and magic. Tai Ji, painting, calligraphy, military strategy, and trance channeling are all Daoist arts. They are practiced to cultivate spiritual growth, seeking perfection of form and timing to invoke the ineffable. People seek out Daoist priests for healing, exorcism, and divination. Priests use ritual and magic to rectify the flow of energy through difficult situations, from drought to demonic possession. Priests care for the local spirits that inhabited their regions, mediating with the spirit world through ceremony and shamanic trance.

Daoist religious observance does not traditionally involve weekly services with hymns or sacraments. There is no missionary mandate in Daoism, no pressure to convert others. Instead, Daoism fosters disciple-master relationships. Disciples train in a number of Daoist arts during an apprenticeship that lasts decades.

MODERN AND POSTMODERN DEVELOPMENTS IN DAOISM

The Chinese governmental authorities repressed all religion during the last half of the twentieth century. Monasteries were closed— often destroyed—and many ancient religious sites were devastated. Temple-trained masters scattered across the world. The Heavenly Teacher sect was the most severely persecuted and remains in exile in Taiwan. Many religious sites, both Buddhist and Daoist, are reopening now for tourism, and monks have been enlisted as Chinese civil servants to operate the sites.

Many Westerners, disaffected with their birth religions, seek refuge in Daoism. Some will identify themselves as Daoists after a single reading of Lao Zi's *Dao De Jing* or popular works such as *The Tao of Pooh*.

With so little known about the Daoist faith in the West, converts have projected onto Daoism various aspects of the "religion they wish they'd had." In the mid-twentieth century, some Western writers saw Daoist sages as beatniks from the Far East who defied authority, rejected society, and got drunk constantly.

Many Western writers have co-opted the Daoist/Taoist arts to sell advancement in this world, as testified by such book titles as *The Tao of Power*, *The Tao of Management*, and *The Tao of Investing*, among many others. Some Western practitioners get caught up in Daoist sexual practices (similar to Kundalini yoga), loving the intense sensations and states of awareness that these practices can generate.

The information age has recently opened the West to a flood of knowledge about Daoism. Daoism is no longer quite the blank slate of the mid-twentieth century. Scholars and practitioners gather at conferences to share insights. Ancient texts are now available to wider audiences. A new generation of Daoist clergy is inventing a style of spiritual support tailored to Western culture and contemporary needs. A Daoist mission from Mount Wudang recently acquired land in Colorado to construct a traditional Daoist temple.

TRADITIONS OF SPIRITUAL GUIDANCE IN DAOISM

The Civilian Parishioner (Lay Daoist)

Most Daoist laypeople—both past and present—seek advice from Daoist clergy for matters such as life planning (e.g., determining auspicious dates to marry or to open a business), healing, and divination. A question Daoist clergy hear frequently is "Why are things going wrong in my life?" Answers to such questions often involve explorations of the consequences of fate rather than explorations of karma or past sins. Our fate is determined from the various alignments of celestial energy when we were born, and it is a force to be embraced and fulfilled, as well as softened (through Daoist practices). Fulfillment of fate permits freedom. For example, following a layperson's divorce, a Daoist spiritual guide might say to him or her, "You were fated to have a marriage end badly. Now that you have gone through that, you are free to craft a relationship of your own choice."

Daoists believe that troubles can arise from disgruntled ancestors whose own issues taint theirs with the ancestors' unfulfilled longings or desires for revenge. These situations can be rectified by rituals (perhaps at the particular ancestor's gravesite). Other hauntings can afflict people, too; *sha* is the term for negative energy picked up in the wilderness. Weakness and diarrhea can be symptoms of *sha* possession. In such cases, a Daoist priest might perform an exorcism. Spiritual guidance is called for to determine what resonance exists between the afflicted person and the spirit that precipitated the possession.

The Apprentice Clergy (Religious Daoist)

The Daoist student undergoes decades of arduous apprenticeship, including focused discipline, endurance, and loyalty to a mentor called a *shifu* or *sifu* (Mandarin and Cantonese, respectively, for "teaching father"). Many weary hours of practice over several years will bring up a host of issues for students. They are expected to endure both the severity of training and the emotional and spiritual issues evoked. The immersion in disciplined cultivation is called "eating bitter," and serves to soften fate by presenting the Daoist with the opportunity to engage his or her spiritual curriculum in the training hall rather than in daily life.

Much Daoist training can involve martial arts—peculiar for a nonviolent religion, but effective in strengthening the spirit and attention. When the mind wanders in meditation, the focus acquired in martial practice assists the practitioner in returning to the present. When inner work brings up frightening issues, young monks have already faced worse while holding their stances in sparring practice against senior students.

During their apprenticeship, as the students seek mastery of their skills, they also acquire mastery of self. Disciplines engaged will vary widely, but all are practiced as a Way: a Dao (Japanese and Korean do, as in *karate do, ju do, ken do, tae kwan do*). Additional training in traditional healing methods (herbal, manipulative, and energetic) gives the student many skills needed to help people. The master has the responsibility of healing both the physical and psychic injuries that a student incurs in Daoist training.

Spiritual Guidance Today

Spiritual guidance has historically been offered primarily to Daoist students, but as lay Daoists develop more communities focused on intensive spiritual practice, we will see a blurring of those traditional boundaries. Spiritual guides who encounter Daoists in their ministries will usually find that Western Daoists often have experience in Daoist arts such as Tai Ji, meditation, and other practices.

SPIRITUAL PRACTICES IN DAOISM

There are two fundamental Daoist practices:

- Silent observation of nature
- Silent meditation (*zuowong*—seated, nonconceptual observation of one's interior world)

Even without access to Daoist masters, scriptures, and training halls, the Dao student may train in the Way using these two practices. Even with all the authentic Daoist training and literature available today, the student will be lost without solid grounding in these two contemplative disciplines.

Other spiritual disciplines include the following:

- *Ceremonial chanting*, especially if one is training in a temple.

- *Study of Daoist scriptures*, both those specific to the lineage and those common to all Daoists, often through the student copying the entire text.

- *Practice of martial arts*, to condition students' bodies and to tone their spirits. Daoists will exhaustively drill with weapons and empty-handed moves, and monks can compete in sparring.

- *Practice of traditional Chinese medicine* (TCM), both as a service to the world and as a model of the universe's invisible workings. The flow of energy through the cosmos is mirrored in the flow of life through the body. The Daoist can influence this flow through acupuncture, herbs, manipulation, and external energy (qi) healing.

- *Practice of internal alchemy* (neidan), undertaking the transformation of life's vital forces into spiritual force.

The major discernment method employed in Daoism is *retroflection*—the observation of the self. Called "returning the light," Daoists turn the light of their awareness back upon themselves, watching their own watching and observing their own observations. Once viewed from within, Daoists can separate themselves from their issues simply by letting go of them. Daoists calm the mind in meditation through deliberate forgetting and relaxation. (See discussion of *wu wei* below.)

Those training in Daoist practices can experience pitfalls, of course—usually when the practices work! As the practitioner gains strength and power, it is easy to feel superior. The ego gains a huge boost in training as one grows in skill and seniority. When practitioners take on students of their own, the adulation and devotion of those students can corrupt teachers. Qigong can help one recover from a night of partying and dissipation and prepare for another night of partying and dissipation. Such misuse is constrained by peer pressure and religious doctrine when within the temple environment. In the West, however, apart from the sacred context and the supervision it provides, adepts can lose their Way.

HOW SPIRITUAL DEVELOPMENT IS UNDERSTOOD IN DAOISM

Daoists use two models to describe spiritual development, the Journey and the Alchemical Way. Both are applied in meditation, providing metaphors for the experiences encountered on the spiritual path.

The Journey

In the Journey model, the Daoist travels metaphorically with various companions on a quest for sacred knowledge. These companions represent those inner forces that the adept must cope with while traveling the Way. Commonly and famously, the Monkey King accompanies a young priest on his Journey to the West (Buddhist India) to recover sacred writings. The adept must cope with the Monkey King, which is a metaphor for the wandering of the mind. The priest (superego) attempts to keep on the Path, while the Monkey is easily distracted and wanders off.

Another version of the Journey has a young boy traveling far in a quest to find and recover his lost ox (water buffalo). The ox-boy wanders, looking for his great beast, tracks the ox, finds it, and tries to lead it home (each of these events represent stages in the quest to harmonize the inner mind), but the ox is mighty and stubborn. These quests lay out the general terrain encountered on the Way of internal cultivation and are common to Daoism and Buddhism. All meditation practitioners know ox and monkey.

The Alchemical Way

In the Alchemical model, the ancient steps of metallurgy become a metaphor for the stages of spiritual growth. The mind is the cauldron in which the raw ore (everything you are: genetics, culture, upbringing, actions, fate) is heated by alchemical practices until the living molten metal separates from the slag (spirit emerges from the dross). Even metals will evolve as they are refined further, their purest form being gold. Progress along the Alchemical Way is seen reflected in the inner light: what color is the background of your mind? Close your eyes for a moment and reflect backward: what color do you see? The transformation of lead into gold occurs in this background radiance.

Daoist Alchemical texts describe the subsequent formation of an "immortal embryo" within the adept's body, a creation that survives after the body dies. Many have pursued Daoist practices and formulae in the quest for eternal life. Indeed, at the highest obtainable state are the Daoist Immortals, radiant beings that have fused their inner forces into a transcendent sainthood. They wander the earth freely, cavort in the clouds, and participate in the heavenly administration.

The modern practitioner understands that all such romantic and heroic images are metaphorical and mythical; they are meant to inform, inspire, and motivate us, while educating us about the challenges of the spiritual path. These images and their stories teach those who are traveling along the Daoist Path what to expect and how to resolve it in order to grow.[2]

COMMON SPIRITUAL ISSUES FOR WESTERN DAOISTS

The Chinese government has attacked Daoists, destroyed their temples, ridiculed their worldview, and has only recently allowed Daoist sites to operate (and only under strict government supervision). Still, the ancient Way is followed in China, parts of Taiwan, South Korea, and Japan (through Shinto—*Shen Dao*, the Spirit Way). Sadly, many masters die without passing on their knowledge to the next generation. You, as a spiritual guide in the West, can do little about such things.

However, following are several issues common to Western Daoists that you can help with.

Wu Wei

Western Daoists often struggle with the principle of no-struggle (*wu wei*) as they attempt to fit Daoist teachings and practices into their lives. Westerners were raised to struggle in order to overcome life's challenging events, while Daoists must relax, accept all events, and be humble. Westerners bring to Daoism residue from their birth religions, seeking in Daoism an alternative model for redemption and salvation rather than seeing an ancient model for harmony and peace. Western Daoists seek immortality to escape dying rather than to prolong their lives and allow full resolution of their fate. Dying with one's fate unfulfilled leaves a ghost behind that can plague the living, and Daoists seek to avoid this through embracing their fates. The extra decades added to one's life by Daoist practices can allow one the time to fully embrace and resolve one's fate.

Power

Daoist practices generate power and can increase sexual attractiveness (*jing*), energy (*qi*), and psychic awareness (*shen*). Adepts can easily misuse these, especially when divorced from the culture of personal probity and restraint customary in residential and religious Daoist training. Many Daoist monasteries are vegetarian or have meat only as a garnish. This makes the monks much less aggressive than does a diet rich in animal protein. Combative training can easily get out of hand when personal rivalries arise. Sexual conquests are readily available as an adept grows in *jing*. Stable love relationships can become unbalanced as one partner develops more personal power than the other.

Misuse of Renewal Practices

Daoist practices provide physiological nurture and renewal, which can aid recovery from excessive partying or overwork. Daoist practices were never intended to provide an antidote to the injuries caused by Western lifestyles, nor were they intended to provide stability for the mentally ill (although they can provide both). Habitual use of such practices to sustain a hedonistic lifestyle is an abuse of the tradition and should be reformed quickly.

Injury

Daoist practices can cause energetic and physiological injuries as powerful internal forces move through the practitioner. Without a teacher to closely supervise a student, practices taken from books and Internet sources can dangerously warp the flow of qi through organ meridians, injuring the practitioner. Masters do not teach unless they can treat the injuries of practice, just as martial arts masters can treat the physical injuries occurring in their training halls.

OFFERING SPIRITUAL GUIDANCE TO DAOISTS

Daoists appreciate ceremony; candles and incense are a nice touch, if they don't set off the fire sprinklers. Offering these to open your spiritual guidance sessions is a fine way to be hospitable to Daoist clients. Daoist scriptures are comforting, readily available, and have interfaith appeal. Being familiar with them will help you guide your Daoist client with sensitivity and authority. On the downside, Daoist icons and altar accoutrements, while a nice touch, are not readily available outside of the Chinese community.

The Hospitalized Daoist

Ill or injured, the hospitalized Daoist will be grateful for your spiritual services. If acupuncture or Reiki therapies are available, please arrange a session. Many people—of all traditions—find scripture comforting when they are ill, and Daoist patients are no exception. Scriptures that Daoists will find most helpful are Lao Zi's *Dao De Jing*, Chuang Zi's *Inner Chapters*, and the first chapter of the *Huainan Zi*.[3]

Divination is important to Daoists and may be facilitated with a copy of the I Ching (*Yijing* or *Zhouyi*). Patients may simply pick any number between one and sixty-four to obtain an initial reading (more details are available if they know how to consult the text themselves with coins or yarrow stalks). Reading the chapter of that number will serve as a powerful tool to initiate conversation on the significance of current events and themes in the patient's life.

Ask about the client's practices; what is the Daoist doing to cultivate the Way? Slow deep-breathing exercises, meditation, and qigong are all possibilities of practices that will help a client cultivate the Way, even in the confines of a hospital bed. If there is a garden available for patients to enjoy, arrange to have your Daoist wheeled out to bask in nature.

In the setting of terminal illness, the Daoist will take comfort from the readings of Chuang Zi (Chuang Tsu) (see note 3). Dying in the depths of winter is more auspicious, for yin is strong and the dead are close. The journey to join the dead is short in fall and winter, easiest at the winter solstice, and progressively longer and more difficult as yang rises toward summer. Dying separates the yin soul (residual emotions) from the yang soul (spirit). The yin soul should quietly disperse into the earth, while the yang soul quietly disperses into the great ocean of Celestial Spirit. Unfulfilled fate and intense or unresolved emotions leave a psychic residue behind the dead. Willows planted near graves bring comfort to the dead, as do regular care and maintenance of gravesites. Spirit money (available in the Chinese community) burned as an offering to the dead brings comfort, redemption, and release to the dead. Encourage your dying Daoist to resolve his or her issues through release. *Let it go.*

The Imprisoned Daoist

The incarcerated Daoist will be disheartened by events and surrounded by hostile energetic influences. The cells, yards, food service, and other spaces will be energetically contaminated by the collective frustrations and rages of so many violent people incarcerated over many years. Ghosts will abound. Meeting spiritual needs in such a place is a high and difficult calling. Daoists will be grateful for a spiritual cleansing ceremony. You can also provide meditation supplies (especially incense), where permitted by authorities. Meditation may be impossibly uncomfortable for your Daoist until you have spiritually cleansed him or her of psychic residues. Provide scriptures and divination services as if in the hospital, teaching Daoist acceptance and harmony as a survival skill to endure confinement.

The Daoist Spiritual Direction Client

Daoists are subject to all the ills of humanity, which may undermine their faith. By virtue of their exotic religion and practices, they may believe that they are exceptional beings above mundane human issues. They may insist that their mundane issues are actually energetic hypersensitivity brought on by practice.

A good spiritual guide can help Daoist clients discern their level of groundedness and the need for balance and harmony. Ask about your client's relationship with his or her teacher and teachings: is your client practicing under the guidance of a living master or just trying exercises from a book or online source? If the latter, encourage your client to find a teacher and a community to provide accountability and guidance.

Is your Daoist client struggling to balance his or her energies? Many dysregulations of energy flow can be treated with acupuncture. Daoist dietary principles (balancing yin and yang foodstuffs with the changing seasons) can also help.

Is your client using Daoist practices as an antidote to his or her out-of-balance lifestyle? If so, some confrontation may be in order. You can certainly be direct and forceful, for a traditional Daoist teacher would probably not be as kind as you will be about such matters.

Has your client made any peace with his or her birth religion and god(s) or simply transplanted Western religious expectations onto an Eastern faith not designed to meet them? If so, you might encourage your client to take care of unfinished business with his or her faith of origin. A renewed review of Daoism and what it can and can't offer to your client is also appropriate.

Is your client continuing to struggle with unresolved family issues that have a negative impact on his or her spiritual health? You might suggest a pilgrimage to the graves of parents and grandparents, where the Daoist can perform the appropriate rituals. Invite your client to tidy up the site and burn "spirit money" (available in any Chinese community) for his or her ancestors.

Remind your Daoist clients:

- *Be calm and quiet.* Fretting is against their religion.

- *Be soft and weak.* The use of force and strength is against their religion.

- *Be modest.* Your Daoist clients are not going to attain immortality and transcend their difficulties. More power will not help. Have them back off the high-level internal alchemy and reengage quiet sitting (nonconceptual meditation) and deep breathing.

- *Be balanced.* Life is not fair, but it can be balanced. Daoism is not about how to avoid troubles but how to cope with them when they arise.

NOTES

1. Zhang Daoling's descendants settled a brief rebellion against the Han Dynasty by becoming Daoist priests, spreading Daoism through China as the Way of the Celestial Masters (Heavenly Teacher) sect. Two persecutions of Buddhists took place in the centuries to follow (fifth and ninth centuries CE), quickly reversed by succeeding emperors. Religious war would not again plague China until the mid-nineteenth century CE, when the Tai Ping rebellion lost twenty million lives in a futile attempt to replace the Buddhist (Ching Dynasty) emperor with a Christian.

2. For more information, I recommend *Dragon's Play* by Liu Ming (Charles Belyea) Berkeley, CA: Great Circle Lifeworks, 1991), and P'u Ming's *Oxherding Pictures and Verses*, translated by Red Pine (Port Townsend, WA: Empty Bowl, 1987), each for an excellent treatment of the Journey. *The Alchemist*, by Paulo Coelho (San Francisco: HarperSanFrancisco, 1994), is told from the Western mystical perspective and quite useful in providing role models and guidance for all alchemists.

3. I recommend the following translations:

   Liu Ming, transl., *Changing: The Heart of the Yijing* (Oakland, CA: Da Yuan Circle, 2005).

Gia-Fu Feng and Jane English, trans., *Chuang Tsu: Inner Chapters* (New York: Vintage Books, 1974). Pages 45, 59, 114, 128, 131, and 136 will provide insight and comfort in the hospice and other terminal-care situations.

Red Pine, trans., *Lao-Tzu's Taoteching* (San Francisco: Mercury House, 1996).

D. C. Lau and Roger Ames, trans., *Yuan Dao: Tracing Dao to Its Source* [*Huainan Zi*] (New York: Ballantine Books, 1998).

RELIGIONS ORIGINATING IN INDIA

Måns Broo, PhD, is senior lecturer at the Department of Comparative Religion, Åbo Akademi University, Finland. His research interests include Caitanya Vaishnava ritual practices, modern middle-class Hinduism, and issues of agency and identity within modern yoga practices. He is also editor of the award-winning Finnish yoga magazine *Ananda*.

Spiritual Guidance in the Hindu Tradition

Måns Broo, PhD

For a spiritual guide, Hinduism presents a unique set of challenges. Of all the world religions, Hinduism often seems the most difficult one for many people to grasp. Having no founder, single authoritative scripture, or unifying leadership, Hinduism often presents a daunting jungle of gods, doctrines, and contradictions. Hindus hold all kinds of beliefs; some Hindus could be called polytheists, calling for the aid of one god or the other depending on the particular need or occasion; others stick exclusively to one god, while yet others are not interested in any gods at all. How is a spiritual guide to make head or tails of all of this?

The search to find a single and unified Hinduism is unrealistic. There has in fact never been any such entity; the term *Hinduism* was coined by the ancient Persians to denote the people living on the other (eastern) side of the Indus River. These people were of course diverse in many ways. Only much later did the term *Hinduism* take on the meaning of a religion and then also as a kind of catchall to denote Indians who were not Muslims or Christians. What scholars of the colonial era knew as religion was naturally based on their understanding of Christianity, and to a lesser degree the other Semitic religions, and they labored hard to fashion out of the bewildering array of what they found in India a religious expression similar to their Western religions. Much of what they came up with was dictated by their and their informants' partisan interests, but some of it has become established as what we could call "textbook Hinduism" and has influenced how primarily urban, middle-class Hindus view their own religion today.

For these reasons, I will begin this chapter by surveying what scholars have commonly held to be the defining ideas of Hinduism. I will follow this with a discussion about the nature of spiritual practice in Hinduism, all the time interspersed with practical advice for the spiritual guide with regard to common spiritual issues. Finally, while discussing the role of the guru in Hinduism, I will give some advice on offering good spiritual guidance to Hindus.

BASIC CONCEPTS TO KEEP IN MIND WHEN GUIDING HINDUS

Hinduism, like Judaism, has long been seen as an ethnic religion; that is, one becomes a Hindu by being born into a Hindu family. Nevertheless, Hinduism has always had its missionary movements, and today most Hindus accept converts. Spiritual guides may therefore meet Hindus with very different cultural backgrounds. Nevertheless, they will have some beliefs in common.

Medieval Indian writers distinguish between the orthodox (*astika*) and unorthodox (*nastika*) on the basis that the unorthodox reject the authoritativeness of the Vedas. Since the unorthodox include the Buddhists and the Jains, and since our colonial scholars thought every religion ought to be based on a book, it is understandable that they thought that adherence to the Vedas offered the definition of a Hindu. Unfortunately, since the Vedas are vast and contain many different doctrines, this definition leaves us with very little concrete information about Hinduism. In fact, compared to Christianity or Islam, Hinduism is not a very bookish religion; there are countless Hindus who have never read a single religious book nor studied the ancient Vedas, which are notoriously difficult to interpret even for the highly learned. Individuals receive religious teachings mainly orally, as organic parts of myths, historical narratives, and family traditions.

However, modern Hindus of the type that a spiritual guide in the United States would be likely to meet would most probably have imbibed the idea of the importance of spiritual literature. There is no dearth of such texts within Hinduism, but today some of the most popular are the Bhagavad Gita, the Durga Saptasati (also known as the Devi Mahatmya), and various forms of the epics Ramayana and Mahabharata. Many Indians are familiar with the contents of the epics, for example, not from reading them, but from watching hugely popular TV serializations. In these cases, emphasizing scriptural study and discussing both its practicalities and its problems—how to navigate between a totally relativistic and a fundamentalist view, for example—could be useful in the process of spiritual guidance.

The ideas of karma and reincarnation are integral to Hinduism. While the mechanics of the so-called law of karma ("as you sow, so shall you reap") hardly need any explanation here, the understanding of its details vary greatly from one Hindu school, or indeed one individual, to the next. Some see almost all human experiences as preordained, while others hold only major life factors such as the type of birth or life span to be determined by actions in a previous life.

With regard to reincarnation, the classical Hindu idea is pessimistic. Since time without beginning, the true self (atman) travels from one life form to another according to its deeds. Since even the most meritorious existences in the world are temporary, they are all unsatisfactory and more or less distressing. For this reason, the ultimate goal for a Hindu is not to accumulate good karma, but to break out of the wheel of birth and death (samsara) once and for all. However, for almost all Hindus, such liberation (*moksha*) is at best a very distant goal. The emphasis is, rather, attaining a good life in the here and now. These two goals, often personified by saffron-clad ascetics and pious householders, represent very different but not necessarily mutually exclusive tendencies within Hinduism.

THE FOUR GOALS OF LIFE IN HINDUISM

By the first century CE, Hindu theologians came up with a way to harmonize the aspirations of the world-transcending ascetic and the socially active, morally astute householder. They saw human life as a process of acquisition, where one begins in youth by acquiring dharma. *Dharma* is a Sanskrit word that is notoriously difficult to translate, with meanings ranging from "nature" to "law," "duty," and "merit." All of these meanings are connected; the idea is that just as the nature of fire is to burn, so every single human being by nature has his or her own duties and laws, which he or she will gain merit by following. Since Hinduism does not differentiate between a religious and a secular side to life, dharma incorporates every practice from how to pray to how to brush your teeth.

Traditionally, Hindu boys of the Brahmin caste would learn about dharma in the context of being *Brahmacharins*, celibate students living in the house of their guru or preceptor. Today, this custom has largely died out, although gurus are still very much a part of Hinduism. Rather, most Hindus learn about dharma from their parents and elders. Depending on gender, caste, geographical location, and sectarian affiliation, the exact form that dharma will take will vary, as will the extent to which such childhood teaching will influence the individual later in life. Hindu culture does not consider it appropriate to disagree openly with one's elders, but Hindus in India are well aware that their relatives in the United States, for example, are not able to live the same kind of Hindu life as they.

From dharma follows the second goal of life, *artha*, wealth. After finishing his education, the Brahmin boy would get married, father children, and become a responsible member of society. As such, he would be expected to make money and, ideally, become wealthy. There is nothing inherently wrong with being wealthy in Hinduism; rather, wealth flows from dharma and enables its possessor to engage in good deeds, such as supporting a local temple or philanthropy. However, wealth can lead more directly to the third goal of life, *kama*, pleasure. For most Westerners, the word *kama* brings up vague ideas of the Kama Sutra and rare sexual pleasures, and those are indeed included within the term. While sex in Hinduism, as in every religion, is restricted in many ways, sexuality that follows the dictates of dharma (within wedlock, most importantly) is seen as not only a legitimate but as a positive force in the world.

Ideally, this kind of pious enjoyment of worldly wealth and happiness is in time supposed to lead the Hindu to realize the transitory and ultimately unsatisfactory nature of this world, and thus to strive for the fourth goal of life, *moksha*, or liberation. Exactly how an individual strives for liberation and what this liberation entails varies from one Hindu school or tradition to the next.

Traditionally, Hindus understood pursuing *moksha* as a kind of return to the first stage of life, where the householder, after seeing his grandchildren, would withdraw from social life and again engage more intensively in spiritual pursuits. Still today, many Hindus consider striving for *moksha* as an aspect of old age, but it is also common for Hindus today to pursue a full but dharmic life in this world while also taking some small, preliminary steps toward *moksha*.

For the spiritual guide, it is useful to figure out where the client situates him- or herself with regard to these four goals. If the client's goals are primarily *artha* and *kama*, cultivating dharma would be the key, that is, performing good deeds in this world. Despite the ways in which Hinduism has tried to harmonize the quests for human and spiritual fulfillment, Hindu practitioners often feel pulled between the two. "I try to devote my spare time to spiritual pursuits, but my husband feels that I should spend more time with the family." "Whenever I take the time to do my yoga, I feel like I am being selfish." The spiritual guide is likely to hear these kinds of statements. In addition to reminding the client of the classical Hindu system outlined above, the spiritual guide could perhaps also point out the need for a balance between "material" and "spiritual" pursuits for people living in the world, emphasizing the way in which spiritual attainments often overflow into other areas of life. If a mother does her yoga, for instance, she may very well have more energy to be a great mother during the rest of the day.

ECLECTICISM WITHIN HINDU SPIRITUAL PRACTICE

Many modern Hindus adhere to an inclusive view of spirituality and spiritual practice (sadhana). The Bengali mystic Ramakrishna (1836–1886) is famous for the metaphor of climbing a mountain that he uses to describe spiritual practice. If one person starts out along the southern slope and another the northern, they will be miles apart and probably not even be aware of each other. However, the higher they proceed, the closer they will come to each other, until they finally meet at the top of the mountain. Similarly, many Hindu teachers hold that what they teach is the highest understanding of reality and will lead to the supreme destination, but other doctrines may do so as well, though more slowly and laboriously.

In practical terms, all of this means that while family traditions are important, the fluid, multilayered nature of popular Hinduism allows a spiritually minded Hindu in today's world to do a good deal of spiritual shopping, so to speak, by listening to various gurus and saints, trying out different practices, and thus gradually creating a customized Hindu package for him- or herself. Such eclecticism is something that a spiritual guide would do well to encourage, but only to a degree, lest the client forget that all serious spiritual practice requires commitment and steady determination over a long period of time. Everything new feels fresh and exciting in the beginning; the real challenge always comes when this first enthusiasm wears off. Distinguishing between a temporary setback and a path that genuinely does not work demands wisdom and detachment from both spiritual guide and client.

PATHS TO LIBERATION IN HINDUISM

Popular Hinduism often distinguishes between three main spiritual paths: karma, *jnana*, and bhakti. Karma here means selfless action, acts that are done from no other motive than a sense of duty. Such actions generate neither merit nor blame, but rather gradually wean the practitioner away from such worldly dualities and selfishness in all its forms. Since selfishness is the one most powerful factor in worldly bondage, a person free from it breaks free from the bonds of birth and death. In classical texts such as the Bhagavad Gita, this path of karma-yoga is presented mainly in terms of dutifully following the socio-ethical duties pertaining to one's particular place within the so-called caste system. Today, many Hindus understand karma-yoga in the context of social service, usually combined with elements of other paths.

Jnana means "knowledge." The teacher today most often associated with this path is Adi Shankara (eighth to ninth century CE), who consolidated the philosophical system of Advaita (non-dual) Vedanta during a brief but immensely productive and influential life. Knowledge of the ultimate substratum of all being—Brahman, identified with the innermost self of every living being—liberates the practitioner from worldly bondage.

This liberating, otherworldly knowledge refers to a mystical insight that cannot be grasped intellectually or easily communicated, but a person who possesses it can pass it to others by creating in them a teachable moment, as it were. For this, Shankara recommends what he calls a fourfold practice. This practice refers first to learning to discriminate between the transient and the eternal; second, to the absence of desire for worldly goals either in this life or the next; third, to the attainment of calm, temperance, renunciation, fortitude, sustained concentration, and faith; and lastly, to an intense desire for liberation. All of these practices run concurrently and are supposed to give the practitioner the prerequisites for serious scriptural study.

Within Vedanta and the path of knowledge, the most important scriptural texts are the Upanishads. Studying these texts follows the threefold system of listening (*shravana*), reflection (*manana*), and deep concentration (*nididhyasana*). First, the student "listens" or reads the texts, ideally under the guidance of a realized teacher or guru, striving to fully grasp their import. Here, an intellectually minded person can find full scope for using his or her mind, by delving deep into the texts and their commentaries. The texts should be read and reread, and a spiritual guide would do well to advise the client to focus on deep study of one text at a time rather than gathering a superficial knowledge of many.

After hearing the text (or, as is more likely today, reading it), the student is advised to reflect on its teachings. Ideally, this should be done by turning over the words of the text in one's head, a practice that points toward the importance of learning sacred texts by heart. There is a Sanskrit saying to the effect that book knowledge is like money lent to a friend: in theory, you do have the money, but were you suddenly to need it, you would be in trouble. Reflection should be done over a significant length of time, so that many different meanings of the text may be gleaned and honed against the stone of experience. Such reflection leads into the third face of scriptural study, deep concentration. Here, the practitioner enters into the full meaning of scripture, such as four so-called great sayings of the Upanishads: "Consciousness is Brahman," "This self is Brahman," "You are that," and "I am Brahman." This is no mere intellectual understanding. The difference between knower, knowing, and knowledge here makes way for liberating insight and union with God.

Bhakti means "devotion," particularly toward a divine being such as Krishna or Shiva. The path of bhakti thus means the cultivation and deepening of a personal relationship with God, through the means of various spiritual practices, such as congregational chanting of God's names (*kirtana*), service of God's image (*archana*), or remembrance of God's form, attributes, and divine activities (*smarana*). By falling head over heels in love with God, as it were, the practitioner comes to live in Him, and material bondage falls away as a matter of course, unless God wants the practitioner to serve Him in the world. Heaven or hell makes little difference for the bhakta—the person who has bhakti—as long as he or she may serve God. Here liberation is not about losing one's identity and merging with God (after all, for love you need two), but rather attainment of one's true, eternal identity as a lover of God, and a blissful, eternal relationship with Him.

According to the Sri Sampradaya—the devotional Hindu tradition best known for the philosopher Ramanuja, eleventh century CE—for a beginner, the central item of the bhakti path is resignation or submission (*prapatti*) to God. Submission is sixfold. First, the practitioner endeavors to accept whatever is favorable to bhakti, such as suitable spiritual practices or keeping the company of like-minded people. Second, having thus created a positive basis, he or she rejects whatever is unfavorable, such as intoxicants, a non-vegetarian diet, or a promiscuous lifestyle (all these details can be gleaned from the bhakti scriptures such as the Bhagavata Purana or from the preceptor).

Two mental determinations follow these two practical stages: to have faith that the Lord will be one's protector and that He will be one's maintainer. This does not mean that the practitioner neglects his or her own safety or finances—after all, which faithful servant wants the Master to have to worry?—but a cheerful resignation to the Lord's will and faith that everything will turn out for the best eventually. Finally, surrendering one's whole self to God and cultivating a humble state of mind constitute the two last aspects of submission, where, having given body and mind to God, the bhakta finally gives his or her heart to God. Such full surrender is exemplified in the scriptures by the milk maidens of Vrindavan village, who, hearing the call of the flute in the middle of the night, left their husbands and infant children and ran into the forest to meet their beloved Krishna.

OFFERING SPIRITUAL GUIDANCE TO HINDUS: THE GURU AND THE SPIRITUAL GUIDE

The spiritual preceptor, or guru, has an important part in all of the above-mentioned practices. The guru is the one who initiates a practitioner into particular practices and sustains that practice with advice taken from his or her personal experience. A famous story told about Gandhi illustrates this idea. At her wits' end, a woman brought her overweight boy to Gandhi and asked the revered Mahatma to tell him not to eat sweets. "Come back in a fortnight," Gandhi said. Mother and child returned duly when the time had elapsed. Hearing about their return, Gandhi briefly looked up and sternly told the boy not to eat sweets before returning to his other business. The mother was happy but also mystified. Plucking up her courage, she asked the great man why he couldn't have spared them those three seconds the first time they met. Gandhi replied, "First I had to stop eating sweets myself."

However, few gurus have the time, opportunity, or even inclination to guide or counsel their disciples personally. Rather, one of the main functions of the guru is to act as a focal point of devotion and as the embodiment of the spiritual ideal that he or she teaches. In many Hindu traditions, the difference between a perfected human being and a god is small or none, so the disciple is often enjoined to view and worship the guru as God. The task of counseling is generally passed on to senior students, parents, siblings, and friends.

The position of being a guru is passed down from one generation to the next either by biological descent or by appointment. Many Hindus feel that a genuine guru must belong to a line of teachers (*parampara*) stretching back to a semi-mythical teacher or saint such as Shankara or Ramanuja. Individuals follow no particular institutionalized systems of "guru training," but when one guru chooses his or her successor, he or she will make the choice from among his or her own students. Gurus or teachers will take into account qualities such as long-term spiritual practice, learning, or exemplary character, though in many cases, institutional belonging is more important than personal qualities. In fact, for many Hindus, the guru is more than just the particular individual holding that title; the position itself demands respect and veneration.

While the spiritual guide is not likely to possess the institutional or individual qualities of a guru, he or she will, by position, become a kind of senior well-wisher for the client—a kind of guru. The guide will do well to remember that Hindu culture considers it rude to disagree with elders, for which reason clients may verbally agree to everything the spiritual guide says, without embracing any of the guide's advice. It is important for the spiritual guide to emphasize the importance of honesty and confidentiality in the relationship. The spiritual guide will never divulge any of his or her discussions with the client, and neither is the guide personally interested in judging the client against some difficult-to-attain otherworldly ideal. Rather, the spiritual guide wishes to be an effective interfaith companion on the path.

With Hinduism's plethora of beautiful and systematic spiritual paths and exemplary saints, Hindu practitioners sometimes tend to downplay personal failings in lieu of keeping an otherworldly goal in sight—for example, seldom revealing disappointments or mistakes to the guru. The spiritual guide can try to overcome this problem by continuously keeping the emphasis on the here and now, while at the same time honoring the spiritual goal of the particular Hindu tradition with which the client identifies. Walking the line between these two aspects may very well prove the essence of successful Hindu spiritual guidance.

RESOURCES

For general introductions to Hinduism, see e.g.:

Flood, Gavin. *An Introduction to Hinduism.* New York: Cambridge University Press, 1996.

Knott, Kim. *Hinduism. A Very Short Introduction.* New York: Oxford University Press, 2000.

For an introduction to Hinduism in the United States, see e.g.:

Mann, Gurinder Singh, Paul Numrich, and Raymond Williams. *Buddhists, Hindus and Sikhs in America: A Short History.* New York: Oxford University Press, 2007.

Goldberg, Philip. *American Veda: From Emerson and the Beatles to Yoga and Meditation—How Indian Spirituality Changed the West.* New York: Harmony, 2010. (A more popular introduction.)

Christopher Titmuss, a former Buddhist monk in Thailand and India, teaches awakening and insight meditation around the world. He is the founder and director of the Dharma Facilitators Programme and Mindfulness Training Course (MTC). He gives retreats, participates in pilgrimages (*yatras*), and leads dharma gatherings. Christopher has been teaching annual retreats in Bodh Gaya, India, since 1975 and has led an annual dharma gathering in Sarnath, India, since 1999. A senior Dharma teacher in the West, he is the author of numerous books, including *Light on Enlightenment, Buddhist Wisdom for Daily Living*, and *Mindfulness for Everyday Living*. A campaigner for peace and other global issues, a poet, and a writer, he is also the co-founder of Gaia House, an international retreat center in Devon, England. He lives in Totnes, Devon, England. Among his websites are www.insightmeditation.org and www.christophertitmuss.org.

The Buddha, Theravada Tradition, and Spiritual Guidance

Christopher Titmuss

A BRIEF HISTORY OF THE BUDDHA

Prince Gautama (*Gotama* in the Pali language), who became known as the Buddha (the Awakened One), was born in Lumbini in the foothills of the Himalayas, on a full-moon night around 563 BCE and died on a full-moon night at the age of eighty years around 483 BCE. Asita, a hermit of the kingdom, predicted that Gautama would become either a great sage or a great king. On a journey from Kapilavasthu, the capital of the Sakyan kingdom, Gautama's mother, Queen Maya Devi, gave birth to Gautama under a sal tree. She died a week after his birth. Thus his father, King Suddodhana and his mother's sister, Maha Pajapati, raised him.

Born into a noble family, Prince Gautama lived an existence wrapped up in cotton wool, so to speak. Hidden from the harsh realities of life, such as aging, sickness, and death, he spent his years in the comfort of palaces and gardens and received dutiful, unquestioning attention from family and numerous servants, who attended to his personal needs. At the age of twenty-nine, Gautama witnessed aging, sickness, death, and a wandering mendicant. He realized the acute vulnerability of the human condition, since all humanity had to endure—without exception—aging, declining health, sickness, pain, and death. The impermanence of life left him deeply troubled.

Finding it pointless to go on living in his sheltered existence, Gautama decided to flee his responsibilities as prince, heir to the kingdom, husband, and father of a week-old boy, named Rahula (whose name means "chains"). One of the old Buddhist texts states that Gautama found it so difficult to leave his wife and son that he could not bring himself to pull back the bedsheet to reveal the face of his little boy. He mounted his horse and rode to the edge of the city, where he dismounted, cut off his shoulder-length hair, and set off on a spiritual search.

Gautama spent time practicing under the spiritual guidance of Alara Kalama, who taught him how to achieve profound mystical states of consciousness and gain mastery over those states. Alara invited Gautama to teach other disciples with him. Despite his depth of experience, Gautama felt dissatisfied and became instead a disciple of Udaka Ramaputta, reputed to be the most advanced teacher in the region. But, again, the former prince felt dissatisfied. Although he gained mastery over these spiritual experiences and could enter them at will, he would then emerge from these states and have to deal with the responsibilities of his daily life. He then left the ashram of Udaka Ramaputta and traveled to Sarnath, where dedicated yogis lived in the forest, about a two-hour walk from Varanasi, the world's oldest city of pilgrimage.

In his search for truth and understanding, Gautama engaged there in intensely rigorous and self-punishing spiritual practices in a determined effort to free himself from his anguish and from all connection with his mortality. Eventually, he realized he felt no closer to the awakening and liberation that he sought, so he left the forest in Sarnath to find his own way. His journey took him to Bodh Gaya in Bihar, northern India, around 180 miles from Sarnath.

In the latter years of his life, Gautama recalled to his friends his awakening at the age of thirty-five in Bodh Gaya. He said that at twelve years of age, he had sat under a tree watching King Suddhodhana, his father, plowing the land in a ceremony to mark the start of the season for growing rice. While sitting under the tree, he felt a deep happiness, a concentration of mind, the capacity to reflect, and inner peace. In Bodh Gaya, he asked himself if this could be the way to awakening and liberation. He acknowledged the importance of this experience as a means to go deep within rather than putting intense pressure on himself.

Gautama then sat under a bodhi tree on a night of the full moon. He recalled his past lives as father, son, prince, heir to the throne, husband, seeker, yogi—and perhaps earlier lives as well—and how these roles arose and passed. He also experienced meditation experiences at a variety of depths and gained access to various realms of consciousness. Most important of all, he woke up to the essential truths of life that human beings face, and he became "the Awakened One"—the Buddha.

After the night of his awakening, he spent seven weeks engaged in sitting and walking meditation to give him time to reflect on the significance of what he had realized. Out of these realizations, insights, and reflections, he formed the body of his teachings called the Dharma. The Buddha then spent the next forty-five years (from the age of thirty-five to eighty) teaching the Dharma in northern India. He encouraged men and women to leave the householders' life for the homeless way of life, yet gave profound teachings to householders and those who lived a nomadic way of life alike.

The Buddha took the Sanskrit word *dharma* (*dhamma* in Pali) from his orthodox religious background, where *dharma* generally meant "duty." The way he used it, it has a threefold meaning:

- Literally "that which upholds or supports"
- A truth
- The teachings of the Buddha

THE THERAVADA TRADITION

Theravada is the oldest tradition of Buddhism, with more than one hundred million followers today, mostly in Burma, Cambodia, Laos, Sri Lanka, and Thailand. Authority for the Theravada traditions rests with the monks. There is a tradition in Thailand of monks taking full ordination for a short period, such as a week, often to make merit or as a form of respect to a recently deceased relative. Others are ordained for months or years or stay ordained for the rest of their lives. Many Theravada monks take care of monasteries and temples in cities, towns, and villages. Other monks teach in schools or live in the forest or in monasteries devoted to Vipassana (insight meditation).

The Theravada tradition relies for its primary authority on around five thousand Pali discourses (suttas) believed to contain the teachings and practices that the Buddha offered. Oral tradition kept the teachings alive for three hundred years after the death of the Buddha. Monks then wrote the teachings down. Western Pali translators in the Theravada tradition have translated all the discourses of the Buddha into contemporary English. They provide an invaluable resource for teaching and for practice. In Sri Lanka in the fifth century CE, Venerable Buddhaghosa wrote lengthy commentaries on the Pali suttas. Other respected monks over the centuries wrote additional commentaries that further formed the Theravada tradition. These commentaries also included the *Abhidhamma*, an analytical interpretation of mind/body processes.

Theravada Buddhism certainly has all the hallmarks of a religion, since it features temples, rituals, ceremonies, chanting, merit making, and a belief in past and future lives. We might say that Theravada Buddhism, at its best, functions like the pod in a pod of peas. We dispense with the pod of the religion of Theravada Buddhism to gain access to the peas. At its worst, the religion of Theravada Buddhism becomes a distraction to the application of the Buddha Dharma, which addresses every major area of our lives.

THE FOUR NOBLE TRUTHS

The foundation of the Buddha's teachings is the Four Noble Truths, more accurately translated as "the Four Truths of the Noble Ones." A practitioner of the Buddha Dharma becomes intimately familiar with the inquiry, reflection, and meditation upon the Four Truths of the Noble Ones, namely:

1. The arising of suffering
2. Causes and conditions for the arising of suffering
3. Complete resolution, also referred to as nirvana or liberation
4. The way to the resolution

The Buddha spoke in Pali. The Pali word for "suffering" is *dukkha*. *Kha* refers to the hole in the hub of the wheel. If the hole is too big, the wheel is loose. If the hole is too small, the wheel endures friction and heat. Just as when a wheel is ill-fitting, so when we do not fit well into the nature of things, when we lack the wisdom to move with events, we suffer in numerous ways, ranging from an unsettled mind to unhappiness and violent behavior.

On the First Truth

Suffering arises, said the Buddha, through not getting what we want, losing what we have, being separated from whom or what we are attached to, and clinging onto aspects of ourselves such as body, feelings, perceptions, thoughts, and consciousness. The Buddha never said, "Life is suffering." He would regard such a statement as a crude generalization that neglects the importance and the value of happiness, serenity, love, appreciative joy, and deep contentment.

On the Second Truth

The Buddha said that suffering arises *only* because there are causes and conditions for it to arise. Suffering does not arise through chance, a punishment from a God, or fate.

On the Third Truth

The Buddha said that the complete resolution of human suffering is through wisdom, realization, and the discovery of freedom, an authentic liberation through non-clinging.

On the Fourth Truth

The Buddha referred to the Way to realization as the Noble Eightfold Path.

SPIRITUAL GROWTH IN THERAVADA BUDDHISM

The Way to realization includes a deep examination of every truth of the Noble Eightfold Path and communicates a great concern for "right" living. In the Pali language the word for *right* is "samma." *Samma* carries the connotation of correct as opposed to incorrect, but *samma* also means "that which is fulfilling." Practitioners of the Buddha Dharma live in accordance with the Way, and the awakened ones live in accordance with the Way, a way that is fulfilling for us and beneficial for others and the world.

The links in the Noble Eightfold Path are as follows:

1. Right understanding, or right view
2. Right intention
3. Right speech
4. Right action
5. Right livelihood
6. Right effort
7. Right mindfulness
8. Right meditative concentration

These links are not sequential steps, like a ladder to spiritual attainment. Instead, spiritual growth is made when due attention is given to each of them as a person is ready and able. In more detail, these links facilitate our spiritual growth in the following ways.

1. Right Understanding, or Right View

Right understanding, or right view, includes the contemplation of the Four Noble Truths in every arena of our daily lives. The first truth is to be understood. The second truth involves letting go and changing conditions that give rise to suffering. The third truth is to be fully realized, and the fourth truth stresses emphasis on development of each link in the Noble Eightfold Path.

2. Right Intention

We learn to keep in touch with our intentions. We work on intentions that cause stress and harm to ourselves or harm to others through body, speech, and acts of mind or acts of the will. Our intentions can carry a variety of feelings, thoughts, and memories that influence and give shape to our intentions. We find intentions in greed, anger, and fear, as well as in generosity, kindness, and fearlessness.

3. Right Speech

We take real notice of what we say and to whom we say it. Right speech requires vigilance and clarity. The Buddha said that on important matters we have to consider the right person, the right place, the right time, and the right subject if we wish to communicate effectively with others.

4. Right Action

The principle of right action shows itself in the depth of clarity and love. We consider our intentions and actions, their results, and our relationship to them. Even noble actions do not guarantee that the results we pursue will emerge. We need the capacity to accommodate the results of actions due to a variety of conditions that we may not have perceived. At times, we have to trust in our intentions and actions even if the outcome is different from what we expected.

5. Right Livelihood

Work constitutes an important feature of many people's daily lives. The Buddha advised against work that caused suffering, such as the manufacture of weapons, the making of poison, and slave labor. Right livelihood considers others and ourselves and requires a degree of maturity and a sense of responsibility. Right livelihood encourages us to question a career focused on position, status, making money, and the exploitation of people and resources. This feature of the Way includes inquiry into one's lifestyle.

6. Right Effort

There are four aspects of right effort. What is worth developing? What is worth maintaining? What is worth overcoming? What is worth avoiding? For example, we see the value of developing and maintaining the Way. We see the value of overcoming addictions and avoiding people and situations that we know are unwise.

7. Right Mindfulness

Mindfulness gives protection. Absence of mindfulness leads to carelessness, "accidents," forgetfulness, and stress. Mindfulness contributes to peace of mind, connection with what is happening, and the capacity to respond. Mindfulness attends to the needs of the body, feelings, states of mind, and Dharma.

8. Right Meditative Concentration

Meditation is a key feature in the teachings of the Buddha. It offers inner depth, calmness, and insight. Through meditation, we becoming less demanding of others and the world. There are daily benefits also to meditative concentration: we can concentrate on what matters, and we have the capacity to focus our attention in the long term on a worthwhile vision.

THE TEACHINGS OF THE BUDDHA

The Buddha formulated his teachings into various groups or categories to make them easy to remember and to show the depth and breadth of his Dharma teachings. He made the teachings practical, down-to-earth, and free from religious rituals, rites, and ceremonies. He emphasized the importance of a "natural" way of life free from the three poisons of the mind, namely greed, hate, and delusion. He refused to offer theories about how the world began or how it will end but kept his focus primarily on the immediacy of human experience and exploring ways to overcome the problems of the self.

The Buddha's teachings address a wide variety of issues facing human existence. Of course, it is not possible to list them all in a short chapter such as this. Following are a few of the most important areas.

Dependent Arising

There is no kind of absolute or transcendental absolutism in the Dharma of the Buddha. The Buddha dropped the religious belief in God. Instead of claiming a God who created the world, or a First Cause, the Buddha proclaimed a teaching he called "dependent arising." Dependent arising is a core teaching of the Buddha. He proclaimed that only causes and conditions bring about life, sentient and insentient, and refuted claims of a Creator God or First Cause to produce existence. Causes have no independent existence, since they depend on causes and conditions as well. Countless contingency factors enable the changing presence of the universe, the world, consciousness, atoms, the material world, past, present, future, life, death, and all experiences, healthy or problematic. There is not a hand of God nor devil nor divine force that shapes events nor any universal agency that dispenses rewards and punishment for beliefs or behavior.

Nagarjuna, the second-century-CE commentator on the Buddha's teachings, wrote in his classic text *The Fundamentals of the Middle Way* (*Mulamadhyamaka-Karika*) in the first verse on causality:

> *No "thing" arises from nothing,*
> *No "thing" arises from itself.*
> *No "thing" arises from another self.*
> *No "thing" arises from both.*
> *No "thing" arises from a metaphysic (such as chance, accident,*
> *   fate, destiny, random selection or the hand of God).*

The Buddha showed the emptiness of any independent self-existence of any "thing. The Buddha said:

When there is this, that comes to be;
with the arising of this, that arises.
When there is not this, that does not come to be;
with the cessation of this, that ceases. (*Samyutta Nikaya* 12.61)

The Buddha referred to the *All*—namely senses and sense objects, consciousness, and its objects. He said to claim anything outside of that as *All* is a theory. The Buddha pointed to the emptiness of self-existence. Again, it is an immense challenge to comprehend deeply the significance of the statement. He used the example of a chariot: Is the chariot the wheels? No. Is the chariot the stand for the driver? No. Is the chariot the steering aid to control the horses? No. If we take away all the parts of the chariot, then there is no chariot. The chariot lacks any self-existence. It is not some "thing." Examining the parts, we also see that the parts have no self-existence. The parts consist of numerous causes and conditions coming together. The Buddha Dharma emphasized realizing the emptiness of self-existence of any "thing." No "thing" is worth grasping onto, including the Buddha, the Dharma, and the Sangha (namely, the noble community of the wise).

Whatever is dependently arising, such as the chariot, shows that no thing whatsoever ultimately exists nor possesses any inherent nature or essence. Events and situations depend on the conditions that allow them to be present and cease when those conditions drop away.

The Middle Way

It is not surprising that, soon after his awakening, the Buddha hesitated to offer such teachings. Belief in God or belief in materialism, or both, had such a grip on human consciousness that he felt it would be "wearisome and a vexation" to teach a Dharma that advocated neither materialism nor God. Under the tree of enlightenment, he had realized the importance of the causes and conditions that give rise to events. He said human beings could not prove the existence of an interventionist God. Not far from the bodhi tree in Bodh Gaya, he met a Brahmin who strongly encouraged him to teach because the Brahmin knew there were human beings with a "little dust in their eyes." The Buddha recognized the truth of what the Brahmin said and then set off to Sarnath to offer teachings on what he called "the Middle Way." He shared the Four Noble Truths with his friends in Sarnath. Like himself, his friends were dedicated yogis who had practiced harsh and extreme methods to try to overcome the problem of the self, the ego.

His friends assumed at first that he had watered down his resolution for liberation until they realized the wisdom of the Middle Way. His five friends followed his teachings and began to travel with him. After this important meeting with his friends, the Buddha walked to Kapilavasthu, the capital, to see his wife, Yashodhara, and Rahula, his six-year-old son. They also recognized the profound significance of his wisdom. He intended to meet his two spiritual teachers to share with them his awakening, but Gautama found that they had both passed away.

The Buddha emphasized a nomadic way of life for those who felt trapped in the role of the householder. Despite an initial reluctance, he became the first teacher in history to call on women to join the Sangha (the community of men and wisdom of noble wisdom), who lived a life of utter simplicity to find and know wisdom of the heart and mind, as well as the profound happiness revealed through a free way of life. As the centuries went by, this nomadic way of life faded due to wars and famines. The institution of monasteries took root with monks observing 227 rules.

When the Buddha spoke to the five yogis, he taught against living in extreme positions, referring to the morbid austerities they had previously practiced. To householders, he also taught against the extreme position of placing self-gratification, self-obsession, and narcissism above all else. With self-gratification, we focus our priorities on securing the maximum amount of pleasurable sensations regardless of the cost to others, our environment, and ourselves. A lack of fulfillment functions as a contributing factor to the desire for self-gratification. Rather than develop our senses to see and hear clearly, as the Buddha expounded, we become beggars at the sense doors in our need to feel good about ourselves.

We can also slide easily into the other extreme, namely self-hate. We put ourselves down, and we have a low sense of self-worth. We feel we are not good enough in various areas of our life such as relationships, work, or levels of intelligence. Our daily lives can swing from the constant need to boost ourselves up to the other extreme of putting ourselves down. The middle way offers a different approach to life.

Ethics

The Dharma addressed ethics as well. We develop ethics to live in integrity and to live in harmony with our deep values. Living ethically requires consistent reflection. We examine ourselves to recognize and determine the way we treat others, near and far. Ethics contributes to right action. In a small number of discourses, the Buddha explained the principles of ethics:

- I undertake the training not to kill.
- I undertake the training not to steal.
- I undertake the training not to engage in sexual abuse.
- I undertake the training not to tell lies.
- I undertake the training not to engage in activities that contribute to heedlessness (abuse of alcohol and drugs).

The principle of ethics means we treat others the same way as we wish to be treated. These principles and practices affect our values and lifestyle, as well as our whole being. Ethics matter far more than the following:

- The vested interests of the nation-state
- The desire for personal accumulation
- Satisfying sexual needs
- Distortion of truth due to the ego's need to get its own way
- Stimulating the mind that makes us act heedlessly

There are also important ethical issues in watching and transforming desire, aversion, and fear. It is an ethic to inquire into the nature of existence, to explore the heart, and to remain committed to realizing our infinite potential.

Reflection

Reflection serves as another important feature for clear comprehension and insight into ourselves, others, and situations. We have the capacity to reflect on our experiences, uncover the process that puts together an experience, and learn from events. Reflection provides us with insights that support us in the present and future. Key to the awakening process, reflection contributes to an authentic sense of staying in touch with the unfolding processes of events, including our inner life. Excessive thinking confirms an underlying stress.

Meditation is an important feature of Dharma practice, since it contributes to calmness of being, harmony of body and mind, inner peace, and equanimity. Meditation contributes to a direct understanding of the Dharma, as distinct from an intellectual one.

Inquiry

The Buddha Dharma also reveals itself as inquiry. Inquiry includes the development of our capacity to listen, ask questions, and respond to a senior in the Dharma. Seniors in the Dharma have nothing to do with age but with depth of experience, realizations, and their capacity in various ways to articulate their understanding. Inquiry reveals itself when we listen totally and attentively to a Dharma talk, ask important questions, and face important questions from another or from within. This inquiry requires a certain trust in the teacher or senior in the Dharma.

Inquiry into experience constitutes another feature of the middle way. One extreme means grasping onto experiences to build up the ego, and the other extreme is rejection of experiences. We engage in meditation, reflection, inquiry, and association with the wise. We regard the bringing together of all of this as an opportunity for an authentic transformation.

Mindfulness and meditative concentration, along with a variety of tools and techniques, enable us to work with our relationship to the body, feelings, states of mind, and the Dharma itself. Insights from our practice empower us to discover much through firsthand experience. It places much responsibility on our capacity to develop and realize truth. Yet, the practice does not slide into a kind of narcissistic view of self-interest through any introversion of meditation and inner reflection.

To put the point more simply, the Buddha Dharma does not convey that the truth is within you, nor in another, past or present, nor above, nor in the book, nor between any of those. Truth dependently arises; insight and wisdom dependently arise.

The Divine

It might appear that the Buddha has renounced the human being's quest for the divine. Far from it. He has taken the concept of the divine and placed it firmly in the heart, where we can realize it (*realize* means "to make real") on a daily basis. He did not speak of love for the divine but rather stated that love *is* divine. Love includes deep friendship and loving-kindness. There is no gap between love and the divine. He gives equal emphasis to the divine as compassion (the act of love to dissolve suffering), appreciative joy and equanimity—the capacity to stay steady and clear amid the challenging dynamics that beset our lives—and life itself. Once again, the Buddha brings the divine down to earth, into the heart, rather than making the divine a religious, remote metaphysical being accessible to the few. There is neither rejection of the divine in the Dharma nor overreacting and grasping onto it as an absolute.

Authentic expressions of love, compassion, appreciative joy, and equanimity confirm the divine within us. Again, we do not have to take up the view that the divine is eternal, immortal, or a step toward something else.

As empowered human beings, we express the divine in the ordinary affairs of daily life, without fear or favor. The power of the divine transforms our way of looking at the world to the point that the fear of enemies, identification with the ambitions of the nation-state, and rage against terror lose their validity. We live without enemies while engaging in direct action, loving, compassionate, appreciative, and equanimous about the outcome. The divine enables us to speak with clear conviction rather than trusting in verbal or physical violence or weapons.

Through the divine abiding, we know and express wisdom of the heart. Through insight and understanding, we find a wisdom of the mind. Wisdom of the heart and mind points to an immediate and direct liberation with its loss of substance to the ego, the notion of "I" and "my."

Wisdom

Readers might get the impression that ethics and meditative concentration consist of practical tools to enable us to cope satisfactorily with our daily issues. While this is correct, the Buddha Dharma goes much deeper than that. The Dharma consists of wisdom teachings. With calmness and meditative concentration, we examine our relationship to roles and actions, to purpose and direction. There are extraordinarily deep layers within. Human beings have the capacity to open and expand consciousness, not only to uncover any dark unresolved forces within needing attention, but to discover the range of experiences that are profound, deep, subtle, and meaningful. The Buddha gave equal attention to worldly matters and spiritual matters.

The Noble Eightfold Path can be divided into three main sections: ethics, concentration, and wisdom. Wisdom is the third aspect of the threefold training. Wisdom means developing our capacity to understand ourselves, others, and situations. If we understand, it means that the situation stands under us—not oppressing our heart and mind, not consuming our thoughts, not tiring us or causing agitation. Wisdom also has the opportunity to arise through directly facing up to the difficult characteristics of existence rather than trying to paint a glossy picture of life on earth. We apply the power of ethics, meditative concentration, and wisdom to daily life.

Theravada Buddhists often place much emphasis on making merit for a better rebirth, as well as devotion to the Buddha, the Dharma, and the Sangha. This serves as a preliminary practice to help Buddhists experience faith and achieve a simple level of happiness. This approach is common in the Buddhist tradition, but the Buddha placed his emphasis on immediate discovery of liberation through non-grasping. This liberation releases an authentic love, compassion, and wisdom. This is the heart of the Buddha's teaching.

SPIRITUAL GUIDANCE IN THE THERAVADA TRADITION

As much as the Buddha encouraged us to attend to our relationship to the world, he equally advocated access to the various depths within. The practitioner may feel quite uncertain about how to respond to these experiences. Senior practitioners in the Dharma offer guidance and wise advice.

It is at such times that the voice of the Dharma teacher matters. The teacher's experience and wisdom stand as an external authority to support those new to the path or with less experience than the teacher over a similar or even longer length of time.

People become Dharma teachers through the invitation of a senior Dharma teacher who recognizes, usually over several years, the practitioner's wisdom and kindness. There is no history of a training course to be a Dharma teacher in the tradition of the East. The teacher, usually the abbot of a monastery of meditators, encourages a practitioner to join the teacher in checking the practice of other monks, nuns, and laypeople; facilitating groups; and giving Dharma talks from time to time. This mentorship approach works well, since it gives the new teacher responsibility while the abbot takes overall responsibility for the Sangha of practitioners. The abbot then encourages the new teacher to move on and impart the Dharma to others as a fully independent teacher.

DHARMA IN THE WEST

As the Buddha Dharma travels from East to West, from the monastery to the home, office, and factory, the teachings and practices find their application. While few Westerners wish to take ordination as Buddhist monks and nuns, increasing numbers of Westerners appreciate the application of Buddhist practices to their daily life. The media often states that the fastest-growing religion or philosophy of life in the West is Buddhism.

The most common form of introduction to the Buddha Dharma in the West occurs in intensive meditation retreats in the growing number of Buddhist centers or rented facilities in numerous Western countries. Books, public talks, and short workshops on Buddhist themes initiate people interested in the Buddha's teachings in ethics, meditative concentration, and wisdom. Introductory classes often serve as a useful stepping-stone to retreats ranging in length from a weekend to a week, three months, or, for a few, three years.

Starting often around 5:30 a.m. and finishing around 10:00 p.m., these retreats, conducted mostly in silence, include a daily Dharma talk, small group meetings with the Dharma teacher(s), one-on-one meetings with the teacher(s), as well as comprehensive meditation instructions and guided meditations. There is no conversion experience in the Buddha Dharma. The Buddha referred to awakening, the Dharma, and the Sangha (those committed to the Way) as the three jewels of existence. He said happiness is the true wealth of existence.

The experience of the intensive retreat in the West inspires many practitioners to practice the principles of mindfulness and insight, love and compassion, in daily life. Numerous small groups meet in countless cities, towns, and villages to sit together in meditation on a weekly basis, share together a Dharma theme, or listen to a recorded talk or DVD. Some practitioners travel to the Buddhist countries of the East or discover the Dharma while backpacking in the East.

The Theravada tradition relies largely on the commentaries, forms, and rituals of the tradition. A number of Asian and Western Dharma teachers have dropped the fifth-century commentaries on the Buddha's teachings. Others draw on books from the Theravada tradition itself. Developments from the Theravada tradition now being applied to life in the West include the following:

- Analysis and contemporary commentaries of the Buddha's teachings
- Fresh applications of the Dharma to Western life
- Conflict resolution
- Formal calm and insight meditation practices
- Green activism
- Inquiry into identity, self, and non-self
- Integration with various traditions, Buddhist and otherwise
- Mindfulness courses for stress reduction
- Dialogue with philosophy, psychology, and science
- Questioning of consumerism
- Reflection on ultimate and relative truth
- Revival of full ordination of women
- Social engagement

SPIRITUAL ISSUES FACED BY THERAVADA BUDDHISTS IN THE WEST

The translation of Buddhism from its native Eastern context to its new home in the West has not always been easy, and some practitioners continue to struggle with religious and cultural aspects of Buddhism. Wise spiritual guides, sensitive to issues that Buddhists practicing in the West are struggling with, can help them overcome many difficult obstacles on their paths and can assist them in developing an effective and rewarding practice. For example, many Westerners are not concerned with a belief in rebirth, whereas most Asian Buddhists take rebirth for granted. Spiritual guides can help Westerners come to their own understanding about rebirth, reminding Buddhists that the Buddha used a provisional language at times about rebirth. See the Kalama Sutta (Discourse) of the Buddha.

Western practitioners have contact with other religious traditions and knowledge of various expressions of spirituality, lifestyle, and psychotherapy. These other traditions and disciplines are not readily available in Buddhist countries. Followers of the Theravada tradition in Buddhist countries may know very little about Mahayana Buddhism and vice versa. There is a more eclectic approach in the West to the Dharma than in the East. Spiritual guides can help make clear the distinctive features of the Buddha Dharma and the Theravada tradition while drawing on the wisdom of other teachings from other traditions and contemporary mind/body disciplines and institutions.

In the Theravada tradition, there is a common view that one will take ordination if one is fully committed to Dharma practice. Western practitioners do not share this view. Spiritual guides can help Buddhists to be very clear about the importance of every aspect of the Four Noble Truths and the Noble Eightfold Path. Some householders experience a calling for ordination and follow through. Some monks and nuns experience a calling to return to the householders' life and follow through.

The expectation of ordination in the East stems from the fact that monasteries served as the traditional resource for the preservation of the teachings over the past twenty-six hundred years. But now the West generates new centers for Dharma and meditation that far outnumber Western monasteries. This is a sign of the lay community coming of age. However, it is still important for practitioners to spend focused time in meditation and in community with others on the same path. Spiritual guides can help direct Buddhists to go on retreats and give them any support required after attending retreats.

The Buddha described the Sangha as those men and women with deep realization. In the East, *Sangha* refers almost exclusively to the Sangha of the ordained in monasteries. The West refers to the Sangha as all practitioners. *Sangha* literally means "community or gathering." There is a general view in the West that monks, nuns, and laypeople are equal partners in the Sangha. Spiritual guides can help make clear the broad use of the concept of Sangha in the West.

In the East, nearly all teachers are ordained monks. There are only a few exceptions in all the major Buddhist traditions. In the West, Dharma teachers are fairly equally distributed between men and women, laypeople and ordained. Spiritual guides can help remind Buddhists that their practice includes listening to the voices of wisdom. The Buddha said there are four kinds of assemblies in the Sangha: monks, nuns (spiritual nomads), and householders, both men and women. Practitioners need to make contact with voices of wisdom and compassion among monks, nuns, and householders.

Despite the broader Western definition of the Sangha, there is a debate in the West about giving full ordination to women. The number of fully ordained Western Buddhist nuns is very small. The situation is similar in the East. Spiritual guides can help Western Buddhists talk through their issues with the patriarchal structures in the religion and can support them as they work for change. Some Buddhist women experience a painful journey. Spiritual guides can both hold their feelings in a sacred context and encourage them to develop their spiritual authority to make their voice heard.

Another important cultural difference in Eastern and Western practice is that Buddhists in Asia generally regard celibacy as part of Buddhist practice. The West generally treats intimate relationships and life as a single man or woman in much the same way. Spiritual guides can help show the development of the Western Dharma in this area. There is the opportunity for spiritual guides to show equal respect for those living a celibate life and those in an intimate relationship as offering equal opportunity for practice.

There is often an attempt to place the Dharma into a Western category such as religion, philosophy, or psychology. The Dharma simply does not fit into such categories. Religion often holds belief as an absolute. Philosophy is the exploration of ideas, and psychology deals with mental well-being. Spiritual guides can help make distinctions clear between Dharma and the Western categories. There is much comparison and analysis between the Buddha Dharma and Western thought. Spiritual guides can remind Buddhists of the value of their firsthand experience to safeguard against getting lost in metaphysics.

OFFERING SPIRITUAL GUIDANCE TO THERAVADA BUDDHISTS

Teachers of the Dharma and meditation encourage their practitioners to examine the range of joyful and painful experiences, worldly and spiritual. Spiritual guides can encourage meditators to "squeeze the honey"—to quote the Buddha—out of these experiences for insight and understanding. What is the essential message in the experience? What are the causes and conditions that brought about the experience? What is the outcome of the experience? What do you want to apply to daily life? A practitioner can explore equally the impacts of the range of joyful and painful experiences. Spiritual guides need to ask short, precise questions to contribute to the resolution and understanding of the Buddhist practitioner's situation.

Some Western Dharma teachers regard their role as being similar to a priest or rabbi. Other Western teachers see their role as a good friend, while applying their authority and wisdom only in certain situations. Spiritual guides can help Buddhists see their own priority in terms of finding a teacher. Some Buddhists benefit from contact with more than one teacher. Dharma practitioners need to keep in mind the essential reference point of ethics, meditation, and wisdom.

Many practitioners of Buddha Dharma are reluctant to call themselves "Buddhists." They prefer to be free from such labels. Spiritual guides can help such people work through their difficulties with labels. Some may wish to stay free from the use of such a label, while others may wish to define themselves as Buddhists.

There are a wide range of Buddhist practices and explorations to open consciousness. Some practitioners get lost in the supermarket of choices or are stuck with a single method. Spiritual guides can help to simplify the practices or expand the sense of practice.

A common thread among most Buddhist practices is giving a great deal of attention to the tendency to cling. (Buddhists use the word *attachment.*) *Clinging* and *attachment* have much the same meaning for many Buddhists. *Attachment* in Buddhism has a different meaning from the use of *attachment* in Western psychology, where attachment of a mother to her child is necessary and healthy. The Pali word for attachment is *upadana*, which literally means "to fuel or inflame." In Buddhism, *nonattachment* means not inflaming a situation within or outside of oneself. Spiritual guides can help Buddhists to see where they are fueling a situation or clinging onto it.

A transformed life includes heart, mind, speech, and body. Spiritual guides help the practitioner address all four of these areas. Meditation contributes to a transformed life expressing love and liberation. It is hard for some practitioners to make sense of important spiritual experiences. Spiritual guides can help to direct the practitioner to respected senior Dharma teachers. The guide needs to ensure that she or he can speak the same language as the practitioner and not try to use another religious or spiritual language, as this often leads to the practitioner feeling misunderstood. Dharma teachings and practices recognize the profound value of communication and the equally profound value of meditative silences in the midst of communication so the right words can emerge from the deep.

May all beings live with wisdom.
May all beings know liberation.
May all beings know an awakened life.

Rev. Daijaku Judith Kinst, PhD, a priest and teacher in the Soto Zen lineage, is professor of Buddhism and Buddhist pastoral care and director of the Buddhist Chaplaincy Program at the Institute of Buddhist Studies in Berkeley, California. She has taught and led retreats in a variety of settings with teachers from Zen and Tibetan Buddhist traditions and is co-founder and teacher, with Rev. Shinshu Roberts, of the Ocean Gate Zen Center in Capitola, California. She is a licensed marriage and family therapist and maintains a spiritual guidance practice for people of all faith traditions.

Richard K. Payne, PhD, is dean and Yehan Numata Professor of Japanese Buddhist Studies at the Institute of Buddhist Studies in Berkeley, California, an affiliate of the Graduate Theological Union, and he is a member of the GTU's core doctoral faculty. He is editor of a number of scholarly series on Buddhism, and his ongoing research focuses on tantric Buddhist ritual. He erratically blogs at http://rkpayne.wordpress.com.

Spiritual Guidance in Mahayana Buddhism

Zen (Chan/Son), Pure Land, Nichiren, and Vajrayana

Rev. Daijaku Judith Kinst, PhD,
and Richard K. Payne, PhD

A BRIEF HISTORY OF MAHAYANA BUDDHISM

Considered historically, all forms of Buddhism derive from the teachings of Sakyamuni Buddha, who was active in the northeast of the Indian subcontinent around the sixth century BCE. This period was one that was economically prosperous, seeing both the establishment of cities and increasing trade. It is worth emphasizing these characteristics of the time, since it is not uncommon that Indian religions are interpreted as a pessimistic, and even nihilistic, rejection of existence on the grounds that human life is filled with pain and suffering. The prosperity and expansion of societies on the subcontinent during these centuries stand in contrast to this representation of Buddhism, one that may be traced more to the influence of the nineteenth-century German philosopher Schopenhauer than to the actual historical record.

Over the course of about two centuries, a number of new religio-philosophical movements were initiated in India. These new movements provided the basis for the later six "orthodox" schools, which accept the authority of the Vedas. These are the Nyaya, Vaisesika, Sankhya, Yoga, Vedanta, and Mimamsa. (The more familiar devotional trends of Hinduism are even later developments, themselves in large part growing out of these six.) The "unorthodox" schools reject the authority of the Vedas and include not only Buddhism but also Jainism and the materialists, or Carvaka (no longer extant). Most of these were based on a new idea of personal liberation. The early, Vedic tradition sought a permanent birth in the heavens with one's ancestors by means of ritual sacrifice. However, the increasingly common idea of repeated rebirth led to the goal of liberation from all rebirth. The goal of liberation from rebirth constitutes a radically different form of religiosity from the idea of salvation from sin.

In one form or another, the goal of liberation from rebirth is shared by most of these movements originating in the last half century BCE. The means by which liberation was sought constitutes the wide range of yogic practices (*yoga* in this case meaning religious disciplines, in contrast to the formal school of Yoga). Such practices include austerities of many kinds, meditative practices, and the renunciation of one's social identity. Arising in this religio-philosophical context, Buddhism shares many characteristics with the other forms of Indian religion that date from this era.

Sakyamuni Buddha: The Founder

All forms of Buddhism are considered by modern historical sciences to derive from the teachings of Sakyamuni, also known as Gautama and Siddhartha. Some specific traditions, however, consider themselves as deriving from other Buddhas. The Pure Land traditions, for example, give particular veneration to Amitabha (Chinese, Omito; Japanese, Amida). Some of the Tibetan traditions consider the Primal Buddha, or Adibuddha, to be the source of their lineage, and still others trace themselves to the teachings of the Great Illuminator Buddha, or Mahavairocana Buddha. There are also variations in the conception of Sakyamuni, such as is found in the Lotus Sutra, where he is presented as the eternal Buddha, and not the temporally limited person his disciples had mistakenly thought of him as being.

Sakyamuni founded an order of monastics, both male and female, known as the *sangha*, a term employed by many contemporary Buddhists to describe their own communities. Only in the past century have laypeople been encouraged to take up Buddhist practice. The more historically normal situation has been for laypeople to support the monastics through donations, or *dana*. Spiritual guidance was traditionally given only by an ordained teacher of one kind or another. Although contemporary discourse treats meditation as the only kind of Buddhist practice, it was in fact just one kind of Buddhist practice. As a consequence, there were a variety of different kinds of teachers, and monastics would receive instruction from several teachers, not only for meditation practices, but also for doctrine and for the rules of the order. Laypeople were generally simply advised to live good lives and to generate positive karma so as to have the opportunity in a future birth to become a monastic and seek liberation. Their instruction often took the form of narratives rather than doctrinal discourse.

Having spread throughout Inner and East Asia, Mahayana Buddhism exists in a wide range of forms. While one frequently encounters geopolitical categories (e.g., Tibetan, Chinese, Korean, Vietnamese, Japanese), such categorization is only useful in considering cultural context. Historically more relevant is the notion of lineage, which is how most Buddhist traditions think about their own institutional form. While all Buddhist lineages consider Sakyamuni to be a key figure in their own lineal descent, some of the Mahayana traditions think of the teachings as originating with an earlier Buddha.

Almost all Mahayana lineages also consider several of the prominent Indian Buddhist teachers as lineal ancestors. Such figures may include Nagarjuna, Vasubandhu, Asanga, Candrakirti, Dignaga, and Dharmakirti. As they developed in Inner and East Asia, lists of lineal founders increasingly diverged. Specific founders will be discussed below under "Major Sects of Mahayana Buddhism."

Development of the Mahayana

In India, Mahayana developed as a series of schools. (For the most part these are only seen as part of the development of Mahayana in retrospect, as the figures developing each did not necessarily think of themselves as part of the same movement.) As historically important as some of these are, the most important ones for the development of contemporary forms of Mahayana Buddhism found in the West are the Middle Way (*Madhyamaka*) school, the Yoga Practice (*Yogacara*) school, and the teaching of the Matrix of Buddha-nature (*Tathagatagarbha*).

The Middle Way school originated with the ideas found in the Perfection of Wisdom literature and was formalized by Nagarjuna. Central to its contribution to Buddhist thought is the idea of the two truths: the identity of conventional and ultimate truth. Conventional truth works within the assumptions of linguistically and socially defined reality, while ultimate truth challenges any assumption of the permanent, eternal, unchanging, or absolute.

The Yoga Practice school is best known for its focus on the dynamics of cognition. In order to explain the continuity of consciousness and of karma across gaps in conscious awareness, Maitreya, Asanga, and Vasubandhu formulated the idea of eight kinds of cognition. These are the five sensory cognitions, the cognition of thoughts, the sense of a separate I, and an unconscious level of cognition that continues despite gaps in conscious awareness.

The third strain of thought influential in the formation of Mahayana Buddhism is the Matrix of Buddha-nature. This was not so much a separate school of thought with identifiable historical figures promoting the theory, but rather an influential idea that contributed to the development of Mahayana practice. The notion of the Matrix of Buddha-nature is that every sentient being—or in some versions of the theory, every *living* being—has the potential to be fully awakened. In some expressions, this was theorized as an actual entity of some kind within individuals, while in others it was asserted that the inherently empty nature of all beings was identical in practitioners and in Buddhas.

By as early as the second century CE, Buddhism was being introduced to China via the trade routes across Central Asia known as the Silk Road. It was then transmitted to Korea in the fourth century, and from there, beginning in the sixth century, it was introduced to Japan. The transmission to Tibet began in the seventh century, becoming much more active in the eighth century.

Central Mahayana Teachings

Central Mahayana teachings include the foundational Buddhist teachings of the Three Marks of Existence and the Four Noble Truths as well as teachings specific to the Mahayana, including the identity of samsara and nirvana, Buddha-nature, an emphasis on the bodhisattva path, and living out the ethical guidelines that are associated with it.

Emptiness, impermanence, and suffering are key doctrinal elements that almost all Buddhists agree on. The teaching of emptiness, a term that is often misunderstood, simply states that all things are interdependent—all phenomena arise in concert with all other phenomena and are therefore dependent on them. All phenomena have no existence separate from that interdependence— that is, all things are empty of inherent or separate existence. The teaching of impermanence states that this interdependent reality is always changing—there is nothing permanent and unchanging; most notably there is no God or entity or metaphysical self that exists outside this interdependent impermanent state. Suffering arises when we live in ignorance of these truths, and we deepen our suffering when we address it by attempting to make what is impermanent permanent. These three teachings, known as the Three Marks of Existence, were originally formulated as a kind of minimal set of beliefs shared by all Buddhists.

The Four Noble Truths express these teachings in a diagnostic-prescriptive format. The first truth acknowledges the actuality of suffering; the second, the source of suffering; the third, the possibility of relief from suffering; and the fourth, the path to relief from suffering. In this form, the Four Noble Truths are based on a medical model of symptom, diagnosis, prognosis, and prescription. More generally, however, this formula describes the character of all existing entities as being the consequence of causes and conditions: when something exists, it exists because of some set of causes and conditions; if those causes and conditions are changed, then that thing will no longer exist; and there is a means by which such change can be effected.

While the Four Noble Truths and Three Marks of Existence are widely accepted by almost all Buddhists, the identity of samsara (the world of suffering) and nirvana (the world or reality of liberation) is an idea more exclusively held by Mahayana Buddhists. This assertion is rooted in the radical analysis of emptiness made by Nagarjuna and the school considered to have been established by him, the Middle Way. Almost all contemporary forms of Mahayana Buddhism include Nagarjuna as one of its lineal figures.

Another pair of key concepts that were introduced into Buddhist thought in medieval India is the ground of consciousness (*alayavijnana*) and the matrix of awakening (*tathagatagarbha*). Although originating separately, these are conflated in Chinese Buddhist thought, creating the idea of "Buddha-nature." The term *Buddha-nature*, frequently misunderstood to indicate an individual personal essence or soul, articulates the identity of the emptiness of both persons and Buddhas. Any fixed nature could not change, and thus the absence of any fixed nature allows the change from ordinary person to Buddha. In most Mahayana traditions, this teaching carries with it the implication that beings are fully capable of realizing this identity.

The bodhisattva path is not unique to Mahayana Buddhism, but an emphasis on it is. A bodhisattva (*bodhi* = enlightenment, *sattva* = being) is a being who is dedicated to realizing awakening in order to alleviate the suffering of all beings. The principles of wisdom and compassion are both operative on the path—the wisdom to see the interdependent reality of all beings and the compassion that arises in consequence of seeing those beings suffering in delusion. The practice of the bodhisattva path is guided by the ethical principles of non-harming and developing increasingly skillful means of alleviating suffering.

MAJOR SECTS OF MAHAYANA BUDDHISM IN THE WEST

For the purposes of this work, we are focusing attention on the contemporary forms of Mahayana Buddhism in the West that have attracted significant numbers of converts or have been in the West long enough that membership includes second-, third-, or even fourth-generation descendants of immigrants who are primarily acculturated to Western society.

Zen (Chan/Son)

Chan, *Son*, and *Zen* are the Chinese, Korean, and Japanese names for the lineages in East Asia that emphasize the practice of silent, sitting meditation as the means of awakening.

Popularized by the works of D. T. Suzuki, the best known of these lineages is the Rinzai (Linji), which employs koan (Chinese, *kungan*) meditation. In this style of meditation, the practitioner contemplates a teaching story and attempts to grasp directly its significance. Understanding then needs to be expressed to the meditation teacher, who confirms the depth of the practitioner's grasp.

The other major sect represented in the West is the Soto (Chinese, *Tsao-tung*) lineage. Rather than meditating on formalized teaching tales, this lineage emphasizes direct confrontation with the mind in its ordinary, daily form. Silent meditation is referred to in this lineage as "just sitting" (*shikan taza*), and the founder of the school in Japan, Eihei Dogen Zenji, equated "just sitting" itself with the awakened mind of the Buddhas.

Zen temples founded in North America to serve immigrant communities drew interest in the mid-twentieth century, and separate Zen centers grew from this interest. Large and small centers of both Rinzai and Soto lineages are widespread in America and Canada, particularly on the East and West Coasts. Most centers are nonresidential; however, residential and monastic centers also exist and provide intensive training to both lay and ordained practitioners. Ordination in the Japanese Zen tradition generally requires a period of monastic training but is not a celibate ordination. In both Chinese (Chan) and the Korean (Son) traditions, ordination is both celibate and monastic.

Vajrayana or Esoteric Buddhism

Esoteric Buddhism, also known as Vajrayana Buddhism or tantric Buddhism, is considered by some to constitute a third form of Buddhism, i.e., in addition to Theravada and Mahayana, while others consider it to be a specific teaching within Mahayana. Despite the common identification of this kind of Buddhism with Tibet, it is found throughout the Buddhist world, having also been transmitted to East Asia, Southeast Asia, and more recently to the West as well. The spread of Vajrayana Buddhism in North America was most profoundly influenced by the Tibetan diaspora. Many Tibetan monastics founded centers and monasteries and traveled widely, teaching in a variety of settings. Multiple lineages are present, some of which have adapted the teachings to Western audiences. The most widely known of these grew from the teachings of the Dalai Lama and from Chogyam Trungpa.

Nichiren Buddhism

Another school of Buddhism was founded in medieval Japan by Nichiren (1222–1282) and focused on the teachings of the Lotus Sutra—most importantly, the single vehicle (*ekayana*) teaching and the idea of the Buddha as having an infinite life span. While several Nichiren lineages exist as monastic traditions today in Japan, and some of these are represented among the immigrant Japanese community, the best-known form outside the immigrant community is a lay organization, Soka Gakkai. Previously known in the United States as Nichiren Shoshu of America (NSA), following the 1991 split between the lay and monastic organizations in Japan, it is now called Soka Gakkai International (SGI). SGI is a lay organization led by President Daisaku Ikeda and is the most ethnically diverse of the four major streams of Buddhism in North America. Members meet in small groups based on geographical area, and these groups in turn form larger area groups. Guidance leaders are chosen from those groups and provide not only guidance in practice but also organizational leadership.

Pure Land Buddhism

Pure Land Buddhism is one of the most widespread forms of Mahayana Buddhism, being found in various forms not only in Japan, the source of most North American Pure Land traditions, but also in China, Korea, Tibet, and Vietnam. It is also, arguably, the least widely represented in contemporary discussions of Mahayana Buddhist practice in North America. Although some scholars have attempted to expand the category, *Pure Land* is usually understood to refer to practices that lead to birth in the Pure Land (Buddha realm) of Amitabha Buddha, the Buddha of Infinite Light and Infinite Life (commonly referred to as "Amida," the Japanese pronunciation). The Pure Land of Amida (*Sukhavati*) is represented in what are called the Pure Land sutras as being produced by the power of Amida's vows following an unimaginably long period of practice. Amida vows that he will not attain full awakening unless such a Buddha realm comes into existence. Described in very florid terms, the most important characteristic of the Pure Land is that once one is born there, full awakening, the attainment of Buddhahood, is assured.

Pure Land emerged as a distinct form of Buddhism at the end of the twelfth century through the teachings of Honen. The sect that continues from that origin is known as Jodo Shu. While there were other forms that arose at this same time, the most prominent of Honen's followers is Shinran, whose form is known as Jodo Shinshu. In the seventeenth century, the shogun divided Jodo Shinshu into two branches, now conventionally known as Higashi Hongan-ji (Eastern Temple of the Primal Vow) and Nishi Hongan-ji (Western Temple of the Primal Vow).

Jodo Shinshu is represented in the United States most prominently by the Buddhist Churches of America (BCA), associated with the Nishi Hongan-ji. The church is over a century old, dating from the end of the nineteenth century, when Japanese immigrants in the United States requested ministers be sent from Japan to serve the religious needs of the immigrant community. Missions were established in both Honolulu and San Francisco, and this division continues into the present—BCA serving the continental United States, and the Honpa Hongwanji Mission of Hawaii serving the island community. In Canada, the related organization is the Jodo Shinshu Buddhist Temples of Canada. Although historically grounded in the Japanese American community, the ethnic makeup of the BCA has become increasingly diverse in the last three decades. There are currently over sixty temples in the BCA, all across the United States. Demographic shifts away from rural communities have led to the closing of some older temples, but in the recent past new temples have been created in areas where population increases have included greater numbers of people interested in Buddhism.

Although no serious research has been done on the matter, Anglo-American converts to BCA seem to be attracted to its more traditionally churchly community orientation, which distinguishes it from the more individualistic character frequently encountered in meditation centers. Most Anglo-American converts seem to have some experience with and may continue to maintain affiliation with other forms of Buddhism but find the church congenial to their own changing situations in life, such as raising families.

GUIDES AND TEACHERS IN MAHAYANA TRADITIONS

Guidance and insight provided by teachers and spiritual friends are important elements of following the Mahayana path. This guidance and the relationship in which it takes place vary greatly; however, the spirit of receiving help along the bodhisattva way is the same. In some Vajrayana lineages, the guru is regarded as awakened, and his or her instruction arises from the enlightened mind. In Zen, the student engages in deep and often strenuous dialogue with his or her teacher, endeavoring to directly encounter and realize the teachings. In SGI, the community of practitioners meet together to discuss the teachings of the president of SGI, and elders in the community provide guidance and counsel. In Jodo Shinshu Buddhism, the minister supports the process of entrusting oneself and one's life to Amida Buddha's vow.

There is also great diversity in how one becomes a guru, teacher, elder, or minister. In the Tibetan Vajrayana tradition, enlightened bodhisattvas choose to be reborn in the form of gurus in order to guide and teach. In addition, other teachers of great insight, both lay and ordained, are recognized and support practitioners with their teachings. In the Zen tradition, though most teachers are ordained, many revered teachers are laypeople. In the Rinzai tradition, teachers have completed an extensive koan curriculum and are authorized by their teacher to guide others in their koan practice. In the Soto tradition, teachers have typically completed many years of practice (including some period of monastic training), study, and close work with their own teacher, resulting in formal authorization to teach. SGI, as a lay tradition, promotes experienced practitioners to leadership positions in which they meet individually with others, guide group practice and discussions, and support the growth of the organization. Jodo Shinshu ministers complete seminary training, enter into guidance relationships with senior ministers, and are then authorized to lead congregations. In each case, the guru, teacher, elder, or minister brings the voice of encouragement, experience, wisdom, and compassion into the life of the practitioner.

DIVERSITY IN MAHAYANA PRACTICE

There is a great diversity of teachings and practices among the various Mahayana traditions. A practitioner of Nichiren Buddhism will have a very different view of spiritual life than one who follows the Pure Land teachings, and this in turn is different from the experience of Zen practice or the many forms of Vajrayana practice. Even within one tradition there can be significant differences; for example, Soto

Zen meditation practice (*shikan taza*) is quite different from Rinzai koan practice. Within a single stream of teachings, the structure and shape of life dedicated to the dharma can vary.

An interfaith spiritual guide meeting with a Mahayana Buddhist client should inquire which Mahayana tradition the client is following as well as how he or she is living those teachings day to day. Is the person ordained or lay? If ordained, does ordination require following the *vinaya* (rules for celibate monks and nuns), or does the ordained person serve as a priest or minister in the midst of ordinary life? Is the client immersed in monastic or intensive residential practice, living alone at a distance from a teacher or community, connected to a sangha and busy with family and work? Is the person an immigrant, the child of immigrants, a convert to Buddhism, or does he or she have a complex religious identity? Has the client studied the tradition at any length, or is his or her affiliation based on an affinity with the practices without substantive exploration of teachings themselves? Each of these factors deeply affects the questions, reflections, difficulties, and longings a practitioner may bring to the spiritual guidance relationship.

THE PRACTICE OF MAHAYANA BUDDHISM

Commonalities exist within and between the four major streams of Mahayana Buddhism prevalent in North America at this time—Zen/ Chan/Son Buddhism, Vajrayana Buddhism (most commonly the many schools of Tibetan Buddhism), Nichiren Buddhism, and Pure Land Buddhism.

Zen Buddhism

Zen Buddhism—both Soto and Rinzai—is marked by a dedication to sitting meditation practice, enacting the teachings in ordinary activities and relationships, and a close relationship with a teacher in the context of the sangha. Both Rinzai and Soto emphasize the importance of practicing with a group. Intensive retreats that include many periods of sitting meditation alternating with shorter periods of walking meditation, formal meal practice done in the meditation hall, regular interviews with the teacher, ritual, the chanting of sutras, and some form of work practice are common and important elements of Zen practice. Most essential, however, is a commitment to a regular practice of sitting meditation and a dedication to bringing the teachings and an awareness of the bodhisattva vow to bear on all aspects of life. The practice is aimed at a direct realization of the interdependent nature of all being, in order to fulfill more completely the bodhisattva vow—the vow to dedicate one's life to liberating all beings from suffering. The bodhisattva vow and following the precepts, which guide the practitioner in how he or she does that, are fundamental to Zen practice. The Rinzai tradition emphasizes personal effort in koan practice to break down habitual ways of perceiving the self and the world and the attainment of *kensho,* a clear seeing into the nature things. Soto practice, based in *shikan taza,* ordinary activity, and service to the sangha, emphasizes the teaching that this moment, just as it is, is already the activity of Buddha—whether we realize it in any given moment or not.

Vajrayana or Esoteric Buddhism

Much of Vajrayana practice focuses on visualizations of varying complexity, all of which are intended to allow practitioners an opportunity to realize their inherent identity with the awakened nature of both themselves and the entire cosmos. The individual practitioner is visualized as identical with a Buddha located at the center of the cosmos, which is arrayed around him- or herself as a mandala. Such visualization practice is usually performed in a very structured ritual form, as is most meditation practice throughout Buddhism. Esoteric Buddhist rituals, however, tend to be more elaborate and are usually based on pan-Indic ritual practices of offerings to deities. In the case of Esoteric Buddhism, however, these ritual practices have been integrated into the broadly based conceptions of ground, path, and goal (i.e., the fundamental human problem being ignorance, the path being practice, and the goal being full awakening identical to that of a Buddha). In Esoteric Buddhist understanding of ritual practice, the practitioner making the offerings is at the same time identified with the Buddha to whom the offerings are being made. The offerings are one's own mistaken conceptions (*jneyavarana*) and misplaced affections (*klesavarana*). Offering serves to purify consciousness of even the deepest, most unconscious delusions, whether conceptual or emotional. This purification then gives rise to awakened consciousness and compassionate being in the world.

Places in which practice is pursued range from small groups to large, established monastic centers. Small groups may gather regularly and only periodically host teachers. At the other end of the scale, large monastic centers often have resident teachers and extensive study, practice, and retreat schedules. Individual practitioners may practice at home on a daily or weekly basis, work infrequently or more closely with a teacher, and do practice intensives ranging from one day to three years or more. Few undertake monastic training and vows of celibacy, though many dedicated lay practitioners do regular retreats.

Nichiren Buddhism

Nichiren Buddhism, most commonly Soka Gakkai International, is marked by devotion to chanting the name of the Lotus Sutra, *Nam-Myoho-Renge-Kyo*. The sound of this chant is understood to be the rhythm of the universe, the "mystic truth" innate in all life, that is, the mutually inclusive relationship of all phenomena. Chanting *Nam-Myoho-Renge-Kyo* expresses the faith that one is identical with this mystic truth and the harmony of all being.

Practitioners commit to chanting every day in order to align themselves and their life circumstances with this truth, to transform their lives and the lives of others through chanting. They are given a *gohonzon*, a scroll with the chant written on it, which is placed on an altar. In addition to chanting at home, both alone and with others, practitioners meet regularly in groups to study and support one another in the practice and are dedicated to spreading the teachings of Nichiren. SGI practice emphasizes directed personal effort. This effort, in the form of chanting, is aimed at changing one's everyday life as well as bringing harmony to the world. As an organization, SGI is actively engaged in efforts to support world peace.

Pure Land Buddhism

The dominant tradition of Pure Land Buddhism in the United States is Jodo Shinshu Buddhism. Jodo Shinshu is a Japanese form of Pure Land Buddhism aimed specifically at lay practitioners. There is no monastic form of Jodo Shinshu practice, nor is meditation generally a part of Jodo Shinshu life. Ministers in the Jodo Shinshu tradition complete seminary and are ordained, lead services, and minister to the community; however, they continue to live and function as laypersons. Temple services take place weekly and include chanting and a short dharma talk, and the temple often serves as a community

center, hosting a variety of activities. Central to the teachings of
Jodo Shinshu are the qualities of gratitude and humility, and the
realization of *shinjin*—a deep entrustment in the reality of Amida
Buddha's vow. The practice of Jodo Shinshu Buddhism takes place
primarily in day-to-day activities in which the practitioner cultivates
an awareness of the foolish nature of human beings—that is, the
consistent human tendency toward selfishness and pride—and
gratitude for all that is, given through no effort of his or her own,
specifically for the assurance of birth in Amida's Pure Land, which
is provided by Amida's efforts, not one's own. It is also central to
Jodo Shinshu Buddhism that one does not earn or create all the ways
one is supported through one's own actions; instead, one benefits in
every moment from the generosity of life, and everything is embraced
by the wisdom and compassion of the vow of Amida Buddha. As a
part of daily life, the practitioner of Jodo Shinshu may say, silently or
quietly, the *nembutsu*, "*Namu Amida Butsu*." The *nembutsu* is not said
in the spirit of petition but in the spirit of gratitude for what is already
present. In this way, Jodo Shinshu Buddhism differs significantly
from Buddhist traditions that emphasize dedicated individual effort
in meditation, chanting, or other forms of practice.

Practitioners of Multiple Traditions

It is not at all unusual for contemporary practitioners to draw from
and practice multiple traditions, both Theravada and Mahayana (the
exception to this are those in SGI). They may have started in one
tradition and shifted to another, or they may have a home base in
one tradition and listen to teachings, engage in daily practices, even
do retreats in another. For example, a person may have started at a
Vipassana center, then heard a Vajrayana teacher they were drawn to
and shifted focus—or vice versa. Or a person may sit zazen at a Zen
center, read books by Pema Chödrön (a contemporary Vajrayana
teacher), and go to a Vipassana center to hear visiting teachers. It is
also not uncommon for people to be religiously active as Christians
or Jews and also be deeply committed to Buddhist practice. Some
of these practitioners identify themselves as being both Christian or
Jewish and Buddhist.

SPIRITUAL GUIDANCE FOR MAHAYANA BUDDHISTS

A spiritual guide who is not a dharma teacher can serve as a sounding
board, guide, and companion to a Buddhist practitioner in the process

of integrating the teachings into his or her life. Specific questions about the tradition or the practice are most often best answered by a dharma teacher or minister. A guide outside the tradition can offer another avenue of exploration. The arc of spiritual development in each tradition may be different in some ways, but there are many questions that remain the same: How are the teachings relevant to my life? What obstacles do I imagine block me from living it out? What does it mean for me to trust the teachings and allow myself to be transformed by them? How do I embody the bodhisattva vow of acting with compassionate wisdom toward all sentient beings? How do I understand myself in relation to the teachings? How do my relationships reflect that relationship? What does it mean for me to embody my understanding in all aspects of my life?

There are a number of important aspects of a life of practice that can be fruitfully addressed in this form of interfaith spiritual guidance. For those raised in a faith other than Buddhism, negotiating the territory between religions can be a tricky process. A spiritual guide can be of great help in this process, providing a place and a relationship in which to ask questions that do not fit easily in a Buddhist context. For example, in Buddhism there is no God of creation, there is no prime mover, no overarching entity that guides the world or individual lives. For the practitioner, it may be very important to talk about his or her understanding of God and creation, perhaps unravel deeply held beliefs that are at odds with the tradition, and honestly assess what are and what are not the guiding principles of his or her life. For example, the practitioner may reflect on beliefs regarding an all-powerful God, or the difference between sinful actions contrary to God's will and ignorant actions that simply lead to suffering.

Entering into a new tradition or community can raise questions of belonging and identity. Even those who are born into a Buddhist tradition may find themselves in need of a place outside of the tradition in which to explore their faith and their place within in it. Spiritual guides can help people find their place within a Buddhist tradition—or multiple traditions, within the sangha, within the organization of the tradition, and, if applicable, with a teacher.

Commitment to a path of any kind naturally involves choice and limitation. A spiritual guide can help clarify this process and support the practitioner to experience this choice as an expression of his or her deepest calling. This process could include, for example in the Zen tradition, taking the bodhisattva precepts and identifying publicly as one who is dedicated to following them. Or a person may choose to follow the path of ordination. These choices can affect relationships with family and friends as well as one's role in the wider community. In some traditions, this would mean a commitment to a celibate monastic path, a choice that is difficult for many to understand even when it is done in a dominant religion.

Buddhism is not immune to painful ethical breaches by clergy, teachers, and other persons in positions of authority. The sense of confusion and betrayal that can result from experiencing such an ethical breach, knowing of it, or hearing about it can be deeply distressing and challenge the foundation of a person's practice and faith. This is particularly true when a practitioner brought to Buddhism a belief that it was somehow more pure or more holy than other religious traditions and therefore immune from such ethical breaches. Companioning people through the spiritual implications of such experiences and supporting them in finding new relationships in their spiritual lives in the face of them is a great gift, and it is a role spiritual guides, sometimes in conjunction with psychotherapists, are uniquely suited to do.

A spiritual guide can explore with the practitioner models of mature Buddhist practice and the ways in which that maturity can be supported and encouraged to develop. All aspects of life can be included—work, parenthood, caring for elderly parents, study, and community service. Developing wisdom, compassion, generosity, meditative depth and concentration, as well as patience, humility, and joy can all be a part of this. The shape and specificity of maturity will differ somewhat according to the tradition, but the clarity and openheartedness of genuine maturity is common to all.

There are some considerations specific to different traditions that need to be handled directly at the beginning of a spiritual guidance relationship. For example, some Buddhist practitioners may have a spiritual practice that is unfamiliar to the guide or, in the case of some Vajrayana practices, cannot be shared outside of the student-teacher relationship. This is particularly important to discuss if the practitioner is coming to spiritual guidance because of distressing experiences that have occurred during the practice. If a practitioner has an established relationship with a teacher, the differences between the student-teacher and client-guide relationships will need to be clarified. If a practitioner considers the tradition he or she is following to be the final or ultimate teaching and the dharma teacher to be the final authority, it is important to clarify differences in the orientation of these two distinct relationships.

Mahayana Buddhists differ widely in the language they use and the shape of the day-to-day relationship they have with the teaching and the path. To discuss with a follower of Jodo Shinshu Buddhism how she can organize her life to make time for greater personal efforts aimed at attaining enlightenment would be as inappropriate as speaking to a Nichiren Buddhist about deepening his trust in the power of Amida Buddha's vow. Sitting meditation, though an important element of many Mahayana Buddhists' lives, is not universal and may not be either significant or present at all in many practitioners' lives. Sensitivity to these differences is essential in building a fruitful spiritual guidance relationship.

Mahayana Buddhist practitioners, in all their diversity, are dedicated to embodying the path of awakening in all aspects of their lives. A spiritual guide outside of the Buddhist tradition can be of great service as a companion on the path and a great help in negotiating the twists and turns that inevitably arise. This is particularly true for those who find themselves integrating multiple religious experiences and identities in a complex world. Aligned with the Bodhisattva vow—taking refuge in the Buddha, the Dharma, and the Sangha—the richness of the path becomes evident and a life dedicated to the Buddha Dharma is made real.

Bharat S. Shah, MD, is the author of *An Introduction to Jainism* and other books to teach Gujarati, English, and Sanskrit. He is also the author of the memoirs *Dawn at Midnight* (about his wife's liver transplant) and *My Life with Panic Disorder*. He has served as president of the Gujarati Literary Academy of North America. He specializes in pulmonary medicine, and lives with his wife of more than forty years in Long Island, New York.

Guiding Jains, People of a Democratic Religion

Bharat S. Shah, MD

HISTORY AND EVOLUTION OF JAINISM

Difficult as it may appear to be, it is easier to conquer the entire world around us than to conquer the one within. We have seen innumerable great heroes, warriors, and emperors rise to glory, only to succumb to temptations and moral lapses causing their downfall. Conquering oneself is difficult partly because it is more attractive to give in to temptations than to thwart them. Our mind is more likely to choose what we like than what we should.

It is a rare person who even attempts to gain control over him- or herself. Most of us would rather appease the demigods or God with prayers, offerings, and sacrifices to achieve fulfillments of our ever-increasing desires, appropriate or otherwise. Over the ages people have worshipped the gods of rain, wealth, beauty, power, or fire. In India, such practices can be traced back to the first books of wisdom, called the Vedas, and this tradition is known as the Brahmanic tradition. The Brahmans were at the height of their power from 1500 BCE to 500 BCE and beyond.

There have always been people who felt that it was futile to spend time in pleasing various demigods whose existence signified nothing more than our ignorance. These gods behaved whimsically, did not always answer our prayers, and were approachable by only a handful of learned men, who were in turn still less approachable. Moreover, the Brahmanic approach made the human effort meaningless. Destiny became the almighty.

Not only ordinary people, but kings and queens, too, were at the mercy of pundits and priests who performed mysterious rituals in a language that nobody else understood. Nor could they be questioned—their authority was absolute. Mighty warriors of the Kshatriya, or the ruling caste, found it unbearable to hand over their power to the Brahman (Brahmin) priests. It is neither fair nor accurate to describe this as a class war for power, although that did constitute a minor part of it.

Many kings and other mighty ones had ample wealth at their disposal. They had innumerable horses, elephants, palaces, beautiful queens, and sizable harems. They had no shortage of servants either. None of these could make them happy. They craved for more, which left them wanting yet more, and feeling yet less happy. They saw that even gods depended on people making some effort on their part, and making more effort improved the outcome. That may have made them question the very idea of trying to please various gods. These thinkers believed in their own effort, and their practices came to be known as the Shraman tradition (*shrama* means "physical labor"), as opposed to the Brahman one.

Shramans chose to control their temptations and give up their desires rather than try to appease various gods to fulfill them. Two such great thinkers arose simultaneously in northeastern India about twenty-six hundred years ago and established two religions that are still being practiced today and are thriving. Lord Buddha established Buddhism, and Lord Mahavir established Jainism.

Both are historical figures. Buddhist scriptures record the moment when Buddha was informed of Mahavir's death. There is no evidence to suggest that they had ever met, even though they both lived in the same state of Magadh, modern-day Bihar, near Kolkata. Bihar is so named because it had innumerable *vihars,* or Buddhist monasteries.

Jainism has been often confused with Buddhism thanks to their similar albeit quite distinct philosophies, similar terminology used, and similarities between names of family members of both prophets and those of their disciples. Jainism and Buddhism are two distinct religions, and Jainism is only recently coming to be known in the Western world. Jainism has not descended from Hinduism either.

There is evidence to believe that when the Aryans came to India, Jainism was being practiced there.

FOUNDER OF JAINISM

The Sanskrit root word for "to conquer" is *ji*. One who has conquered the self with all its desires and temptations to achieve the pure and absolute knowledge or the truth is a Jina (pronounced "jin" which rhymes with "pin"). Followers of Jinas are Jains,[1] and their religion is Jainism, named after its followers. The Jain tradition considers Jainism to be prehistoric. It believes in several successive lineages of twenty-four Tirthankaras, each of whom established and reestablished the religion.

Tirthankaras establish the congregation, or *tirtha*, consisting of Jain monks (sadhu, "one who strives"; *sadh*, "to strive"), nuns (sadhvi), and civilian men (*shravak*, one who listens to the preaching by sadhus and sadhvis; *shru*, "to listen"), and women (shravika). Collectively these four are called *sangh* or *sangha*, the term used by the Buddhists also. Indian philosophy compares worldly bondage to an ocean. *Tirtha* is the dock from which the soul embarks on the journey across the ocean to its ultimate salvation, or *moksha*. Not all Jinas are Tirthankaras, while all the latter are Jinas.

There is no one single founder of Jainism. Its Shraman tradition traces itself to antiquity, during which innumerable founders and re-founders have established the religion repeatedly. The last two prophets, Parshvanath (the penultimate one), and Mahavir Swami[2] (the last one) are historical, and they existed between 700 and 600 BCE. Fewer than one hundred remaining monks of the older prophet happened to meet those of Mahavir, and they soon joined the new order. The older tradition preached celibacy but did not list it among its four major vows. Celibacy became the fifth major vow in later tradition.

Mahavir means "great warrior" or "conqueror of the self." (The reader is probably familiar with *Mahatma*, or the "great soul.") Mahavir was born as Vardhaman, meaning "incremental," as the material and spiritual prosperity of his parents increased with his birth. While he was still in the womb, his mother Trishala saw fourteen dreams:

1.	An elephant	Wisdom, stability
2.	An ox	Strength
3.	A lion	Leadership, prowess
4.	Laxmi	The godess of wealth, both material and spiritual riches
5.	A garland of flowers	Fragrance of virtue
6.	The moon	Cool comfort to the soul
7.	The sun	Brightness, warmth, knowledge
8.	An orange flag	Striving, austerity, renunciation
9.	A pot full of water	Life, perfection, enrichment
10.	Lotus lake	Detachment, rising above the mud
11.	An ocean	Diving into the inner waters for riches
12.	A divine airplane	Higher destination
13.	A heap of gems	Reaching the true wealth, salvation
14.	Smokeless fire	Pure, sheer, perfect knowledge, *moksha*

Vardhman Mahavir was conceived and delivered like any other child, to a local royal couple. When the rain god Indra doubted the power of the newborn child, Mahavir pressed his great toe to earth to make the Himalayas tremble, one of the many miracles attributed to him.

At age twenty-eight, after his parents' death, he sought permission from his older brother to relinquish worldly attachments, but at his brother's request, he waited two more years. Once the mind gives up the world, then it scarcely matters whether one lives in a palace or in a forest.

At age thirty, he gave up his wife, a daughter, the palace, ornaments, and clothing, and he literally pulled off all his hairs with his own hand. He went to a forest, fasted for weeks and months on end, and suffered extreme hardships and tortures with equanimity, staying in meditation all the while. There were many important events that took place during this period of forging. We will look at a few of them.

Chand Kaushik, the Snake

Vardhaman (Mahavir) was warned by the local people against venturing on a path through a dense forest. It was inhabited by a ferocious venomous snake that was sure to bite. Mahavir went there, and the snake did bite, but it was surprised to see milk rather than blood oozing out of the wound. Vardhaman's compassion and mercy were flowing for the snake.

Vardhaman calmly looked at the bewildered snake and uttered only two words: "*Buzz, buzz!*"[3] It means, "Learn, learn!" He thereby reminded the snake that the latter was an angry monk, Chand (meaning "angry") Kaushik, in its previous birth, who had accidentally killed a female frog by inadvertently stepping on it and later neglecting to atone for the sin.

A young disciple of the monk reminded him once too often, and Chand Kaushik blew his top. He grabbed his walking stick and chased the younger monk in the dark monastery, where Chand Kaushik hit his head against a pillar and died instantly. Since he had died while in a very angry mood, he was born again as a venomous snake.

Vardhaman reminded it of its previous birth by saying, "Learn, Chand Kaushik, learn! You were a great monk and teacher, far advanced in practicing penance and austerity, all of which were nullified by your anger. Still you do not give up your anger. If not now, when will you learn?"

Torment by the Cowherd

Once when Vardhaman was standing in deep meditation, a cowherd was grazing his cows nearby. The cowherd had to leave for the town to run some errand, so he asked Vardhaman to keep an eye on his cows. Vardhaman, meditating deeply, did not hear him, and the cows wandered off. Not seeing the cows on his return and suspecting that Vardhaman had stolen them, the cowherd started yelling at Vardhaman, who still did not hear him.

The cowherd got furious and asked, "Are you deaf?" Still not getting any reply, he got two sharp sticks of bamboo and hammered them into Vardhaman's ears and left. Vardhaman still did not respond. When a few villagers found Vardhaman later and pulled the sticks out, he screamed with pain. He advised the villagers not to pursue the cowherd and explained to them why that event had happened.

Vardhaman was a king in one of his previous births, and the cowherd was his court musician who would play his instrument to put the king to sleep. Once the musician continued to play even after the king had fallen asleep. The king was furious, and he ordered molten lead to be poured into the musician's ears so that he would realize how painful the noise can be to a sleeping king. Vardhaman was being paid back for that action. Even he was not immune from the law of karmas.

Compassion for the Enemy

A demigod named Sangam, to break Vardhaman's deep meditation, inflicted severe torments on the latter when Vardhaman was about to achieve his salvation, or the *Keval Gnan*. Vardhaman knew that he was about to be free and was destined to be a Tirthankara. However, he started worrying about Sangam. How many births would he have to go through and suffer to pay back the sin accrued by torturing a Tirthankara-to-be! Tears flew from Vardhaman's eyes, even for the one who was treating him like an enemy.

MAHAVIR THE PREACHER

The purpose of such severe penance was to shed the already accumulated karmas. Good and bad karmas do not cancel one another out. They have to be paid for sequentially. At age forty-two, Vardhman became Mahavir, having achieved the *Keval Gnan*, or sheer knowledge, the smokeless brightness.

Mahavir started preaching, thereby becoming an Arihant[4] and a teacher. He preached for thirty years, during which he ordained thousands of sadhus and sadhvis and guided hundreds of thousands toward his path of salvation. Again, there are many interesting stories from this period of his life, but we will look at two and note some points.

Mahavir's Compassion

Mahavir's congregation included the local king, Shrenik, as well as the local butcher, Mahavir's preaching of extreme nonviolence notwithstanding. The king and the butcher both were entitled to do what they chose and yet were worthy of Mahavir's compassion.

Fate of King Prasanna

For many days, on his way to see Lord Mahavir, King Shrenik saw a monk practicing severe austerities and meditating.

"What would be the fate of that monk?" he asked Mahavir.

"He will go to the seventh and the darkest hell," replied Mahavir.

"Hell!" Shrenik could not believe his ears.

"Yes, now the sixth one, now the fifth, fourth … now the first," Mahavir continued.

"He will go to the first heaven, now second … third … sixth … heaven," Mahavir went on. Then Shrenik heard the divine drums and other musical instruments and looked at Mahavir, askance. Lord Mahavir enlightened him:

"The monk is an ex-king, named Prasanna Chandra. He gave his throne to his child and left to pursue his spiritual goal. While in deep meditation, he overheard a couple of his townsfolk talking about his kingdom being attacked by an enemy and the inability of the child king to fight back. Prasanna was stirred up and was mentally fighting the battle, killing his kingdom's attackers mercilessly. Oh, Shrenik, that is when I told you that he was destined to go to the seventh hell."

"Prasanna soon lost all his weapons and started fighting with his bare hands. Then he saw the enemy king near him. Prasanna engaged in a duel and knocked the enemy down. Not having any weapon in his hand, Prasanna reached for his protective headgear with which to smash the enemy's head," Mahavir continued.

"Prasanna felt his hairless bald head—the head of the monk that he was, who had relinquished his family, kingdom, and wealth and taken the spiritual path. He realized the grave mistake he had made, that he had betrayed his vows. He felt penitent, overcome with sorrow, and started atoning for his missteps. That is when I told you that he was coming out of the hell and was ascending the steps to heaven. He has reached the *Keval Gnan*, and the gods have come to celebrate the event."

Shrenik kept looking at Mahavir, who went on, "Shrenik, the mind is very powerful. Our attitudes and thoughts can determine our destiny and adjust it very rapidly. Do not ever let bad thoughts enter your mind. All violence occurs first in your mind. That is why one should become nonviolent in thought, speech, and action."

MAHAVIR'S WORD, THE JAIN HOLY BOOK

Mahavir died at age seventy-two. His disciples, led by his chief disciple, Gautam, compiled his teachings in twelve books. These were lost and then were re-created into fourteen volumes, which had to be rewritten years later as forty-five Agamas ("coming down" through the ages), most of which are known and available today. The Agamas constitute the canonical literature of Jains. Instead of being written in the classical Sanskrit language, these are written in the dialect of the local people. They are meant mainly for the monks to study and to preach about. The head monk, the acharya, gives discourses on these. However, a civilian reading these on his own may not be able to obtain its full benefit.

Jainism does not have one single holy book to live by. When pressed to name one, Jains most commonly name the Tattvarth Sutra.

THREE MAIN INDIAN SCHOOLS OF THOUGHT

Indian culture is hard to distinguish from its religions. There are three main schools of thought: Hinduism, Jainism, and Buddhism. The last two are relatively recent Shraman offshoots, while the first is the oldest. All three claim to be without a discernible beginning.

Indian philosophy revolves around an immortal soul, as pure as the great cosmic soul. In India, the soul gives up the body, rather than the body giving up the ghost. This soul is trapped into an otherwise nonliving body, which subjects the soul to endless misery—birth, death, grief, disease, old age, and emotional pain. The soul is in the grip of ignorance, which makes it body-centered, forgetting its lofty origin.

Bodily and worldly pleasures are illusions; desires fulfilled lead to more desires, misguided struggles and strivings, distracting the soul from its pursuit of freedom, the *moksha* (literally "liberation"), or the nirvana (a word used mostly by the Buddhists in this sense). One has to learn to control one's mind, thoughts, desires, speech, and actions, withdrawing them from shallow pleasures and channeling one's energies into achieving real and lasting spiritual pleasure and bliss.

PRACTICE OF JAINISM

Jainism is best known for its extreme nonviolence. Mahatma Gandhi was influenced by it. All life is similar, and nobody likes to suffer or be killed. Vegetarianism automatically follows from this respect for all life forms. Animal sacrifice it is to be refrained from for the same reason. Avoiding any kind of violence either by thought, by speech, or by action is the right way to live and strive for salvation. All desires and violence begin in the mind. Therefore, controlling the mind is of paramount importance.

Disagreements, differences of opinion—especially intolerance for the opinions of others—lead to violence. Jainism advocates an approach that balances a multiplicity of viewpoints and avoids extremism. This "non-one-ended-ism" is called *anekantavada* and is Jainism's greatest offering to solving the problem of violence. *Anekantavada* facilitates respect, tolerance, and harmony and has kept Jains away from unnecessary quarrels. Jainism is not a proselytizing religion—that is, it does not seek to convert anybody, although one is welcome to follow this path and become a Jain. An attempt to convert someone amounts to disrespecting his or her religion, implying that there is something wrong with the latter religion and hence needs to be replaced with a better (i.e., "our") religion.

Nonviolence, truthfulness, non-stealing, non-hoarding, and celibacy are Jainism's five principal recommended vows (of the total twelve), which are absolute for monks but more limited for civilians. Marital sex is not considered a sin. The purpose of celibacy is spiritual, as is that of vegetarianism and yoga (literally, *a union* of soul with the great soul). Physical exercises are only the visible part of the yoga.

Nonviolence (*ahinsa* or ahimsa) extends to humans, animals, minute life forms in air and water, plant life, and inanimate objects. The *ahinsa* applied to the minutest life forms and inanimate objects (non-disruption) is known as *jayana* (nurture), or protecting the environment from waste, overuse, senseless destruction, and squandering of resources.

The Jain worldview can be described in detail under nine subheads called Nine Fundamentals, or Nine Elements:

1. *Living.* This is the soul—pure, pristine, shining, weightless, the abode of knowledge, and freedom.
2. *Nonliving.* This is the body, made of humors and incapable of doing anything without the soul. It acts like a cage to bind the free soul.
3. *Sin.* This refers to bad deeds committed by the soul, which tie the latter to the body.
4. *Merit.* This is the opposite of sin. Good deeds also bind

the soul to the body. This is worth understanding. One is rewarded for merits by being assigned to heaven, and for sin, to hell. From neither of these entities can the soul strive to be free. Hence, neither is desirable. One cannot stop all deeds, but there is a way out of bondage, as we shall see later.

5. *Influx.* This refers to inflow of karmic particles, potentially, but not necessarily (see below), binding the soul to the body.

6. *Outflow.* This is shedding off the karmic particles by the soul. Influx and outflow both are of no consequence as such, as long as they do not stick to the soul. They are made important by our likes and dislikes (see below).

7. *Bondage.* The soul is bound to the body by karmic particles, with help from the likes and dislikes, both of which act like sticky grease, thereby making the karmic particles stick to the soul and in turn shrouding the soul in a veil of ignorance.

8. *Shedding Off.* The not-so-sticky karmic particles are washed away by practicing detachment. However, those already attached firmly can only be shed by fasting, meditating, and living through the good and bad times (our karmas) with equanimity. Practicing penance, observing austerity, and tolerating afflictions without bitterness are the way to do this.

9. *Salvation.* This is the *moksha,* when the soul achieves its freedom. *Moksha* does not lend itself to description, even by the Lord.

SPIRITUAL GROWTH IN JAINISM

Jain scriptures describe fourteen spiritual steps, symbolically described in the fourteen dreams Mahavir's mother had during her pregnancy (see above), that a soul has to climb to reach its salvation, or *moksha.* They are called *gunasthanas* [5] or virtue stations. The first rung of that ladder is ignorance! Ignorance of the soul, of its true nature, is the root cause of our problems. The soul forgets its pure and shining nature and falls to temptations of the body, which makes it suffer through innumerable births, rebirths, and deaths. The soul can achieve liberation from the worldly woes by acquiring proper knowledge and striving to free itself by shedding its bad karmas or deeds.

Awareness of ignorance is the first step toward knowledge. Of course, ignorance is not knowledge, not even its first step. Let us say that we are wandering around a building, hoping to enter it. This is the ignorance. Even if we see the building, we cannot go to its terrace. Then we see a ladder, grab it with our hands, and look up to the terrace. That is the first virtue station; everything before that was sheer ignorance.

One has to climb the ladder, rather than just holding on to it. That requires true information, true perception, proper conduct,[6] plus striving and forging through accordingly. The upward journey is not guaranteed. The soul may make mistakes and fall back and even entirely drop off the ladder into total ignorance. Progressively, the soul has to develop immunity to temptations, free itself from the likes and dislikes that act as the grease that makes the karmas stick to the soul, find the inner wealth to reach the fourteenth and final station.

The final station is the state of enlightenment, of pure, perfect *Keval Gnan* (sheer or perfect knowledge), without any qualms or doubts, the fire without the smoke. From then onward, all actions are carried out with total disinterestedness, without any likes or dislikes. New karmas cannot bind this soul, it is liberated, it has become a Jina. All Jains aspire to become a Jina, and only in one's earthly, human life can one achieve it—not in heaven, nor in hell; nor can plants or nonhuman animals succeed. Human birth is the golden opportunity for the soul to liberate itself.

MAJOR SECTS OF JAINISM

Jainism is a democratic system. Mahavir presented the fundamental principles, taught about the ramifications of various spiritual issues, and made the individual responsible for his or her own discernment and commitment. There are no commands like "Thou shall not …!" The closest exception is when Mahavir admonished against laziness and apathy. He told us (addressing his chief apostle Gautam), "Listen, Gautam, never be indifferent!"

It is no wonder that free thinking encourages different interpretations of Mahavir's words and practices and has led to the formation of many sects, based on whether their followers go to temples or not, whether their idols are made of plain stones without eyes, whether their monks wear white clothes (*Svetambara*, or white-clad) or none at all (*Digambara*, or sky-clad). There are other smaller sects, too. All these sects follow the same path as preached by Lord Mahavir.

MODERN AND POSTMODERN DEVELOPMENTS IN JAINISM

Although quite ancient, Jainism is modern in its attitude. It does not have a caste system, it treats men and women equally, it does not believe in a creator God or in an agency to dole out punishment for sins. Its preaching regarding tolerance and the environment are relevant today, even after at least twenty-six hundred years.

Since Jain monks respect life in soil, air, fire, and water, they do not travel before sunrise or after sunset, during the rainy season, or by any vehicles. That provides them ample opportunity to meet Jains and other people and be close to them. At the same time, monks do not stay in one place for more than three consecutive rainy seasons, preferably only one.

At present Jainism is practiced mostly in the middle western states of India, with a sizable population of Jains in the south, and in the east in and around Kolkata. Jains have migrated to Africa, Europe, and the United States. In the United States, as of 2010, there are 150,000 to 200,000 Jains. There are close to one hundred Jain centers, with more than fifty ornate Jain temples.

A few maverick monks have crossed the ocean by air (a forbidden act for monks) to come to the United States, to the great consternation of the local communities in India. Their contribution in furthering Jainism among the second-generation immigrant Jains is enormous. A few Westerners have also chosen to practice Jainism.

In Jainism, the congregation, or the sangh, has the final say. It can, and it has, commanded its greatest monks to accede to its orders in the interest of the greater good. The Federation of Jain Associations in North America (JAINA) has drawn up a code of conduct for the monks and others coming to America.

SPIRITUAL GUIDES, MONKS, AND CIVILIANS IN JAINISM

The Jain way of teaching and learning has always been through the word of mouth, from the guru (teacher) to the disciple. This was especially so before the written word came. There were no schools or seminaries for monks. They were taught by senior monks and by civilian scholars. A newly ordained monk spends several years studying Jainism, other religions, and scriptures, excels in maintaining an impeccable character, and practices severe austerities, to achieve the status of an *acharya*,[7] which makes him qualified to deliver sermons to the sangh.

There is no single head of the religion. The *acharya* is the head of a partcular order. There are several independent orders. They do meet off and on, but mainly they keep on carrying out their duties of helping people, teaching them, leading religious festivities and observances, ordaining new monks and nuns, and inspiring the civilians into building temples and monasteries.

Civilian teachers are important because they are free to travel abroad and carry out the educational duties of the monks and nuns who do not use any vehicles. They cannot ordain new monks.

Jain monks in India today do not keep any money or possessions, except a few essential books, one or two pairs of non-stitched cotton or woolen garments, and a walking stick to help them negotiate their path and for support, regardless of the monk's age. They go barefoot in every kind of weather and gather food by going from door to door, just enough for that day. Monks do not keep any food after sundown. They cannot collect all their food from only one household. They do not bathe or brush their teeth the way we do, but just clean them with a minimal amount of water instead.

Civilian *shravaks* and *shravikas* put on clean clothes and go to the temple to worship the idol of a Jina or just to say prayers without physically worshipping the idol. The Jinas do not give anything, nor do they remove anybody's sins or offer forgiveness or punishment. Prayers to the Jinas are only praises, without asking for any favors. Worship helps one to strive to become a Jina.

Shravaks and *shravikas* go to the *upashraya* (monastery) to listen to the *acharya* give religious discourses, especially during the rainy season, the monsoon that runs for four months from mid-June through mid-October, during which monks do not travel. The civilians practice nonviolence, support charities, and operate animal shelters, schools, and hospitals.

FESTIVALS AND OBSERVANCES IN JAINISM

Since Jainism advocates giving up worldly pleasures, it might seem as though its festivities are no fun at all. To those who are initiated, however, there is a great deal of excitement. There are religious processions, parades welcoming the *acharyas* to the town or bidding them farewell, installation of new idols, consecration of new temples, opening of public libraries and dispensaries, and exhibitions of dioramas of religious stories. Day to day, small and large observances at the temple or in the *upashraya* can keep Jains physically and spiritually occupied or may even overwhelm them.

The Anniversary of Lord Mahavir's Birth

The anniversary of Lord Mahavir's birth is observed every year by children and young adults staging a variety of programs related to his life. It is celebrated as World Peace Day in many countries. It comes in the middle of the summer in India.

Mahavir's Death, or Nirvana Day

The anniversary of Mahavir's death, or Nirvana Day, is observed on the last day of the Hindu (Vikram) calendar year, the day before the New Year. There is chanting in the temples and festive fireworks outside. Since Mahavir achieved nirvana (or salvation) on that day, lamps are lit in houses and on buildings. This is known as Diwali, or the Festival of Lights. Many cultures and religions share this festival.

The New Year

Mahavir's chief disciple, Gautam, was away when Mahavir left this world. When Gautam learned of Mahavir's death, he broke down and cried like a child. On further contemplation, he realized that Mahavir was free from all attachments and had taught Gautam to be likewise free. Attachment, even to Mahavir, was not desirable. The next day, Gautam achieved the *Keval Gnan*, and that day is celebrated by Jains as the New Year, a celebration of *gnan*, or knowledge.

Paryushana

Paryushana (meaning "staying put") is the greatest observance by the Jains. It is an eight-day religious fast (similar to Lent for Christians), which occurs in the middle of the monsoon season. Monks do not travel during the rainy season, because rivers are running high, and roads are muddy and teaming with creatures. During the eight days of Paryushana, *sharavaks* and *shravikas* observe fasts without any food and often without any water, from one day to up to two months (yes, sixty days, without anything at all). The purpose is to withdraw from everything and focus on the word of the Jinas. The *acharya* reads from the holy Kalpa Sutra, describing the life of Mahavir and a few others. When Mahavir's birth is read, a big celebration ensues.

Just after Paryushana, the civilians visit other temples within, say, a hundred-mile radius, to assess and repair the ravages of the monsoon. Monks compose books during this period and dedicate them to the sangh.

Samvatsari. On the last day of Paryushana, Jains do the annual review of their conduct, atone for their transgressions, and seek forgiveness from each other.

JAIN TEMPLE CODE OF BEHAVIOR

Non-Jains often do not adequately appreciate the role of the temple or the role of idol worship for Jains. (There is no Jain equivalent of the Christian word *pagan*, the Muslim word *kafir*, or the Jewish word *goy*. Those who do not practice or belong to the religion are simply called non-Jains.) Idol worship for the devoted is what the flag is to a patriot. One does not just adore a stone or a piece of fabric. These objects stand for another idea or image. In other words, one does not admire the window, but rather what it shows.

The temple represents our body, and its inner sanctum represents our heart. The idol represents the Lord, whom we want to invite and establish in our heart. Jain temples are very ornate, appropriate for one's body. They display carvings that may be sensual, nude, and even depicted as engaging in sexual acts. These are properties of the body. Once inside the temple, one leaves these behind. The innermost sanctum, which houses the idol, represents our heart, and it has no decorations. There are plain walls and maybe a lamp.

Jain temples are extremely clean, since there is no food permitted in them. Only clean clothes are permitted. To worship the idol physically with saffron or with flowers, one dresses up almost like a surgeon, with a mask, too. Singing devotional songs is welcome, but generally there are no lectures or Sunday schools in the temple; these are held in the monasteries.

SPIRITUAL DISCIPLINES IN JAINISM

The monastic code of conduct has been alluded to before. In addition, monks go from house to house to obtain food. That is called *gochari*, meaning "as the cow grazes." Cows do not denude an area of grass, but take a little from here and a little from there. Monks do not make food for themselves but eat whatever is offered to them. Even if the food contains bitter cucumber, an indigestible garnish, or other unpleasant ingredients, monks cannot throw it away but must eat it, for fear of hurting the soil life.

Civilians are encouraged to become a monk or nun for a day or for a week. It is not possible for civilians to advance beyond a few *gunasthanas*, or virtue stations, because their lives do not permit them to be totally free of all violence or worldly attachments—desires, likes, and dislikes. There is no compulsion to be ordained.

Jains contribute to seven fields of charities: monks, nuns, civilian men, civilian women, temples, monasteries, and a general-purpose fund. The first two support the basic necessities of monks and nuns, their discourses, and their medical care. Nothing is given directly to monks or nuns. The next two categories support poor civilians and provide them with food, education, shelter, and jobs.

Money earmarked for temples is sacrosanct, and it cannot be diverted to anything else. It is used for building new temples or for the renovation of old ones. Funds given for monasteries are applied toward building new monasteries and other similar facilities and for their maintenance. The general-purpose fund is unrestricted, and it can be used for any suitable purpose.

COMMON SPIRITUAL ISSUES FOR JAINS

Finding Balance

Jainism is often wrongly perceived as being very strict. Jainism does advocate undertaking progressively more strenuous practices; however, it always advises one to consider the time, the place, and one's limits before jumping into any severe practice. Spiritual guides can help Jains discern whether a spiritual practice is appropriate or balanced and whether it will be helpful or harmful to the client in the long run.

Discerning Issues around Violence

Jainism's approach to vegetarianism is difficult for many people to understand. A superficial understanding of Jainism may lead to questions like, "The plants are alive too. Why do you eat them?" There is a long spectrum of life, and Jains try to move toward decreasing any kind of killing. Spiritual guides can help Jain clients discern how to decrease violence in every aspect of their lives.

Jainism's nonviolence is often misconstrued by its followers and others as devaluing agriculture, police work, and national defense. Spiritual guides can help Jains balance their idealism with life's practicalities.

Some Jains mistake and equate nonviolence with cowardice and passivity. Spiritual guides can help their clients appreciate the courage and heroism involved in protecting and honoring all beings.

Discerning Financial Faithfulness

Often an extravagant amount of money is channeled into building temples and performing rituals, at the expense of providing housing, food, and heath care to the congregation. Spiritual guides can hold Jain clients accountable to their own highest ideals, tending to the needs of both the congregation and the poor in a balanced and equitable way.

Reverence versus Worship

With its innumerable Tirthankaras (who are not gods), Jainism is often misconstrued as being a polytheistic religion. If at all, it is an atheistic religion. Jains do not believe in God, the creator, or any agency that can take away or forgive sins or that gives out boons when pleased. Jinas are free souls, without a body, and hence they cannot listen to anybody's prayers or answer them.

Idol worship is the most ill-understood tenet of Jainism. Idol worship reminds one of the ultimate goal of the soul itself to become a Jina by shedding its burden. It is a kind of meditation on one's true nature. Idol worshipping is like having training wheels that one has to outgrow. The idol is not God, any more than the flag is the nation or a photograph is the grandma. Idol worship is a window to look through, rather than to be looked at. Spiritual guides can remind Jain clients of these crucial points, help them to be wary of blind idolatry, and encourage them to be able to explain these concepts to non-Jains.

Adapting to New Cultures

Many of the traditional practices of monks and nuns are nearly impossible to carry out in modern cities with high-rise buildings, locked doors, and impossible walking distances. Not traveling by vehicles makes contact with a greater number of people difficult. Not brushing or bathing is of dubious value. *Acharyas* not using electric loudspeakers deprives their listeners of the word of the Jinas. Spiritual guides can help Jains discern appropriate ways to live out their faith in new and bewildering contexts.

Jainism is not known much outside India, thanks to its low-key, non-proselytizing approach. Mahatma Gandhi transformed its doctrine of *ahinsa* into a social and political force. Second-generation Jains outside India, and even within India, are hardly conversant with languages like Sanskrit, Ardha-Magadhi, and Gujarati, in which Jain scriptures are written. Spiritual guides can encourage second-generation Jains to become scripturally literate and knowledgeable about their culture and faith.

THINGS TO REMEMBER WHEN WORKING WITH JAINS

- Jainism is an ancient faith that is at least six hundred years older than Christianity and twelve hundred years older than Islam. It has a long and august tradition.

- Jainism provides a very good support system for its followers.

- Although it is a minority, the Jain community is relatively rich and powerful in its native India. It is small in numbers, but large in its influence in part because of its peaceful, tolerant approach and its emphasis on education.

- Jainism respects other viewpoints and religions and appreciates the same in return.

NOTES

1. *Jain* does not rhyme with *pain*. This "ai" sound does not occur in English. It can be approximated by saying "a" as the first "*A*" in *America*, immediately followed by "i" as in *inn*.
2. *Nath* and *swami* both mean "the master."
3. *Buzz*, with "u" as in *put* and "zz" as in *pizza*.
4. Meaning "whose all internal enemies are destroyed." *Ari* means "enemy;" *hant* sounds somewhat similar to "hunt" in English, but with a dental *t*.
5. *Gun* rhymes with *put*.
6. These three are collectively known as "three gems," any of which can lead the soul to its salvation.
7. The head monk who sets the example by practicing (*aa-char*) what he preaches.

Siri Kirpal Kaur Khalsa is a practicing Sikh, the founder of an interfaith worship organization, and the author of *Sikh Spiritual Practice: The Sound Way to God.* She has spoken about Sikhism on televised interfaith panels. She lives in Eugene, Oregon, with her non-Sikh husband.

Spiritual Guidance in the Sikh Tradition

Siri Kirpal Kaur Khalsa

AN OVERVIEW OF SIKH HISTORY AND BELIEFS

The Punjab region—a land rich in many cultures and faiths—today straddles the India-Pakistan line. Here, Hinduism and Islam converge—sometimes in battle, sometimes in glorious cultural fusion. Into this milieu in 1469 CE, a boy was born to a Hindu family, a boy who became Guru Nanak Dev ji, the founder of Sikhism.

As a boy, Nanak liked to meditate and serve people. He continued these traits as he grew up, married, and had two sons. In 1496, he stepped into the local river to take his morning bath and disappeared for three days. When he returned, he was enlightened. Sikhs ("disciples") gathered about him, and so he became Guru Nanak. (*Guru* means "enlightener" or "teacher.")

Guru Nanak spoke and sang of the oneness of God, who is formless, genderless, and wrath-less. God is the only reality, totally present throughout creation and also infinite beyond comprehension. We exist only within God; we have no reality independent of God. Because Guru Nanak spoke and sang that all creation exists in God's will, he emphasized the folly of religious intolerance and false divisions such as caste. He taught his Sikhs to live in the world—as householders in service to humanity—rather than to retreat from it. He exposed the folly of all forms of idolatry and superstitious practice. He emphasized the importance of meditation and service to others. While his teachings included karma (the law of cause and effect) and reincarnation, he taught that meditation burns off karma and is therefore the route out of the cycle of rebirth. While Guru Nanak's message included elements of Hinduism, Islam, and other faiths, it is a separate revelation.

Guru Nanak traveled widely—all over India, down to Sri Lanka, at least as far north as Tibet and southern Russia, and at least as far west as Mecca. As he traveled, he taught and sang. A Muslim-born musician named Mardana accompanied Guru Nanak on his early journeys, as did a Hindu named Bala.

Before Guru Nanak merged into the final light, he ordained his most devoted disciple as the next Guru, bypassing his two sons. Sikhs credit Guru Angad, the second Guru, with the creation of Gurmukhi script, used today for the Punjabi language. He devised it to write down Guru Nanak's many songs and poems, including Japji Sahib (literally, "Great Recitation for the Soul")

Guru Angad passed the torch on to a devout elderly Sikh, who became Guru Amar Das, the third Guru. Guru Amar Das was truly egalitarian—abolishing the practice of sacrificing widows on their husband's funeral pyres, creating a priesthood that included women, and instituting the practice of *langar*, the Sikh communal meal. Sikhs had always fed people, but *langar* extended the practice, requiring people from all walks of life to sit down and eat together, a novel innovation for its time. Guru Amar Das was also an accomplished poet, his best known work being Anand Sahib (literally, "Great Bliss")

Guru Amar Das had a devout daughter named Bibi Bhani. One day, while Guru Amar Das was meditating, Bibi Bhani noticed that the chair he was sitting on was about to topple. Rather than disturb her father, Bibi Bhani held his chair for the duration of the meditation, injuring her hand in the process. Guru Amar Das was so moved by his daughter's sacrifice that he said he would grant whatever she requested. She asked that the position of Guru remain in her family line. Guru Amar Das granted this wish, appointing Bibi Bhani's husband the next Guru, with the understanding that all Gurus to come would be Bibi Bhani's descendants.

Bibi Bhani's husband was called Guru Ram Das, a man of great humility and service. When they married, the Mughal emperor Akbar gave Bibi Bhani a large tract of land as a wedding present. On this land, Guru Ram Das built the city of Amritsar and laid the foundation for the Harimandir Sahib, known to the world as the Golden Temple. Guru Ram Das was also a poet, his most famous work being the *Lavan*, the Sikh wedding song.

Arjan Dev, the youngest son of Guru Ram Das and Bibi Bhani, became the fifth Sikh Guru. Guru Arjan Dev completed his father's work on the Golden Temple and was a very prolific poet. He compiled the Siri Guru Granth Sahib, including his own poems, the poems of all the previous Gurus, plus the poems of many other saintly people from several religious traditions—Hindu, Sufi, Sikh, Muslim. So the Siri Guru Granth Sahib was intended as an interfaith document and was compiled by one of the saints who wrote the words. Nearly all of the included poems—called *shabads*—are intended to be sung.

Guru Arjan Dev was martyred at the end of five days of torture in 1606. His son Hargobind became the sixth Guru. At his father's request and due to increasing hostilities in Punjab, Guru Hargobind became the first of the Sikh Gurus to wear a sword (actually, he wore two—representing the spiritual and temporal realms) and the first to arm his Sikhs. So from him was born the Sikh warrior saint tradition.

The seventh and eighth Gurus both died young. Guru Har Rai, a grandson of Guru Hargobind, lived just long enough to recognize the profundity of his youngest son, who became Guru Harkrishan at age five and returned to the Light at age eight.

Before becoming the ninth Guru, Guru Teg Bahadur—the youngest son of Guru Hargobind and the uncle of Guru Harkrishan—spent twenty years in deep meditation. Guru Teg Bahadur was another Guru poet, but we cherish him most for his martyrdom. In 1675, he gave his life so that members of another religion could worship in peace.

And so the torch passed to Guru Teg Bahadur's son, who became Guru Gobind Singh, the tenth Guru, a great general and the last of the Sikh Gurus in human form. More than any of the Gurus that followed Guru Nanak Dev ji, Guru Gobind Singh was responsible for the way we practice Sikhism today.

Guru Gobind Singh added his father's poems to the Siri Guru Granth Sahib, thereby creating its current form. Though Guru Gobind Singh was a noted poet in his own right, he added none of his own works to the Siri Guru Granth Sahib, with the possible exception of two couplets. His poetry and poems created under his patronage were compiled in a separate volume after his death.

Most importantly, Guru Gobind Singh established the amrit ceremony (Sikh "baptism" or initiation) in 1699 with five men who passed a supreme test of courage and devotion. Each year we celebrate this event—the birth of the Khalsa—on its anniversary in mid-April on Vaisakhi, an Indian harvest festival. Amritdhari Sikhs—those who "take amrit" and live up to the requirements of this initiation—become Khalsa (rhymes with "salsa"), or Pure Ones. Around the same time, Guru Gobind Singh also abolished the priesthood established by Guru Amar Das, because with the passing of time, that priesthood had become increasingly corrupt.

With the establishment of the amrit ceremony, Sikhs gained a code of conduct, called the *Rahit*. The poems in the Siri Guru Granth Sahib contain plenty of admonitions to meditate and to keep the company of the holy, but little in the way of lifestyle "do's and don'ts." Guru Gobind Singh changed that and required his Khalsa Sikhs to live to the *Rahit*, which was formally written down in 1945.

Living to the *Rahit* includes following a dress code, reciting certain *shabads* from the Siri Guru Granth Sahib and the works of Guru Gobind Singh daily, living as warrior saints in the defense of the weak and vulnerable, and following such principles as making a living honestly and sharing what we have with others. It also includes four *kurehits*, the "thou shalt nots" of Sikhism:

1. No hair cutting
2. No sex outside a legal, monogamous marriage
3. No tobacco, recreational drugs, or alcohol
4. No meat eating (though there is some debate that certain types of meat are allowable)

Engaging in any of these four things "breaks amrit," but the other requirements mentioned above are not so stringent.

Guru Gobind Singh's four sons all predeceased him. The two youngest were martyred by being bricked up alive, and the two older ones died in battle. So, in 1708, when Guru Gobind Singh was dying of wounds inflicted by an assassin, he ordained the Siri Guru Granth Sahib as the eleventh and ultimate Sikh Guru. It is our Guru today.

As of 2014, there are an estimated twenty-five million or more Sikhs worldwide. Most of these are ethnically Punjabi, and most still live in India. But increasingly, people of other ethnicities and countries find themselves attracted to the Sikh path. The majority of these are the direct or indirect students of Yogi Bhajan, who came to

North America in 1969 to teach yoga. For his students who wished to become Sikhs, he established Sikh Dharma after he became the Siri Singh Sahib, an extremely high honor. In this capacity, he established a group of ministers to provide inspiration and leadership for Sikh Dharma communities. Invariably, Yogi Bhajan's students practice yoga. This is not true of most Punjabis, some of whom view yoga as unsuitable for Sikhs.

Sikhs have no denominations. All Sikhs worship with all other Sikhs.

SIKH SPIRITUAL PRACTICES AND DISCIPLINES

Sikh spiritual practice is similar to many of the world's other religions in that it includes outward signs of piety, prayer and devotional practices for the inner life, and communal worship and celebrations. But of course the specifics of these practices are very distinctive to Sikhism. Below is a description of the most common ways Sikhs practice.

Bana

Every morning in addition to my regular clothes, I put on thigh-length underwear (*kacheras*) and a steel bangle (*kara*). I comb my uncut hair (*kesh*) with a wooden comb (*kanga*), coil my hair up, and crown it with a turban after inserting the comb in my hair first. I add a small steel sword (*kirpan*) to the ensemble. (Well, actually I carry a Swiss army knife. We'll get to the reason for that discrepancy later.) I have just donned *bana*, a discipline required of Amritdhari Sikhs by Guru Gobind Singh and the Sikh practice most obvious to outside observers.

Sikh men and women follow the same rules for the five *k*'s—*kesh, kanga, kacheras, kara,* and *kirpan.* Western Sikh men and women both wear turbans as well, but among Punjabis usually only the men wear turbans. Instead, Punjabi Sikh women cover their heads with a long scarf, called a *chuni.* Western Sikh women also wear *chunis,* usually over a turban, especially in public. Men do not wear *chunis.*

Bana has two polar-opposite pitfalls. Because it is so obvious, wearing *bana* can put a practicing Sikh at odds with society. Some Sikhs crumple under society's pressure, cut their hair, and take their *bana* off. I'll be discussing this phenomenon at length later. On the other hand, because *bana* is so obvious, some Sikhs become fanatics about it and miss the real heart of our religion, our practices for achieving union with God and Guru—*banis, naam simran, sangat, seva,* and *paths.*

Banis

The Siri Guru Granth Sahib, the Sikh Guru, is composed entirely of devotional poems similar to psalms. *Banis* are those poems that devout Sikhs recite or read out loud every day. Here's a quick guide to each *bani*.

We recite Japji Sahib by Guru Nanak Dev ji in the morning, thereby activating our souls and elevating our spirits. Also in the morning, we recite three works by Guru Gobind Singh: Jaap Sahib, Tav Prasaad Swaiyay, and Bayntee Chaupaee (these aren't included in the Siri Guru Granth Sahib). Reciting these three *banis* instills courage and the can-do attitude of a warrior saint. We recite Anand Sahib by Guru Amar Das in the morning for happiness.

In the evening, we recite Rehiras Sahib—which is a composite of several poems by several Gurus—for renewal. It's also recommended for marital harmony and prosperity. We recite Kirtan Sohila—another composite—at bedtime, for peace and harmony. Shabad Hazaaray—another composite—is an optional *bani* that unites the longing soul with the Beloved. Sukhmani Sahib by Guru Arjan Dev is also optional. Reciting it comforts the mind and grants fulfillment.

Reciting *banis* helps unite the consciousness of the reciter with the Guru's consciousness. Because our Guru literally *is* Word, we become the Guru when we recite the Guru's words with devotion. Keep this list of *banis* in mind when providing spiritual guidance to Sikhs.

Sadhana (*Simran*)

Devout Sikhs rise early for sadhana, disciplined spiritual practice. Sadhana practices vary, but usually include (1) reciting *banis*; (2) chanting Mul Mantra, the opening section of Guru Nanak's Japji Sahib; and (3) chanting God's Name. Chanting God's Name is called *nam simran*, which means "name remembrance." So, besides chanting out loud, *nam simran* also includes the Sikh practice of remembering God's Name silently on the breath—inhaling the Name of God, exhaling the Name of God—throughout the day.

Seva

However, Sikhs do not withdraw from the world to practice contemplation. They also live in the world as householders, marry and have children, earn their livings honestly, and share what they have with others. Sharing includes *seva*, or selfless service. Forms of *seva* include feeding people, helping anyone in need, and helping out with Sikh services.

Sangat

Like people of most faiths, Sikhs worship in congregations, the word for which is *sangat*. The whole experience of *sangat* allows us to keep the company of the holy in the presence of the Guru. A Sikh place of worship is called a gurdwara, literally "the Guru's door." Because we see all creation as God's handiwork, we do not have any particular day of the week set aside for worship. Many gurdwaras are open for services daily. In North America, for convenience, we often worship on Sundays.

Gurdwara services are open to everyone. In case you ever attend such a service, you should know that we remove our shoes and cover our heads before entering. We sit on the floor, so dress accordingly; pantsuits are better than tight skirts, for instance. (Some gurdwaras will provide a chair for the crippled or infirm.) When sitting on the floor, please sit in such a way that the bottoms of your feet do not point directly toward the Siri Guru Granth Sahib, which is always under a canopy.

Our services consist primarily of singing *shabads* from the Siri Guru Granth Sahib and other approved works by Sikh saints and poets. The musicians range from *ragis*—highly skilled in the classic Indian melodic modes called *ragas*—to kids in the *sangat* who just know one or two *shabads*. Because we prefer to let each person have his or her own experience, you won't hear preaching, but sometimes a *ragi* weaves a spoken story from Sikh history in between the stanzas of a *shabad*. We usually tell stories from Sikh history on *gurpurbs*, those days that commemorate special events in Sikh history: Guru Nanak's birthday, Vaisakhi (the birth of the Khalsa), and others.

At the end of each service, we all stand while one person gives an *ardas*, a prayer or supplication for the whole *sangat*. Then one person reads a random passage from the Siri Guru Granth Sahib out loud. After this, we cup our hands to receive a sweet—similar to warm cookie dough—to remind us of the sweetness of the Guru's word. And then we all sit down together and share *langar*, the meal from the Guru's kitchen as instituted by Guru Amar Das. Though men and women sit on opposite sides of the room during a Sikh service, we sit together during *langar*.

Akhand Path and *Sehaj Path*

Another way we connect with the Guru is to read it out loud all the
way through. Many gurdwaras host a weekly *akhand path,* or unbroken
reading of the Siri Guru Granth Sahib, a process that takes forty-eight
hours in the original Gurmukhi or seventy-two hours in translation,
and requires a relay of several readers. An *akhand path* invariably ends
with a gurdwara service. A *sehaj path* is the more relaxed, go-at-your-
own-pace version, usually accomplished by a single person or a small
group.

Sikhs typically hold *akhand paths* or *sehaj paths* to bless new
marriages, new houses, or any new venture or to console the bereaved,
as well as just for the Guru's blessing. It's always good to let the word
of the Guru point us in the right direction.

SPIRITUAL DEVELOPMENT IN SIKHISM

Sikhs have two general ways of looking at spiritual development, each
model having three forward stages and one retrograde stage.

The first model of spiritual development is more general, offering
a description of four types of people based on the teachings of the
Siri Guru Granth Sahib. A *manmukh* is an egotist, someone who
thinks only about him- or herself and the material world. Although
a *manmukh* has no true interest in God or spiritual matters, he or
she might attend religious services for self-serving reasons. A *sunmukh*
is a seeker, someone who is interested in the spirit and the divine
but who hasn't arrived at a high level yet or who doesn't know it's
possible to go for the spiritual gold. The average churched person is
a good example. A *gurmukh* is someone whose face is turned toward
the Light, who speaks divinely and focuses on the Infinite God. Sikhs
consider all true saints of all religions to be *gurmukhs.* The retrograde
person is a *baymukh,* a person who has (perhaps) been a *gurmukh,*
seen the Light, and walked away from it. The most famous *baymukh* of
all time in any tradition is Judas. The Siri Guru Granth Sahib makes it
clear that a *manmukh* can turn into a *gurmukh*—and vice versa—without
any intervening steps if God so wills.

Among ourselves, Sikhs use a more observable model of spiritual
development, based entirely on practice and depth of commitment
to the Sikh path. *Keshdhari* Sikhs do not shave or cut their hair.
Keshdhari men invariably wear turbans. People in this group look like

Sikhs, but if they haven't taken amrit, then their commitment to the Sikh path is not yet complete. Most people in this group engage in other Sikh practices, though not all do. Non-*keshdhari* Sikhs shave and cut their hair, which means they are cutting their radiance and conforming neither to God's blueprint for creation nor to *Rahit*, the Sikh code of conduct. Although they may perform other Sikh practices and attend Sikh services religiously, they neither look like Sikhs nor maintain a commitment to the *Rahit*. Retrograde Sikhs are called *patits*. *Patits* were once practicing Sikhs but have since cut their hair and now engage in whatever selfish worldly activities they please. *Patit* is a harsh term, meaning "apostate," "corrupt person," or "sinner." Sikhs don't like to call people "sinners," so we generally reserve this term for those who run off with community funds and/ or someone's spouse and then slander practicing Sikhs. *Amritdhari* or Khalsa Sikhs have fully committed to the Sikh path by going through the amrit ceremony. They are invariably *keshdhari* and never cut or shave their hair, so they look like Sikhs. They are usually good at the rest of Sikh practice as well.

Among ourselves, this second model of spiritual development is the one we use most regularly and the one that explains most cogently what our most pressing issues are.

TRADITIONS OF SPIRITUAL GUIDANCE IN SIKHISM

A few years ago, when there was no public gurdwara in Salem, Oregon, I opened my home to anyone who wished to visit the Guru or experience a Sikh service. Two Punjabi men who had not had access to the Guru for upward of two years came to my house during this time, and both of them broke down and sobbed after I ushered them into the Guru's room and began reading from the Guru for them. A devout Sikh without access to the Guru can feel very bereft indeed.

The one defining characteristic of all Sikhs is that we seek spiritual guidance from the Siri Guru Granth Sahib. Though most of a Sikh service is singing, the high point of each service is the random reading of a *shabad* from the Siri Guru Granth Sahib, called a *hukam*, literally "command." Each of us holds the lesson from the *hukam* as our spiritual guidance for the day.

Many of us meditate in the morning to receive God's guidance. Generally, we follow this meditation with a *hukam*, allowing the

Guru to tell us whether the guidance we've received really is divine inspiration or just ego talk.

So, for instance, on a day that I feel like writing, but worry that I should be doing other things, my *hukam* for the day might be the *shabad* by Guru Nanak that contains these lines:

> *If my mind becomes the paper and my mind an inkpot,*
> *And if my tongue becomes the pen,*
> *I would write with care the praises of the True Beloved God.*[1]

In this case, I happily spend the day writing.

But suppose the Guru isn't available or we need human input. In those cases, we can turn to a variety of helpers.

First, notice that Sikhs don't need ministers or priests to hold any service, except to legalize our marriages; even there, many Sikh couples prefer to legalize their marriages with a civil ceremony before or after the religious one. What we do need are musicians and people with sufficient know-how for each portion of our services. Although you may hear someone called a "Sikh priest," in practice Sikhs have no priests. Guru Gobind Singh abolished them. A person being called a priest is most likely one of the following.

A *granthi* is a caretaker for the Granth (i.e., the Siri Guru Granth Sahib). Usually this person lives in or near a gurdwara, but the term also applies to anyone who sits behind the Guru during a worship service. A *jethadar* is a group leader—sometimes of a Sikh temple, sometimes of a Sikh musical group. *Gyani* literally means "one who knows." Preferably, this person "knows" God and can impart that wisdom, but it may just refer to someone who knows how to set up and perform all aspects of a Sikh service. Often, though not always, a *gyani* is also a *granthi* and/or a *ragi* (a musician who has mastered the Indian *ragas*). Correspondence courses exist for training *gyanis*.

Bhai Sahib and *Bhai Sahiba* ("Revered Brother" and "Revered Sister") are honorary titles bestowed on particularly fine *ragis* or people who have performed great services to Sikhism. *Singh Sahib* and *Sardarni Sahiba* are other honorary titles for men and women, respectively. These are also the titles for Sikh Dharma ministers, people who provide inspiration, leadership, and often guidance for the community. Young Sikhs are trained for this ministry in a boarding school near Amritsar, India. Older aspirants for the Sikh

Dharma ministry need recommendations from five current ministers, usually after taking a yearlong correspondence course.

If we have Sikh protocol issues, the people I've just mentioned are often enough the ones we turn to. We may turn to them for our troubles as well. But even for issues of Sikh protocol, we may just as well turn to whoever's handy with the necessary know-how. We take our troubles sometimes to family members, but usually to saintly people, to people we admire or even revere, people we think are real *gurmukhs*. So, if a Sikh comes to you for spiritual guidance, either the Sikh has no recourse or it's an enormous compliment.

COMMON SPIRITUAL ISSUES FOR SIKHS

As practicioners of a minority religion in North American, Sikhs can often encounter clashes between their deeply held beliefs and the general culture. It is important for a spiritual guide to be aware of areas where such conflicts may arise.

Bana versus Society

Sikhs respect those who grow their hair to its full length, who never shave, who wear turbans. Western society does not. Consider the following examples.

Sometimes society's disapproval of our dress code takes an economic form. A turbaned Sikh may have difficulty landing a job. For instance, the U.S. military generally refuses entry to Sikh men because of perceived problems of beards interfering with gas masks. (Ironic, given that Sikhs are warrior saints and have served with distinction in the militaries of India, Great Britain, and Canada.)

Sometimes society's disapproval of our dress code takes the form of hate crimes. A Sikh man was the first fatality in the 9/11 backlash. Our children are often teased, threatened, and bullied by ignorant classmates. I myself have been spat at.

You can imagine how much fun it is being a turbaned Sikh going through an airport security checkpoint—especially a turbaned Punjabi man with the usual brown skin and thick accent.

And you can bet that no turbaned Sikh woman appears on any popular magazine's "best dressed" list. Our uncut hair—with or without a turban—runs counter to fashionable coifs and curls. Our unshaved legs and unshaved underarms run counter to the pressures of Madison Avenue and adolescent peer groups.

Many Sikhs stand firm in the face of such pressure, but not all do. I know several Sikh women who ceased to be Sikhs because they wanted to be fashionable. I know Sikh men who cut their hair in order to get jobs. I've met Sikh families who cut their sons' hair rather than let them stand up to school bullies. And I've talked to several people who ran away from the Sikh path out of fear.

Remember that for us haircutting is no small thing. It runs counter to all we hold holy. A Sikh whose lack of commitment to the *Rahit* manifests in haircutting collapses to the bottom of our spiritual development heap.

Should a Sikh with issues surrounding haircutting or the turban or *bana* in general come to you, acknowledge the person's dilemma and let him or her know that you (and many other people) don't approve of bad behavior toward Sikhs. And, if the Sikh doesn't know what his or her rights are, please let the person know.

Uncut Hair versus Surgery

Suppose you are a practicing Sikh. You've made a commitment never to shave or cut your hair. You feel that haircutting and shaving are disrespectful to God, that haircutting and shaving are tantamount to spiritual castration, and anyway, your word is given. What do you do when you need surgery?

Well, what most of us do is accept God's will and have the surgery, even if it requires shaving. Most of us feel that hair-shaving for surgical purposes does not break amrit. But it's still an enormous decision, and most Sikhs don't deal with it nonchalantly. Some Sikhs do feel that surgical shaving breaks amrit, making it even more difficult.

If a Sikh comes to you with this dilemma, you can tell the person why shaving may be acceptable for surgery, but never minimize what the person is going through. No statements like "Oh, it will grow back!" No jokes like "The shave and haircut are free." If you're working in a hospital setting and are able, make sure that the Sikh having surgery gets to make an informed choice, except in life-and-death emergencies, of course.

Warrior Saints versus Society

While some movies and novels glamorize warrior saints, Western society and its laws and customs make it nearly impossible to be one. So say you're a twelve-year-old boy, a devout Sikh, and you've just taken amrit. You're honor bound to wear your *kirpan*, the short steel sword. You take it to school. What happens? You'll probably be suspended or expelled. The school district won't honor your *kirpan*, so you either have to break your word or forgo a public education.

You're a middle-aged *amritdhari* Sikh woman. You walk downtown with your *kirpan* plainly in view. What happens? People tend to act as if you're a rabid dog.

Unfortunately, Sikhs who carry their *kirpans* where they aren't noticeable and won't alarm passersby run afoul of laws against carrying concealed weapons. It's nearly impossible to get a license to carry a concealed *kirpan* in some locales; I've tried. Some Sikhs get around this by wearing a little sword as jewelry, and it's the reason some of us, including me, carry Swiss army knives. But the whole purpose of the *kirpan* is to save lives. Suppose you do use your *kirpan* (or your Swiss army knife) to tackle someone who's threatening you or someone else. You'll probably be exonerated, but you may have to spend some time in jail first.

If you are a pacifist, you yourself may have issues with the whole concept that saints may also be warriors. Please understand that Sikhs are taught to use force only as a last resort. And please be aware of your own orientation when dealing with practicing *amritdhari* Sikhs.

One final thing: Many Sikh women have issues with being a warrior. For them, being a warrior is not feminine or glamorous. Many women have left the Sikh path because they couldn't handle the requirement of carrying a sword and because they didn't see how graceful and noble being a strong Sikh woman can be. It's similar to the problem of wanting to be a fashion plate: what society promotes conflicts with what the *Rahit* requires.

Banis versus Institutions

Banis are part of our daily spiritual self-care, but reciting *banis* can conflict with institutional routine. I know of a case where an elderly Sikh living in a care facility was sedated because he kept mumbling, especially in the morning. What the man was actually doing was reciting his *banis*. Once the care facility folks understood what the man was doing, they gave him the space to "mumble" every morning.

You should understand that Sikhs are family-oriented people, and if a Sikh is too incapacitated to read or recite their own *banis*, family and friends will often read or recite the *banis* for the patient. This brings the blessings of both *sangat* and Guru to the bedridden Sikh. So please allow family and friends to do this. Don't shoo them out.

A suggestion: if you live and work in an area with a large Sikh population, keep some recordings of *banis* handy. Musical recordings of assorted *shabads* and *Mul Mantra* are good, too.

Despondency, Lack of Fulfillment, or Spiritual Malaise

Sikhs are usually pretty cheerful people. We tend to be active and to have rich family lives. But like everyone else, we may have our moments of despair, despondency, feelings of unfulfillment, and spiritual malaise. We may respond to these problems in many ways, from "Am I really worthy to receive the blessings of God and Guru?" to "Why is this happening to *me*?" Your compassionate presence, insight, and understanding may be all a suffering Sikh needs. But the following is some additional help.

The first thing I tend to do when a Sikh comes to me with this sort of problem is ask about the person's spiritual practice. I inquire, "Do you meditate and read your *banis*?" I remind the person to remember the Name of God on the breath—inhaling the Name of God, exhaling the Name of God. In doing so, I usually also explain how to breathe deeply, allowing the diaphragm and belly to expand on the inhale and contract on the exhale. Typically, the person admits to having slacked off, then nods and decides to get into (or back into) spiritual practice. That's often all that's necessary.

Specific *banis* to recommend include Japji Sahib to release spiritual malaise, any of the *banis* by Guru Gobind Singh (especially Jaap Sahib) to release feelings of defeat and despair, Anand Sahib for happiness, and Sukhmani Sahib for fulfillment. You could also recommend a *sehaj path*, the personal complete reading of the Siri Guru Granth Sahib.

And attitude matters. A Sikh woman once talked with me about some problems she was having with her husband. I asked if she was doing her *banis*, and she told me she was doing them more than she had been. I suggested she be grateful. "Oh," she said, "I never thought of that!" Her problems resolved.

Marriage and Marital Troubles

Most Sikh marriages are arranged by the parents. Cutting desire out of the marital equation cuts out a great deal of marital neediness. So please do not react in horror if a Sikh mentions being in an arranged marriage or about to undergo an arranged marriage.

Sikhs view marriage as the union formed when two souls become one. We view our wedding ceremony as a wedding with God. If you think that through, you'll realize that Sikhs view divorce as a last resort. So, recommending divorce to a Sikh isn't advisable unless the person consulting you is abandoned or facing potentially lethal violence. However, if your client brings up divorce as an option, you can certainly discuss it.

Although the Sikh religion allows remarriage, most Sikhs are Punjabi, and Punjabi culture opposes remarriage. Though, again, if your client brings up the option of remarriage, feel free to discuss it. *Banis* for easing marital problems include Anand Sahib for happiness, Rehiras Sahib for marital harmony, Shabad Hazaaray for union with the Beloved, and Sukhmani Sahib for inner peace and supporting the spouse.

Death, Dying, and Grief

Because Sikhs do not believe in a vengeful or wrathful God and because we see death as a natural end, death holds little terror for us. Because Sikhs do not believe in heaven or hell, except as states of mind, we have no fear of hellfire. We are taught to prepare for this end throughout our lives by being *jiwan-mukta*, "liberated while alive."

Although we believe in reincarnation and the law of karma, we also believe that meditating, reading *banis,* and following the Guru's teachings burn off karma so that we may end the cycle of birth and death and return home to God, all of which make it comparatively easy for a Sikh to face death.

A woman once told me that she went to visit an elderly Sikh man with the view to being his caregiver. His face was so radiant and luminous that her own fear of death disappeared and her view of death radically altered. She didn't become his caregiver, since he died within twenty-four hours of her visit. You could say that he was *her* caregiver!

None of this means that dying is easy on anyone. This same elderly Sikh man told his son, "I'm going to be going through some tests, and when I pass them, I'll graduate."

As you've probably figured out, we get through the tests of physically dying by reciting *banis* (or having family or friends recite them for us), by meditating, and by accepting God's will. In particular, Sikhs hope to be reciting Japji Sahib or chanting God's Name when we "graduate." Sikhs who need comforting as they face the inevitable may also recite or listen to Sukhmani Sahib. Jaap Sahib by Guru Gobind Singh can help release any fear.

The same things that make dying easier for Sikhs also help us through grief. We chant Japji Sahib and Kirtan Sohila as part of our death rites when the deceased is cremated. When a family member dies, the family often hosts an *akhand path* or a community *sehaj path* to provide the comfort of the Guru's word for the whole *sangat* as well as themselves. Sikhs also often recite Sukhmani Sahib for two or more weeks following a death. With death as with everything else, we turn to the Guru, and the Guru gives us comfort.

OFFERING SPIRITUAL GUIDANCE TO SIKHS

When talking with your Sikh clients, please keep the following in mind.

Sikhs dislike being mistaken for Muslims or having our religion called a branch of Hinduism. Sikhism is a separate revelation. We tend to be sensitive about this issue.

Keep in mind that most Sikhs are Punjabi, and Punjabi culture is not Western culture. For instance, many Punjabi women will only make private appointments with other women. Keep in mind, too, that Punjabi English isn't much like what we speak in North America, so what you think you've heard isn't necessarily what's really being said. For elderly Punjabi Sikhs, you may need a translator.

All Sikhs are family oriented, but Punjabi Sikhs are family oriented to the max. In India, the family takes care of the patient in hospitals at night, so if you work in a care facility, you may need to explain about visiting hours.

And notice that all Sikhs are hospitable, but Punjabi Sikhs are so hospitable that they may wish to share food with you and may want to know all about *you* before being willing to talk about themselves. Let them. Sharing is part of our religion.

NOTES

Siri Kirpal Kaur Khalsa wishes to thank the following for providing information, inspiration, and helpful suggestions: Bhai Sahiba Bibiji Inderjit Kaur Puri;

Dr. Balkar Singh, SS; Guru Sangat Kaur Khalsa; Dr. Guru Singh Khalsa, SS; Harbhajan Kaur Khalsa, SS; Har Darshan Kaur Khalsa, MSS; Hari Jiwan Singh Khalsa, SS; Karta Purkh Singh Khalsa, SS; Sat Kartar Kaur Khalsa-Ramey, SS; Sat Kirin Kaur Khalsa, SS; Sat Kirpal Kaur Khalsa; Satmitar Kaur Khalsa, SS; Shiva Singh Khalsa, SS; Siri Vishnu Singh Khalsa; Surinder Singh; and her husband, Jim Waldon.

1. Guru Nanak, Raga Sorath, Siri Guru Granth Sahib, Khalsa Consensus Translation, p. 636; available at www.sikhs.org/english/eg_index.htm.

RESOURCES

Dhillon, Harish. *The First Sikh Spiritual Master: Timeless Wisdom from the Life and Teachings of Guru Nanak.* Woodstock, VT: SkyLight Paths, 2006.

Khalsa, Siri Kirpal Kaur. *Sikh Spiritual Practice: The Sound Way to God.* Ropely, Hants, UK: Mantra Books. 2010.

Macauliffe, Max Arthur. *The Sikh Religion*, Vol. 1–6. London: Forgotten Books, 2008.

www.sikhnet.com

www.sikhs.org

RELIGIONS
ORIGINATING
IN THE
MIDDLE EAST

Ervad Soli P. Dastur was born as the last of eleven children in the small village of Tarapur, India, to a priestly family from Udwada. Soli was admitted to the M. F. Cama Athornan Institute boarding school to complete his priestly studies as well as high school. During his nine years at the boarding school, Soli completed all the requirements for becoming Navar and Martab and was initiated as a priest in the Holy Iranshah Atash Behram in Udwada. He had to also pass the final examination of Saamel required by all initiated priests from Udwada to be able to perform all inner and outer liturgies. Soli is fully retired and lives with his wife of forty-eight years, Jo Ann, in University Park, Florida. He performs religious ceremonies all over Florida and the rest of the United States. He is an avid tennis player and dabbles with the computer in his free time.

Spiritual Guidance in the Zoroastrian Religion

Ervad Soli P. Dastur

Zoroastrianism is an ancient faith that has deeply influenced world history, especially Western culture and religion. Ironically, despite its profound influence, few people are familiar with its tenets and teachings. Although Zoroastrians are not highly visible in contemporary society and are few in number, they are found in nearly every part of the world. Every major city has a Zoroastrian community, and psychotherapists, hospital chaplains, and other emergency and helping professionals will, on occasion, have the opportunity to encounter and assist Zoroastrians.

A BRIEF HISTORY OF THE ZOROASTRIAN RELIGION

The founder of the Zoroastrian religion was Zarathushtra (or Zoroaster, in Greek). The exact date and place of his birth is highly contested, but most agree that he was born somewhere in eastern Iran between 1700 BCE and 1200 BCE.[1]

According to the prophet Zarathushtra, an interesting celestial drama is being played out: the soul of the Mother Earth cries out to her creator, Ahura Mazda, complaining that the affairs on earth have been taken over by evil people. She fervently beseeches him to send a strong warrior to fight against these evil people and restore

truth and justice in the world. Ahura Mazda asks his two helpers if
they know anyone who can help Mother Earth, but they do not have
any suggestions. Then Ahura Mazda himself says, "We know such
a holy person, Zarathushtra Spitama, who has heard and followed
our teachings and who will fulfill Mother Earth's wishes!"[2] And so
Zarathushtra was sent to this earth to fight evil and to help good
people.

His mother's name was Dughdova, and his father's name was
Pourushaspa. Legend has it that he laughed at his birth.[3] There
was an aura around him. According to the Zoroastrian scriptures,
"The entire Nature cried out: 'Hail to us, for us is born an *aathravan*
[priest], Zarathushtra Spitama!'"[4] The wicked priests were worried
about his birth because of all the signs, and they devised a number of
ways to kill him, but to no avail.

At the age of twenty, Zarathushtra left his home and went to the
Ushi Darena mountain (a place holding divine intellect) to meditate
and be in communion with his God, Ahura Mazda (Wise Lord). After
ten years on the mountain, he finally received the Divine Knowledge
from Ahura Mazda and was instructed to spread his religion to the
world.

He came back to his hometown and preached the new religion,
but he was shunned by all, even his own family and friends.
Zarathushtra was very dejected and cried out, "To what land shall
I turn, whither shall I go? I am forsaken by kinsmen and nobles.
Neither do my people like me, nor do the wicked rulers of the land.
How then, shall I please Thee, Ahura Mazda?"[5] Finally, his first-cousin
Maidhyoimanha became his first disciple.

Zarathushtra searched in vain for a king, governor, or chief to
be his sponsor. Finally, he traveled to Balkh (Bactria) whose king,
Vishtaaspa, was known for his wisdom, justice, kingly glory, and
hospitality to strangers. Vishtaaspa received Zarathushtra with
admiration and respect. Zarathushtra was holding the Adar Burzin
Fire in his right hand and a sapling of a cypress tree with a message
inscribed on each leaf: "Vishtaaspa! Accept Zarathushtra's religion!"

When Vishtaaspa asked him to explain his religion, Zarathushtra
responded, "Believe *only* in one God, Ahura Mazda [Wise Lord]!
He has sent you a messenger, his prophet. Forsake all other gods,
superstitions, and magicians. Live a life of *humata* [good thoughts],

hukhta [good words], and *hvarshta* [good deeds]. Propagate the religion throughout your kingdom!" After many trials and tribulations, Vishtaaspa and his whole family and court accepted Zarathushtra's religion, and his eldest son, Asfandyaar, fought many battles to propagate Zarathushtra's religion all over his kingdom.

Zarathushtra married Havovi and had three sons and three daughters. When he was seventy-seven years old, he was killed by a Turanian enemy soldier while he was praying in the Balkh fire temple.

DEVELOPMENT OF ZOROASTRIANISM SINCE ZARATHUSHTRA

Not much is reported about the religion after Vishtaaspa. We next hear about the religion during the Achaemenid Empire established by Cyrus the Great (559–331 BCE). In the inscriptions at Persepolis and Behistoon, we find evidence of the Zoroastrian religion during this dynasty. However, Alexander of Macedonia defeated the dynasty in 330 BCE and suppressed the religion, first by torching the magnificent buildings of Persepolis and then by massacring the clergy, thus destroying much of the religion's oral tradition.

After Alexander and his Selucid generals, the Parthian Empire came to prominence and ruled for almost five hundred years (250 BCE–226 CE). They were the main force to stop the eastward spread of the mighty Roman Empire. The Zoroastrian religion was in shambles at this point, but the later kings tried to gather all the available remnants of the religious books.[6]

The last Iranian dynasty, the Sassanian (226–641 CE), revived the Zoroastrian religion and established it as the court religion. Under this dynasty, the religion reached its zenith, and most of its current extant literature was compiled during this time. The dynasty was ruthlessly overthrown by the Arabs in 641 CE, destroying much of the tradition.

Some Zoroastrians left Iran around the tenth century and settled on the west coast of India. Known as Parsis (originally from the province of "Pars" in southern Iran), they prospered over the centuries and played a very prominent role in Indian history. Currently, however, there are fewer than one hundred thousand Parsis left in India.

There are three major sects of Parsis in India, each of which follow different religious calendars. Apart from this, however, their beliefs, prayers, and rituals have remained identical over the years. Mumbai (formerly Bombay) is still the major city for the Parsi population (around sixty-five thousand). Parsis have migrated in recent decades to Pakistan, the United Kingdom, the United States, Canada, New Zealand, Australia, and nearly every part of the world. There are still around thirty-five thousand Zoroastrians living in the original country, Iran. Ever since the breakup of the Soviet Union, many groups in newly formed independent countries like Tajikistan, Turkmenistan, Uzbekistan, Kyrgyzstan, and Russia have claimed to have Zoroastrian lineage and profess to follow the Zoroastrian religion.

ZOROASTRIAN SCRIPTURES

Zarathushtra is traditionally acknowledged as the author of seventeen hymns called the Gathas, written in the old Avestan language, which has been extinct for many centuries. They were composed in poetic form so that they could be easily memorized, and thus they were kept intact by the Zoroastrian *mobeds* (priests) over many centuries. Eventually, they were written down using diverse scripts. The Gathas present Zarathushtra's teachings about how a human being should follow the path of *Asha* (righteousness, truth) using his or her God-given precious gift of *Vohu Mana* (good mind) to discern good and evil in this material world.[7]

Zarathushtra's followers wrote many other scriptures, including Yasna, Visperad, Vendidad, and Yashts. Later religious books report that there were twenty-one volumes of knowledge compiled by the later Zoroastrian scholars.

During the Sassanian times, most of the extant Avestan literature was translated in the Pahlavi language, which was the language of the court. We have some pieces of this Pahlavi literature, as well as others written in later centuries after the Arab conquest. These are the only remaining scriptures of the religion.[8]

BASIC TEACHINGS OF THE ZOROASTRIAN RELIGION

The most important teachings of the Zoroastrian religion are the principle of *Asha* and the proper use of the God-given ability for humans to discern good from evil, right from wrong, known as *Vohu Mana* (good mind).

The Principle of *Asha*

The Gathic term *Asha* is related to the term *Rta* in Vedic Sanskrit, and to the term *Arta* in Old Persian. It has traditionally been given the meaning "truth," but equally often "right." *Rta*, which is under the control of the divinity Varuna in the Rig Veda, has quite frequently been translated as "order," that is, the underlying scheme of existence. In Iranian thought, *Asha*, and later, *Arta*, was also viewed as the principle of justice. We have, therefore, at least four meanings justifiably associated with *Asha*: truth, the order underlying the universe, right as the most general term of moral correctness, and justice as the moral principle of the social system.[9]

Asha is a sublime attribute of Ahura Mazda, next to *Vohu Mana* in hierarchy. Ahura Mazda, *Vohu Mana*, and *Asha* are the divine triad.

In his Gathas, Zarathushtra presents two worlds: the ideal world (the *mainyu* world), and the material or physical world (the *gaetha* world). First, Ahura Mazda created the ideal existence and then created the material world, which could evolve toward the perfection already envisioned.

Within this material world, there are two spiritual mentalities (*mainyus* in the Gathas), sometimes thought of as dynamic forces, particularly in the later literature, and endowed with personalities. These are the good and the evil. The good is called *Spenta Mainyu*, the benevolent mentality. The evil (not actually named in the Gathas) is *Angra Mainyu*.[10]

The conflict between the two spirits can only be understood in terms of *Asha*. In the material world, the good spirit is good precisely because it promotes *Asha*, that is, it brings the world toward the state of ideal perfection. The evil spirit is evil precisely because it attempts to frustrate the progressive realization of *Asha*.

It is in this aspect of Gathic theology that we can see why *Asha* is interpreted as "truth." It is the true picture of the form of ideal existence and also the ideal toward which the conflicted world evolves. It is the ideal truth underlying all existence. In this same framework, we can see how *Asha* is interpreted as "right." That action is right which is in accordance with *Asha*, and which furthers the realization of *Asha*.

This is the doctrine of natural law that provides the basis for moral life and moral judgment. In that sense the ethics of

Zarathushtra is founded on a natural-law theory of apprehending and applying *Asha,* and not a prescriptivist theory that gives a set of moral rules to obey.

To the extent that the physical world is comprehensible and harmonious, it is in accordance with *Asha.* This is why *Asha* is interpreted as "order." This is what we come to understand progressively in the advance of scientific knowledge. For the comprehension of this process, we must now refer to the faculty of understanding—that is, the good mind (*Vohu Mana*).

Vohu Mana (Good Mind)

The good mind is a divine attribute that is possessed by human beings. In contemporary language, we might say that it is the rational capacity to grasp both facts and ideals: to understand, to discriminate, and to judge. The mind, in understanding nature, grasps its laws—that is, the order (*Asha*) underlying the facts of experience. The mind through its power to discriminate can recognize when *Asha* has been violated because it can grasp *Asha* in the abstract.[11] Then the mind can judge what is true (i.e., in accordance with *Asha*) and promote it, thereby dispelling evil, which is called falsehood (the opposite of *Asha*). It is the good mind that enables us to be moral and vanquish falsehood—"to deliver Falsehood into the hands of Truth."[12] Moral responsibility demands individual reflection (including consideration of the implications of one's intended actions) and discriminating judgment, all operations of the good mind.

In performance of action, discrimination between right and wrong is not entirely enough. Gathic theology introduces the concept of the good will, more accurately put as the spirit of benevolence, called *Spentaa Aarmaiti.* It is a divine attribute that, with varying degrees of zeal, inclines humans toward doing good, that is, actualizing *Asha. Spentaa Aarmaiti* has two aspects. One is what we have just seen: benevolence, goodwill, or even kindness. The other is the inner consciousness of being required to do right, an aspect that is usually articulated by the word *piety.* Both these conceptions have their content in *Asha.*[13]

The opposite of *Asha* is *Druj,* which is not just translated as "falsehood," but also as "deceit," the activity of perpetrating falsehood. The deceivers violate *Asha,* which in the social context is a disturbance of the principle of just recompense, and thus generate disharmony and conflict. It is in this context that *Asha* is interpreted as "justice." The ideal social structure where *Asha* prevails (in its interpretation as justice) is the worthy or holy society. In Gathic, it is *Khshathra Vairya*, which may be interpreted as "ideal dominion."

The individual whose life is inspired by the realization and the will to live according to *Asha* is not only morally vindicated, but is free of malice and free of regret, thereby reaching a state of justified contentment and well-being. This state is *Haurvataat*, "well-being," or in its exalted form, "perfection." As individuals live this form of life, a good society approaches the ideal state (with progressively reduced coercion).

Zoroastrian scripture views the immortal soul of the individual who has realized *Asha* in thought, word, and deed as reaching a state of eternal bliss.[14] The Gathic term for this is *Ameretaat*. This state is sometimes called the state of best consciousness.

The relationship of *Asha* to the other five significant concepts (*Vohu Mana, Spentaa Aarmaiti, Khshathra Vairya, Haurvataat,* and *Ameretaat*) is a pivotal aspect of the philosophical theology of the Gathas and hence of the Zoroastrian religion.[15]

VOHU MANA (GOOD MIND) AND ASHA IN DAILY LIFE

Based on the principles of *Asha* and *Vohu Mana*, Zoroastrians strive to live by the following principles in their daily life.

Righteousness Is the Watchword

Zoroastrianism teaches a universal morality. Rightness of deeds is grounded both in good mind (*Vohu Mana*) and in truth-with-justice (*Asha*). Righteous deeds should be performed selflessly and with love (*Aarmaiti*), for right action, mind, and heart operate in unison. This is well expounded by Zarathushtra, when he wrote:

> *Such are, indeed, the Saviors of the Earth.*
> *They follow Duty's call, the call of Love;*
> *Mazdaa, they listen unto Vohu Mana;*
> *They do what Asha bids, and Thy commands;*
> *Surely, they are the Vanquishers of Hate.*[16]

Thus, in Zoroastrian ethics, rightness and wrongness are determined by *Vohu Mana* and *Asha* as the yardsticks. To simplify the matter,

Zarathushtra formulated the oft-quoted maxim: "Good thoughts, good words, and good deeds." This maxim describes the principle of *Asha* in action and the Zoroastrian creed in daily life.

One of our most important prayers, the Yatha Ahu Vairyo, states:

Just as an Elected Leader acts according to her/his will,
So does a Religious Leader, due to her/his righteousness.
The gift of Vohu Mana (Good Mind) is for those working for
Ahura Mazda in this world;
He who acts to be the protector and nourisher of the poor, accepts
Ahura Mazda as the sovereign ruler.[17]

This prayer has three main points:

1. Elected leaders and religious leaders act according to their own wills, depicting the principle of the separation of state and religion.
2. Those who work for Ahura Mazda receive the gift of *Vohu Mana* (good mind).
3. Those who protect and nourish the poor enhance the sovereignty of Ahura Mazda.

The last one, helping the poor, is the hallmark of Zoroastrians all over the world. In India, the tiny Parsi (Zoroastrian) community is so famous for their charitable deeds that it is often said of them, "Parsi! Thy name is Charity!"

Justice Shall Be Done to All

The law of *Asha* ensures that happy consequences accrue to good acts.[18] An individual reaps what he or she sows. Everybody receives his or her *Mizhdem* (accrued consequences). "Reward" and "punishment," although freely used in translations of the Gathas and in common parlance, are not appropriate substitutes for *Mizhdem*. Ahura Mazda stands beyond revenge and punishment. He is, exclusively, goodness. *Mizhdaa*, or consequences, denote the accrued fruitions of one's acts, earned by performances: the best existence for the righteous and the worst for the wicked.[19] *Asha* also guarantees the final victory—of righteousness over falsehood—that evokes God's omnipotence.

Righteousness is the best of all that is good and is the radiant goal of life on earth. One must live righteously and for the sake of righteousness alone. Worldly rewards should not be our motivation, but duty for the sake of duty constitutes selfless service.

In another very important prayer, Ashem Vohu, we pray:

Righteousness is good!
It is the best!
It is happiness!
Happiness to him/her
*   who is righteous for the sake of the best righteousness!*[20]

The realization process of good's triumph over evil is gradual and not abrupt. A dutiful human being, as a coworker of God, should spread righteousness and eradicate falsehood for the advancement of the world and the progress of human beings toward perfection. Sometimes the good feel that there is no justice of God. However, we have a saying: "God's cane has no sound!" He acts unseen, and justice is eventually delivered by him! In Zoroastrian tradition, truth is justice, and justice is in *Asha*.

The final aim of all Zoroastrians is well presented in the last paragraph of another beautiful prayer, Hosh Baam:

Through the best Righteousness!
Through the excellent Righteousness!
May we see Thee!
May we surround Thee!
May we become one unto Thee![21]

What a wonderful way to express the final wish of all of us!

Divine or Natural Law of *Asha*

The divine or natural law of *Asha* connotes the eternal, immutable law that governs the universe. It regulates both the spiritual and the corporal worlds. In Zoroastrianism, natural law and divine law are the same. The law of *Asha* is as changeless as God, yet it regulates change in the world and determines world dynamism. It organizes the gradual refreshment or renovation (*fresho kereti*) of the world.

Asha represents the causative law—the relation between an individual's actions and their consequences (*Mizhdaa*). In Zoroastrianism, it is one's actions that determine the direction of one's life and one's fortune. An individual is free to choose his or her course of action and set its consequences in motion. Thus, the consequences of each action are predetermined, but the choice of action for people is not. Thus, the fate of human beings is not preordained. Once the choice is made, the direction of life is set. The consequences of an individual's acts—thoughts, words, and deeds—will follow in accordance with the law of *Asha*. This is God's will and God's justice.

Nothing can change the operation of the law of *Asha*. No mediation is possible. Nobody, not even the prophet, can intervene or mediate. Each action generates its consequence. There can be no addition or subtraction of the consequences. Repentance cannot alter the course of justice, either.

Although the Gathas state only the principle, the later Avesta defines in detail the character of certain types of behavior. Certain norms of conduct are highly recommended, and some acts are strictly forbidden. Wrath (*aeshma*), violence (*rama*), falsehood (*drauga*), deceit, (*druj*) are evil acts. Honesty (*Arsh Manangha*), fulfillment of promises (*mitra*), compassion (*merezehdika*), and charity (*rata*) are acts of piety.

Conceptualization of the moral norms set out in the Gathas helps to provide a better understanding of the ethical contents of the law of *Asha*.

Liberty

A human being's liberty is the most precious of God's bounties. It is the natural right of every person. Human liberty is so sacrosanct that God does not curtail our freedom even with regard to our choice of religion. In the Gathas we read:

> *Hearken with your ears to these best counsels:*
> *Gaze at the beams of fire and contemplate with your best judgment.*
> *Let each person choose his creed, with that freedom of choice which*
>   *each must have at great events:*
> *O ye, awake to these my announcements![22]*

Few other prophets have invited believers to weigh the tenets of their faith with reason and good mind.

The right of liberty is also reflected in the Zoroastrian concept of the God-human relationship. In Zoroastrianism, the human being is God's coworker, and not a slave, nor a child. Hence, neither the owner's right nor paternal authority can constrain a person's freedom of choice. The restraining forces are an individual's moral convictions or conscience (*daena*), and good mind (*Vohu Mana*).

Equality

The equality of males and females is unreservedly admitted. In all his sermons, Zarathushtra addresses man (*naa*) and woman (*naairi*) separately and on equal footing. In a sermon addressed to his daughter Pouruchista, Zarathushtra teaches young men and women to consult with their inner selves with wisdom and love (*aarmaiti*) before entering the uniting bond of marriage. No discrimination is allowed. Human beings—irrespective of sex, race, or color—are equal. The only superiority of individuals to each other relates to their righteousness. That is the only test for distinction.

Human Rights

In the words of Professor John R. Hinnells, "Zoroastrianism is the first religion that has taken a doctrinal and political stand on the subject of human rights and has condemned limitations or curtailment of those rights under any pretext."[23]

Although "human rights" is a modern phrase and idea, the concept of human rights as a system of values and ideas is engrained in Zoroastrianism. The Gathas condemn tyrannical and unjust rule and advise the faithful not to submit to oppressive rulers.

Body (*tanu*) and soul (*urvaan*) are inviolable, and their integrity should be respected. Physical and mental assaults are repugnant acts. Nothing should be done in contravention of this law. The Gathas state:

> *In full accord with law shall all men act,*
> *The law that forms the basis of all life,*
> *With strictest justice shall the Ratu judge,*
> *Whether it be the true man or the false;*
> *Against the false in him he shall with care*
> *Weigh all the truth that with it has been misled.*[24]

The concept of slavery is alien to Zarathushtra's teachings and no caste system or class privilege is recognized in the Gathas. The best evidence of this is provided by Zarathushtra's prayer for Kavi (Gushtaaspa), wherein he hopes that some of the king's sons would go into agriculture, some into the military, and some work for the religion. The class privileges that existed in the time of the Sassanians were contrary to Zarathushtra's teachings.

Protection of the Environment

Concern for creation is an aspect of *Asha*. The later Avesta states that defilement of soil, water, air, and fire in any form or degree is considered a trespass against nature and a transgression of the law of *Asha*. This protective attitude has its origins in the Gathic understanding of life and the material world. Matter and life are blessings from God and as such are worthy of reverence. This joy-producing world is being sustained by Ahura Mazda, and as his coworkers, human beings have a responsibility to act wisely and gratefully in preservation of the world. Zoroastrians acknowledge the importance of keeping nature free from pollution. The natural elements are essential for existence and progress, and human beings must act as the guardians of nature. Anybody who acts in breach of this trust encroaches upon the law of *Asha* and will encounter misery.

Active and Constructive Life

Idleness begets evil. Divine wisdom, righteousness, and moral courage flourish in an active life. The prophet teaches his disciples to be both active and productive:

> *O Wise Jaamaaspa Hvogva, I have taught*
> *That action, not inaction, higher stands.*
> *Obeying then His will, worship through deeds;*
> *The Great Lord and Guardian of the Worlds,*
> *Through His Eternal Law discriminates*
> *Who are truly wise and who unwise.*[25]

Monasticism, celibacy, asceticism, and self-mortification have no place in Zoroastrianism. The function of Ahu (the Lord) is to preserve life and vitality, to give human beings an opportunity to enhance their moral apprehension. The aim of life is happiness—*ushtaa*. Life is the battlefield between good and evil, and human beings should act as warriors of good. This activism of life is well illustrated in our Visperad prayer:

> *O Zoroastrian Mazdayasnaans!*
> *Hold your feet, hands, and understanding in readiness,*
> *For the purpose of doing proper, timely, charitable works, and*
> *For the purpose of avoiding improper, untimely, and uncharitable*
> *works.*

Practice good industry here.
Help the needy and relieve them from their needs.[26]

This has been fondly called the Zoroastrian Creed.

Progress and Modernity

Asha is the law of progress. It is an organic law and capable of accommodating modernity without any change in its essence. The Gathic principles are general. For instance, these principles guide humans to respect the environment. In disposing of the dead, Zoroastrians are free to use the method that is least harmful to the environment, meeting the exigencies of time and place.

The Gathas teach humans to be mindful of their physical and mental health. With acquired knowledge and advances in health sciences and technology, one must make decisions as to one's diet and the type of meat or drink one consumes.

The Gathas recommend against submission to unjust and despotic rulers. With the experiences and the knowledge acquired by social scientists, a Zoroastrian should be able to decide on the best system of government. *Asha* is the law of progress and is consistent with modernity. Zoroastrians in diaspora will succeed if they exercise good thinking, *Vohu Mana,* and tread the path of *Asha,* as our ancestors did and our co-religionists are doing in Iran, India, and Pakistan.

TRADITIONS OF SPIRITUAL GUIDANCE IN THE ZOROASTRIAN RELIGION

Religious guidance, for typical Zoroastrians, in the form of monthly consultation (or weekly confession to a priest, as is practiced in the Roman Catholic tradition) is a very foreign idea. The main principle of the religion—using your God-given good mind (*Vohu Mana*) with the principles of *Asha* (righteousness, truthfulness)—places a personal responsibility on each Zoroastrian to be a good person, and he or she is accountable for all his or her actions and cannot be absolved from them by confessing to someone.

Understanding this, how does a Zoroastrian obtain spiritual guidance? Before we address this question, let us look at the daily life of a typical Zoroastrian in her home, Mumbai, in the Parsi/Irani community.[27] Her name is Anaahitaa, and she lives with her family in a *baug* (a Zoroastrian colony or neighborhood), which has an *agiyaari* (fire temple) nearby. All over Mumbai there are more than forty such fire temples, and so they are in easy reach for most Parsis and Iranis.

Anaahitaa will visit her nearest *agiyaari* at least four or five times a month on special holy days; her very devout relatives may visit daily before going to work. Usually, a *mobed* (priest) is present to take care of people's religious needs. Anaahitaa washes her face and hands and performs the Kushti prayer before entering the prayer hall. She then brings a piece of sandalwood as an offering to the holy fire in the sanctum sanctorum, places it on the threshold, and takes a pinch of holy ash from a ladle and places it on her forehead. The sandalwood is taken by the *mobed* and is offered to the fire.

Inside Anaahitaa's home there is a sacred nook lighted by a floating candle, which burns perpetually. The nook is adorned by photos of Zarathushtra, *Farohar* (or *Faravahar*)—a Zoroastrian symbol depicting a winged human figure that represents the guardian spirit—and departed relatives of the family. This is the place where Anaahitaa and her family do their prayers each day, usually by themselves, each fulfilling his or her religious duties.

On holy days, Anaahitaa and her family will go to the *agiyaari* to attend a special ceremony, performed by the *mobeds*. This is followed by a short *hum bandagi* (congregational prayer) recited by all present.

Six times a year, Anaahitaa and her family attend special *gahambar* (seasonal) celebrations performed in outdoor *baugs* (celebration halls) where a *Jashan* ceremony is performed, followed by a community feast. These are the occasions to commemorate the six creations of Ahura Mazda, and every Zoroastrian is required to celebrate them in community.

The last ten days of the religious calendar are holy days for all Zoroastrians. Special ceremonies are performed in the *agiyaaris* for the departed souls of family members, and many devout Zoroastrians attend them, performing their own individual prayers during the ceremonies. The eleventh day is the Zoroastrian New Year, Navroze, celebrated with new clothes, prayers, food, visiting neighbors, and merrymaking.

Mobeds are not formally trained to provide spiritual guidance, as in other religions. However, they learn some skills from their elders by osmosis. It was a *mobed* who taught Anaahitaa her daily prayers, and *mobeds* are the ones who prepare children for their *Navjote* (initiation) ceremonies.

RELIGIOUS LIVES OF ZOROASTRIANS IN DIASPORA

Most of the traditions Anaahitaa and her family follow in India are also followed by her distant relations in the diaspora, with a few major differences. Unless they live in big metropolitan cities in the United Kingdom, North America, Australia, or New Zealand, they do not have a formal *agiyaari* close by, such as Zoroastrians in India do. Usually, in major cities like New York, Chicago, Toronto, Houston, Los Angeles, and San Francisco, a religious place usually referred to as *Dar-e-Meher* is set up similar to an *agiyaari*, but the fire is not kept burning continuously. Usually, such places are too far for many Zoroastrian families and hard to reach for all functions.

Because of that, the private nook in the home takes the place of the *agiyaari* for many families. The community gets together in the form of Sunday religious classes and for celebrations of holy days, usually in such big cities.

Zoroastrian associations have been formed in many cities in North America, and the Federation of the Zoroastrian Associations of North America (FEZANA) has been formed to look after the needs of these individual associations, as well as all Zoroastrians in North America.[28] An annual FEZANA general meeting is hosted by different association cities, with a North American Zoroastrian Congress every two years in North America, and a World Zoroastrian Congress with all Zoroastrian groups of the world every four to five years.

OFFERING SPIRITUAL GUIDANCE TO ZOROASTRIANS

Though a very ancient and influential religion, Zoroastrianism is neither well known nor well understood. Whenever possible, it is best for Zoroastrians to seek spiritual guidance from a *mobed* in their own community. When, however, this is impossible—such as in crisis situations, hospital emergency rooms, or when a Zoroastrian is undergoing psychological counseling or is, perhaps, estranged from his or her community or religion—people of other faiths may find themselves in the position of offering care to Zoroastrians. In these circumstances, non-Zoroastrians may find it instructive to keep in mind the following:

Spiritual Discernment

Zoroastrianism is a religion that emphasizes spiritual discernment. A Zoroastrian is responsible for choosing between right and wrong, and she is solely responsible for the choice and its consequences. Discernment is the most important spiritual discipline in the Zoroastrian faith and is considered a holy act. A spiritual guide can listen to his Zoroastrian clients as he processes the choices before them aloud and can hold sacred space as he seeks the divine will in discerning between the paths before them. He can hold the ideal of *Asha* before them and bear witness to the unfolding of *Vohu Mana* (good mind) as they discern. A spiritual guide should expect to experience the Holy in such discernments, since good mind is one of the ways that Ahura Mazda manifests goodness in the world. A spiritual guide should remember that "good thoughts, good words, and good deeds" are foundational to Zoroastrian spirituality and have significant bearing on any act of discernment.

Partnership with God

Zoroastrians stand before God with dignity. Spiritual guides should keep in mind that Zoroastrians see themselves as partners with God in the work of creation, not as slaves or children. There is a dignity inherent in those who fully identify with their Zoroastrian faith. They approach Ahura Mazda as friends in a relationship of mutual respect and reciprocity. Spiritual guides can remind Zoroastrians who feel defeated of their partnership with God and their responsibility for the fate of the world. They can help clients refocus their energies from the small concerns of their own lives to Ahura Mazda's project of resisting evil and moving the world toward perfection.

Individual Responsibility

Human beings are responsible for their own actions. Zoroastrians fully embrace their freedom of choice and understand the responsibility to choose what is right and good to be a primary discipline of their faith. A Zoroastrian believer is responsible to God alone for his actions. No other person is responsible for his actions in this life, nor can any person absolve him of his sins or intervene with God on his behalf. Judgment (rendered on the fourth day after death on the Chinvat Bridge) will be based on one's actual actions, not on one's intentions, and remorse cannot alter one's destiny. However, repentance that leads to good thoughts, good words, and good deeds can, given time, shift the balance of one's life and eternal destiny. Spiritual guides can remind Zoroastrian clients that their decisions matter in the grand scheme of things.

NOTES

1. Some scholars think he might have lived even earlier.
2. The Gathas, Yasna 29.
3. He was born on the sixth day Khordad and the first month Farvardin of the Zoroastrian calendar, which is known as the Khordad Sal.
4. Farvardin Yasht 94.
5. The Gathas, Yasna 46.1
6. Especially Vologases I (51–77 CE).
7. The Gathas are preserved within the Yasna scripture as chapters 28–34, 43–51, and 53.
8. A very good reference for all our scriptures can be found in the excellent website "Avesta–Zoroastrian Archives," compiled by Joseph Peterson: www.avesta.org.
9. *An Introduction to the Gathas of Zarathushtra*, ed. Dina G. McIntyre. Available at http://www.zarathushtra.com/z/article/dgm (accessed January 20, 2014).
10. This term appears in post-Gathic Avesta and becomes *Ahriman* in the Pahlavi texts. The doctrine of the two spirits appears in Yasna 30, verses 3–5, with a reference to their followers in verse 6. Another reference to the two appears in Yasna 45, verse 2, where the personality interpretation is persuasive.
11. That *Asha* can be grasped by the good mind is indicated in Yasna 28, verse 6.
12. Yasna 30, verse 8.
13. This close connection finds expression in the following sections of the Gathas: Yasna 32, verse 2; Yasna 43, verses 1 and 10; Yasna 46, verse 16; Yasna 49, verse 2.
14. Yasna 46, verse 10.
15. Farhang Mehr and Kaikhosrov D. Irani, "Asha (God's Will)," in *An Introduction to the Gathas*, ed. McIntyre.
16. Gathas, Yasna 48.12, Taraporewala translation.
17. Ervad K. E. Kanga, *Khordeh Avesta* (1880), corrected English edition, 2013, trans. and ed. Ervad Maneck Furdoonji Kanga. Available at www.avesta.org/kanga/ka_english_kanga_epub.pdf.
18. Yasna 44.19, 51.15, 53.6.
19. Yasna 51.13
20. Ervad K. E. Kanga, *Khordeh Avesta.*
21. Hosh Baam, trans. Faramroze Patel, for the Avesta classes at M. F. Cama Athornan Institute, Mumbai.
22. Gathas, Yasna 30.2, Dinshaw Irani translation.

23. John R. Hinnells, "Theory and Practice of Human Rights in Zoroastrianism" (presented at the Fourth World Zoroastrian Congress, Bombay, 1985).

24. Gathas, Yasna 33.1, Taraporewala translation.

25. The Gathas, Yasna 46.17, Taraporewala translation.

26. Chap. 15, verse 1.

27. The Parsi community consists of the Zoroastrians who migrated in the tenth century from Iran after the Arab conquest. They settled in the western state of Gujarat, finally concentrating in Mumbai later on. Iranis are Zoroastrians who migrated from Iran much later, during the eighteenth and nineteenth centuries. Both communities follow essentially the same religious principles; however, they follow different religious calendars. From this main stronghold in Mumbai, as well as from Iran, many Zoroastrians migrated to Pakistan, England, the United States, Canada, Australia, New Zealand, and almost all corners of the world. This is known as the second diaspora of the Zoroastrians. Zoroastrians in diaspora are very closely aligned with their co-religionists in India and Iran but have developed their own daily lifestyles to assimilate in their surroundings.

28. Please refer to www.fezana.org for more details.

RESOURCES

Many of the Zoroastrian dasturs (highly qualified *mobeds*) and scholars have written books offering guidance to Zoroastrians on how to live a faithful and productive life. One of the best of these is *Homage unto Ahura Mazda*. This excellent book, in the form of daily thoughts, was written meticulously by a great scholar, Dastur Dr. M. N. Dhalla, who was the head dastur of the Anjuman (Zoroastrian community) in Karachi, Pakistan, over a long period of time until his death. The full text of the book is available for free online at www.zarathushtra.com/z/article/dhalla/index.htm. For those who find themselves in the position of working with Zoroastrians on a regular basis or who are simply interested in exploring our historic faith further, I recommend this book with a whole heart. Its wisdom is such that I believe it would be inspirational to people of all religious traditions.

Karen L. Erlichman, MSS, LCSW, provides psychotherapy, spiritual direction, supervision, and mentoring in San Francisco, California. Karen is a core faculty member in the Spiritual Guidance Program at Sofia University in Palo Alto, California, as well as an adjunct faculty member at the Starr King School for the Ministry and the Chaplaincy Institute for Arts and Interfaith Ministries. Karen is passionate about creating diverse and welcoming spaces for exploring identity, spirituality, and community. To find out more about Karen, visit her website: www.karenerlichman.com.

Dan Mendelsohn Aviv, PhD, has been engaged in Jewish learning as an educator, lecturer, professor, and published scholar for almost twenty years. Having spent three years creating an alternative model for informal education, he recently returned to his greatest passion, classroom instruction. He is also an itinerant blogger at http://thenextjew.com, an inchoate podcaster, MacBook zealot, and most important, a proud spouse and father of three.

Spiritual Guidance in the Jewish Community

Karen L. Erlichman, MSS, LCSW,
with Dan Mendelsohn Aviv, PhD

> Make for yourself a holy teacher,
> and you acquire for yourself a friend.
> —*Pirke Avot* (Wisdom of the Sages) 1:6

A BRIEF OVERVIEW OF JUDAISM

The Jewish religion has existed around the world since 2000 BCE and is a monotheistic religion whose sacred texts include the Torah and the rest of the Hebrew Bible (sometimes referred to by others as the Hebrew scriptures or Old Testament), Talmud, and other writings. For some, Judaism is a religion; for others, it is a culture or ethnicity whose core ethics and values have roots in the Jewish religion.

According to a commonly told joke, Jewish history might be summed up in a pithy maxim involving food: "They tried to kill us; they failed. Let's eat." Though much of Jewish history has been steeped in peril and threat and commemorated by festive meals, it is also a story of piety, perseverance, and passion. The first Jews, Abraham and Sarah (c. second millennium BCE), as the Bible reports, left everything at God's behest to establish a nation in the backwater of Canaan. Their family would grow over generations into a tumultuous clan and eventually find themselves indentured and enslaved by Pharaoh in Egypt. Under the leadership of Moses, the Jews would be freed and, as the Bible recounts, bound by a covenant with God at Sinai. After conquering (or, as some archaeologists have argued, infiltrating) Canaan and establishing what would eventually be a monarchy, the Jewish people would rally around a centralized Temple sect of animal sacrifice and pilgrimage, much to the dismay of the prophets, who averred that God, who is not a carnivore, hungered instead for human kindness. This call was often left unheeded.

After being uprooted by Babylonian conquerors and exiled from the Promised Land in the sixth century BCE, the Jews continued to believe in the strength of their covenant with God. This dramatic departure, however, necessarily forced innovations to Judaism never conceived before: the synagogue as new locus of Jewish communal life and the Torah as the record of revelation and God's law. These changes remained even after the return to the Land of Israel. Canonizers of Torah became interpreters and continued their work of entrenching the Torah as Judaism's authoritative text alongside the renewed Temple-based religious practices.

Even after the Second Temple was destroyed by the Romans in the first century CE, Jews within Judea and without had long partaken of a new Judaism. They were already well versed in synagogue life and extra-Temple worship. Rabbis and their communities, and their communities' local traditions, were framing the Jewish present. The devastation wreaked by the failed Bar Kochba Revolt (132–135 CE) would not only entrench rabbinic authority, but add to it a strong pacifist streak as well as a posture of accommodation to foreign authorities until the day of the Jews' ultimate redemption. An esoteric offshoot of this tradition, steeped in mystical interpretations of Torah, eventually coalesced into a movement around the sixteenth-century sage Rabbi Isaac Luria, who would popularize the Kabbalah and its "search for meaning" in a world rife with expulsions and rampant persecution. It was this "search for meaning" that would also prompt Rabbi Yisrael ben Eliezer, or the "Baal Shem Tov" (literally "Master of the Good Name"), to establish a similarly spiritualized movement in Eastern Europe in the eighteenth century. His followers, known as Hasidim, or "Pious Ones," included the unlearned looking for spiritual revival as well as the scholarly elite looking for an entrée into mystic practice.

While Eastern European Jews continued to suffer from violent attacks, pogroms, and anti-Semitic outrages, Western European Jews would become emancipated and enlightened. Modernity brought freedom to Jews in the West, but it also relegated the once-binding rabbinic law to a matter of choice. With modernity, the individual was a citizen, not a subject or cog in a communal wheel. In this spirit, Reform Judaism emerged in Germany, positing the mutability of Jewish law and rabbinic authority, alongside Conservative Judaism, which did not take such a far-reaching position.

The Shoah (Holocaust, 1939–1945) would change everything, sweeping up Jews from East and West alike in waves of Nazi persecution and annihilation. With the virtual destruction of European Jewry, the focus of world Judaism shifted to those who built lives in the New World of North America and those who chose to create a truly new Jewish world under the Levantine skies of Palestine. The North American Jewish community of the twenty-first century is arguably the most well-established, well-accepted, well-educated, and well-meaning iteration in the history of the Jewish people. And Israel, the dream willed by Theodor Herzl and the Zionist movement, is a developed country barely seven decades old, though not without complex sociopolitical challenges within and outside its borders.

There are five major identifiable denominations within Judaism. In addition to the Conservative and Reform movements mentioned above, there are also the Orthodox, Reconstructionist, and Jewish Renewal movements. There are different branches of Orthodox Judaism as well, some of which include ecstatic, contemplative, and mystical practices such as Kabbalah, Mussar, and meditation (these are also found in other Jewish denominations). Each of the denominations in Judaism has its own interpretation of Torah and other sacred texts and of halacha (Jewish law), as well as Jewish liturgy, ethics, rituals, and practices. Jewish clergy include rabbis and cantors; other Jewish spiritual leaders, such as *kohanim* ("priests"), predate the rabbinate.

A respectful understanding of Judaism must include awareness of the pernicious history of anti-Semitism and its impact on the evolution of Jewish culture and religion. The majority of American Jews describe themselves as "unaffiliated," meaning they do not closely practice the Jewish religion, but they report a strong sense of Jewish identity and culture. Some cultural Jews are also active in Buddhism, Unitarian Universalism, Wiccan and Pagan communities, Sufism, and Hinduism.

Historically, Jews around the world have participated in various kinds of cross-cultural, multi-faith, and inter-spiritual pollination, while maintaining sturdy theological roots. In addition, over the last twenty years there has been a rebirth of Jewish meditation, now an integral practice in many mainstream congregations and closely aligned with Jewish spiritual guidance.

After reading this short summary of Jewish history, one might regard this narrative as rather sad, but to paraphrase Jewish historian Salo Baron, there is also "repeated joy as well as ultimate redemption."[1] Though it might be somewhat depressing to rehash how "they tried to kill us," there is consolation in "their" failure. And that consolation comes in the best form possible: a celebratory repast with family and friends, heralded by the well-known toast of "*L'chaim!*"—"To life!"

SPIRITUAL GUIDANCE IN JEWISH DENOMINATIONS

Spiritual companioning has long been part of the Jewish community, as illustrated in our opening quotation from *Pirke Avot*, a collection of ethical rabbinic teachings from the Mishnah (part of the Talmud). Throughout time there have been Jewish spiritual guides who have served spiritual seekers and students in a variety of capacities, and the contemporary practice of Jewish spiritual guidance has evolved as a result of a potent confluence of factors and conditions.[2]

Within Orthodox Jewish communities, especially within yeshiva study settings (almost exclusively male), the role of the *mashpia* (spiritual guide) has been that of a spiritual guide and mentor, with little to no specific training in spiritual guidance per se. In the more contemporary mainstream Jewish denominations (Conservative, Reform, and Reconstructionist), there have been individual spiritual guides who completed formation or training programs in other wisdom traditions who brought the practice of spiritual guidance back to their communities.[3]

Since its inception in the early 1990s, the contemporary Jewish healing movement has provided fertile ground for laypeople and clergy to discover spiritual guidance; since then, three specifically Jewish spiritual direction training programs have emerged. All three are distance-learning or low-residency programs: Lev Shomea ("Listening Heart"), Morei Derekh ("Teacher/Guide along the Path"), and Hashpa'ah ("Spiritual Guidance"). Hashpa'ah is specifically under the umbrella of the Aleph Jewish Renewal movement's training program for rabbis and rabbinic pastors.

Currently there is an international network of several hundred Jewish spiritual directors from around the world, representing the full spectrum of Jewish denominations from Orthodox to Renewal to independent, including lay, ordained, and secular spiritual guides.[4]

Jewish spiritual guidance is offered in a variety of modalities and settings. For some, the practice is integrated into an individual's organizational role; for others, they might have a "private practice" of providing spiritual guidance for individuals, groups, and organizations. Some are also therapists, coaches, or healers. In contemporary Judaism, there is also a growing movement of independent *minyanim* and *chavurot* ("fellowships" and spiritual communities) that either include spiritual guidance or are ripe for the inclusion of spiritual guidance.

SPIRITUAL PRACTICES IN JUDAISM

There is a vast range of spiritual practices that are useful when offering spiritual guidance to Jewish people. Many are framed in the context of the Jewish calendar, the seasons, and across the life span; others are embedded in the fabric of everyday life, such as daily prayers and rituals. Some are commandments (*mitzvot*), while others are customs that have evolved over time. These practices include rituals and related liturgy for the many Jewish holy days, as well as the monthly new moon (Rosh Chodesh) and weekly Sabbath (Shabbat).

The following are a few examples of Jewish spiritual practices that are especially relevant for spiritual guidance:

> *Remembering and observing the Sabbath* is not only a mitzvah (biblical commandment); it is a contemplative model of unplugging

from the demands of daily life that lends itself beautifully to spiritual guidance.

The study of Torah and other sacred Jewish texts and lifelong Jewish learning are also essential to Jewish practice and can be incorporated beautifully into spiritual guidance sessions for individuals or groups. Inspired by the Catholic *lectio divina*, Jewish spiritual guides often use *kriyat ha'kodesh*, a meditative practice for engaging with sacred texts.

Meditation, and specifically the practice of *hitbodedut* ("self-seclusion"), with roots in Hasidism (a more mystical branch of Orthodox Judaism founded by the Ba'al Shem Tov), has become part of nearly every Jewish denomination. In contemporary Judaism, several visionary spiritual teachers introduced meditation to congregational life across the United States. Jewish meditation can also incorporate sacred texts, chanting, music, or *kriyat ha'kodesh.* There is also a meditation practice that involves focusing on a specific Hebrew letter or on the Tetragrammaton, the unpronounceable name of God.

Tikkun olam, or the healing and repair of the world, is central to Jewish theology and practice. While at first glance it may not appear to be a spiritual practice, many secular Jews claim social justice activism as their primary spiritual practice.

Tzedakah is often mistakenly translated as "charity"; in fact, it actually comes from the root for the word *justice* or *righteous behavior* and is referred to as such in sacred texts. The mitzvah (commandment) of *tzedakah* is often referred to as the highest mitzvah one can do and was considered by the sages to be a spiritual practice connected to *tikkun olam.*

Additional spiritual practices in Judaism include various candle-lighting rituals (on Shabbat, Hanukkah, and other holidays), *mikveh* (spiritual bathing/purification ritual), hand-washing ritual and blessing, and others.[5]

DISCERNMENT

While there is not a Jewish equivalent to the word *discernment,* there are particular rituals and practices that affirm the deep listening that is at the heart of discernment. For example, one of the central spiritual practices for the Jewish High Holy Days offering a framework for discernment is *cheshbon ha'nefesh.*

Cheshbon ha'nefesh, or "accounting of the soul," is done every year during the month of Elul, the thirty days leading up to Rosh Hashanah, and helps us to hold the tension between living such fragmented, complex lives and our journey toward *shleimut,* or wholeness. Contemporary Mussar practitioner Alan Morinis has outlined a practice of *cheshbon ha'nefesh* that uses *middot,* or spiritual traits, as benchmarks.

Mussar is a Jewish psycho-spiritual path with origins in the tenth and nineteenth centuries. Mussar, which literally means "ethics/ morality/punishment" and implies taking on a personal moral or spiritual discipline, is a collection of contemplative practices and exercises that have evolved over the past thousand years, including meditation, chanting, and other methods that provide a framework for cultivating inner balance. Mussar teaches that every person has a pure soul of divine light and offers tools to help release or transform the barriers that prevent that inner light from shining through and to engage that light in everything that we do in the material world.

Alan Morinis has long been a faculty member in the Morei Derekh training program, and Mussar practice is an essential resource for many Jewish spiritual directors. Morinis recommends writing a list of thirteen *middot,* thirteen qualities you wish to observe in yourself—such as gratitude, equanimity, or compassion. Every morning you chant and meditate on each of these *middot,* and every night before going to sleep you should journal and reflect on any thoughts, feelings, or experiences you have had during the day in relationship to these qualities, thus creating a daily accounting practice for the soul. The meditation and reflection aspects of this practice are quiet spaces in which you can listen more contemplatively for inner guidance and clarity.

The Shema prayer, which is perhaps the liturgical heart of Judaism, is considered by some to be a touchstone for discernment practice. As Rabbi David Teutsch writes, "The Shema is called *kabbalat ol malchut sha'mayim,* [which means] we 'receive upon ourselves the yoke of the sovereignty of Heaven.' To proclaim God as ours and as one is to acknowledge fealty to the divine will—and the Shema is a time to listen. We listen in order to discover God's will."[6]

There are many Jews who consider themselves cultural or secular Jews, spiritual but not religious, agnostic or atheist, yet have a strong sense of Jewish identity and values. They may be unfamiliar with some of the above concepts and practices. Some also explore Buddhism, yoga, aikido, meditation, and other spiritual traditions, in addition to or instead of affiliating with a synagogue or other Jewish organization.

HOW SPIRITUAL DEVELOPMENT IS UNDERSTOOD IN JUDAISM

Jewish spiritual development is understood theologically as a lifelong practice, rather than a one-dimensional linear process of maturation. There are a number of thematic narratives that provide a framework for spiritual development, and there are some related practices that offer tools for spiritual formation. Following are a few examples.

Action as Spiritual Formation

The primacy of behavior and action over thought and rhetoric is a core Jewish theological teaching. A well-loved and often quoted biblical phrase, *Na'aseh v'nishma*—"We will do and we will hear/understand" (Exodus 24:7)—reflects this benchmark of spiritual development and identity. Judaism's strong commitment to *tikkun olam*—the healing and repair of the world—has influenced many secular Jews to claim social justice activism as their paradigm of spiritual development.

Journey

The narrative of journeying is perhaps one of the most powerful spiritual development models in Judaism. In her seminal article "Spiritual Transformation: A Psychospiritual Perspective on Jewish Narratives of Journey," Barbara Breitman discusses the spiritual journey as a practice of letting go of all that is familiar in order to get where one is going—highlighting the paradoxical tension of exile and homecoming.[7]

Moreover, Jewish spiritual development can be traced along the path of the Jewish calendar and throughout the life cycle, with explicitly identified milestones (e.g., bar and bat mitzvah) and time periods (e.g., the month of Elul, the period of the Omer) and their associated spiritual practices.

From *I* to *We*: Becoming a People

Judaism often sees spiritual development as a collective process, a tribal oneness, and nearly all of Jewish liturgy is written for the grammatical collective *we*. This reflects the Jewish theology of becoming a people with a shared unifying identity. As such, many Jewish clients in spiritual guidance wrestle with questions about identity, belonging, and community.

Jewish Mystical Perspectives on Spiritual Development

In Kabbalah, a Jewish mystical tradition, there are a number of tools and practices for spiritual development. In addition to ancient and contemporary Mussar resources and having a *mashpia* (spiritual guide), Estelle Frankel's book *Sacred Therapy: Jewish Spiritual Teachings on Emotional Healing and Inner Wholeness* is an invaluable guidebook for understanding and applying kabbalistic resources for spiritual guidance.[8] In *Sacred Therapy*, Frankel posits the kabbalistic interpretation of the Creation story as a central narrative and metaphor for spiritual growth and development, with every human being as a holy spark of the Divine.

COMMON SPIRITUAL ISSUES FOR JEWISH PEOPLE

Spiritual issues for Jewish people do not exist separately from Jewish culture and experience, particularly the history of anti-Semitism and the impact of the Holocaust on contemporary Jewish identity. The following is a list of issues and themes to consider in working with Jewish clients (some of them may apply to non-Jews as well, but certainly need to be considered in a Jewish context).

- Discomfort or skepticism about the existence of God or the use of God language or prayer language
- Cultural (and atheist) Jews versus religious or spiritual Jews (some refer to themselves as "bad Jews")
- Images of the Divine[9]
- Healing from experiences with anti-Semitism
- Internalized anti-Semitism
- Attachment to suffering as a response to trauma
- Trauma and safety issues
- People drawn to Judaism who weren't born Jewish (may or

may not be in relationship with a Jewish spouse or partner), including converts

- People who are bored, disillusioned, disappointed, or frustrated with their synagogue, rabbi, tradition, or even God

- Secular Jews who are spiritual seekers, or who had a life-changing event (e.g., death of a loved one, illness, near-death experience, breakup) that caused them to search out their Judaism

- Jews who might feel alienated from mainstream Judaism (e.g., lesbian, gay, bisexual, and transgender Jews, Jews of color, Jews partnered with non-Jews)

- Jewish activists, artists, and healers who might not be religious per se but who express their Jewishness through their craft or vocation

- Feeling like an outsider; wanting to belong but feeling ambivalent about it

REFLECTION AND INQUIRY FOR SPIRITUAL GUIDES WORKING WITH JEWISH CLIENTS

Participating in a multi-faith peer supervision group and having individual Jewish colleagues with whom you can consult are invaluable resources for spiritual guides working with Jewish clients. It can be very affirming, useful, and comforting to have a colleague with whom you can be completely open about your questions and concerns, without fear of judgment or offense.

The following is a sample list of topics and questions for self-reflection regarding working with Jewish clients in spiritual guidance; they are designed to stimulate internal inquiry and practical exploration. There is no single answer to each question; a particular Jewish client might respond in a very unique manner, but the themes may resonate for many people. You might take some time to reflect on these questions, perhaps even journal about them and share them with your supervisor, in an interfaith peer consultation group, or with a trusted colleague.

What questions might you ask in an initial spiritual guidance session with a new Jewish client?

Do Jews view their identity or affiliation as religious, ethnic, or cultural? How might this affect their experience in spiritual guidance?

How might issues of assimilation come up with a Jewish client, either directly or indirectly?

Why might there be a high prevalence of trauma symptoms among Jewish clients? How might that present itself in spiritual guidance?

How might internalized oppression and its many manifestations (low self-esteem, disconnection from Jewish community, mistrust of non-Jews) come up in spiritual guidance?

What countertransference issues might come up in working with Jewish clients? How might these issues be best addressed in supervision?

What transference issues might arise for Jewish clients?

How is your meeting space or office explicitly and implicitly hospitable or hostile to Jewish clients (e.g., icons, images)? What about your voicemail message, email signature, website, and any forms you use? What modifications might be helpful to create a more welcoming physical environment?

How would you work with a client who discusses his or her attraction to Judaism and/or interest in converting? Are you familiar with local resources that might be useful?

What is challenging for you about working with Jewish clients regarding their experience of family boundaries and obligations?

How do you understand the concepts of *home* and *family* for Jews?

Words and language (e.g., Yiddish, communication styles) are often essential aspects of Jewish identity. What if you don't understand something they are saying; how should you ask?

Issues of money and fees, and assumptions about class and money, are intertwined with anti-Semitism. How do you feel discussing your fee with Jewish clients?

Community and tribal affiliation are core identity issues for Jews. How do these themes come up in working with Jewish clients?

What are some of the unique challenges for Jews in interfaith relationships? How might you explore this with a Jewish spiritual guidance client or with the non-Jewish partner in an interfaith relationship?

What are some of the "nuts-and-bolts" practical issues for your work with Jewish clients? For example, are you aware of any Christian-normative language on forms and other paperwork?

What is your familiarity with Jewish holy days and seasons? Specifically, how do they affect spiritual guidance, not only as themes, but also in your sensitivity to and awareness of them? Are you familiar with the major Jewish holidays? Minor holidays?

For many Jews, social justice, or *tikkun olam* (sacred activism) is their form of prayer. How does this challenge and/or affirm *your* definition and experience of prayer?

What are some of the developmental life-cycle events that bring Jews to spiritual guidance (e.g., illness, bar/bat mitzvah, marriage, loss)? Why would they be spiritual catalysts?

OFFERING SPIRITUAL GUIDANCE TO JEWISH CLIENTS

In addition to the above background knowledge and questions for reflection, here are a few practical tips and ideas to consider in working with Jewish (and multi-faith) clients:

- Different branches of Judaism understand God differently (e.g., omniscient God [Orthodox] versus immanent God [Reconstructionist]), and their liturgy and practices reflect these theological differences.

- If you lead spiritual direction groups or retreats, remember to check the Jewish calendar for holiday dates, and whenever possible, make every effort not to schedule retreats in conflict with Jewish holidays. Include some intentional language in publicity materials that acknowledges this issue.

- When retreats are held over a Saturday (Shabbat), it would be wonderful to include some language in outreach materials that explicitly describes the retreat as spiritual practice (as opposed to *work*), acknowledging a commitment to respecting Jewish Shabbat practice.

- If you are part of a congregation or organization, consider creating a subcommittee or advisory task force whose primary task is to review materials (print, web, electronic) for content, images, messages, and language that invite and welcome a religiously and ethnically diverse constituency.

- Develop a library of resources that includes poetry, music books, and other items from many faith traditions.

- Consider the conscious and unconscious assumptions that might be present regarding how different religious, racial, and ethnic groups understand images, language, and concepts like *soul, ministry, formation,* and *spirituality.* These words don't always translate theologically for every faith tradition.

EMBRACING THE PRACTICE OF NOT KNOWING

When I was in graduate school studying to be a social worker, one of the seminal textbooks on cultural diversity in clinical practice was *Ethnicity and Family Therapy,* edited by Monica McGoldrick, Joseph Giordano, and Nydia Garcia-Preto.[10] While a groundbreaking anthology in many ways, it also perpetuated many stereotypes about families from different racial and ethnic backgrounds.

This experience left a painful imprint in my memory; consequently, in this chapter on spiritual guidance in the Jewish community, particularly given the long-standing history of anti-Semitism, I encourage readers to be mindful of the pitfall of stereotyping that might lead to unintentional hurt or bigotry.

Interfaith spiritual guides do not have to become experts in the world's religions. We do, however, need to be attentive to and mindful of our blind spots and committed to lifelong learning about people whose cultural or faith traditions are different from our own.

Pirke Avot 3:2 states, "When two people sit together and exchange words of Torah, the Shechinah [Divine Presence] dwells with them." Often it is at the very threshold of our differences that we encounter the Sacred in relationship with one another. I have had the experience of working with guides and supervisors who are Jewish as well as others from different faith traditions. All of these relationships offered me potent, enriching peaks and troughs in sameness as well as in difference. Humbly embracing the practice of not knowing can be a gentle resting place in the spiritual guidance relationship where that divine presence is felt by both guide and seeker.

NOTES

1. Salo Baron's obituary in the *New York Times* refers to a 1975 interview where he said that "suffering is part of the destiny" of the Jews, "but so is repeated joy as well as ultimate redemption" (www.nytimes.com/1989/11/26/obituaries/salo-w-baron-94-scholar-of-jewish-history-dies.html).

2. There are many different terms used to describe the practice of spiritual guidance, including *spiritual direction* (traditional), *spiritual companioning*, and *spiritual mentoring*, each one hoping to capture the essential qualities of this practice. For this chapter, I will use primarily *spiritual guidance* and *spiritual direction*, particularly since the latter is connected to the tradition and the international community of practice.

3. The term *ministry* is not used by Jewish spiritual guides, as it is not syntonic with Jewish theology or lexicon. Because there isn't an exact equivalent term, the word *practice* is most often used.

4. Rabbi Amy Eilberg, the first woman rabbi ordained by the Conservative movement in 1980, trained at the Shalem Institute and became one of the first co-directors of Morei Derekh, along with Linda Thal, EdD. In addition to her role as co-director, Rabbi Eilberg was one of the founding leaders of the Jewish healing movement, which attracted many Jews to spiritual direction training. Rabbi Eilberg and Dr. Thal were instrumental in bringing spiritual guidance to the Reform and Conservative movements, particularly for rabbinical students.

   Rabbi Jacob Staub and Barbara Breitman, co-founder of Lev Shomea and a psychotherapist with a long-standing interest in pastoral care and counseling, advocated for the inclusion of spiritual direction at the Reconstructionist Rabbinical College (RRC). Since then, RRC has offered spiritual guidance to its rabbinic students, as well as coursework that prepares them to offer spiritual guidance as part of their rabbinate post graduation.

   In the Jewish Renewal movement, with roots in feminism and the activist movements of the 1970s, founder Rabbi Zalman Schachter-Shalomi has long advocated for spiritual guidance as a sacred and necessary practice in the Jewish community. While the Jewish Renewal movement was not developed with the goal of becoming a denomination per se, over the last four decades it has created ordination programs for rabbis, cantors, rabbinic pastors, and now spiritual guides in its Hashpa'ah program.

   In 1997 the groundbreaking book *Jewish Spiritual Guidance* by Carol Ochs and Kerry Olitzky was published, followed by the Jewish Lights anthology *Jewish Spiritual Direction: An Innovative Guide from Traditional and Contemporary Sources*, edited by Lev Shomea co-directors Rabbi Howard A. Addison and Barbara Eve Breitman, MSW; and close to a dozen articles about Jewish spiritual guidance have been published in *Presence: An International Journal of Spiritual Direction*.

5. There are many books with information about Jewish spiritual practices; for example, *The Tapestry of Jewish Time: A Spiritual Guide to Holidays and Life-Cycle Events,* by Rabbi Nina Beth Cardin; *Jewish with Feeling: A Guide to Meaningful Jewish Practice,* by Rabbi Zalman Schachter-Shalomi; and *Seasons of Our Joy: A Modern Guide to the Jewish Holidays,* by Rabbi Arthur Waskow.

6. From *Kol Haneshamah: Prayerbook for the Days of Awe* (Elkins Park, PA: Reconstructionist Press, 1999), 713.

7. Barbara Eve Breitman, "Spiritual Transformation: A Psychospiritual Perspective on Jewish Narratives of Journey," in *Jewish Spiritual Direction: An Innovative Guide from Traditional & Contemporary Sources,* ed. Howard Avruhm Addison and Barbara Eve Breitman (Woodstock, VT: Jewish Lights, 2006), 171–196.

8. Estelle Frankel, *Sacred Therapy: Jewish Spiritual Teachings on Emotional Healing and Inner Wholeness* (Boston: Shambhala Publications, 2004).

9. According to Jewish theology and texts, we cannot "see" God. Theologically we are God's partners, we are *b'tzelem Elohim* (created in the divine image), but we do not have an image of God per se. Therefore, praying with icons is not part of Jewish practice. However, there many different names for the Divine in Judaism (e.g., Adonai, Elohim, and others), as well as verbal and literary images and metaphors for God.

10. Monica McGoldrick, Joe Giordano, and Nydia Garcia-Preto (eds.), *Ethnicity and Family Therapy,* 2nd ed. (New York: Guilford Press, 1996).

RESOURCES

Books and Articles

Addison, Howard Avruhm. "Reciprocal Grace: The Vocabulary of Jewish Spiritual Direction." *Presence: The Journal of Spiritual Directors International* 10, no. 1 (2004): 28–32.

Addison, Howard Avruhm, and Barbara Eve Breitman, eds. *Jewish Spiritual Direction: An Innovative Guide from Traditional & Contemporary Sources.* Woodstock, VT: Jewish Lights, 2006.

Breitman, Barbara E. "Reclaiming 'Love' and the Song of Songs as a Center for Jewish Theology: Implications for Spiritual Direction with Jews." *Presence: The Journal of Spiritual Directors International* 10, no. 3 (2004):19–26.

———. "Tehom El Tehom Koreh / Deep Calls to Deep (Psalm 42:8): Contemplative Christianity and the Emerging Practice of Jewish Spiritual Direction." *The Reconstructionist* 67, no. 1 (Fall 2002): 17–26.

Cardin, Nina Beth. *The Tapestry of Jewish Time: A Spiritual Guide to Holidays and Life-Cycle Events.* Springfield, NJ: Behrman House, 2000.

Erlichman, Karen. "Reflections on Spiritual Direction and Tikkun Olam." *Tikkun* 20, no. 3(2005): 62–63.

Frankel, Estelle. *Sacred Therapy: Jewish Spiritual Teachings on Emotional Healing and Inner Wholeness.* Boston: Shambhala Publications, 2004.

Friedman, Dayle A., ed. *Jewish Pastoral Care: A Practical Handbook.* Woodstock, VT: Jewish Lights, 2010.

Green, Arthur. *These Are the Words: A Vocabulary of Jewish Spiritual Life.* Woodstock, VT: Jewish Lights, 2004.

Gusfield, Chaya. "May Their Memory Be for a Blessing: A Report on Jewish Spiritual Direction Groups for the Grieving." *Presence: The Journal of Spiritual Directors International* 14, no. 1 (2008): 23–28.

Hoffmann, Jennifer Jinks. "What to Expect in Jewish Spiritual Direction." *Presence: The Journal of Spiritual Directors International* 13, no. 4 (2007): 47–51.

Kaufman, Susie. "Finding Your Voice in Torah." *Presence: The Journal of Spiritual Directors International* 16, no. 1 (2010).

Lew, Alan. *This Is Real and You Are Completely Unprepared: The Days of Awe as a Journey of Transformation.* Boston: Little, Brown, 2003.

Milgram, Goldie. *Seeking and Soaring: Jewish Approaches to Spiritual Direction.* New Rochelle, NY: Reclaiming Judaism Press, 2009.

Morinis, Alan. *Everyday Holiness: The Jewish Spiritual Path of Mussar.* Boston: Trumpeter Books, 2007.

Ochs, Carol. *Our Lives as Torah: Finding God in Our Stories.* San Francisco; Jossey-Bass, 2001.

———. *Reaching Godward: Voices in Jewish Spiritual Guidance.* New York: URJ Press, 2003.

Ochs, Carol, and Kerry M. Olitzky. *Jewish Spiritual Guidance: Finding Our Way to God.* BookSurge Publishing, 2009.

Schachter-Shalomi, Zalman. *Jewish with Feeling: A Guide to Meaningful Jewish Practice.* Woodstock, VT: Jewish Lights, 2013.

Taylor, Bonita E., and David J. Zucker, "Nearly Everything We Wish Our Non-Jewish Supervisors Had Known about Us as Jewish Supervisees." *Journal of Pastoral Care and Counseling* 56, no. 4 (Winter 2002): 327–338.

Waskow, Arthur. *Seasons of Our Joy: A Modern Guide to the Jewish Holidays.* Boston: Beacon Press, 1991.

Weiss, Zari. "Jewish Spiritual Direction." *Presence: The Journal of Spiritual Directors International* 5, no. 2 (1999): 29–34.

Zucker, David, T. Patrick Bradley, and Bonita E. Taylor. "The Chaplain as an Authentic and an Ethical Presence." *Chaplaincy Today* 23, no. 2 (Autumn/Winter 2007): 15–24.

Organizations and Websites

Aleph: Alliance for Jewish Renewal: www.aleph.org/hashpaah.htm

Awakened Heart Project for Contemplative Judaism: www.awakenedheartproject.org

Ayeka: Adult Education for the Soul: www.ayeka.org.il

Institute for Jewish Spirituality: www.ijs-online.org

Lev Shomea: www.jewishspiritualdirection.com

Mussar Institute: www.mussarinstitute.org

My Jewish Learning: www.myjewishlearning.com

Yedidya Center for Jewish Spiritual Direction (and Morei Derekh spiritual direction training program): www.yedidyacenter.org

Ozgur Koca is an adjunct professor of Islamic studies at Claremont Lincoln University in Claremont, California. His studies focus on Islamic philosophy-theology, Islamic mysticism, contemporary religion and science discussion, environmental ethics, interreligious discourse, and contemporary Islamic movements and ideologies.

Muslims and Spiritual Guidance

Ozgur Koca

I slam is a monotheistic and Abrahamic religion. Adherents consider the Qur'an, the sacred scripture of Islam, to be the verbatim word of God and Muhammad to be the last prophet of God. Muslims do not see Muhammad as the creator of Islam. They view him as the last restorer of the pristine monotheistic message revealed to other prophets throughout history.

Islam is the second largest religion in the world, with 1.5 to 1.6 billion followers. There are two major denominations of Islam: Sunni and Shia. Sunni Islam accounts for 85 to 90 percent of all Muslims. Shia Islam accounts for 10 to 15 percent. The two sects share the same fundamental beliefs and engage in many of the same practices.

These two groups separated from each other in the early years of the Islamic community for political reasons. The passing of Muhammad led to a dispute over selecting the new leader of the community. Shia Islam believes that the political and religious leadership of the Muslim community is vested in the family of the Prophet Muhammad. Sunni Islam rejects this view and holds that the method of choosing leaders must be the consensus of the Muslim community. This political schism later took a religious turn and continues to this day.

BASIC BELIEFS IN ISLAM

The Unity of God (*Tawhid*)

At the heart of Islam stands the reality of God, the One, who is at once transcendent and immanent, greater than all we can conceive or imagine, yet, as the Qur'an attests, is closer to us than our own "jugular vein," that is, consciousness. God is, on the one hand,

218

incomparable, unique, infinitely distant from us and, on the other hand, accessible, near, and infinitely close to us.

The Multiplicity of Revelations: Books and Prophets (*Nubuwwa*)

According to Islamic belief, God has sent many prophets to guide humanity and the core of their message is the same. The Qur'an, the central sacred text of Islam, explicitly affirms the divine origin of Christianity and Judaism.

> Say ye: we believe in God and that which is revealed unto us and that which was revealed unto Abraham, and Ishmael, and Isaac, and Jacob, and the Tribes, and that which Moses and Jesus received, and that which the prophets received from their Lord. We make no distinction between any of them, and unto Him we have submitted. (Qur'an 2:136)

Moreover, the Qur'an hints at the possibility of revelations other than Judaism, Christianity, and Islam. "Verily we have sent messengers before you [O Muhammad]. About some of them have we told you, and about some have we not told you"(Qur'an 40:78).

The Qur'an attests that its source is the same as other divine revelations. The same source manifested itself in different forms, languages, and modes in many different places and times before the Prophet of Islam, Muhammad. The same message, like a seed, gradually unfolded throughout the sacred history of humanity. Islam, for Muslims, represents the consummation of this process and the most perfect form of the primordial faith that was revealed to Abraham, Moses, Jesus, and others. This understanding of the history of the revelation allows Muslims to feel intimacy toward other faiths, while at the same time affirming the uniqueness of their own faith.

Islam sees itself in the long line of the Abrahamic tradition and as a continuation of Judaism and Christianity. In other words, Islam does not view itself as a new religion. Therefore, Hebrew prophets such as Moses and important Christian figures such as Mary and Jesus are deeply venerated figures within the religious universe of Islam. It is an obligation for Muslims to believe in and respect them. Muslims see them as paragons of virtue and desire to emulate their qualities in their lives. They name their children after these great men and women. Many stories and the characters we find in the Hebrew and Christian scriptures (such as Adam, Cain, Abel, Zechariah, Elias, Solomon, David, John the Baptist, Jesus, Moses, Noah, Abraham, and others) can also be found in the Qur'an. There are many similarities between the biblical and the Qur'anic narratives, but there are also sometimes profound differences.

The Prophet of Islam, Muhammad, according to Muslims, is not merely a "conduit" transmitting the divine message to humanity. He is also the most able interpreter and the most perfect embodiment of the divine revelation, the Qur'an. Therefore, the Prophet's sayings and acts (hadith) were carefully recorded in large collections in the eighth and ninth centuries. Throughout the Islamic intellectual history, hadith literature has been regarded as the second most important source after the Qur'an.

Life after Death (*Maad*)

Muslims believe that this world is not an end in itself. This world is a means to attach ourselves back to God. We are here to know, love, and serve God. To this end we are equipped with great potential. The realization of this potential is our mission. The potential is great, the mission is cardinal, the stakes are high. We humans find ourselves in the midst of this great challenge and opportunity. We will be held accountable for our deeds, sayings, and even silences.

This life is a starting point of a journey heading toward eternity. The mercy and compassion of God are always with us during this journey. However, the love and mercy of God do not totally negate the role of human effort in striving for eternal happiness. The nature of this infinite journey will also be determined by the way we live our lives.

BASIC PRACTICES IN ISLAM

There are five basic practices in Islam that are considered obligatory for all believers: testimony (*shahadah*), daily prayers (*salat*), charity (*zakah*), fasting in Ramadan (*sawm*), and pilgrimage to Mecca (*hajj*).

Basic Islamic beliefs (the unity of God, the unity of truth, the multiplicity of revelations, life after death) help us discern that we, human beings, are created by God, that our existence in this world is sustained by God, and that we have a purpose and the potential to realize that purpose. We are finite beings who need to attach ourselves to the Infinite God in order to quench our thirst for infinity.

Out of this realization that our life has a purpose, that this world is a message from God, and that we need the Infinite to go beyond ourselves, a desire flows forth to establish the link between the human spirit and God. Religious practices such as fasting, supplications, prayer (in its myriad forms), and charity serve precisely this purpose of relating the human spirit and its creator.

Testimony (*Shahadah*)

The *shahadah* is professing that there is only one God and Muhammad is God's messenger. The first part of the *shahadah* is the declaration of the oneness of God (*tawhid*). The second part professes that the true understanding of God as one, transcendent, and immanent is possible through revelation. By the oneness of God, Muslims mean that God is the only creator and sustainer of the universe, divinity is not shared by any other being (idols, humans), none has the right to be worshipped (praying, invoking, asking for help) except God, and all of our acts must be dedicated only to God in order to seek God's approval, mercy, and love.

Prayer (*Salat*)

Salat is the practice of formal worship in Islam. *Salat* consist of five daily prayers. These prayers are performed at the prescribed times during the day: *fajr* (dawn), *zuhr* (noon), *asr* (afternoon), *maghreb* (after sunset), and *isha* (late night). Muslim wash themselves before the daily prayers (*wudu*) and face Mecca during the prayer. The spiritual function of *salat* is to help a person contemplate and communicate with God. With five daily prayers, the life revolves around God. The believer lives in the joyful presence of God (*ikhsan*). *Salat*, if it is properly performed, becomes a journey leading a person toward a higher realization of the blessings of God (*shukr*), the remembrance of God (*zikr*), and moral ascendance.

Charity (*Zakah*)

Zakah is the practice of charitable giving. It is obligatory for Muslims who have accumulated wealth (*nisab*) and thus are able to do so. *Zakah* consists of giving up 2.5 percent of one's wealth to help the needy. If *salat* establishes a relation between human spirit and

God, *zakah* establishes a relation between a person and his or her neighbor on the basis of giving and compassion. *Zakah* is a way to express our concern for the well-being of our fellow creatures. In charity, we transcend the predicaments of egoism and selfishness. By performing *zakah*, we dethrone ourselves from the center of the world and put another person there.

Fasting in Ramadan (*Sawm*)

Ramadan, the ninth month of lunar calendar, is a time of joy, generosity, compassion, and breaking bread with others. Fasting in Ramadan involves abstaining from food, drink, and sexual activity from dawn to dusk. However, true fasting involves more than this. Abstaining from eating and drinking is not an end in itself but rather a means. By disciplining the body, fasting paves the way for a self-transformation, spiritual cleansing, and realization of a higher ethical standard. Good deeds, kindness, and helping others become fruits of this transformation.

Fasting is an act not only of the stomach, but of the whole body. Eyes refrain from looking at anything that is blameworthy; tongues refrain from lying, backbiting, abusive speech, hypocrisy, hateful speech, and so on. If fasting is understood and practiced properly, Ramadan becomes a time to practice self-control, kindness, and self-discipline to be a better person and to improve our relationships with others.

During this month, Muslims break the routine of their lives. After long hours of thirst and hunger, one realizes that there is nothing mundane in this world, nothing is banal. Everything is unique, special, and miraculous, especially the things we take for granted. From this follows a sincere thankfulness and appreciation of many things we take for granted.

Fasting helps individuals to feel the pain of the less fortunate. Fasting gives individuals a chance to empathize. During long hours of thirst and hunger, individuals realize how it feels not to be able to find food to eat or water to drink, how it feels to be affected by famine or disasters. It helps us to cultivate empathy with the suffering of others and thus to restore compassion to the center of all morality and religion. Compassion leads to charity. Fasting helps develop a very important skill: patience. During long hours of fasting, by refraining from eating, drinking, and sexual activity, individuals practice patience and learn to wait for an end and to strive toward a goal with perseverence. Thus, fasting provides individuals with an opportunity to transcend overindulgence and to reconsider their bad habits related to consumption.

Pilgrimage to Mecca (Hajj)

Hajj is the pilgrimage to Mecca. Every able-bodied Muslim who can afford to do so must make hajj at least once in a lifetime. Two to three million Muslims participate in this annual pilgrimage. Hajj is a demonstration of Muslim solidarity. People from all over the world, of different colors, ethnicities, and nationalities, gather together, dress in the same clothing, participate in the same rituals, and display a spirit of unity, solidarity, equality, and harmony. As the pilgrims of all colors, races, and ethnicities revolve around the same center (*Kaaba*), they realize that diversity in unity and unity in diversity is possible.

As such, hajj also strengthens the idea of community (*ummah*). In religious language, *ummah* refers to supranational collective identity and solidarity of Muslims and universal brotherhood that goes beyond the boundaries of race, ethnicity, and language. *Ummah* also refers to a type of society where justice and love feed each other and enrich an individual's journey to God.

ISLAMIC SPIRITUALITY: SUFISM

Sufism, or *tasawwuf*, is the inner and spiritual dimension of Islam. The Arabic root word for *sufi* is *suf*, which is a rough wool garment worn by ascetics and prophets in the Near East, symbolizing detachment from the worldly pleasures and dedication to God.

Sufism: History and Sufi Orders

The earliest Sufi circles were formed around individuals of intense piety. These individuals called for piety, introspection, and ethical analysis as a reaction to the increasing worldliness and moral decadence that arose out of the unparalleled accumulation of wealth and power in the early Islamic community.

The outstanding Sufi masters of the ninth and tenth centuries such as Abu Yazid al-Bistami and Junayd al-Baghdadi later became known as the first formulators of the Sufi doctrines and the organizers of the Sufi movements. Toward the end of the tenth century, some important manuals emerged summarizing Sufi doctrines and practices. In the eleventh century, the famous Islamic scholar al-Ghazali, in his magnum opus *The Revival of Religious Sciences* (*Ihya al-Ulum ad-Din*), argued that Sufi doctrines and practices have a basis in the Qur'an and the prophetic tradition (sunna) and are thus compatible with Islam. They do not contradict Islamic law and are necessary for the perfection of one's religious experience. Al-Ghazali's view has been the mainstream position for centuries among Muslims.

The most decisive forms of organization in Sufism are Sufi orders. A number of outstanding individuals, such as Abd al-Qadir Jilani, Bahauddin Naqshbandi, Ahmad Rufai, and others, who lived in twelth and thirteenth centuries developed spiritual methods (*tariqah*) to attain nearness to God. Later generations named their orders after these individuals (Qadiriyye, Naqshbandiyye, Rufaiyye, Suhrawardiyye, Chistiyye). Some Sufi orders are regional, such as Shadiliyye in North Africa; some are spread throughout the Muslim world, such as Qadiriyye. They have different methods and practices, such as the loud recitation of the divine names in Rufaiyye, in contrast to the silent recitation in Naqshbandiyye. Their attitudes toward politics and economics vary as well. Some are politically active; some are passivist and quietist.

In recent years, the influence of Sufi orders has also been felt in the West. Branches of some Sufi orders that originated in Islamic countries are now active in major urban cities throughout Europe and the United States. Sufi masters such as Rumi and Ibn Arabi are becoming increasingly known in the West.

There are differences as well as these similarities between Sufi orders and their counterparts in other religious traditions. For example, the participants of Sufi orders do not observe celibacy. They have less hierarchy and formality than do other forms of Islam. Sufi lodges are usually located in large cities, not in distant and isolated locations, symbolizing the Islamic understanding of perfection, which is, as the Prophet Muhammad states, "to be with God, within people."

Sufism, for most of Islamic history, has been a crucial aspect of Muslim societies. However, modern Islamic revivalist movements developed a quite negative attitude toward this form of spirituality and mystical practice, believing that Sufism, due to its otherworldly tendency, precludes Muslims from much needed political and economic activism. They also view Sufism as an innovation (*bid'a*) and a foreign intrusion adulterating the pristine message of Islam. Therefore, such movements sought to eradicate Sufism once and for all because of its excesses.

Some Muslim scholars such as Ahmad Sirhindi and Waliyyullah Dehlavi, appreciating the value of this form of spirituality, attempted to reform Sufism. These movements seek to purify Sufism, weed it of its excesses, and redefine it by emphasizing a spirituality that incorporates worldly action into it. In their philosophy, the world is not an obstacle; on the contrary, it is a ladder. Individuals go to God not by circumventing the world but by walking through the world in the presence of God. The distinction between earthly action and heavenly pursuit disappears.

Sufism and Spiritual Development

Various scholars have defined Sufism in many ways. Junayd al-Baghdadi, a famous Sufi master, defines Sufism as a method of attaining "self-annihilation in and subsistence with God."[1] Abu Muhammad Jarir describes it as "resisting the temptations of ego."[2]

Sufis believe that they are striving to acquire the state of perfection, *ihsan*, which they believe is the culmination of religious experience. According to the Islamic tradition, the definition of the term *ihsan* comes from a dialogue between Gabriel and Muhammad. Gabriel asked Muhammad about *ihsan*, that is, human perfection and the utmost goal of religion. Muhammad answered that *ihsan* is "to worship God as though you see Him, and if you cannot see Him, then indeed He sees you."[3] This hadith clearly calls Muslims to strive to attain a higher consciousness of God and to live as if they are in the presence of God.

A Sufi's primary concern is to acquire a profound awareness of God, of being in the presence of God. Sufis usually see a complementary relation between "inner/spiritual" and "outer/ritual" aspects of religion. Although they primarily focus on the inner/spiritual side, they support and deepen their search with a profound respect for and application of the outer/ritual side of religion. To use Rumi's analogy, a religious practice resembles a fruit with its kernel and shell. Shell and kernel compose the totality of a fruit, and their togetherness yields the desired result. Still, we do not want to get stuck forever in shell. We desire to go beyond shell to taste kernel and sap. To use an example, fasting is a multifaceted religious ritual. Now, abstaining from eating and drinking is a physical act; this is the outward aspect of fasting. It paves the way for the attainment of the realization of a spiritual goal attached to it; this is the inward aspect of fasting. The spirituality of fasting involves a deeper understanding of the human condition. In fasting, we realize how needy, how weak, how fragile, how finite we are. We are finite and we yearn for the Infinite. Departing from physical thirst and hunger, we intimately witness our spiritual and existential thirst and hunger for infinity. Herein we attain a deeper consciousness of the Divine, start smelling the alluring perfume of the Divine, and we escape from our finitude to the bosom of the Infinite and quench our spiritual thirst and hunger.

COMMON ISLAMIC SPIRITUAL PRACTICES

What do Muslims do in order to make spiritual progress? The simple answer is that they undergo a set of physical and spiritual practices and perform certain acts. These practices include the daily canonical prayers, fasting, pilgrimage, charity, and obeying the general moral injunctions of Islam, which bear resemblance to those of Judaism and Christianity.

Muslims also try to follow the sunna of the Prophet. Sunna includes the sayings, deeds, and silences of the Prophet Muhammad. The close followers of the Prophet seek to emulate sunna not only physically but also spiritually. Here the routines of one's daily life are transformed into sacred rituals.

Another source of spiritual guidance and sustenance is the frequent recitation of the Qur'an. Recall that Muslims believe the Qur'an is the verbatim word of God. Therefore, reading the Qur'an brings nearness to God and constitutes an essential part of Muslim practice. As the Prophet himself said, the goal of this contemplative recitation is to reach a state of awareness in which one feels as if the Qur'an were being revealed to the reciter at the moment of recitation.

The practices I have mentioned so far are commonly observed by all Muslims. There are also practices specific to Sufism. The most of important of them is *dhikr*, or invocation, remembrance, and mention. The *dhikr* involves contemplative repetition of divine names, prayer, or formula sanctified by the Qur'an and sunna. The Qur'an says, "All the beautiful names belong to God" (Qur'an 7:180, 59:24). Traditional scholarship tends to categorize the beautiful names (*asma ul-husna*) as the names of Beauty (*Jamal*) and the names of Majesty (*Jalal*). These categories refer to the feminine and masculine dimensions of the Divine. The names of Majesty include the Just, the Majestic, the Reckoner, the Giver of Death, the Victorious, and the All-Powerful. The names of Beauty include the All-Merciful, the Forgiver, the Gentle, the Generous, the Beautiful, and Love. Such verses as "My mercy has encompassed everything" (Qur'an 7:156) and "God has written mercy upon Himself" (Qur'an 6:12, 6:54) indicate that the names of Beauty take precedence over the names of Majesty.

To reach the named, God, one must recite the names in a state of contemplation. A specific name for a specific individual is chosen under the guidance of a qualified master. A person must be present with all of his or her being in the invocation to truly benefit from it. The *dhikr* can be performed both individually and communally. The communal *dhikr* is usually performed by Sufis in an audible manner and in unison. These gatherings, it is believed by Sufis, bring great grace and fortify their inner life.

ISLAM AND SPIRITUAL GUIDANCE

Islam is not a clerical religion. When a Muslim is in need of guidance regarding religious matters, he or she will usually turn to the canonical sources of Islam (the Qur'an and hadith) independently. However, if a Muslim does not feel confident about interpreting these sources in regard to his or her specific situation, then he or she may turn to someone with the necessary ability, knowledge, and character. This could be an imam, a scholar, an opinion leader, or even a friend. This person's opinion could be perceived as binding depending on his or her relation with the inquirer.

In such a situation, a person may seek a fatwa. A fatwa is a legal opinion regarding Islamic law (shariah). It is issued by an Islamic scholar who, ideally, knows the Qur'an and hadith in depth, uses the methodology of jurisprudence (*usul al-fiqh*) carefully, is acquainted with traditional sources and discussions, and understands the complexities of the current context.

A fatwa is not necessarily binding unless there is a consensus among scholars (a condition rarely achieved!). Islamic law has a highly decentralized, non-hierarchical, soft, and diverse structure. Therefore, if there is a divergence of legal opinions on any given issue, a Muslim may prefer one of these opinions over others, according to the circumstances. This legal plurality is one of the important factors allowing Muslims to live faithfully according to the principles of their religion while adapting to new environments.

COMMON SPIRITUAL ISSUES FOR MUSLIMS

The major spiritual problems Muslims struggle with—especially those who live in non-Muslim-majority countries—may be summarized as follows:

- There is an unfortunate tendency to mariginalize Muslims, especially in countries where they live as a minority. Islam has been unfairly depicted as a religion preaching violence. However, Islam is a universal religion calling its followers to peace, mercy, and justice.

- Contacts with Western culture led to many subtle changes in the Muslim community. This created tension within families between subsequent generations. Muslim communities are struggling to find an efficient way to interact with their surrounding cultures in mutually enriching ways without losing their distinctive and valuable qualities. Such interaction continues to be a challenge, and it remains to be seen how Muslims will handle it.

- There is an obvious tension between Islamic law and theology and the modern secular philosophies and ways of life. There is a great need for elaboration of Islamic law and theology to answer the challenges and transcend the predicaments of the modern secular way of life. The lack of such important teaching leads to intellectual, social, and—consequently—spiritual problems. There is an urgent need for the expression of Islamic law and theology in terms of the most advanced intellectual culture of the times. There are promising developments, but there is much work to do.

OFFERING SPIRITUAL GUIDANCE TO MUSLIMS

Modern lifestyles emphasize activity over contemplation. Like other spiritual methods, Islamic spirituality advises us to go beyond the noise, distractions, and transient pleasures to contemplate our own center—as well as the world—where one can find God. But this is not to say that Islamic spirituality calls for a total detachment from the world. "There is no monasticism in Islam," as the Prophet Muhammad himself repeatedly asserted. To remember and to invoke God does not require a formal and organized withdrawal from the world. A distinction is made between inner detachment and outer detachment. Individuals must be detached inwardly from the world, because in their inner reality and heart they should attach themselves to God. But outwardly individuals should live socially active lives. For Muslims, the model of the life of the Prophet displays the perfect integration of inner detachment from the world and active involvement in the world. The goal is to be in the world but not of the world.

In times of darkness and challenge it is wise to remind Muslims of such Qur'anic verses as "Who, when afflicted with calamity, say: 'Truly, we belong to God, and truly we shall return to Him.' They are those on whom are blessings and mercy from God, and they are the ones that receive guidance" (Qur'an 2:156–157).

There are some practices that are widely observed by Muslims to attain spiritual depth. Muslims observe practices that Islam mandates, which include the daily canonical prayers, fasting, pilgrimage, charity, and obeying the general moral injunctions of Islam. They also follow the outward (physical) and inward (spiritual) sunna of the Prophet. In addition, contemplative recitation of the Qur'an occupies a central place in Muslim spirituality. Finally, there are myriad forms of the remembrance of God (*dhikr*). In the broadest sense of the term, all religious practices can be seen as different forms of *dhikr*, for they help us remember God. In the remembrance of God, Muslims find tranquility and ease. As the Qur'an says, "Behold! In the remembrance of God, do hearts find satisfaction" (13:28). There is consensus on the value of these four types of practices among all Muslims.

NOTES

1. Cited in Fethullah Gulen, *The Emerald Hills of the Heart: Key Concepts in the Practice of Sufism* (Clifton, NJ: Tughra Books, 2011), xiii.

2. Ibid.

3. *Sahih Bukhari*, vol. 1, bk. 2, no. 47.

Wendi Momen, PhD, studied economics and international relations at the London School of Economics, of which she is now a governor. She is a founding member of the European Bahá'í Business Forum (ebbf), is a magistrate, and sits on a number of boards relating to social issues including health, the advancement of women, interfaith work, and philanthropy. She is the author of twelve books and a consultant to the Bahá'í Office for the Advancement of Women in the United Kingdom.

Moojan Momen, MB, BChir, was born in Iran but was raised and educated in England, attending the University of Cambridge. He has a special interest in the study of the Baha'i Faith and Shi'i (Shia) Islam, both from the viewpoint of their history and their doctrines. His principal publications in these fields include *Introduction to Shi'i Islam; The Babi and Baha'i Faiths 1844–1944: Some Contemporary Western Accounts;* and *The Phenomenon of Religion* (republished as *Understanding Religion*). He has contributed articles to *Encyclopedia Iranica* and the *Oxford Encyclopedia of the Modern Islamic World.* He is a Fellow of the Royal Asiatic Society.

Spiritual Guidance in the Bahá'í Faith

Wendi Momen, PhD, and Moojan Momen, MB BChir

The Bahá'í Faith is a religion that has spread to every country of the world and is practiced by some five to six million believers. It is based on the teachings of Bahá'u'lláh, who claimed to be the latest in the line of the prophets or founders of the religions of the world sent to guide humanity in the stages of its development. The central theme of his message is that this is the time for humanity to transcend all the divisions and conflicts that it has created and to come together in one united, peaceful, global community.

A BRIEF HISTORY OF THE BAHÁ'Í FAITH

The Bahá'í Faith was founded by Bahá'u'lláh (1817–1892), which means "the Glory of God." Although he was from Iran (Persia), he was exiled from this country and spent almost all of his ministry in exile in what was then the Ottoman Empire, first in Baghdad (now in Iraq), then Istanbul and Edirne (now in Turkey), and finally in Akka (or Acco, now in Israel). Bahá'u'lláh was preceded by the Báb (1819–1850), which means "the Gate." The Báb founded a religious movement that caused an upheaval throughout Iran and the surrounding countries. It was as a follower of the Báb that Bahá'u'lláh was exiled from Iran to Baghdad in 1853. As he was leaving Baghdad, he claimed to be the religious figure that the Báb had prophesied, and in later writings, he claimed to be the Promised One of all religions.

Bahá'u'lláh appointed his son, 'Abdu'l-Bahá (which means "Servant of the Glory"; 1844–1921) to succeed him as leader of the Bahá'í Faith and authoritative expounder of the Bahá'í teaching. During the ministry of 'Abdu'l-Bahá (1892–1921), the Bahá'í Faith spread to North America and Europe and even reached Australia, Japan, and China. 'Abdu'l-Bahá appointed his grandson, Shoghi Effendi (1897–1957), as head of the Bahá'í community and authorized interpreter of the Bahá'í scriptures. Shoghi Effendi spent much of his ministry (1921–1957) building up the Bahá'í administrative order and spreading the Bahá'í Faith to all parts of the world.

PRINCIPAL TEACHINGS OF THE BAHÁ'Í FAITH

The principal teaching of the Bahá'í Faith is that all the religions of the world come from one source, which is called God in English. Each of the founders of the world's religions has come to renew the spiritual message that focuses on the need for human beings to detach themselves from the things of this world and to develop themselves spiritually. In addition to these spiritual teachings, each of the founders has brought a social teaching that is suitable for the time and place to which he came. It is as a result of this that there are variations and apparent conflicts in the teachings of the world religions.

Bahá'u'lláh claims to be a new teacher sent by God, not for the purpose of creating yet another religion but rather for the purpose of bringing unity to the human world and to religion. Bahá'u'lláh emphasized the need to appreciate that "the earth is but one country and mankind its citizens"[1] and that we need to put aside all the causes of conflict and separation that afflict the human world and move toward unity and peace on a global scale.

In his writings, Bahá'u'lláh called for the establishment of the Universal House of Justice, and since 1963 the Bahá'í world has been led by this elected body. It has continued the process of spreading the Bahá'í Faith such that there are now Bahá'í communities in almost every country of the world, but it has also turned its attention to developing the distinctive attributes of Bahá'í community life. In the course of the developments of the last few decades, Bahá'í community life has become much less centralized and at the same time more systematic and focused at the community level.

In the course of Bahá'í history, various individuals aspiring to leadership themselves have challenged the leadership of the Bahá'í community, but they have never attracted a sizable number of followers, nor have they created an alternative Bahá'í tradition. Today, 99 percent of Bahá'ís in the world belong to one community headed by the Universal House of Justice.

TRADITIONS OF SPIRITUAL GUIDANCE IN THE BAHÁ'Í COMMUNITY

The Bahá'í Faith differs from most other religions in that it does not have any individual professional religious leaders. There are thus no priests, no learned class, no professional spiritual guides in the Bahá'í community and consequently no formal preparation for individual ministry. There are no different traditions or schools of thought regarding spiritual guidance in the Bahá'í community, and indeed, given the emphasis on unity and forestalling the development of splits, cliques, and sects in the Bahá'í Faith, any such schools are unlikely to develop in the future.

Although Bahá'u'lláh abolished religious leaders, he provided for the continuation of the functions of religious leadership, pastoral care, and spiritual guidance in the Bahá'í community. The role of religious leadership is fulfilled by the Bahá'í administrative order. Elected bodies at the local ("local spiritual assemblies"), national ("national spiritual assemblies"), and international (the Universal House of Justice) levels provide the authority structure in the Bahá'í community. Individuals are elected to these bodies but do not hold any personal power or authority. The Universal House of Justice appoints the other arm of the administrative order, which is composed of individuals who provide counsel and guidance to communities and to the elected bodies at each level.

In addition to the spiritual practices described in the next section, the main way of obtaining spiritual guidance in the Bahá'í community is through consultation. The Bahá'í Faith has a very precise and developed consultative process. It involves bringing a group of people together in a spirit of prayerfulness and unity to consider a matter or a problem. After the facts are ascertained, there is discussion about the spiritual principles that are relevant to the issue. Then there is a free-ranging discussion about the issue itself. In the course of the discussion, everyone is encouraged to express his or her opinions without becoming attached to them or feeling that he or she must defend them. A person's opinion may be developed by the group and grow into a concept that is very different from the original idea. Out of this emerges an answer that has the benefit of the contributions of the whole group.

This consultative process is used by a group in studying passages of scripture, by the Bahá'í institutions in decision making, and by families, and it can be used by an individual gathering together a group of friends to consult about a personal problem or, if there is need, for spiritual guidance. Bahá'u'lláh says,

> In all things it is necessary to consult.... The intent of what hath been revealed from the Pen of the Most High is that consultation may be fully carried out among the friends, inasmuch as it is and will always be a cause of awareness and of awakening and a source of good and well-being.[2]

Bahá'u'lláh also calls consultation "the lamp of guidance which leadeth the way and the bestower of true understanding."[3] 'Abdu'l-Bahá says, "The purpose of consultation is to show that the views of several individuals are assuredly preferable to one man, even as the power of a number of men is of course greater than the power of one man."[4] 'Abdu'l-Bahá also says, "Man must consult in all things for this will lead him to the depths of each problem and enable him to find the right solution."[5] Consultation for Bahá'ís' is not a therapeutic activity, nor is it one where one person gives direction to another person. It is a mutual, interactive process in which everyone is equally involved in seeking the truth. Each person has a part of the truth, and the process is designed to enable each to contribute this portion to the final result.

This consultative process is not only a way of obtaining spiritual guidance. Participating in it can assist one's spiritual progress. The qualities an individual needs to cultivate for good consultation are also qualities that help individuals progress spiritually. 'Abdu'l-Bahá lists these qualities as "purity of motive, radiance of spirit, detachment from all else save God, attraction to His Divine Fragrances, humility and lowliness amongst His loved ones, patience and long-suffering in difficulties and servitude to His exalted Threshold."[6] 'Abdu'l-Bahá also writes of the need for "courtesy, dignity, care, and moderation"[7] as a precondition for consultation. In short, consultation both provides a way of obtaining guidance for progress along the path of spiritual development and helps one to acquire some of the virtues of the path.

In addition, Bahá'u'lláh appointed 'Abdu'l-Bahá to be the perfect exemplar of the Bahá'í teachings as well as their expounder. His life of selfless service to others, kindness to all, universal love, and championship of the advancement of women and the rights of the oppressed is set before the Bahá'ís as an example of how to give practical application to spiritual truths such as justice, unity, equality, and love. When Bahá'ís wonder what to do in a particular circumstance they often ask, "What would 'Abdu'l-Bahá do?" and look to situations in his life that will shed light on their own responses.

HOW SPIRITUAL DEVELOPMENT IS UNDERSTOOD IN THE BAHÁ'Í FAITH

Bahá'ís do not have the same concept of a static state of salvation or liberation as is found in many other religions, nor do they have a belief in heaven and hell as final and permanent destinations for human beings after death. Rather, Bahá'ís see the birth of a human being as the start of a long spiritual journey that goes on throughout a person's life and extends after death. Progress along this path is through the acquisition of divine attributes—such virtues as love, justice, patience, trustworthiness, and contentment. Human beings have the potential for manifesting all these divine attributes (and this, for Bahá'ís, is the meaning of the statement from the Jewish scriptures that man is "made in God's image"). Each attribute, moreover, can be manifested to ever higher degrees of perfection.

The goal of this journey is the state of being sufficiently imbued with these attributes so that one is worthy of entering into, and abiding in, the divine presence. Salvation is thus a process of ascent on this journey rather than a state of being. For Bahá'ís, therefore, "heaven" is when one is drawing closer to the journey's goal, just as "hell" is when one is moving away from it.

There are a number of implications of the Bahá'í model of spiritual growth. One person may seem very spiritually advanced but may not be making much progress in spiritual development and so would be in a more perilous spiritual state than another who may seem less spiritually advanced and yet is making great progress. We are not therefore in a position to judge other people. (It is difficult enough to judge our own position.)

Spiritual progress is not aquired through book learning or by listening to a spiritual guide but by trying to live one's life in accordance with the values laid out in the Bahá'í scriptures. Bahá'í community life gives many opportunities for consultation, which provides both guidance for the spiritual path and the means to make progress along it. The greater the diversity of those engaged in the process of consultation, the more viewpoints there are on the subject being discussed, causing more light to be shed on the matter and increasing the chances of arriving at a beneficial conclusion. This may be one reason why the leaders of the Bahá'í Faith have encouraged as many people from varying ethnic, religious, and social backgrounds as possible to be involved in the Bahá'í community and to become active members.

The presence of people from such varying backgrounds in the Bahá'í community does, however, inevitably lead to tensions as people from different cultures and temperaments focus on a problem in the course of consultation. This is the reason that consultation is carried out in a spirit of prayer and with a focus on spiritual values. Here again, as the overarching theme of unity constrains Bahá'ís to transcend their differences and strive toward an appreciation of the viewpoint of the other, they learn valuable spiritual lessons and make spiritual progress.

The key factor in maintaining unity is the concept of the Covenant. The Covenant is a spiritual contract as a result of which Bahá'ís are free to hold their own opinions on theological matters (but can never claim authority for their views) and agree to submit to the authority of the Bahá'í institutions when it comes to community action. This concept of the Covenant thus serves the same function in teaching the individual humility and detachment from one's own fond notions that in other religious traditions is fulfilled by having an authoritative spiritual master.

SPIRITUAL PRACTICES IN THE BAHÁ'Í FAITH

The main spiritual practices for Bahá'ís are prayer, reading of the scripture, meditation, repetition of the Most Great Name of God, fasting, striving every day to bring one's behavior into accordance with the Bahá'í teachings, teaching the Bahá'í Faith to others, service in the work of the Bahá'í Faith and in carrying out one's trade or profession, and pilgrimage. Apart from fasting and pilgrimage, these are to be carried out daily. Several of these are sources of guidance for Bahá'ís.

Prayer

One of the laws of Bahá'u'lláh is that the individual must pray every day. Bahá'u'lláh has given Bahá'ís three personal obligatory prayers from among which a Bahá'í chooses one to say every day: a short prayer to be said once a day between noon and sunset; a medium-length prayer, which includes ablutions and ritual actions such as bowing, the raising of hands, and kneeling, to be said three times a day; and a long prayer, which is to be said once every twenty-four hours and includes ritual actions. The obligatory prayers are preceded by ablutions, that is, washing the hands and face, and by turning toward the Qiblih, the place where Bahá'u'lláh is buried, at Bahji, outside Akka in present-day Israel. The obligatory prayers are to be said privately, with pure-hearted devotion. There is also an obligatory prayer for the dead. One person reads this prayer at a funeral while others stand. The Bahá'í scriptures include a large number of other prayers and supplications that may be said at any time a person feels the need to pray. These include prayers for guidance, assistance, help in times of difficulty, protection, healing, spiritual development, purity, selflessness, forgiveness, thanksgiving, and praise of God. Many prayers are for the well-being of others, such as one's parents and children, one's community, and the whole of humanity. There are also many prayers for special occasions and activities such as marriage, traveling, meetings, and assistance in teaching the Bahá'í Faith, as well as prayers to be read during the fast. All prayers are powerful, but the highest prayer is the one that seeks nearness to God.

Bahá'ís generally use the prayers found in the Bahá'í scriptures, believing them to be more powerful spiritually than other prayers, but they sometimes offer spontaneous prayers from the heart in private. Bahá'ís believe that in prayer one's attention is turned away from the physical world and toward the spiritual. One converses with God and establishes a connection with God, and the balance between the physical and the spiritual is restored to one's life. Bahá'ís believe that through prayer one enlarges one's spiritual capacities. Bahá'ís strive to memorize prayers from the scriptures, and many such prayers have been set to music.

A main purpose of prayer is to remind one of the purpose of one's life. Prayer provides people with guidance and direction, grounds them, and gives them a sense of where they are in relation to the whole of creation. It enables them to know themselves better: "Whatever duty Thou hast prescribed unto Thy servants of extolling to the utmost Thy majesty and glory is but a token of Thy grace unto them, that they may be enabled to ascend unto the station conferred upon their own inmost being, the station of the knowledge of their own selves."[8]

Daily Reading and Recitation of Scripture

It is also the responsibility of a Bahá'í to read a passage from the sacred scriptures each day, at least each morning and evening, with reverence, attention, and thought. As the Bahá'í Faith has no clergy, personal reading of the scriptures is a primary way to obtain spiritual guidance from the highest source of guidance available to human beings, the word of God. Bahá'u'lláh has indicated that such reading should not be so excessive that it causes fatigue but rather should be reflective and followed by meditation on what has been read.

Meditation

Bahá'u'lláh enjoins Bahá'ís to meditate prayerfully on a passage of the Bahá'í scriptures daily. The purpose of meditation is that the individual may understand the teachings more deeply, fulfill them more faithfully, and convey them more accurately to others. Such meditation is a personal activity and not generally done as a group. The Bahá'í Faith does not prescribe formulas, techniques, or practices of meditation, although the Bahá'í teachings describe some features and conditions of meditation that may be applied to reach the meditative state: silence, a temporary withdrawal from the world, and turning one's spirit toward the divine kingdom. For Bahá'ís, meditation is speaking with one's own spirit. One puts certain questions to one's spirit and the spirit answers:

> The light breaks forth and the reality is revealed. The spirit of man is itself informed and strengthened during meditation; through it affairs of which man knew nothing are unfolded before his view. Through it he receives Divine inspiration, through it he receives heavenly food.[9]

Through meditation, spiritual truth is revealed.[10]

Repetition of the Most Great Name of God

Bahá'ís are to repeat the Greatest Name, Alláh-u-Abhá (God the Most Glorious), ninety-five times each day. One purpose of this practice is to develop the power of concentration, which, when rightly directed, can lead to knowledge, understanding, and illumination. The repetition of the Greatest Name provides a focus for prayer and meditation and draws the power of divine assistance toward us.

Fasting

Bahá'ís abstain from food and drink from sunrise to sunset for nineteen days a year (those under fifteen years of age, over seventy, ill, pregnant, fasting, or traveling are exempt from this aspect of fasting). The Bahá'í scriptures explain the fast both is a symbol of and results in purification, self-discipline, coming to understand the sufferings of the poor of the world, and the control of self and passion. It thus plays a role in an individual's spiritual development. The fasting period is one of meditation and prayer and of spiritual recuperation. During this time, Bahá'ís strive to make necessary readjustments in their inner lives, and they are striving to refresh and reinvigorate the spiritual forces latent within them.[11]

Pilgrimage

Bahá'ís, if they are able, go on pilgrimage at least once in their lifetime, which at present (since access to Bahá'í holy sites in Iran and elsewhere is not possible) is to the shrines of Bahá'u'lláh and his herald, the Báb, in the Haifa-Akka area. Here they pray, seek guidance, and develop their spiritual capacities. Through visiting the shrines and the buildings associated with the lives of the central figures of the Bahá'í Faith, a Bahá'í pilgrim achieves a sense of closeness to God and Bahá'u'lláh and returns home spiritually renewed and reinvigorated.

Personal and Community Development

Bahá'u'lláh states that the purpose of these spiritual practices is not the arbitrary exercise of power on the part of God but is rather to guide and assist human beings in what will best help them to develop their spiritual reality. As they practice these spiritual disciplines, they acquire spiritual attributes, draw nearer to God and love God more deeply, and will find in their daily lives numerous opportunities to practice and perfect them. A person's daily life must be consistent with his or her spiritual life. Spiritual practices are meaningless if they do not result in spiritual development, and spiritual development must show itself in a person's day-to-day life. However, Bahá'ís are to follow these practices not for any hope of reward or fear of punishment, but out of love for God.

In the last two decades, the Universal House of Justice has been developing the capacity of Bahá'ís at the local level to work with others in their neighborhoods to build community and contribute toward the advancement not only of their local community but of civilization itself. This aspiration is being achieved through the study of training materials by Bahá'ís and others around the world, which gives them the abilities to meet with others in their homes to share prayers and study the scriptures together, to provide classes for children and programs for young people, and to offer devotional gatherings for their friends.

These activities develop community spirit, give confidence and skills to those who are often ignored, particularly women and younger people, and inspire reliance on group consultation for decision making. Periodic gatherings for reflection on the progress made enable people to learn from one another and to use their own experiences and that of others to decide what steps to take next. Guidance thus comes from the group and community as a whole.

When functioning well, this program of grassroots community development enables people to seek and use the experiences of one another to address the needs of their neighborhoods—be that a communal well or a place for teenagers to meet—solve local problems, and develop the skills required to sustain the prosperity and advancement of that community. Visiting others in their homes to share prayers and study the scriptures together is also a way of providing pastoral care. In this way personal spiritual development and community development go hand in hand.

COMMON SPIRITUAL ISSUES FOR PEOPLE OF THE BAHÁ'Í FAITH

According to Bahá'í teachings, tests and difficulties are opportunities for spiritual progress.

> Naturally there will be periods of distress and difficulty, and even severe tests; but if that person turns firmly towards the Divine Manifestation, studies carefully His Spiritual teachings and receives the blessings of the Holy Spirit, he will find that in reality these tests and difficulties have been the gifts of God to enable him to grow and develop.[12]

Bahá'ís believe that God does not test a person beyond his or her capacity. Bahá'ís are not to seek tests for themselves, nor do they practice self-harm as a way to achieve spiritual enlightenment or salvation. They are not to be the cause of tests for others. However, individuals may well, by acting badly or through negligence, bring difficulties upon themselves. Further, Bahá'ís accept that some unpleasant things that happen are just accidents, not deliberate "tests" from God. In all these circumstances Bahá'ís believe that one can learn how to respond to such difficulties in ways that contribute to one's spiritual development. In this sense, then, difficulties and the learning that comes from responding to them can be a source of guidance.

The kinds of spiritual tests Bahá'ís tend to face are probably similar to those faced by people in other faiths: living up to the teachings of the religion, maintaining good relationships with others, accepting authority, keeping the ego in check, and dealing with crises of faith. For some Bahá'ís, these may be manifest in the following ways:

- Difficulty accepting and applying some of the laws of Bahá'u'lláh

- Difficulty understanding why certain things happen (e.g., natural disasters, abuse of children) or do not happen (e.g., people not restored to health)

- Difficulties with guidance offered by the Bahá'í institutions or with the institutions themselves

- Difficulties with other members of the Bahá'í community (e.g., perception that another person is not following the Bahá'í teachings correctly, personality clashes—this is particularly challenging because the main purpose of the Bahá'í Faith is to create unity, and to be in disunity with another person or with the community itself can be a source of much distress for Bahá'ís)

- Effects of disunity, backbiting, rumormongering, and similar acts that negatively impact an individual and the community as whole

- Personal crises of faith arising from any of the above, personal or family difficulties, things not going the way one would wish, or inner spiritual conflicts with one's own ego

OFFERING SPIRITUAL GUIDANCE TO BAHÁ'ÍS

Bahá'ís can be advised to turn to the resources in their own religion for guidance and spiritual sustenance, including the following:

- To follow the example of 'Abdu'l-Bahá

- To draw on the power of divine assistance

- To pray and carry out the other spiritual practices

- To meditate on the guidance found in the Bahá'í writings

- To consult with others, including their local spiritual assembly, to find a way forward

Given that Bahá'ís believe in the oneness of the founders of the major religions of the world, advice can also be offered from other religions. This should, however, be advice based on the scriptures of these other religions, since it is these that Bahá'ís regard as divinely inspired, rather than the words of professional religious leaders.

Keep these things in mind as you offer spiritual guidance to Bahá'ís:

- Bahá'ís do not have clergy and do not have mediators (other than Bahá'u'lláh, the Báb, 'Abdu'l-Bahá, and Shoghi Effendi) between themselves and God.

- Bahá'ís are encouraged to seek truth for themselves through studying both the Bahá'í scriptures and the scriptures of other religions, through the experiences of themselves and their communities, through consultation, and through investigating science.

- The role of a person guiding Bahá'ís is to point out these sources of guidance and to be one of the individuals with whom they might undertake the Bahá'í process of group consultation.

NOTES

1. Bahá'u'lláh, *Gleanings from the Writings of Bahá'u'lláh*, trans. Shoghi Effendi (Wilmette, IL: Bahá'í Publishing Trust, 1983), 250.

2. *The Compilation of Compilations*, prepared by the Universal House of Justice 1963–1990 (Sydney: Bahá'í Publications Australia, 1991), 1:93.

3. Bahá'u'lláh, *Tablets of Bahá'u'lláh Revealed after the Kitáb-i-Aqdas* (Haifa: Bahá'í World Centre, 1978), 168.

4. *Compilation*, 1:97.

5. *Lights of Guidance: A Bahá'í Reference File*, 2nd ed., comp. Helen Hornby (New Delhi: Bahá'í Publishing Trust, 1988), 228.

6. 'Abdu'l-Bahá, *Selections from the Writings of 'Abdu'l-Bahá* (Haifa: Bahá'í World Centre, 1978), 87, no. 43.

7. *Compilation*, 1:95.

8. Bahá'u'lláh, *Gleanings*, 4–5.

9. 'Abdu'l-Bahá, *Paris Talks* (London: Bahá'í Publishing Trust, 1967), 174.

10. Bahá'u'lláh, *The Kitáb-i-Íqán*, trans. Shoghi Effendi (Wilmette, IL: Bahá'í Publishing Trust, 1989), 8.

11. Shoghi Effendi, quoted in Bahá'u'lláh, *The Kitáb-i-Aqdas* (Haifa: Bahá'í World Centre, 1992), 176–77.

12. From a letter written on behalf of Shoghi Effendi, in *Living the Life* (London: Bahá'í Publishing Trust, 1984), 18–19.

RESOURCES

'Abdu'l-Bahá. *Paris Talks*. London: Bahá'í Publishing Trust, 1967.

————. *Selections from the Writings of 'Abdu'l-Bahá.* Haifa: Bahá'í World Centre, 1978.

Bahá'u'lláh. *Gleanings from the Writings of Bahá'u'lláh.* Translated by Shoghi Effendi. Wilmette, IL: Bahá'í Publishing Trust, 1983.

————. *The Kitáb-i-Aqdas.* Haifa: Bahá'í World Centre, 1992.

————. *The Kitáb-i-Íqán.* Translated by Shoghi Effendi. Wilmette, IL: Bahá'í Publishing Trust, 1989.

————. *Tablets of Bahá'u'lláh Revealed after the Kitáb-i-Aqdas.* Haifa: Bahá'í World Centre, 1978.

The Compilation of Compilations. Prepared by the Universal House of Justice 1963–1990. 2 vols. Sydney: Bahá'í Publications Australia, 1991.

Lights of Guidance: A Bahá'í Reference File. 2nd ed. Compiled by Helen Hornby. New Delhi: Bahá'í Publishing Trust, 1988.

Living the Life. Prepared by the Universal House of Justice. London: Bahá'í Publishing Trust, 1984.

CHRISTIAN DENOMINATIONS

The Very Reverend John A. Jillions, PhD, has been the chancellor of the Orthodox Church in America since late 2011. Previously, he served parishes in Australia, England, Canada, and the United States. He was a founding director and first principal of the Institute for Orthodox Christian Studies in Cambridge, England, until 2014, and was an associate professor at the Sheptytsky Institute of Eastern Christian Studies at St. Paul University in Ottawa, Canada.

SPIRITUAL GUIDANCE IN EASTERN ORTHODOX CHRISTIANITY

Very Rev. John A. Jillions, PhD

> And they returned to Jerusalem with great joy, and
> were continually in the temple blessing God.
> —*Luke 24:53*

> For as many of you as were baptized into Christ have
> put on Christ. There is neither Jew nor Greek, there
> is neither slave nor free, there is neither male nor
> female; for you are all one in Christ Jesus.
> —*Galatians 3:28*

> Whoever finds his life will lose it, and whoever loses
> his life for my sake will find it. —*Matthew 10:39*

"*… As many of you as were baptized into Christ have put on Christ.*" These words are sung at the baptism of every Orthodox Christian, and they encapsulate the essence of Orthodox Christian spiritual guidance. The aim of spiritual life in the Orthodox Church is to "put on Christ," to shape human life according to Jesus Christ and in so doing to discover the true and unique self God has desired for each human being from before the creation of the world. This is the Christian paradox of losing one's life in order to find it.

Why follow Christ at all and not some other great spiritual teacher? Because of the empty tomb. From the beginning, Christianity was not just about a teacher of spirituality, but about witnessing the empty tomb and the risen Jesus, and understanding that the human race now has a crucified Savior. This claim remains "foolishness" (1 Corinthians 1:18), but it is a persistent faith that God shares in the death of his creatures and by so doing destroys the ultimate power of death. That inexplicable encounter with the victorious crucified Christ still happens today to countless people, transforming their existence, desires, sins, sufferings, and, above all, death, into the taste, the hope, the possibility of an eternal joy that nothing and no one can take away. This ineradicable resurrection joy is at the heart of Eastern Orthodox Christianity and colors all experiences and events within it.

A BRIEF HISTORY OF EASTERN ORTHODOX CHRISTIANITY

Orthodox Christians identify themselves as the direct historical successors to the Christian church founded in response to the life, teaching, death, and resurrection of Jesus Christ in first-century Jerusalem. Indeed, many of the places named in the Christian scriptures—the source document of early Christianity—have had a continuous Orthodox Christian presence since that time, including, among other places, Jerusalem, Damascus, Thessalonica, Corinth, and Athens. The center of Orthodox Christianity moved to Constantinople (modern Istanbul, in Turkey) in the fourth century (along with the move of Emperor Constantine from Rome) and spread throughout the Eastern Roman Empire and beyond. Today the largest number of Orthodox Christians are found in Russia, Ukraine, Georgia, Greece, Romania, Bulgaria, Lebanon, Syria, Albania, Serbia, Egypt (the Coptic Orthodox Church), Armenia, and Ethiopia. But there are sizable populations of Orthodox Christians throughout the world.

Saint Paul's letters, the earliest documents of the Christian scriptures, witness to the early emergence of a Christian way of life, a way centered on following the crucified and risen Christ.

> For I decided to know nothing among you, except Jesus Christ and him crucified. (1 Corinthians 2:2)

> I have been crucified with Christ; it is no longer I who live, but Christ who lives in me; and the life I now live in the flesh I live by faith in the Son of God, who loved me and gave himself for me. (Galatians 2:20)

> Have this mind among yourselves, which is yours in Christ Jesus ... who emptied himself, taking the form of a servant, being born in the likeness of human beings. And being found in human form he humbled himself and became obedient unto death, even death on a cross. (Philippians 2:5, 7–8)

The crucified and risen Jesus remains even today the essential focus of Orthodox Christianity. Although there are some important theological differences among some of the Orthodox churches, they share a sense of historical continuity with the early church and place huge value on preserving the ancient Christian tradition.

The Orthodox have a deep sense of belonging to the church as a mystical human-divine body that brings together clergy and laity in an encounter with God through prayer and the "mysteries" (sacraments), especially the Eucharist (Holy Communion). The churches are highly liturgical and emphasize the role of bishops, in collaboration with the faithful, in guiding the church spiritually both to preserve the tradition and to respond to new questions under the guidance of the Holy Spirit in an ever-evolving "living tradition." What undergirds this communal aspect of the church is the conviction that every believer is called to be personally committed to the life of faith and prayer and thus to participate in the ongoing discernment of the Spirit's voice in his or her own life and in the life of the whole community. Indeed, Orthodox Christians regard "the acquisition of the Holy Spirit" (Saint Seraphim of Sarov) as the goal of the Christian life, leading to complete transformation called *theosis* or *divinization*.

Followers of Christ from the beginning came from all walks of life, but from the start there was powerful encouragement to single-minded devotion and—for those who discerned this as their calling—giving up the otherwise good and blessed state of marriage and family life. While celibacy of the clergy was never required in the East (except for bishops, from the fourth century onward), the community often viewed monks and nuns as the ideal Christians, and their example and teaching over the centuries have exerted deep and lasting influence on the Orthodox Christian understanding of spiritual guidance. Such emphasis can be found not only in the monastic literature that remains the bedrock of teaching on Orthodox spiritual guidance (*The Philokalia* and *The Ladder of Divine Ascent*, for example), but also in the living connection that is made with men and women who are trained by long practice in this tradition and who have themselves been under the direction of an experienced practitioner who has also been shaped by the Orthodox Christian tradition of spiritual living and knows it well.

Countries where Orthodox Christianity has traditionally been strong without exception also have deeply rooted monastic foundations. In recent years, monastic life has experienced a lively revival throughout the Orthodox world, and in many places parish and monastic life flourish side by side, with married clergy and laity visiting monasteries for times of retreat and spiritual guidance. In countries like Greece, for example, it is normal for a pious Orthodox believer to attend a local parish but also to go to a monastery periodically to visit with his or her spiritual father or mother for conversation, confession, and spiritual refreshment.

Most Orthodox churches also share the burden of having lived as severely restricted or persecuted minorities for much of their history, although there are sad chapters too of persecuting others. Martyrdom has also been called "the seed of the church," because the steadfastness and joy of the martyrs in every generation powerfully inspires others to follow the Christian way.

Orthodox Christians remember the martyrs of the first centuries of the church regularly, but martyrdom also affected the church years after these early centuries. The effects of persecution by the Ottoman Empire—most notably the Armenian Genocide of 1915–1923—are still being felt today in parts of the Orthodox world. The Orthodox churches of Russia and Eastern Europe live with the memory of systematic persecution by the Communist regimes that only ended in 1990 with the collapse of the Soviet Union. Churches and monasteries were closed; priests, monks, nuns, and faithful laypeople were persecuted, imprisoned, and killed. Freedom of religion was stamped out. In the Soviet Union alone, some five hundred thousand Orthodox Christians were put to death in Stalin's prison camps. All of this continues to have an effect on the renewed spiritual life of Orthodox Christians. Today, Orthodox Christians still live as embattled minorities in Muslim countries like Egypt and Syria and often view the new local freedom movements with alarm because there is evidence of increased persecution of Christians, many of them Orthodox, by local populations.

In the Western countries where most of this book's readers live, Eastern Orthodox Christians are very much a minority. In the United States, for example, there are only about one million Orthodox believers, and they fall into a wide array of churches that usually attach an ethnic identifier to the word *Orthodox*: Greek Orthodox, Russian Orthodox, Armenian Orthodox, and so on. In the public mind, Orthodox churches are still predominantly viewed as ethnic churches, and in practice that is largely true for many immigrant-based congregations, where the church is known mainly for its connection to the needs and aspirations of particular ethnic communities. The cultural norms that have helped shaped these particular churches and their expression of Eastern Orthodox Christianity may play a greater or lesser role in the life of the person coming for spiritual direction, depending on his or her own upbringing and how immersed he or she may have been in the ethnic community. Cultural influences, intertwined with religion and folk practices, may play a bigger role than the Orthodox faith as such in the life of a given person. Thus, in speaking with anyone who comes from an Orthodox background, practitioners need to determine his or her mix of influences. Is the person a deeply faithful Orthodox Christian who has a spiritual father or confessor, goes to church, receives the sacraments, prays regularly, keeps the fasts and feasts? Or is he or she Orthodox in the sense of belonging to an ethnic group, going to church on occasion with parents or grandparents, and generally identifying as "Orthodox" without being especially committed to the tenets and practices of the faith? The practitioner needs to be as sensitive culturally as religiously because in most Orthodox cultures, belonging to that culture presupposes that one is Orthodox.

Many of these ethnic Orthodox Christian communities are well assimilated into American culture, with English being their dominant language, and with children and grandchildren and parents and grandparents fully at home in the United States. Mixed marriages are increasingly the norm among Orthodox Christians in the United States, cross-pollinating these formerly predominantly ethnic communities. In addition, there are a growing number of Orthodox churches that have no formal ties at all to any one ethnic tradition and refer to themselves as pan-Orthodox. Their services are in English, or the *lingua franca* of the region, and their membership reflects a wide range of ethnic backgrounds. In these parishes, numerous parishioners may have converted to the Orthodox faith, and there are many parishes established in recent decades that are almost entirely made up of newcomers to the faith. There has been growing recognition among the various Orthodox churches that there is need for a single, unified Orthodox Church in North America, and steps are being taken by the highest leadership (the bishops) to move in this direction. The oldest of these bodies, the Orthodox Church in America (which traces its roots to 1794 in Alaska) received its independence from the Russian Orthodox Church in 1970 in order to help the project of forming a united Orthodox Church in and for North America.

There are numerous church groups calling themselves Orthodox, and this may be confusing to anyone trying to sort this out. However, there are two broad categories of Orthodox churches:

1. Those that accept the teachings of the Council of Chalcedon (451 CE) and are in communion with the Patriarch of Constantinople; these are usually called "Eastern Orthodox."

2. Those that did not accept Chalcedon and left the larger body after 451 CE are called "Oriental Orthodox" and include the Armenian, Coptic, Ethiopian, Syrian, and Indian Orthodox churches.

Today these two families of churches see themselves as close relatives, and while there is still no formal communion between them, they are closer to each other than either is to any other Christian body.

While there were a number of church divisions in the early centuries, the main body of Christians remained unified until the eleventh century. Then, due to growing theological and administrative divergences, but also geographical, political, and cultural alienation, the two halves of the church—western, under Rome; and eastern, under Constantinople—separated from each other and gradually became known as Roman Catholic (the west) and Orthodox (the east).

In the sixteenth century and later, there were various attempts by the Roman Catholic Church to re-assimilate parts of the "lost" eastern church that fell within their political sphere by permitting them to keep their eastern practices while giving allegiance to the Roman pope. Large numbers of these churches exist to this day and are known as Eastern Catholics, Eastern Rite Catholics or—mostly pejoratively—"uniates." The largest among these is the Ukrainian Catholic Church. Although not recognized as Orthodox by the Orthodox Church, it continues to identify itself as Orthodox in faith and practice (sometimes using the phrase "Orthodox in communion with Rome" to describe itself).

The Orthodox churches today have a very strong sense of identity. Although they participate actively in interfaith and ecumenical bodies, the Orthodox claim that it is the Orthodox Christian path that is the perfect expression of God's will for human beings. This does not mean that the Orthodox cannot learn from others and draw closer to others on the basis of shared insights and experience of spiritual guidance. Orthodox Christians themselves may stray far from that path and live it very poorly, while others live what they have to the full and far outstrip the Orthodox in their demonstrated, self-emptying, joyful love of God, human beings, and all creation. Such love is the aim of spiritual guidance, which must point beyond itself. Yet as a teaching, Orthodox Christians regard the Orthodox Christian way as the spiritually safest and most direct and complete path to the fullness of life that God envisions for human beings by God's grace and through no innate worthiness of the Orthodox.

Still, even ecumenical dialogue is a concession too difficult for some Orthodox traditionalists to accept. They fear that such contacts and dialogue will erode the identity of the Orthodox Church and its firm reliance on a well-tested tradition of prayer and guidance and produce instead a spiritually dangerous syncretistic mix.

While there is a strong Orthodox identity among those who remain committed to the faith, many people of Orthodox background drift away, often because their churches do not address the spiritual needs and life situations of their families, because they (and/or their families) do not feel at home in an ethnic church, or simply because the demands of an Orthodox Christian way of life may not fit with their circumstances and choices. Those raised in a markedly ethnic church have had little education and formation in the Orthodox spiritual tradition and so may look elsewhere for spiritual nourishment and guidance. These are precisely the sort of individuals who might seek the assistance of spiritual directors reading this book, who in turn could help these individuals reconnect with their own deep Orthodox tradition of prayer and spiritual development.

TRADITIONS OF SPIRITUAL GUIDANCE IN ORTHODOX CHRISTIANITY

"You are all one in Christ Jesus." Two broad patterns of living an Orthodox Christian way of life have evolved—one for monastics, and one for those who live "in the world." This distinction is only partly accurate, of course, because there are plenty of monastics who live outside monasteries and plenty of laity and clergy living "in the world" whose manner of life could be called an inner monasticism. Monks and nuns commit themselves to chastity (celibacy), poverty, and obedience to a spiritual father. Their ultimate aim, especially through communal life, is to live out the Gospel teachings of Jesus aimed at a love of the other based on love of God "with all your heart, with all your soul, and with all your strength." Saint Basil the Great (329/330–379), one of the founding teachers of monastic life, taught that the early Christian Jerusalem community illustrated the ideal monastic community.

> And they devoted themselves to the apostles' teaching and fellowship, to the breaking of bread and the prayers. (Acts 3:42)

> And all who believed were together and had all things in common; and they sold their possessions and goods and distributed them to all, as any had need. And day by day, attending the temple together and breaking bread in their homes, they partook of food with glad and generous hearts, praising God and having favor with all the people. (Acts 3:44–47)

Monasteries evolved—and still function in many places in the Orthodox world—not only as communities of worship and prayer, but as centers of social work serving numerous needs in the local community. While each monastery has its own character, ethos, and liturgical life, there are no monastic orders as such (unlike the Roman Catholic Church's monastic structure), and all Orthodox monastic life follows the monastic tradition generally developed over the centuries. Indeed, apart from the specific vocation to celibacy, the monastic way is simply the Christian way. A widely known story about Saint Anthony the Great (c. 251–356), the founder of monasticism, underscores this:

> It was revealed to Abba Anthony in his desert that there
> was one who was his equal in the city of Alexandria.
> This man was a doctor by profession and whatever he
> had beyond his needs he gave to the poor, and every
> day he sang "Holy, Holy, Holy" with the angels.[1]

The message here is that individuals who live in the world and who
carry out their vocation in the spirit of the Alexandrian doctor mirror
Anthony's monastic life. Although Orthodox literature on spiritual
guidance remains dominated by the monastic model and has not
developed the theme of a spirituality for clergy and laity "in the
world," there is a well-developed liturgical tradition of prayers and
blessings for almost every occasion: study, travel, work, home life,
meals, illness—even for the planting of vineyards and the blessing
of bees. Every aspect of life is brought together in an all-embracing
vision of sanctity. Monk, nun, bishop, priest, male or female—all
are one in Christ Jesus and called to the same vocation to "put on
Christ."

How is this vocation meant to be lived in practice? How is spiritual
guidance given and by whom? Regardless of the wide diversity of
cultures and personal callings, Orthodox Christians share a number
of assumptions about these questions, beginning with placing this
entire process in the context of the church.

Orthodox Christians do not see the church merely as a human
institution that exists for better or for worse to organize a response to
the religious needs of people. Orthodox Christians understand the
church to be a divine-human reality, the Body of Christ. To put it
in theological terms, while Christ himself is understood to be one
person in two natures—perfect God and perfect humanity—the
church as his Body is also two natures—perfect God but *imperfect*
humanity. So while one could easily point to the imperfections of the
church throughout history, the Orthodox would want to balance this
with the conviction that God himself is also at work in the midst of
the sinful, earthly, all-too-human dimension of the church.

So the sacraments of the church, Orthodox Christians believe,
do convey something of the divine gift of God himself. They insist
on the very materiality of the sacraments—water, bread, wine, oil,
a priest, a building—as testimonies to their faith in God's presence
within creation and history. This is the center of the Christian claim,

that God has entered history and has taken on the human life in all its beauty and ugliness and become flesh. This witness to faith in "God with us" is equally signaled by the prominence of icons in the Orthodox Church. The icon is a testimony to faith in the God who became a fleshly, visible human being and in so doing transformed the nature of humanity and creation. As the Gospel of John puts it, "No one has ever seen God; the only Son, who is in the bosom of the Father, he has made him known" (John 1:18). This is not the place for a deeper exposition of Orthodox theology, but without some appreciation of this incarnational faith, it is impossible to understand the Orthodox approach to the church and to spiritual guidance. The church is not a secondary aspect of spirituality for the Orthodox, but central. Indeed, for the Orthodox, if it is missing the material, sacramental, incarnate, fleshly, historical dimension, spirituality cannot be *Christian* spirituality.

The church is the embodiment of Christ's promise to his disciples, "Lo, I am with you always, even unto the end of the world" (Matthew 28:20). The church in this sense is inseparable from Orthodox thinking on spirituality. Tradition is the life of the Spirit in the church; it is vivifying, like a palm tree planted by streams of water, "ever full of sap and green" (Psalm 92:14). This also means that the saints of the past, defined as those widely recognized by others as inspired by the Spirit of God, are very much alive in the consciousness of the church. They live with us in a continuous present. Hence the teachings of the saints are not in the past at all, but nourish the church's life now. This sense that in God the past is alive helps explain why it is that the Orthodox give so much attention to the saints and aren't necessarily looking for new, up-to-date ways of spiritual guidance.

If one is trying to live this Orthodox Christian way, what are the various dimensions of that way? One of my teachers, Father Thomas Hopko, dean emeritus of St. Vladimir's Orthodox Theological Seminary (Crestwood, New York), once told me that he learned the answer to this question from his mother when he was seven years old: go to church, say your prayers, remember God. These form a solid three-legged stool for spiritual guidance. If you are helping to guide an Orthodox Christian, you might offer them the same advice, as amplified below.

Go to Church

Orthodox individuals should find an Orthodox church where they can feel at home with the priest and the parishioners. No community will be perfect, and one of the tasks in spiritual life is learning how to live and care for others, "especially those who are of the household of faith" (Galatians 6:10). They need a parish where they can attend not only to their own and their family's spiritual needs and "healing of soul and body," but where they can contribute to the building of a vibrant, welcoming, forbearing, outward looking, Christlike community. As one of the prayers before communion says, "Unite all of us to one another who become partakers of the one bread and cup in the communion of the Holy Spirit" (Liturgy of Saint Basil).

The life of the parish will become an essential part of their spiritual life, because that is where they will participate in the sacraments, prayer, and communal life and service of the church. Orthodox Christians aim to put the church life at the center of their lives and build their other activities around it. Even if this goal doesn't always work out in practice, Orthodox Christians are aware of this as their aim. Saturday vespers, Sunday Divine Liturgy, feast days and fast days, Great Lent (before Easter), the Easter season—this liturgical rhythm runs like an underground stream in the consciousness of Orthodox Christians. In fact, the prayers of the church will become part of them as they hear and memorize them and allow them to shape their spiritual life. So, while they may mostly hear these prayers in church, they are equally personal prayers.

The most frequently heard prayers in church are the psalms, which are often the basis of personal prayer. The church is thus the place where they will hear the scriptures read, or chanted, which is normal practice among the Orthodox. While the Orthodox Church encourages personal reading of the Bible as an element of spiritual guidance, individuals read the Bible with the church context in mind, since it was the *church*, as a community, that over time recognized and interpreted the Bible as a witness to its faith. Whether one speaks of the community of the Hebrew scriptures or the Christian scriptures, the community of faith existed before the written biblical texts, which emerged from the community's experience of God's revelation. Hence the community's experience as the people of

God is the proper context for reading, hearing, and interpreting the Bible. At the heart of that experience for Orthodox Christians is the life in Christ experienced in the church.

The parish church is also the place where individuals will most likely experience confession, the sacrament of penance. Personal, one-on-one confession, usually with a priest or a monk, is a key part of spiritual guidance. Confession creates an opportunity for the individual to look at his or her life in the light of Christ, and it allows the church to come to know the person at his or her deepest point.

Actual practice of church life can vary significantly among the Orthodox churches, so a given group of Orthodox Christians may have widely differing experiences. For many, confession and the words of the priest at particular moments in their life can be life changing. Yet others may never have been encouraged to go to confession. Some parishes require formal confession every time a person desires to receive communion. Others expect parishioners to go to confession "regularly" (loosely defined), and others leave the matter entirely up to the individual. For some communities, the norm is to go to the local parish priest for confession. For others, a visiting monastery priest—or a visiting monk-priest—serves as confessor. The form of confession varies as well. Personal confession usually takes place in the church, privately, standing with the priest before an icon, but publicly visible to all. But it might also take place in the priest's office. Confession is sometimes practiced in a communal way: in front of a group of people coming to confession, the priest says a number of prayers and then gives a meditation that prompts everyone to reflect on how he or she falls short of the Gospel teachings. The priest then calls individuals forward to say privately what is on their heart before saying a final prayer of forgiveness and reconciliation. Confession is especially sought out and expected by Orthodox Christians during Great Lent, the most intense period of spiritual effort in the Orthodox calendar, when Orthodox Christians are expected to attend more services, fast, renew their personal prayer, and address personal struggles and sins that keep them from living in a Christlike manner.

The primary aim of confession is repentance, forgiveness, and healing. Confession provides the person a place where, before God and the church—witnessed by the priest—he or she can confess sins, commit to a change (repentance), and receive assurance of forgiveness. "If we confess our sins, he is faithful and just, and will forgive our sins and cleanse us from all unrighteousness" (1 John 1:9). Although this is the first aim of confession, most Orthodox also avail themselves of confession to seek spiritual advice. In practice this is the main avenue for personal spiritual guidance in the Orthodox Church, although counseling is also a regular feature of parish life.

The highlight of the church year is Great Lent and Holy Week, all leading to "the feast of feasts," the resurrection of Christ, commonly called Pascha, or Easter. There are numerous special services, particularly every day in Holy Week (the week commemorating Christ's final days before his crucifixion, burial, and resurrection). Complicated calendar differences from ancient times mean that Orthodox Easter is usually celebrated on a different Sunday than is Western Easter, but each celebrates the resurrection of Christ. This is an especially exuberant feast among the Orthodox, with the constant exchanging of the Paschal greeting, "Christ is risen—Truly he is risen!"

Say Your Prayers

Jesus said, "When you pray, go into your room and shut the door and pray to your Father who is in secret; and your Father who sees in secret will reward you" (Matthew 6:6). Regular, disciplined personal prayer "in secret" supports and reinforces participation in church liturgical life, and vice versa. While spontaneous prayer is possible, Orthodox Christians build their personal prayer life around a "rule of prayer" that usually includes a number of traditional prayers, psalms, and scripture reading. There are prayer books with collections of prayers for morning and evening, during the day, before and after communion, before study, before work, and before meals, among other times. Many Orthodox Christians memorize a selection of prayers. Some teachers recommend that a person develop a set number of prayers daily as "the rule." Others recommend a set time for prayer, focusing more on attentiveness to content than the number of prayers. A period of silence can be included during prayer or at the end of the time of prayer.

The rule of prayer will vary tremendously depending on a person's individual circumstances. Needless to say, the "rule" of a retired senior citizen and that of a mother of a brood of preschoolers may look quite different. Whatever the precise content or timing of the "rule," commitment, to daily time alone with God—when phone, computer, television, etc., are turned off—is necessary for a spiritual life.

Remember God

The earliest text in the Christian scriptures is Saint Paul's first letter to the Thessalonians (written around 50 CE), and it includes the instructions, "Rejoice always, pray without ceasing, give thanks in all circumstances" (1 Thessalonians 5:16–18). Saint Paul envisions the Christian as someone who is constantly remembering that God is everywhere present. He or she has an unbroken sense of God's presence and seeks as much as humanly possible to be aware of that presence. The early monastic writers took the words "pray without ceasing" literally, and over time, in addition to periods of worship in church and times of regular personal prayer, they developed ways to keep the remembrance of God alive through the constant repetition of short phrases from the psalms or a brief form of words built around the name of Jesus. Such practice evolved into what has become known among many Christians of East and West as "the Jesus Prayer." The most commonly used form of this prayer is this: "Lord Jesus Christ, Son of God, have mercy on me." Some add at the end "a sinner." The prayer is widely known because it is the focus of the the nineteenth-century Russian spiritual classic *The Way of a Pilgrim*. Indeed, this tradition is known as "prayer of the heart." The constant repetition of this prayer throughout the day—driving, walking, doing chores—eventually can allow remembrance of God to bubble up naturally, like an ever-flowing spring of fresh water.

HEARING GOD'S VOICE

Spiritual guidance is an essential aspect of an Orthodox Christian's life. It most often comes through the priest of the local parish but may also be sought out from monks, nuns, and laypeople whom others recognize as having a gift for guiding others. There is little formal training in spiritual guidance other than personal experience with a spiritual guide. While there is much caution in the tradition about pursuing a spiritual life with no guidance, there is an equal or greater amount of caution about the damage that inexperienced, self-appointed, prideful guides can cause to individuals. Every Sunday liturgy includes the phrase "Put not your trust in princes and sons of men, in whom there is no salvation" (Psalm 146:3). God himself is the guide, and though he uses many and various ways and people, individuals can't lose sight of that direct connection everyone has with God. People need to be taught to pay attention to their own feelings, reactions, and warning bells to prevent them from falling prey to misguided guidance. The premise of Orthodox Christian spiritual guidance is that if someone is living out the spiritual path of the Orthodox Church, he or she will learn to hear God's voice and he will lead them beside still waters and restore his or her soul.

NOTES

1. Saint Anthony 24, in Benedicta Ward, *Sayings of the Desert Fathers* (London: Mowbrays, 1975).

RESOURCES

Bloom, Anthony. *Beginning to Pray*. Denville, NJ: Paulist Press, 2002.

Markides, Kyriacos C. *The Mountain of Silence: A Search for Orthodox Spirituality*. New York: Doubleday, 2001.

Schmemann, Alexander. *For the Life of the World: Sacraments and Orthodoxy*. Crestwood, NY: St. Vladimir's Seminary Press, 1973.

Ware, Kallistos. *The Orthodox Way*. Crestwood, NY: St. Vladimir's Seminary Press, 1979.

Bruce Lescher, PhD, is adjunct lecturer in Christian spirituality at the Jesuit School of Theology of Santa Clara University in Berkeley, California. He has been involved in the ministry of spiritual direction for over thirty years. He has also taught courses on spiritual direction at the Graduate Theological Union, Berkeley, and St. Michael's College, Burlington, Vermont.

Spiritual Direction in the Roman Catholic Tradition

Bruce Lescher, PhD

A BRIEF HISTORY OF ROMAN CATHOLICISM

Like all Christian denominations, the Roman Catholic Church traces its origin to Jesus of Nazareth, who lived in Palestine in the early part of the first century. During this turbulent time, the Jewish people suffered under occupation by the Roman army, and they were restless for a leader who would free them from this oppression. Various "messiahs," leaders claiming to liberate the Jewish people, arose on the scene, though they were often crushed by Rome's military might. Jesus was different from these messiahs. He preached the "good news" that the kingdom of God, a social order based on justice and peace, was both coming in the future and was already present. He preached the abundance of God's love, and he reached out to the outcasts of his society: lepers, gentiles, people who collected taxes for the occupiers, and even the hated Samaritans. His teachings were a threat to the Jewish leaders, who had reached an accommodation with Rome, as well as to local Roman officials, and he was executed as a criminal, dying the slow, excruciating death of crucifixion.

Jesus's followers took up his teaching and began to understand Jesus as an embodiment of the Divine. Initially, they were a sect within Judaism, but within a generation after Jesus's death, hostility between his followers and synagogue leaders developed, and Jesus's followers were expelled from synagogues around the year 90 CE.

Early Christian writings, especially the letters of Paul, indicate that early Christian communities were loosely organized and that leadership in these communities followed the customs of the local area. Over time, the Christian community developed a tripartite structure of governance. Bishops administered a geographical region, the basis of what today are dioceses in the Catholic Church. Priests, also called presbyters, led local assemblies. They were assisted by deacons and deaconesses, who served the physical needs of churches, such as caring for the poor. Within the community of bishops, the bishop of Rome held a certain prominence. Undoubtedly this is because Peter, the leader of the twelve apostles after Jesus's death, eventually moved to Rome. Over time this office evolved into what is today the papacy, so that the pope is seen as the "first among equals" among the bishops.

The church, which began in the Middle East, gradually became one of the dominant cultural forces in Western Europe and from there spread to the various European colonies around the world.

SOME BASIC BELIEFS OF ROMAN CATHOLICS

Today there are over a billion people who belong to the Roman Catholic faith. Summarizing the major beliefs of such a vast population in a few pages is a daunting task indeed. However, foundational beliefs of the Roman Catholic faith include the Trinity, creation, incarnation, the sacramental principle, and the teachings of scripture and tradition.

Like other Christians, Roman Catholics believe that the one God is a community of three persons, commonly called Father, Son, and Spirit (or, alternatively Creator, Redeemer, Sanctifier). This implies that God is about loving relationship: within Godself, between God and humans, and indeed between God and the created world, the cosmos.

Catholic theology asserts that there are two important self-expressions of the Divine: the first is creation, and the second is redemption. In both of these, the Trinity acts to express love. The created world is an expression of the Divine; indeed, the book of Genesis affirms over and over that God delighted in creation and "saw that it was good." Medieval theologians looked upon the natural world as a second bible, a place where people could "read" the signs of God's presence. Humans, then, are entrusted with stewardship to care for this beautiful cosmos. Redemption flows from the incarnation, in which the Son took on human flesh in Jesus of Nazareth, who taught, as the Gospel of John proclaims, "the way, the truth, and the life." Catholics believe that if you want to know something of what God is like, see how Jesus lived his life—a life of reaching out to outcasts, proclaiming a message of peace and justice, speaking truth to power, and even giving up his life for those he loved.

The "sacramental principle" claims that the sacred is contained in the ordinary. This principle operates in two ways. In a more narrow sense, Catholics communally celebrate seven sacraments—baptism, confirmation, Eucharist, reconciliation, marriage, ordination, and anointing of the sick. In these rituals common materials—such as water, oil, bread, and wine—become the means of grace, the basis for a ritual encounter with God's bounty. Most of these sacraments mark a rite of passage or a time of significant transition in a person's life. This "narrow" sense of the sacramental principle leads naturally enough to a wider sense: that common, everyday life is shot through with hints of the Divine. The divine presence permeates the natural world, the gifts and talents of each person, the joys and sufferings of quotidian life, the movements toward justice and peace found in society. A powerful symbol of this is the story of Moses found in the book of Exodus, where God reveals to Moses that God has heard the suffering cries of the Jewish people and Moses is called to work with God in liberating them.

Finally, Catholics believe that the Holy Spirit guides the Christian community through both scripture and tradition. Scripture comprises the sacred texts contained in the Bible, and the teachings contained therein guide the church community through the centuries. Generally, Catholics do not take a literal approach to interpreting the scriptures, recognizing the need to take into account the literary form that the author employs in order to understand what the text is trying to say. "Tradition" is composed of matters handed down from generation to generation that are not contained in the scriptures. Catholics believe that just as scripture can be inspired by God's Spirit, so this process of handing down can also be guided by the Spirit. When bishops meet in council to decide important issues, for example, their decisions carry significant teaching authority. As another example, some of the beliefs that Catholics hold about Mary, the mother of Jesus, come from tradition.

TRADITIONS OF SPIRITUAL GUIDANCE IN ROMAN CATHOLICISM

One can imagine the long history of spiritual guidance as a stream. When a particular form of guidance begins (is dropped into the stream, so to speak), it continues in some form into the present day; it influences the flow downstream.

The first form of what could be recognized as "spiritual direction" in Roman Catholicism emerged from the men and women who moved into the desert in the fourth century, the so-called desert mothers and fathers. In the early fourth century, women and men began to move into the Egyptian and Syrian deserts to practice a more radical form of Christianity. This was an inherently dangerous undertaking, both physically and spiritually. The desert would be a physically challenging place to live. But, more to the point, it was the place where, living in the stark environment of silence and solitude, one confronted one's "demons," those aspects of self one would rather not acknowledge. So a newcomer to this way of life was expected to have a "father" (*abba*) or "mother" (*amma*) to whom he or she turned for guidance. This elder was someone gifted with discernment, one who could "read the spirits" and advise the newcomer on the ways of the Spirit. This relationship between novice and elder was informal, not determined by institutional structures, and highly personal. The newcomer was expected to tell the *abba* or *amma* what was going on in his or her stream of awareness: thoughts, feelings, sensations, images. The elder, in turn, would give a word of advice to the newcomer. Finally, the novice was expected to obey the advice of the elder.

As more people moved into the desert, this informal arrangement began to take on institutional structures, so that by the seventh century nearly all monastic communities were guided by a rule, the most famous being the Rule of Saint Benedict. One can still see the seeds of the relationship of guidance that developed in the desert, but now they were wrapped in more formal structures. A woman or man joining a monastery received guidance in a variety of ways. Members of the community owed obedience to an abbot or abbess, just as the newcomer had owed obedience to the elder. But other sources of guidance were also available. Community members were guided by the teachings found in scripture, especially the Christian scriptures; by the rule, which outlined a way of life; or by decisions of the community meeting as a whole. In addition, an elder was usually assigned to a newcomer to introduce her or him to the communal life.

By the High Middle Ages (twelfth and thirteenth centuries), the Roman Catholic Church had accumulated great political and cultural power and rivaled kings, queens, and local nobility in influence. Abuses sometimes resulted from the temptations of wealth or power. Reform movements, calling Christians to a more Gospel-centered way of life, sprang up, usually emphasizing the need for a life of poverty and of preaching the Gospel. These movements attracted many laypeople and also drew some clergy. Two of the most famous reformers were Dominic Guzman (1170–1221), founder of the Dominicans, and Francis Bernadone (1181–1226), founder of the Franciscans. Other communities sprang up around charismatic women such as Hadewijch of Antwerp (early thirteenth century) and Catherine of Siena (1347–1380). These women guided their communities with their wisdom, counseled people from all walks of life, and eventually put their teachings into writing; they often claimed to have direct contact with God and so were able to work around the ecclesiastical structures that excluded them from positions of official authority.

A significant development in spiritual direction resulted from the teaching of Ignatius of Loyola (1491–1556), the founder of the Society of Jesus (the Jesuits). As a young man, Ignatius sought the life of a royal courtier—seeking to excel in service to local nobility, in the use of arms, and in romance with the ladies. He was grievously wounded in a battle and, during his convalescence, underwent a religious conversion, so that he decided to serve under the banner of Jesus Christ rather than under a secular prince. Ignatius lived at the dawn of modernity, and rather than imitate medieval asceticism, he struggled to find spiritual practices that made sense in his culture. He kept a journal of his experiments and gradually shaped his teaching into a book called the *Spiritual Exercises*, which spoke to the spiritual longings of the people of his time. He devised a series of exercises that could be practiced in various formats, such as an intense period over thirty days, or spread out over a longer time if a person was unable to leave his or her home setting. The exercises help people get in touch with their deepest desires and see how these relate to their commitment to follow Jesus. The person making the retreat would meet daily with a retreat director (hence the link to spiritual direction), who would listen to what was happening with the retreatant and suggest next steps. Central to these exercises was the discernment of spirits: was the retreatant moving in the direction of greater love and service, or moving in a selfish and destructive direction?

Ignatius's spiritual exercises grew in popularity in his time and are enjoying a renaissance in the early twenty-first century. As a form of retreat, they were designed not only for members of religious orders but also for women and men living everyday lives, busy with their families and professions. Ignatius emphasized the importance of "finding God in all things." This gave rise to an Ignatian style of spiritual direction that is still widely practiced today. Many, if not most, spiritual direction training programs in North America study this Ignatian style, which consists of listening closely to the inner movements that a person is experiencing rather than telling the person what to do.

The sixteenth century saw the beginning (in 1517) of the Protestant Reformation as theologians such as Luther, Calvin, and Zwingli criticized the abuses they found in the Roman Catholic Church. The pope responded to the Reformation by calling the bishops into the Council of Trent, which met in twenty-five sessions between 1545 and 1563. The church of the Counter-Reformation confronted the division of Christendom and the developing culture of modernity with a defensive style, circling the wagons, as it were, and distinguishing Catholic teachings from those of the Reformers. As part of this overall stance, Roman Catholic spiritual direction began to move into the confessional, where a penitent confessed his or her sins to a priest. Thus, for many Catholics, spiritual guidance came to be seen as the purview of the clergy, and the focus of the conversation would be aligning oneself with the moral teachings of the church. For many Catholics who lived in the four hundred years between 1550 and 1950, their spiritual director was also their confessor.

By the mid-twentieth century, many Catholics could see that the church's Counter-Reformation strategy no longer spoke to the modern world. So, in 1959, Pope John XXIII announced his intention to call another ecumenical council, a meeting of bishops from around the world. This council, known as Vatican II, met in four sessions between 1962 and 1965. The bishops sought to open a dialogue between the Catholic Church and the modern world and spoke of the church as a "pilgrim people," a people on a journey, not as a people who had "arrived" and had all the answers. The bishops urged a "return to the sources," to the scriptures, the early theologians, the master spiritual teachers. This theological and pastoral revolution has significantly affected the practice of contemporary spiritual direction in Roman Catholicism.

For many Catholics, contemporary spiritual direction is no longer seen as the purview of the clergy, to be carried on within the sacrament of penance. Rather, spiritual direction is understood as a charism (a gift of the Spirit) given to some Christians, be they clergy or laity. In fact, most spiritual directors today are laypersons. One sign that a person has this gift is that others spontaneously seek out him or her for advice. In addition to having the call to this ministry, a spiritual director is also expected to have some training in both knowledge of this ministry and skills in how to practice. The skills are honed through a process of supervision. There is now even a professional guild, Spiritual Directors International.

The various models of spiritual direction summarized here can still be found in the "stream" of Roman Catholic practice. Some Catholics seek spiritual guidance within the sacrament of penance. The emphasis on personal charism found in the desert tradition and medieval lay communities is echoed by authors like Tilden Edwards. Monastic practices are discussed by Sister Joan Chittister, among others. The Ignatian style has been popularized by William Barry and William Connolly.

SPIRITUAL PRACTICES IN ROMAN CATHOLICISM

The spiritual practices fostered within Catholicism are common to most other spiritual traditions. A traditional tripartite division is prayer, fasting, and almsgiving, to which one could today add a fourth: guidance.

Prayer

Prayer is the lifeblood of spiritual practice and essential for anyone seeking spiritual direction. Catholicism emphasizes both personal and communal prayer. In terms of personal prayer, there is no one "right" way to pray. Over their two-thousand-year history, Catholics have given witness to diverse styles of prayer. Examples include rote repetition of verbal prayers, such as the rosary; discursive reflection, using one's mental capacities with a scripture passage or a teaching; use of imagination to re-create biblical scenes; mantra-like repetition of a holy word; and imageless, wordless silence. The challenge for the believer is to find a style that "works" for him or her. Communal prayer is also essential in Catholicism. Participation in the Sunday celebration of the Eucharist is expected of all Catholics, though as it is lived today this practice is not as common as it once was. Other forms of communal prayer include chanting psalms in common (the monastic practice is called "the office," but laypeople also participate in this prayer form); belonging to a local prayer group, often based on scripture study; and for those who find it meaningful, participating in a charismatic prayer service, where the gifts of the Spirit, such as speaking in tongues, are celebrated.

Fasting

Under the rubric of fasting come various forms of ascetic practice. These are aimed at curbing our propensity to satisfy selfish desire. Such practices can be cast in a negative light (i.e., doing something because it is unpleasant or you don't like it), but the deepest tradition here emphasizes freedom. We seek to free ourselves from unhealthy attachments so as to live in harmony with our deepest desires. In the past it was common for people to induce physical discomfort— for example, by wearing abrasive cloth like burlap or wearing a small chain around one's waist—but now most Catholics see such practices as abusive. Today several practices could fall under this category: abstaining from food, literally fasting; abstaining from sleep, or vigiling during the night; abstaining from sexual activity; or in situations where one is presented with a choice, choosing the less appealing option. In a more positive light, a person might fast from the distorting influence of television or other media or from the negative self-talk that stifles his or her gifts; these can be fasts that lead the practitioner to being open to the call to social justice.

Almsgiving

The tradition of almsgiving is a rich vein in the Catholic spiritual tradition. The great spiritual teachers, such as Teresa of Ávila (1518–1582), insist that the goal of the spiritual life is love. Prayer and fasting have the potential of focusing our practice on ourselves, so almsgiving is an important balance. This love of others can take many forms: the self-giving of mutual spousal love, unselfish service to family members, especially children, or volunteering with a church or social agency. Since the 1960s, the Catholic Church has particularly emphasized the "preferential option for the poor," emphasizing the important scriptural theme that outsiders to the social structure (in the Hebrew scriptures these are orphans, widows, strangers) have a special claim on God's concern. So today "almsgiving" might involve working to overcome unjust systems as well as alleviating the suffering of the victims of those systems. A person who focuses only on prayer and fasting has an incomplete spiritual practice.

Guidance

Today a fourth category that could be added to these traditional three is guidance. How do we make decisions that lead to a life of generative love? In the past, people might rely on churches or local communities to provide guidance, but in the twenty-first century, with so many people alienated from churches and denominations, this question becomes ever more important. Several practices fall under this rubric. One is called *examen*, which means taking a few minutes each day to review the day's events to see where you are experiencing God's call and how you are responding. Another is discernment, which involves the effort to find the presence of the Spirit amid the various thoughts, feelings, and impressions that flow through your awareness and to come to decisions that are in harmony with the Spirit. A third is guidance itself, which can take many forms, from talking with a trusted friend over a cup of coffee or meeting with a group (such as a prayer group or a Quaker clearness committee) to seek out God's will, to meeting with a spiritual director. A seeker who is not checking his or her intuitions with some trusted other runs a serious risk of getting lost in self-delusion.

Avoiding Pitfalls

In considering these practices, we also need to be aware of pitfalls that are inherent in them. Perhaps the most pervasive danger is illustrated by the Pharisees in the Christian scriptures: deriving a sense of self-righteousness because one engages a practice, rather than focusing on the goal that the practice is meant to foster—in this case, love.

For prayer, people can pat themselves on the back because they do pray, or they can try to convince others that their method is the one everybody should try. For fasting, people can look down upon those who appear more lax in their practice. They can also fall into a distorted spirituality that says that the body and pleasure are always bad, so "if you like it, it's a sin." For almsgiving, people can suffer from the illusion that they have the "goodies" to give to the less fortunate rather than seeing the gift that the "other" has to offer them. The gift of the outsider is that he or she sees the failings of the social structure more clearly than do those who benefit from the structure.

SPIRITUAL DEVELOPMENT IN ROMAN CATHOLICISM

Within the Christian tradition, there are two fundamental understandings of spiritual development, which are not mutually exclusive. The "Saint Paul model" posits that people undergo a sudden and profound conversion that sets their life on a new path; the song "Amazing Grace" captures just such a sense. The "gradual model" posits that people's spiritual development is slow, taken in small steps, and worked out in daily living. The Roman Catholic tradition affirms the gradual approach while not denying that the Saint Paul experience sometimes happens. There is an oft-quoted saying of Saint Thomas Aquinas (1225–1244) that "grace builds on nature." So, God's grace works with the talents, flaws, and foibles of any particular individual to bring out that person's gifts toward loving service of others. We grow in holiness through the day-to-day struggles with our personal failings, shortcomings, and self-destructive tendencies, as well as our gifts and successes.

Given the breadth of writings from the great mystics, Catholics have any number of road maps for spiritual development. One, developed by the early theologian Origen (185–232), describes the spiritual journey in three stages. Beginners tend to use their mind and intelligence to reflect on a passage of scripture or a teaching, which Origen would label *meditation.* Once a person has undergone conversion, then he or she moves toward a prayer rooted in feelings— not only thinking about a Gospel story, but beginning to fall in love with Jesus (affective prayer). Finally, those who develop further in the spiritual journey begin to pray out of silence, as their prayer resembles a simple, wordless awareness of the presence of the Divine (mystical prayer). A seminal insight here is that people's prayer changes as they develop spiritually, and so a spiritual director needs to pay particular attention during the tender time of transition when someone's prayer is changing. When a person is experiencing frustration with the way he or she has been praying, has he or she gone off the path, or is the Spirit calling him or her to a deeper faith?

Other models abound. Gregory of Nyssa (353–395) wrote about *epektasis,* a perpetual ascent from the light of reason into a transcendent darkness, which itself is a mysterious form of knowing; here the knowledge of God never ends—the more one knows, the more one wants to know. Benedict (480–547) taught his monks about the twelve degrees of humility, each exhibiting a higher level of virtue. Bernard of Clairvaux (1090–1153) wrote of the four degrees of love: narcissistic love of self, love of God for one's own sake, love of God for God's sake, love of self for God's sake. Ignatius of Loyola (1491–1556) built his *Spiritual Exercises* around four weeks that involve sorrow for sin, conversion to discipleship, the suffering of the cross, and the triumph of resurrection. Teresa of Avila (1515–1582) described spiritual development in terms of seven stages of prayer in her masterpiece *The Interior Castle.* Her friend John of the Cross (1542–1591) wrote about an ascent toward God, in which one goes through dark nights, followed by illumination, to the heights of contemplation. Contemporary authors, such as James Fowler, Kathleen Fischer, and Elizabeth Liebert, build their theories of spiritual development on the work of developmental psychologists.

A typical modern practioner, then, has a wide variety of road maps from which to draw. The spiritual director may assist the practioner in finding a model of spiritual development that fits.

COMMON SPIRITUAL ISSUES FOR ROMAN CATHOLICS

At present, Roman Catholics constitute about 17 percent of the world's population, nearly 1.2 billion people. Speaking of "common spiritual issues" for such a vast population is a hopeless task. This section will focus, then, on North America, a society marked by the postmodern turn.

Roman Catholicism's relationship to postmodernity is perhaps more complex than it is for most Christian denominations. On the one hand, Catholicism appears profoundly out of sync with the contemporary world; official church teaching, which probably does need to be distinguished from the views of many practicing Catholics, rejects the ordination of women, views homosexuality as intrinsically disordered, and contradicts contemporary attitudes about sexuality on a range of issues, from birth control to premarital sex. The sexual abuse crisis has brought to light the shortcomings of the church's ministers and even more the failure of bishops to protect victims. For all these reasons, many people, and young adults in particular, find the Catholic Church's teaching irrelevant.

On the other hand, scripture and tradition give Catholics a place to stand outside mainstream culture from which they can critique it. Catholicism understands the individual person as made in the divine image, and so it has maintained a sense of social justice in the face of the rampant consumerism that marks so much of the contemporary world. Through the sacramental principle, Catholicism has preserved artistic expression such as architecture, music, painting, and sculpture. Its rituals involve material objects, beautiful environment, and movement, not only reflection on the written word. The church has also kept alive the mystical tradition and the emphasis on spiritual practices. Other Christian denominations have in fact looked to Catholicism when seeking to revive their own spiritual practices.

How to provide spiritual direction to a person caught in this confusion? Contemporary society is posing questions, such as the ordination of women, which the tradition has not addressed before. New experiences may eventually lead to new teachings. One can, then, begin with the experience of the person seeking direction: Where does this person experience the Divine? And how does this person's experience relate to the tradition? Catholic theology has always acknowledged a "hierarchy of truths," so that some teachings (e.g., the Trinity and incarnation) are more important than others. Is this person's experience in conflict with those fundamental truths? The church has also recognized the primacy of individual conscience. For example, many LGBTQ Catholics would say that the tradition is simply wrong in condemning their orientation and that they, too, are part of the pilgrim church, and their sexuality does not violate their conscience. So, the suggestion here is to place the person's experience in dialogue with the church's tradition and see where the resulting discernment leads.

Finally, postmodernity and globalization have provoked another approach to religion: fundamentalism. This represents a rejection of moral and religious relativity and an assertion of truths about which one can be certain. This resurgence of fundamentalism can be seen across all religious traditions in the early twenty-first century. This same tendency can be seen in many young Catholics, who are seeking a solid basis for their moral and spiritual grounding. Here the spiritual director might encourage a person to become familiar with the breadth of this two-thousand-year tradition, which is home to a wide variety of theological positions and spiritual practices. Much of current fundamentalist approaches represent a recent (nineteenth century) viewpoint and are not reflective of the long history of the tradition.

For spiritual directors who have read this chapter, thank you for your service to seekers, whatever their religious tradition. This chapter summarizes some of the history, practices, and understandings of people with a background in Roman Catholicism. They, more than some, may appreciate your assistance in sorting through the questions posed by postmodernity. May you assist them both in realizing their full potential as persons and in offering their gifts to the world.

RESOURCES

Barry, William A., and William J. Connolly. *The Practice of Spiritual Direction.* Rev. 2nd ed. New York: HarperCollins, 2009.

Guenther, Margaret. *Holy Listening: The Art of Spiritual Direction.* (Lanham, MD: Rowman & Littlefield, 1992).

Houdek, Francis J. *Guided by the Spirit: A Jesuit Perspective on Spiritual Direction.* Chicago: Loyola Press, 1996.

Ruffing, Janet K. *To Tell the Sacred Tale: Spiritual Direction and Narrative.* Mahwah, N.J.: Paulist Press, 2011.

Rev. N. Graham Standish, PhD, MSW, is pastor of Calvin Presbyterian Church in Zelienople, Pennsylvania, and an adjunct professor at Pittsburgh Theological Seminary, focusing on spirituality and congregational life. He is author of six books and numerous articles and is a contributor to five books. He is also a therapist, spiritual director, and teacher (www.ngrahamstandish.org).

Spiritual Guidance and the Reformed Tradition

Rev. N. Graham Standish, PhD, MSW

MARTIN LUTHER AND HIS NINETY-FIVE THESES

On October 13, 1517, a young, obscure German monk named Martin Luther changed the world. No one had expected greatness from this man who spent his days studying scripture and teaching Greek in the town of Wittenberg.

As a member of the Augustinian order, Luther had been steeped in the writings, teachings, and monastic rules of Augustine, an early bishop of the Christian church, who was responsible for shaping much of the church's thinking on sinful human nature. Because Augustine had been consumed with his own sinfulness, his order institutionalized a deep concern with sin and purity—a concern that the young monk from Germany would share so deeply. Once ordained to the priesthood in 1507, Luther spilled wine on the altar whenever he celebrated Mass. His nervousness embarrassed him and convinced him of his sinfulness. What could he do to overcome it? He felt hopeless.

Part of his problem was the theology of the Catholic Church at the time, a theology influenced by Augustine. In Luther's time, the Catholic Church taught that a person must earn his or her salvation; God's grace isn't free. Salvation and eventual entry into heaven had a cost. Individuals could give money to the church for big projects either to earn entry into heaven or at least to carve out less time in purgatory. The doctrine of indulgences permitted people to purchase grace for a hefty sum or to earn their salvation through ascetic practices.

In the early 1500s, the Roman Catholic Church used the doctrine of indulgences as a massive fundraiser for building St. Peter's Basilica in Rome. The church sent clerics throughout Europe to sell thousands of small scrolls, all bearing the papal seal and bound with a red ribbon. Each scroll conferred an indulgence upon the person, promising limited grace that pardoned him or her for a portion of sin. Purchasing one or more scrolls promised the purchaser a decreased amount of time spent in purgatory (a place where sin is purged and the person is prepared for heaven) and hastened entry into heaven.

This whole theology of indulgences bothered the young Luther. He wondered how the church, or any person, could determine whether a deed was good enough to wash away sin. How could anyone determine if she or he had accumulated enough good deeds? He obsessed about this. He saw himself as among the worst of sinners, even though he was a priest, and he believed he was unfit for heaven. Certainly a wrathful God wouldn't forgive him for his sinfulness, even though he had done everything he could to outdo others in good works. He wanted a guarantee of forgiveness, but he worried that he would never be clean enough in the eyes of God. How could he, such a terrible sinner, do enough good to be rid of the stain of sin?

He tried everything to expiate his sin: he prayed fervently; he studied the Bible; he confessed and confessed and confessed. Still, all he could see in himself was sin. The more he tried to get rid of sin, the more he agonized over how deep it was. He was certain that he was too sinful to be an effective priest and that God would eventually strike him down. He fell into the depths of despair.

As a scholar of the Christian Scriptures and a reader of Greek, the monk read and prayed over scripture daily. One particular day, as he was working his way through the letters of Paul, he came across a passage in Paul's Epistle to the Romans. He had read it many, many times before, but this particular time he read it with fresh eyes. One particular sentence caught him: "For there is no distinction, since all have sinned and fall short of the glory of God; they are now justified by his grace as a gift, through the redemption that is in Christ Jesus, whom God put forward as a sacrifice of atonement by his blood, effective through faith" (Romans 3:22–25). He wondered whether this was true. Was this the real path to God? Are we really saved by grace as a free gift? If this was true, then the church has been straying from the Gospel for over one thousand years.

What did the young monk do? He did what any religious scholar in his time did to make people aware of a new theological idea: he invited people to debate it. Luther went to All Saints Church in Wittenberg and nailed his proposal, ninety-five theses titled "Disputation of Martin Luther on the Power and Efficacy of Indulgences," onto the church door. He hoped that his proposal might lead to an orderly debate. He did not anticipate the church's response.

In his "Ninety-Five Theses," Luther argued that grace and salvation were free gifts given by God, unearned, accessed only through our faith in God, and that purchasing indulgences was merely a good act with no saving power. He was telling the church and the faithful that the practice of selling indulgences did nothing to get us into heaven or keep us out of hell. This idea rocked the church. Luther not only challenged almost one thousand years of church doctrine, but his ideas seriously threatened the church's fundraising efforts for building a holy basilica in Rome—a building that is still treasured today.

The church was so angry with Luther that it not only excommunicated him but also tried to have him killed. Luther went into hiding, yet his "Ninety-Five Theses" were printed, published, and distributed widely throughout Europe. By now, not only were the church's fundraising efforts threatened, but people were leaving the church and joining new movements based on Luther's message that we are saved by grace, not works. Martin Luther's insight led to an explosion of faith rooted in the Bible rather than in ecclesiastical tradition.

The courage of Luther's willingness to debate, as well as his insights into what he believed scripture taught, had a wide-ranging impact on people's understanding of God's grace, salvation, and serving God. Certainly Luther wasn't the first Christian to have discovered that the church's teachings were at odds with scripture. Others had made similar discoveries centuries before. Yet Luther's bold assertions pushed the church to confront the fact that it had let go of a crucial Christian belief, which is that Christians do acts of compassion to reflect God's love, not to procure it.

During Luther's time, the Roman Catholic Church allowed churches to use only one translation of the Bible, a centuries-old version translated solely into Latin. The church believed that scripture was so holy that only those ordained or in religious orders were holy enough to read it, and then only in Latin.

Besides Luther, others were determined to translate the Bible into their own languages so that the laity could also be inspired by it. Even one hundred years before Luther lived, others were committed to translating the Bible into a language that people could read themselves rather than Latin, which many individuals could no longer read or understand. For example, John Wycliffe, in England, during the fourteenth century was burned at the stake for daring to translate the Bible into common languages. Among those sharing this determination were Christians in Switzerland such as the Swiss pastor Huldrych Zwingli in Zurich, the German Martin Bucer in Strasbourg, and the Frenchman John Calvin in Geneva. These were the early heroes of the "Reformed" Protestant movement. They were determined to build on what Luther had offered to the world—a Christian faith grounded in scripture. While Zwingli and Bucer were approximately the same age as Luther, Calvin was twenty years younger and became influential in the 1530s. Among those who call themselves "Reformed" (whom others often call Calvinists), John Calvin has been the most influential.

JOHN CALVIN AND THE REFORMED TRADITION

John Calvin was born and raised in Noyon, in the northern border region of France.[1] As a teen, he had been assigned as a chaplain to the cathedral in Noyon, and as a young adult, he studied law at the University of Orleans. In the 1520s and 1530s, Protestant sympathizers were being persecuted in France, so Calvin broke with the Roman Catholic Church around 1530 and accepted an invitation from Martin Bucer in Strasbourg, Switzerland, to help him form a Protestant church there.

Later, Calvin moved to Geneva, Switzerland, where he sought to take the Protestant Reformation a step further. He wanted to bring scripture to bear on everyday religious and political life. For him, it wasn't enough that the laity read scripture. He wanted to apply scripture to the communal life of congregations, towns, and cities. He wanted to bind Christians to the kind of communal living that can be found in Acts, as well as in Paul's epistles.

Beginning with its publication in 1536, John Calvin's *Institutes of Christian Religion* became the seminal work on extending scripture to create a political structure for the local church and the community. Calvin continued to edit and revise his *Institutes* over the next twenty years. These *Institutes* remain influential for all the denominations that harken back to the Swiss Reformation. These denominations include all Presbyterian denominations, the United Church of Christ,[2] the Disciples of Christ, the Reformed Church, the Christian and Missionary Alliance Church, and even many independent, nondenominational evangelical churches that maintain the theological and political influence of Calvin.

All of these denominations consider themselves "Reformed," which is a term that is explained in the phrase *ecclesia reformata, semper reformanda*, or "church reformed, always being reformed." What this means is that the Reformed Protestant movement and its people had undergone a reformation of faith, yet were still always open to the ongoing movement of Christ and the Holy Spirit that leads us to continual transformation and reformation. In other words, the Reformed movement understands itself and its individual members as having been reformed by God's grace and Spirit and as always ready to be reformed again. To grow spiritually means to be open constantly to God's reforming work. The primary foundation of that reformation is Christ's Word in scripture.

REFORMED SPIRITUALITY

In many ways, Reformed Christianity is a theological movement with spiritual implications. I say this in this way because it helps us understand how a Presbyterian or a Congregationalist or a Christian Missionary and Alliance member might approach spiritual growth. The Swiss Reformation was very much an intellectual movement with practical outcomes. The attempt of the Reformation's leaders was to unite people in a stronger theology rooted in a deeper understanding of the Bible. John Calvin himself was a biblical and legal scholar. He approached the Bible with a sense of scholarly understanding, reading the original Greek and Hebrew texts of scripture in those languages, and translating them into German and French. When he read scripture, he wasn't just trying to apply it to his life then and there. He delved into it, trying to understand who wrote a book or passage, what was going on at the time of the writing, and what the writer meant. He wanted people to read the Bible with a rigorous mind. While Calvin cared about prayer and spiritual growth, he approached both topics intellectually. This is important to understand because it explains why those coming from the Reformed tradition can be so "heady" in their approach to spirituality. Individuals in Reformed-style churches can sometimes get caught up in theological debates, which allows them to mask subtly their spiritual yearnings and struggles, using intellectualization to repress their spiritual restlessness. Theology is a discipline that helps explain spiritual experiences. It gives structure to what can otherwise be mystifying. However, sometimes Christians substitute theological thinking for spiritual practice and awareness, and that's often a problem for those of the Reformed tradition seeking spiritual guidance. They approach God mainly with their heads and struggle with a spirituality of the heart and body.

A Reformed spiritually is, above all else, a biblically informed spirituality. It is not rooted so much in centuries-old traditions of "this is how we do things," but in an ever-ongoing process of "this is what Christ is saying to me now." Because Reformed spirituality is always biblical, it is very difficult to distill a Reformed approach to simple tenets (although many Reformed thinkers try to do so). The Bible is able always to speak afresh to people of any age. This has been the experience of Christians throughout history when they have been allowed to read scripture. The center of a Reformed spirituality is to live out scripture in our age, our context, and our daily situation.

The implication of this approach to spirituality and life is the understanding that to grow spiritually we must be rooted in scriptural guidance. This means that to be spiritual guides with Reformed Christians we must be similarly rooted in scripture. A spiritual guide who has been trained in all the "right" guidance techniques will still struggle if she or he does not have a fairly solid foundation in understanding scripture, as well as having had an experience of grappling with how to apply scripture to daily life.

SPIRITUAL GUIDANCE IN THE REFORMED TRADITION

There are particular beliefs that are central to a Reformed understanding of spiritual growth, and understanding them can help to form a Reformed approach to spiritual guidance.

Sin and Grace

The Reformed approach is very clear in its teachings about both sin and grace. From a Reformed perspective, we understand that sin is our primary problem. Our sin separates us from both God's love and God's will, not because God pushes us away, but because in sin we push God away. Defining *sin* is very difficult. The Greek word for sin in the Christian scriptures is *amartia*, or *hamartia*. The word literally means "missing the mark." It's a Greek archery term that describes an arrow that has been shot but has gone wide of the mark. When we sin, we may aim at what God wants, but we miss the mark God has set for us. Or, we aim at other marks instead of those at which God wants us to aim. Sin is anything that causes us to miss the mark God has set for us. Another way of thinking about sin is to use the Reformed theologian Paul Tillich's well-known definition, which is that sin is an estrangement from God.[3] It is any thought, action, or inaction that leads us to become alienated and estranged from both God and God's will. This is a broader definition that takes into account not just our behavior but our motivations.

While much of what John Calvin wrote about had to do with the reality of human sin and our total depravity because of sin, he was always very careful to point out that sin is nothing compared to God's grace. Calvin said, "It can all be summed up like this: Christ is given to us by the goodness of God; we grasp and possess him by faith; then we obtain a twofold benefit. First, when we are reconciled by the righteousness of Christ, God becomes a gracious Father instead of a judge. Second, when we are sanctified by his Spirit, we reach after integrity and purity of life."[4] For Calvin, out of our faith in God, sin is overcome as we become reformed through the free gift of God's grace working in our lives.

The Reformed tradition always emphasizes both the reality of sin and the greater reality of grace. To grow spiritually in the Reformed tradition means to grow ever more in a faith that opens us to God's grace. We cannot overcome sin through our own means alone. It requires a faith in God that opens us to the work of God's grace. The problem for many Reformed Christians is the tendency to emphasize sin over grace. It's very easy to become judgmental about someone's sin in spiritual guidance, whether it is the person's extramarital affair, his struggle with online porn, her constant in-fighting with family and church members, his constant defensiveness, and more.

A spiritual guide needs to recognize that her Reformed client's struggle with sin is also the guide's struggle with sin and that her task as a spiritual guide is to point the person toward God's transforming grace. This means recognizing that what leads the person to live a more whole and holy life is not a teeth-gritting struggle to overcome sin by means of personal strength and effort, but an encounter with God's grace that leads to conversion and transformation.

The Reformed understanding of transforming grace is articulated throughout scripture. In the Gospel of John, for example, Jesus explains this process to a teacher named Nicodemus:

> Now there was a Pharisee named Nicodemus, a leader of the Jews. He came to Jesus by night and said to him, "Rabbi, we know that you are a teacher who has come from God; for no one can do these signs that you do apart from the presence of God." Jesus answered him, "Very truly, I tell you, no one can see the kingdom of God without being born from above." Nicodemus said to him, "How can anyone be born after having grown old? Can one enter a second time into the mother's womb and be born?" Jesus answered, "Very truly, I tell you, no one can enter the kingdom of God without being born of water and Spirit." (John 3:1–5)

This passage teaches the spiritual guide to assist her Reformed client to "see the kingdom of God" at work all around him and to invite him to become open to God's transforming power so that he can live in this kingdom.

So our task as guides is not necessarily to implicate our clients in their moral failings, but to help open our clients up to God's grace, which does the transforming. The client still has to work on his moral and ethical struggles, but we guides recognize that he will get only so far on his own efforts alone. God's grace is needed if he is to grow and become more open to God, and so our task as guides is to help lead the person to open up to God's grace by working on the person's faith—the person's trust in God.

Surrender

The emphasis on trust in God leads to another general tenet of the Reformed tradition, and therefore of Reformed spiritual guidance.

To grow spiritually means to be willing to surrender ourselves to the Trinity—to the Creator's purpose for us, to Christ's presence in and around us, and to the Spirit's ongoing work in and through us. The Reformed point of view recognizes that we all resist God's will and work in our lives. We do it without thinking about it because we want to be in charge; we want to dictate the terms of our lives, even if that means falling into self-destructiveness. The Reformed perspective teaches that until we surrender to Christ's saving presence and work in our lives, we will always be a bit insecure and uncertain about our lives. The way to overcome this unease is to give ourselves over to Christ's presence. To overcome sin requires God's transforming grace, but the way to become open to this grace is through surrender to God.

Surrender can either be slow or sudden. Sudden surrender is that immediate, whole-person desire to give ourselves over completely to Christ. This experience is often called a "born-again" or conversion experience. Slow surrender is the ongoing struggle to become transformed by God over time. Either way, the point of surrender is to become completely open to God's grace. From the point of view of spiritual guidance, it means that the guide needs to be constantly inviting the client to surrender a bit more, a bit more, a bit more to God's grace. Part of the answer to anyone's struggle is the fact that she hasn't given her will over to God. You need not be shy about pointing this out to her. In fact, it will be helpful to explore the struggle to surrender by saying, "Let's look at how you resist the Spirit," "I notice that you have a hard time putting aside your will in order to let God's will work," or "What keeps you from surrendering your will to God's will?"

Again, those in the Reformed tradition gain inspiration for this by looking at scriptural models, such as John 15:1–5, in which Jesus says:

> I am the true vine, and my Father is the vinegrower. He removes every branch in me that bears no fruit. Every branch that bears fruit he prunes to make it bear more fruit. You have already been cleansed by the word that I have spoken to you. Abide in me as I abide in you. Just as the branch cannot bear fruit by itself unless it abides in the vine, neither can you unless you abide in me. I am the vine, you are the branches. Those who abide in

> me and I in them bear much fruit, because apart from
> me you can do nothing.

This passage gives us a model of surrender that says that unless we abide, or live, in Christ, we cannot bear fruit in our lives. As guides, our task is to help those we are guiding find ways to surrender, if only in small steps, so that they can live more in the vine.

Calling

Central to the Reformed tradition is the idea that everyone has a calling from Christ that is unique to that person's life and situation. In some Christian traditions, the idea of call, or "vocation," is limited to careers in religious occupations such as pastor, priest, or religious order. John Calvin believed that everyone has a unique calling in life and that pastors, elders, and deacons are ordained because their calling is to specialized public ministry. That's not the same as saying that a pastor's calling is holier than another person's calling. A pastor's, elder's, or deacon's calling is functional in the sense that it is an ordination to a function in the church. This function does not make the person holier than non-clergy, only set apart.

The Reformed tradition recognizes that God uses all people to do God's work in the world. According to Calvin, "But because [God] does not live among us physically (Matt. 26:11), to make his will clear from his own lips, he uses the ministry of men, making them his substitutes. He does not transfer his rights and honor to them, but does his work through them, as any workman would use a tool for his purpose."[5] In other words, each and every one of us has a calling, which is to serve God in our context.

Every career and work is part of that calling. So, the mother and father are called to be parents and spouses. The policeman, doctor, engineer, television producer, and more are all called to do what they do. The question is always the extent to which they seek God's call and will in each of their "vocations." The more they seek God's voice to lead them in what they do, the more they are able to let what they do embody Christ's presence, the Spirit's work, and the Father's purpose.

So, what are the implications of the idea of "calling" for the spiritual guide? The implications are that the guide has a primary responsibility to help the client constantly seek God's calling in her life. Questions helpful in any session are "What do you sense God is calling you to do?" and "How is God calling you to be?" These are profound and fundamental questions because they get right to the core of who and what we serve in life and how we live out that service.

So many people are growing up and learning to serve their own desires or the desires of the larger culture without ever asking whether these are desires that God has called them to serve. Seeking to discern a call is not that prominent a theme among the culture at large, and even among Christians it has become less prominent. As a guide, though, I become responsible for holding the client accountable to seeking to discern that calling. I'm going to consistently ask the client what he senses God calling him to do, what's getting in the way of his ability to sense this calling, and what would help him ascertain the call.

Sovereignty of God

A final Reformed tenet that will be primary for those seeking to offer spiritual guidance to clients in the Reformed perspective is the idea that God is in charge of everything, which Reformed Christians refer to as "the sovereignty of God." Ultimately, Reformed Christians all agree that God is in charge of everything, God has created everything for God's purposes, and to become mature means to offer ourselves, sin and all, to God's purposes for us and for the world.

One of the Reformed doctrines that seems to cause a stir among those who aren't from the Reformed tradition, but that reflects this idea that God is sovereign, is the idea of *predestination,* or, in biblical terms, *election.* Calvin and the other Reformers developed this belief from the apostle Paul, who had mentioned it in his letters to the Romans, Timothy, and Titus. Jesus also uses this term in the Gospels to designate those chosen by God. The underlying idea of election or predestination is that God chooses who is or isn't saved. Paul used the term *election,* while the Reformers used the term *predestination.*

Either way, the point is that only God has the power to choose who will or won't be saved. God has all the power. God gets to choose, not us, and God's choice is based on God's criteria, not the power of our good deeds. Calvin was trying to set the beliefs of the Reformed movement apart from the Roman Catholic Church, which taught that good deeds were needed for salvation. Predestination trusts in God's sovereignty rather than our works: "God is in charge of choosing my destiny, and since God is a God of grace, I will trust in God's choice." Predestination is a doctrine rooted in God's sovereignty over everything. Salvation is God's work, not ours.

Many people, Christian and non-Christian, argue that because of predestination, they could never become Presbyterian or part of any other Reformed church. They say that they don't believe in predestination because they believe in free will. Predestination believes in free will, too. Predestination is not the same as predetermination, which is the idea that God predetermines every action we take and that we are simply puppets on a string. Predestination says that we have the freedom to choose how we will live, as well as the extent to which we will allow grace to live in us. But God gets to choose, based on whatever criteria God uses—we believe the criteria is love and grace—whether or not we will be saved. Those in the Reformed tradition often disagree, and even argue, over who God predestines for salvation. Some would say that God chooses everyone. Others say that God chooses only some. Others still, who believe in "double predestination," say that God chooses ahead of time to send some to heaven and some to hell. John Calvin had a simple way of dealing with all of these disputes. He would say that we can never know for sure whether or not God has chosen us but that if we are attracted to prayer, worship, reading scripture, and serving God, that's evidence that we have been chosen.

Why all this talk about predestination? Because it is a concept emphasizing that God is in charge of everything and Lord over all. Also, since God is love and loves each of us deeply, we don't have to work to get God's attention or procure God's forgiveness. God already loves and forgives. So predestination teaches that what's left for us is to surrender and trust God to lead us. For those of us serving as spiritual guides, this means that part of our task is to help people learn to trust in God's power and grace. It means that part of what we do is to help people to have hope in their lives, to know that even though life might be difficult, God has a purpose for each and every person, and God is using God's power to mold the universe to God's purpose. Each of us has a calling in this purpose. Our sin does not have the power to obstruct it, and grace can lead us into it. So, the task of the spiritual guide is to help those being guided to realize that God is calling them to a grace-filled life and to help them become open to that life.

As a spiritual guide, my role isn't to determine whether or not a person is saved. My role is simply to encourage my client to trust in God's power and to do whatever he can to live in it. The point is simply to help the client to see, accept, and trust that God is everything.

EXPECTATIONS OF THE SPIRITUAL GUIDE IN REFORMED TRADITIONS

Determining what makes a Reformed approach to spiritual guidance different from all others is not an easy task. Every Christian tradition emphasizes much of what the Reformed tradition does. Certainly Roman Catholic spiritual guides encourage their clients to live according to the guidance of scripture. Episcopalian and Anglican guides emphasize that God is sovereign. Lutheran guides emphasize God's grace in response to our sin. Evangelical and Pentecostal guides emphasize the need for surrender.

What makes the Reformed tradition helpful for spiritual guides probably is the simplicity of its aim. Reformed clients recognize scripture as their primary authority and so guides need not be as concerned with also helping the person fit into the mold of the Reformed tradition. The focus is always on the extent to which an individual is listening for God's calling in her life, surrendering to that calling, trusting in the power of God, and allowing grace to lift her up rather than wallowing in sin, guilt, and more.

At the same time, Reformed clients will have expectations of spiritual guides. They need to be familiar with scripture to a great extent, meaning that they should read the Bible regularly. The Reformed tradition does not demand memorization of the Bible or argument over finer points of interpretation. There is freedom of interpretation within the tradition, not one overbearing interpretive stance. Still, the Reformed client will expect spiritual guides to have taken on the struggle with how to live out scripture in their lives so that they can help others to live out scripture in theirs.

NOTES

1. Biographical information taken from Herman J. Selderhuis, *John Calvin: A Pilgrim's Life* (Nottingham, UK: InterVarsity Press, 2009).
2. The United Church of Christ was created in 1957 by the merger of German-heritage Evangelical (Lutheran) and Reformed (Calvinist) churches with

English-heritage Congregational and Christian (related to the Disciples of Christ) churches.

3. Paul Tillich, *The Essential Tillich: An Anthology of the Writings of Paul Tillich*, ed. F. Forrester Church (New York: Macmillan, 1987), 165.

4. John Calvin, *The Institutes of Christian Religion*, eds. Tony Lane and Hilary Osborne (Grand Rapids, MI: Baker Book House, 1987), 181.

5. Ibid., 243.

Susan S. Phillips, PhD, executive director and professor at New College Berkeley (part of Berkeley's Graduate Theological Union), is a University of California, Berkeley–trained sociologist as well as a spiritual director and supervisor. She teaches in San Francisco Theological Seminary's Spiritual Direction Institute, supervises New College Berkeley's Group Spiritual Direction Program, and is the author of *Candlelight: Illuminating the Art of Spiritual Direction.*

Spiritual Guidance in the Evangelical Christian Tradition

Susan S. Phillips, PhD

For hundreds of years the word *evangelical* has been a changeable yet resilient descriptor of a doctrinal and cultural stream within Christianity, enduring through history and across geography as nations and denominations have formed. The label has been potent and at times politicized, embraced, and rejected for a multitude of reasons. As an adjective deriving from Greek, *evangelical*, like *gospel*, its theological cousin of Old English provenance, has pointed to the centrality of Christian Scripture and communicated the joy that faith bestows. Literally, *euangélion* (*eu* = good + *angelion* = message) means "good news" (gospel). In the sixteenth century, William Tyndale wrote that *evangelical* signifies "good, merry, glad, and joyful tidings" that make the heart glad and the person "sing, dance, and leap for joy."[1]

Today most evangelical Christians would introduce themselves as merely "Christian" when meeting someone from whom they hope to receive soul care. Nevertheless, they have been shaped by a particular tradition that has theological, historical, and cultural components, all of which affect how they seek and receive spiritual guidance.

A BRIEF HISTORY OF EVANGELICAL CHRISTIANITY

Theology

The Gospel of Jesus Christ is the foundation, guide, and hope of those who claim the name "evangelical." A number of key affirmations flow from this Gospel grounding. Evangelicals embrace a Christian orthodoxy that affirms Jesus's nature as fully divine and human and the sanctification and salvation—by grace alone—of those who love and follow him. The Bible is viewed as the supreme authority in understanding God (theology) and in living in accordance with God's truth and love (discipleship). Faith is arrived at by conversion, a transformation of one's self through relationship with the Holy One who was made known, most clearly, in Jesus Christ. Evangelicals believe in the priesthood of all believers, that every individual is called to a life saturated and informed by faith and God's call to care for the world, especially those in need. In this way, evangelicalism is a form of Christian spirituality, for it is concerned with the lived experience of the one who follows Jesus Christ in everyday life. The evangelical tradition is marked by a transdenominationalism, or ecumenism, that recognizes fellow Christians by their commitment to God's Good News rather than membership in a particular religious affiliation.

The Reformation Period

Some evangelical historians claim that *evangelical* can be used to refer "to all those movements in history that have attempted to restore a vital historic Christianity to the church at those moments when the church has become dead in spirit or has departed from the faith."[2] Lists of such historical movements might include monastic renewals prior to the Reformation as well as medieval upsurges of spirituality. However, a brief overview of the word's use usually begins in the early sixteenth century when *evangelical* was used to describe European Protestants, as distinct from Roman Catholics. In particular, the Protestants who followed Martin Luther used the term during the Reformation to distinguish themselves from the Calvinists, who were designated as "Reformed," and a number of Lutheran synods in Europe and the United States still officially identify their bodies as "evangelical." The word is used to denote Protestants today in parts of Latin America, Europe, and the Middle East, where it distinguishes Protestants from Roman Catholics and from Orthodox Christians.

The Great Awakenings

In the seventeenth century, members of the Puritan party in the Church of England who identified with the Reformation called themselves evangelicals. In those early years, evangelical Christianity was a hybrid of the Reformed emphasis on doctrinal orthodoxy and the pietist emphasis on the state of a person's heart and his or her "personal relationship" with God. In the eighteenth century, evangelicalism as a movement was born through transatlantic revivals led by John and Charles Wesley in England and by George Whitefield and Jonathan Edwards in the American colonies. The revivals were the seedbed for international evangelicalism, which is thriving today in a variety of manifestations, such as the World Evangelical Alliance.

The eighteenth century revivals had a significant effect on Christian spirituality in that they placed great emphasis on the life-changing experience of conversion. So much attention was placed on one's own salvation by conversion—and the related mission of bringing others to conversion—that attention to spiritual formation and spiritual disciplines, such as spiritual guidance, were neglected. Evan Howard summarizes this period's effect on American evangelicalism: "From the various revivals of this period, and from the 'revivalism' that developed from them, evangelicalism has inherited … an interest in the experience of initial conversion, an ecumenical openness to those of kindred experience, and an orientation toward evangelism and missions."[3] Many scholars see this First Great Awakening (c. 1734–1750) as a precursor to and democratic force in the American Revolution.

Expressive of Jesus's call to be salt and light in the world, American evangelicalism has been committed to activism on a number of social and political fronts, never in a univocal fashion, and with a distinct change in tenor over the centuries. In nineteenth-century America, evangelicals were known by the religious fervor of the Second Great Awakening (1800–1840) and their commitment to working for social welfare (e.g., prison reform, orphanage establishment, abolition, the creation of hospitals and schools) and missionary endeavors. The Third Great Awakening (1880–1910) extended the commitment to missionary work and the implementation of the Social Gospel.

The Modern Period

In the early twentieth century, the term *evangelical* (sometimes prefixed with *neo-*) was adopted by American post-fundamentalists, including Billy Graham, Fuller Theological Seminary, Wheaton College, and a large number of parachurch organizations. This manifestation of evangelicalism in the United States is seen by its adherents as maintaining biblical orthodoxy (in contrast, evangelicals believe, to the stance of liberal Protestantism), as well as social engagement and cultural literacy (in contrast, evangelicals believe, to the stance of Christian fundamentalism).

In the late 1970s, the Religious Right developed in the United States, claiming itself the "moral majority" and striving to bring American evangelicals into the Republican Party (some have called this period a Fourth Great Awakening). Prior to that time, evangelicals had been predominantly Democratic, but by the year 2000, 68 percent of white evangelicals (who make up one-quarter of the U.S. population) voted for George W. Bush for president, and in 2004, 78 percent of them voted for him. Frances FitzGerald claims that "white evangelicals have become the GOP's most reliable constituency, and they normally provide about a third of the Republican votes."[4] Partisan association with the word *evangelical* has caused socially and politically liberal evangelicals to abandon it.

Postmodern Evangelicalism

Many American evangelicals in the early twenty-first century who disassociate themselves from the contemporary politically partisan use of the word embrace the worldwide fellowship of evangelicals (this includes the most rapidly growing churches in the world today, along with the Pentecostal churches). Some of these Christians identify themselves as "progressive evangelicals," "post-evangelicals," or as part of the "emerging church movement."

The emerging church is characterized by evangelical roots, a desire to be prophetic (to some degree provocative and anti-establishment), and concern with orthopraxy (how to live according to the Gospel and to "be and do church"). The concern with the lived experience of faith has a deep history in the tradition, but over the centuries it became contained (possibly entombed) within a modernist paradigm of thought that focused on reasons for faith and propositions of truth, rather than on what we today call "spirituality."

Those offering spiritual care and guidance to evangelical Christians encounter significant differences in orientation across the generations. Older evangelicals who became adults just after World War II are interested in apologetics, the reasons for faith that can then be offered to nonbelievers in the hope of their conversion. Evangelicals who were young adults in the 1970s through the 1990s are characterized as more pragmatic, less convinced by objective evidence for the claims of faith, largely ahistorical in their religious identification, and more attentive to experience.

Christians identifying with the evangelicalism of the new millennium, whether using the word *evangelical* or not, retain belief in the truth of Christ, yet, in keeping with their postmodern leanings, are less sure that they know the whole of that truth. They are relationally focused and praxis oriented, emphasizing devotion and right living. They are also more open to spiritual understandings and practices from the whole history of the Christian church, especially the premodern church, and these include contemplative practices of prayer and worship, adaptations of monasticism, pilgrimage, and spiritual direction. Progressive evangelicals tend to be politically liberal—more often part of the Democratic Party, with interests in the abolition of modern slavery, AIDS prevention worldwide, and the relief of global hunger.

UNDERSTANDINGS OF SPIRITUAL DEVELOPMENT AND GUIDANCE IN EVANGELICAL CHRISTIANITY

The recently published *Dictionary of Christian Spirituality*, edited by scholars at evangelical seminaries, contains entries for spiritual direction, formation, and mentoring, as well as ones devoted to early saints of the church and pre-Reformation practices, such as *lectio divina* and the Ignatian prayer of *examen*. This signals a tremendous shift within the evangelical tradition toward spiritual formation and the disciplines that aid it. It marks a response by the evangelical tradition to a need felt by many Christians.

A Gap in Spiritual Development

In the late twentieth century, historians observed a "sanctification gap" in evangelical Christianity, a deficit in attention to the believer's experience in the days and years between the moment of conversion and ultimate expectations of a life after death.[5] Indicating a persistence in this gap, in 2009, while reflecting on thirty years of spiritual formation ministry, Richard Foster lamented that the "overall dysfunction in our culture is so pervasive that it is nearly impossible for us to have a clear vision of spiritual progress."[6]

This gap widened over the centuries, for immediate post-Reformation concerns with piety and communal practices of devotion indicate keen attention to sanctification. In the sixteenth and seventeenth centuries, Puritan ministers counseled people with psychological problems as well as those with spiritual and moral ones. Puritan ministers counseled (often in tandem with physicians), offered behavioral advice (e.g., be active, avoid solitude, spend time with friends), spiritual guidance, and scriptural counsel. Some of the guidelines that shape present-day spiritual direction are evident in Puritan practice. For example, a Puritan minister wrote that a minister "must identify himself with his consultants, sharing their sorrow and their tears, and he must be a good listener who guards their secrets and, where the conscience is unduly disturbed, is not censorious."[7]

Through the first centuries of the United States, spiritual guidance diminished in priority in the life of American clergy, and on the whole, Christians were left without spiritual guidance. Evangelical Christians have been slow to acknowledge the need for soul care and have also been wary of the burgeoning secular psychotherapeutic professions. As Wesley Tracy put it, "One of the problems with evangelical spirituality is that Christians have no one to talk to."[8]

The Rise of Modern Evangelical Spiritual Guidance

Beginning in the 1920s with Anton Boisen's challenge to the American church to become involved in people's emotional ills and health, there was born a movement to train clergy in counseling theory and techniques. In the early 1930s, the Council for Clinical Pastoral Training was formed with the help of Seward Hiltner, and in the 1940s Rogerian client-centered therapy was endorsed by the pastoral counseling movement. Evangelicals were slower to embrace psychotherapy, but by the 1970s some evangelical seminaries were emphasizing counseling and establishing counseling centers. By 1982, the impulse toward counseling had become so much a part of evangelical Christianity that a professor of psychology at evangelical Fuller Theological Seminary's Graduate School of Psychology could write of "God's gift of Christian psychology to the church."[9] The amount of time evangelical pastors spent counseling parishioners increased by 300 percent between the late 1950s and late 1970s, up to just under ten hours a week. By 1981, 53 percent of all Protestant seminaries in the United States required students to take a course in the area of pastoral care and counseling.[10]

The secular mental health professions' gradual acceptance of spirituality (an acceptance widespread throughout the culture during the past thirty years), the training of clergy in soul-care practices of various kinds, the rise of laypersons trained in Christian spiritual guidance, including the arts of spiritual direction, mentoring, paraprofessional counseling, and discipling, have contributed to the rapprochement between psychotherapy and Christianity in the United States. Just as laypeople were involved in soul care during the early Protestant period, so, too, they were significant in the development of late-twentieth-century soul-care practices.

Sanctification and Guidance

For evangelical Christians, the Good News of Jesus Christ offers the grounding vision of spiritual progress. Scripture claims we are to be "sanctified by the Spirit to be obedient to Jesus Christ" (1 Peter 1:2). We are enjoined to follow Christ (John 21:19), grow in grace (2 Peter 3:18), and become rooted and grounded in love (Ephesians 3:17). According to Christian historian William Bouwsma, "The essential element in the Christian idea of adulthood is … the capacity for growth, which is assumed to be a potentiality of any age of life."[11] Yet, as Dallas Willard, a prominent exponent of evangelical spiritual formation, claims,

> We have for most of the twentieth century been in a period of time when, in all segments, the Christian churches have been distracted from the central task of teaching their people how to live the spiritual life in a way that brings them progressively to enjoy the character of Christ as their own.[12]

In short, evangelical churches have neglected spiritual formation, and that neglect has extended to spiritual guidance.

SPIRITUAL PRACTICES IN EVANGELICAL CHRISTIANITY

Evangelicals are committed to revival and reformation. Revival is a rekindling of life, and the early revivalists were caught up in a spontaneous freshening of God's Spirit, though most of them had been baptized participants in Christian fellowship for their whole lives. They experienced an awakening of their souls to God's forgiveness and grace, and that awakening spilled out to the world in movements of reform. The spark of revival ignited intentional efforts to restore the liveliness of Christian faith through engagement in missions, disciplines, and worship.

Spiritual Disciplines

Spiritual disciplines are means of God's grace that reform the heart of the believer, shaping and sanctifying the person's soul in the way of faith, hope, and love. They are ways of keeping the soul fueled, on track, and progressing after the initial spark of conversion has taken place. Disciplines of spiritual guidance that have been embraced by evangelical Christians include Bible study, pastoral counseling, and hearing believers' testimonies. These disciplines affect personal and corporate spiritual formation, but engagement in these disciplines is to be voluntary and is, on the whole, uncoordinated by churches. Today there is a kind of ancient-modern movement afoot among evangelicals through which some people are rediscovering the spiritually salutary possibilities of ancient spiritual disciplines, such as observing weekly or occasional Sabbaths from work, observing daily hours for prayer, and making pilgrimages, as well as those disciplines that are more explicitly in the domain of seeking guidance, such as slowly praying biblical passages, engaging in spiritual direction, and living in intentional quasi-monastic communities.

There have been those on the contemporary evangelical scene, Richard Foster and Dallas Willard included, who have strongly advocated for attention to spiritual formation and its associated disciplines. During the past twenty years, evangelical seminaries have offered courses on spiritual disciplines for those studying to be clergy as well as for interested laypeople. Evangelical para-church organizations, like InterVarsity Christian Fellowship for college students and Young Life for high-school-age Christians, now regularly teach spiritual disciplines to their members, and InterVarsity Press's new imprint Formatio is dedicated to books about Christian spiritual formation.

One of the disciplines becoming increasingly familiar to evangelicals is spiritual direction, an ancient practice that has been rediscovered by evangelical Christians in the past thirty years. Into our circus-like culture of caffeinated performance and narcotized consumption, spiritual direction extends a quiet space for listening for God, to one's self, and to another person. Dietrich Bonhoeffer, a theologian greatly admired by evangelicals, wrote that "the first service that one owes to others in the fellowship consists in listening to them…. But Christians have forgotten that the ministry of listening has been committed to them by Him who is Himself the great listener and whose work they should share."[13] That "first service" is increasingly acknowledged as necessary by evangelical Christians.

SPIRITUAL ISSUES IN EVANGELICAL CHRISTIANITY

Evangelicals seeking spiritual guidance come with many issues common to most Christians. What follows is a discussion of some issues that may have a particular coloration for evangelicals.

Understanding of Scripture

Evangelical Christians are biblically literate and receptive. "Jesus loves me, this I know, for the Bible tells me so" is a song deep in the hearts of those in this tradition. They want to know how spiritual direction is sanctioned by their scriptural faith, and they also resonate with insights drawn from scripture. They are, in this, akin to the two people who were met by Jesus on the road to Emmaus a few days after Jesus's execution. Jesus drew them out by asking what they were talking about. He listened and did so in such a way that they were in touch with the complexity of their thoughts and feelings—hopes, fears, and confusion. When he spoke, he spoke to them concerning their "issues" and did so through the lens of scripture (Luke 24:13–35).

A spiritual guide working with evangelical Christians would be well served by studying scripture in a spiritual way. Many evangelicals have heard scripture preached in a way that leaves them with a list of do's and don'ts, but no real insight into the particular challenges they face. How does scripture offer exemplars, images, and metaphors that help us navigate our lives today? In our time-stuffed culture, people have few opportunities to reflect on scripture in this way, much less to view their own lives through those reflections.

Sin and Grace

In the gap between the real and the ideal in our lives—that place of sanctification—we all fall short of God's glory (Romans 3:23) and don't behave as we know we ought to behave (James 4:17), yet we trust that we are being transformed into Christ's image by God's grace (2 Corinthians 3:18). An evangelical Christian understands sin to be real in a way that some segments of our culture deny. An evangelical Christian also affirms belief in a God who is love, forever welcomes the repentant wanderer (as did the father in Jesus's parable of the prodigal son), and calls us to forgive and love our enemies.

Evangelicals often have an overdeveloped sense of their own sinfulness. They may experience themselves as unforgivable and sometimes have come to this impression as a result of the teachings and actions of Christian communities in which they have participated. A spiritual guide can be an exemplar of loving attention to what's real for the one listened to: both that person's genuine sin and also his or her fundamental belovedness. Evangelical Christians, like all Christians, long to know and be known by the One who has called them by name, and who loves and redeems them. Practices of spiritual guidance can attune people's hearts to the voice of the One they seek, whether they hear that voice through scripture, community, tradition, creation, or prayer. Evangelical Christians may need encouragement to release their guilt and receive the gift of God's love.

Unmediated Prayer and Agency

As descendants of the Reformation, evangelical Christians affirm each believer's direct relationship with God through Jesus Christ by the Holy Spirit. Qualms about spiritual guidance develop around the possibility that someone else will presume to come between the believer and God, either as a vehicle of confession or as a channel of instruction. Jesus invites each of us to pray to the One who is our Father in heaven. Each of us is examined by God who is the "knower of hearts" (Acts 1:24), and a spiritual guide accompanies the other as his or her heart is opened before God. So, too, God's grace searches, cleanses, and shapes the spiritual guide's heart. Both the spiritual guide and the one being spiritually guided bow before the One who seeks our hearts. In practices of guidance, one person offers to be a sounding board, amplifying the prayers and spiritual experience of the other, as Eli did for Samuel in the quiet of the night (1 Samuel 3).

Just as the relationship with God is unmediated in evangelical and many other kinds of Christian theology, in keeping with the professional ethics of spiritual direction, the directee's relationships with other people and institutions are unmediated as well. Spiritual directors adhere to an ethic of confidentiality and would not intervene in a directee's family or in that directee's relationships within the church, even by way of telling the directee what is the right thing to do. A director accompanies the other in listening and discerning. Despite the word *director*, a spiritual director in the evangelical tradition understands that the true director is God and the key relationship is the one between the directee and the divine Director. Despite believing in the individual's own direct relationship with God, evangelical Christians may be familiar with more didactic spiritual guidance and will press the spiritual director to exert more authority.

Discipleship and Mission

Missional has become a much loved word in evangelical circles. It is sometimes used in contrast to *devotional* in a way that devalues spiritual experience and practices as self-centered and passive (similar criticisms have been leveled at contemplatives throughout the history of the church). People coming from this ecclesial culture often display signs of burnout. They have been running on empty, trying to be good missional Christians, pouring out to others and seldom stopping to receive. Sometimes, to their chagrin, they experience "compassion fatigue" even while they are steadfastly trying to express compassion.

What is helpful for many Christians, and may be experienced in a relationship of spiritual guidance, is the image of being rooted and grounded in love (Ephesians 3:17). There is an organic flow of grace into and through the Christian, and that is the foundation of discipleship. The person is filled and nurtured by the Holy Spirit and, in turn, becomes fruitful, or missional, in the world. Spiritual guidance can allow for spiritual rehydration and revitalization of calling and mission.

A related issue that can arise regarding spiritual guidance among evangelicals is the understanding of the contours of the guide's mission. Is it all right for a spiritual guide to be someone other than a pastor? Ought Christian spiritual guidance to be professionalized, entailing confidentiality or fees? In general, spiritual guides will do well to have thought through these issues and allow opportunities for safe, open conversations about them.

Community

Evangelical Christians believe in the priesthood of all believers and the community as God's holy habitation. A one-on-one relationship in spiritual guidance is the smallest form of the faithful "two or more gathered in my name" (Matthew 18:20). Many spiritual disciplines embraced by evangelicals are communal: worship, prayer meetings, table fellowship, small groups, conferences, Sunday school classes, and Bible studies. One-on-one guidance poses questions about accountability to the larger fellowship, the possibility of going off track in terms of orthodoxy and/or intimacy, and bringing an idea of soul care established by the larger therapeutic culture into Christian circles.

A spiritual guide caring for an evangelical Christian is helped by maintaining an awareness that the person being attended to is part of the communion of saints throughout history and around the globe, as well as part of the local chapter of that communion, whether actively involved or not. Community has eroded radically in the past fifty years or so in much of the industrialized world. However, Christianity is a community-based faith and, therefore, today is increasingly countercultural. To retain consciousness of community while meeting with an individual is a crucial exercise of sociological imagination when working with evangelical Christians.

THE CHARACTER OF EVANGELICAL CHRISTIAN SPIRITUALITY

When an evangelical Christian arrives for spiritual guidance, it is likely he or she might not mention the word *evangelical*. What will be apparent is respect for the authority of scripture, fluency in biblical language, some history of church participation, an awareness of sin, and a longing to experience and exemplify God's grace and love. Though the word *evangelical* has become a cultural construct, many evangelical Christians have not allied their religious understandings with political movements, parties, or positions.

Evangelicals are communal and missional, in that they want to follow Jesus Christ in daily life, and that means in their homes, places of work, the marketplace, the public square, and among their brothers and sisters in Christ. Following Christ is a matter of being spiritual—seeking and knowing the One who says, "Follow me." While the word *evangelical* connotes rigidity and closed-mindedness to some people, those qualities are cultural accretions. Following depends on attentiveness, perseverance, and responsiveness. It also requires desire. At the core, an evangelical Christian is one who longs to hear Christ's glad tidings and dance for joy.

NOTES

1. Quoted by Bruce Hindmarsh, "Contours of Evangelical Spirituality," in *Dictionary of Christian Spirituality*, ed. Glen G. Scorgie et al. (Grand Rapids, MI: Zondervan, 2011), 146.
2. Robert E. Webber, *The Younger Evangelicals: Facing the Challenges of the New World* (Grand Rapids, MI: Baker Books, 2002), 14.
3. Evan Howard, "Reflections on the Study of Christian Spiritual Life," *Journal of Spiritual Formation and Soul Care* 1, no. 1 (Spring 2008): 16.
4. Frances FitzGerald, "The Evangelical Surprise," *New York Review of Books* 54, no. 7 (April 26, 2007): 2, www.nybooks.com/articles/archives/2007/apr/26/the-evangelical-surprise.
5. See Richard F. Lovelace, "The Sanctification Gap," *Theology Today* 29, no. 4 (1973): 363–69.
6. Richard Foster, "Spiritual Formation Agenda: Three Priorities for the Next 30 Years," *Christianity Today* 53, no. 1 (January 2009): 29, http://www.christianitytoday.com/ct/2009/january/26.29.html.
7. Winthrop S. Hudson, "The Ministry in the Puritan Age," in *The Ministry in Historical Perspective*, eds. H. Richard Niebuhr and Daniel D. Williams (San Francisco: Harper and Row, 1956), 198.
8. Wesley D. Tracy, "Spiritual Direction in the Wesleyan-Holiness Tradition," in *Spiritual Direction and the Care of Souls: A Guide to Christian Approaches and Practices*, eds. Gary W. Moon and David G. Benner (Downers Grove, IL: IVP Academic, 2004), 128.
9. C. W. McLemore, *The Scandal of Psychotherapy: A Guide to Resolving the Tensions between Faith and Counseling* (Wheaton, IL: Tyndale House, 1982), 13.
10. Robert R. King Jr., "Evangelical Christians and Professional Counseling: A Conflict of Values?" *Journal of Psychology and Theology* 6, no. 4 (Fall 1978): 276–81.
11. William J. Bouwsma, "Christian Adulthood," in *Adulthood*, ed. Erik H. Erikson (New York: W. W. Norton, 1978), 85.
12. Dallas Willard, foreword to *Spiritual Formation as if the Church Mattered*, by James C. Wilhoit (Grand Rapids, MI: Baker Academic, 2008), 2.
13. Dietrich Bonhoeffer, *Life Together* [1938], trans. John W. Doberstein (New York: Harper and Row, 1954), 98–99.

RESOURCES

Bonhoeffer, Dietrich. *Life Together* [1938]. Translated by John W. Doberstein. New York: Harper and Row, 1954.

Bouwsma, William J. "Christian Adulthood." In *Adulthood*, edited by Erik H. Erikson, 81–96. New York: W. W. Norton, 1978.

FitzGerald, Frances. "The Evangelical Surprise." *New York Review of Books* 54, no. 7 (April 26, 2007). www.nybooks.com/articles/archives/2007/apr/26/the-evangelical-surprise.

Foster, Richard. "Spiritual Formation Agenda: Three Priorities for the Next 30 Years." *Christianity Today* 53, no. 1 (January 2009): 29. http://www.christianitytoday.com/ct/2009/january/26.29.html.

Hindmarsh, Bruce. "Contours of Evangelical Spirituality." In *Dictionary of Christian Spirituality*, edited by Glen G. Scorgie et al., 146–52. Grand Rapids, MI: Zondervan, 2011.

Howard, Evan. "Reflections on the Study of Christian Spiritual Life." *Journal of Spiritual Formation and Soul Care* 1, no. 1 (Spring 2008): 8–26.

Hudson, Winthrop S. "The Ministry in the Puritan Age." In *The Ministry in Historical Perspective*, edited by H. Richard Niebuhr and Daniel D. Williams, 180–206. San Francisco: Harper and Row, 1956.

King, Robert R., Jr. "Evangelical Christians and Professional Counseling: A Conflict of Values?" *Journal of Psychology and Theology* 6, no. 4 (Fall 1978): 276–81.

Lovelace, Richard F. "The Sanctification Gap." *Theology Today* 29, no. 4 (1973): 363–69.

McLemore, C. W. *The Scandal of Psychotherapy: A Guide to Resolving the Tensions between Faith and Counseling.* Wheaton, IL: Tyndale House. 1982.

Scorgie, Glen G. et al., eds. Dictionary of Christian Spirituality. Grand Rapids, MI: Zondervan, 2011.

Tracy, Wesley D. "Spiritual Direction in the Wesleyan-Holiness Tradition." In *Spiritual Direction and the Care of Souls: A Guide to Christian Approaches and Practices*, edited by Gary W. Moon and David G. Benner, 115–36. Downers Grove, IL: IVP Academic, 2004.

Webber, Robert E. *The Younger Evangelicals: Facing the Challenges of the New World.* Grand Rapids, MI: Baker Books, 2002.

Willard, Dallas. Foreword to *Spiritual Formation as if the Church Mattered*, by James C. Wilhoit, 9–11. Grand Rapids, MI: Baker Academic, 2008.

Robert A. Rees, PhD, teaches Mormon studies at Graduate Theological Union in Berkeley and the University of California, Berkeley. Dr. Rees has been active in religious and Mormon studies over the course of his academic career. He has served as the editor of *Dialogue: a Journal of Mormon Thought* (1970–1976) and as chair of the Sunstone Foundation, and he has published a wide variety of scholarly articles, personal essays, editorials, and poetry. He is the editor of *A Readers' Book of Mormon* (2008) and *Why I Stay: The Challenge of Discipleship for Contemporary Mormons* (2011). Previously he taught at UCLA and UC Santa Cruz and was a Fulbright Professor of American Studies in the Baltics.

Spiritual Guidance in Mormonism (The Church of Jesus Christ of Latter-Day Saints)

Robert A. Rees, PhD

A BRIEF HISTORY OF MORMONISM

Most scholars consider Mormonism the first indigenous American religion to emerge out of the Second Great Awakening of American religious fervor (c. 1800–1830). The evangelical fires that swept the Eastern Seaboard to the edge of the frontier, especially in the region of upper New York that has come to be known as "the Burned-Over District," found ministers, itinerant preachers, camp meeting evangelists, and self-styled prophets competing intensely for the souls of their countrymen and women.

Mormonism was born out of this cauldron of holy conflagration when the young American frontiersman Joseph Smith, troubled by the sectarian conflict that raged not only in his own region, but in his own family and in his own heart, sought divine direction as to which church he should join. Taking literally the apostle James's admonition that any who lacked wisdom should ask God, who would give liberally to all who asked (James 1:5), the fourteen-year-old Smith went to a grove of trees near his father's farm to seek divine guidance. In response to his quest, he had a vision in which God the

Father and Jesus Christ appeared to him. In response to his question as to which church he should join, he was told by God that he was to join none of them and that God had a great work for him to do, the particulars of which would be revealed to him later. This First Vision, as it is called by Mormons, was the beginning of many divine visitations Smith was to experience over the ensuing years. These included visitations by Moroni (the last prophet of a group of Israelites who immigrated to the New World 600 BCE and who kept a sacred history called the Book of Mormon); John the Baptist, who restored what Mormons call the Aaronic or lower priesthood, including the authority to baptize; Peter, James, and John, who restored the Melchizadek or higher priesthood, including the keys to the apostleship; Moses, who restored the keys of the gathering of the Israel; Elias, who restored the keys to bring to pass "the restoration of all things" (Doctrine and Covenants 27:6); Elijah, who restored "the keys of the power of turning the hearts of the fathers to the children, and the hearts of the children to the fathers" (Malachai 4:5–6; Doctrine and Covenants 27:9); and at least one additional appearance of Jesus Christ.

These visions and visitations constitute for Latter-Day Saints the restoration of the primitive church of Jesus Christ, including all of the authority, teachings, principles, doctrines, and ordinances that had been lost during what some theologians refer to as the "Great Apostasy" or "the Great Falling Away," the period lasting from the crucifixion of Christ until, more or less, Smith's own time, therefore necessitating a restoration of these very things. It also included a restoration of certain ancient Hebrew rites and doctrines. Thus, the latter-day "restoration" included not only the true doctrine as taught by Christ and his apostles, but the authority of the priesthood to organize a church, ordain ministers, proselytize, baptize converts, receive revelation, and administer all of the ordinances of the Gospel and necessary affairs of the church.

On the basis of the spiritual guidance Smith received, Mormons believe that God called him to be the prophet to usher in the new "dispensation of the fullness of times," the final dispensation before the return of Christ. Smith organized the Church of Christ (later, the Church of Jesus Christ of Latter-Day Saints) on April 6, 1830, with only a handful of followers. The church he established grew rapidly, especially through proselytizing initiatives in the United States, Canada, and Great Britain.

As the new church grew in size, it also attracted controversy and notoriety. With new revelations and the establishment of what other religionists considered a radical, even heretical, form of Christianity, Smith and his followers began to experience persecution, especially from other denominations. In the face of such persecution, they moved from western New York to Ohio, to Missouri (where the governor issued an order to "exterminate" the Mormons), and finally, during Smith's time, to the banks of the Mississippi River in western Illinois, where they established the city of Nauvoo (meaning "the beautiful"), which at the time was more populous than Chicago.

Controversy and persecution continued to plague Smith and his followers, especially as the church increased in size and political power. One of the most controversial doctrines Smith introduced was the practice of polygamy. Smith and other church leaders took multiple wives in what they considered a restoration of the form of marriage practiced by ancient Hebrew patriarchs. The official denial of and secrecy surrounding the practice, as well as internal conflicts over other issues and external persecution, resulted in Smith and his brother Hyrum being killed by a mob while jailed in nearby Carthage, Illinois.

Following Smith's murder (or martyrdom, in Mormon terms), persecution of the Mormons continued. Initially, there was confusion and controversy as to who should be the new prophet-leader of the church. After several years of uncertainty, the leadership of the church, the "mantle of the prophet," passed to Brigham Young, a charismatic leader and colonizer who saw one of his primary tasks as helping his people escape persecution and finding a safe haven where they could practice their religion. Young led the Mormons across the Plains, over the Rocky Mountains, and into the Great Salt Lake Basin in the Utah Territory in what has been termed the longest religious migration since the time of Moses, thus earning Young the sobriquet "the Mormon Moses."

Young established a central community in Salt Lake City and then immediately sent colonizers into various parts of the American West—California, Arizona, Nevada, New Mexico, Idaho, Colorado, and Utah—as well as southern Canada and northern Mexico), where they established Mormon outpost communities. In an effort to establish social, economic, and political as well as religious autonomy, the Mormons organized enterprises throughout these colonies, including communal farms, mercantile and manufacturing enterprises, and other self-sustaining activities aimed at making the Mormons completely independent and self-sufficient.

These efforts were largely successful but not without their trials, tribulations, and failures. With the westward expansion, the discovery of gold in California, and the attraction of rich repositories of natural resources throughout the West, what was originally a territory inhabited mainly by Native Americans soon drew hundreds of thousands and eventually millions of adventurers, pioneers, prospectors, and entrepreneurs, many of them passing through Mormon territory.

The diminishing isolation of the Mormons and their increasing political and economic power, as well as their religious practices, brought unwanted attention from the United States government. The continuing practice of polygamy, called, along with slavery, one of the "twin relics of barbarism," finally caused President James Van Buren to send federal troops to enforce the nation's anti-bigamy laws and to punish those who continued to practice polygamy. Many Mormons went underground, and some went to prison. Faced with these challenges and the prospect of disenfranchisement, coupled with the opportunity to gain statehood, in 1890 the Mormon prophet-president Wilford Woodruff issued a proclamation announcing the end of polygamy. Although some Mormons moved to Canada or Mexico to keep their polygamous families intact, eventually polygamy ceased to be practiced among Mormons and today is considered grounds for excommunication from the church. Nevertheless, some splinter groups, most prominently the Fundamentalist Church of Jesus Christ of Latter-Day Saints (FLDS), much to the dismay of the Mormon Church, have continued this form of marriage and family life to this day.

If the nineteenth century brought isolationism and defensiveness for Mormons, the twentieth brought accommodation and assimilation. With Utah being admitted to the Union in 1896, Latter-Day Saints could be said to have entered the modern world. Although often conservative in their social and political orientation, in some ways

Mormons proved to be progressive. For example, Utah, while still a territory, granted women's suffrage in 1870, being the second state in the Union to do so (behind Wyoming in 1869). However, during the twentieth century and lasting to the present, Mormonism can be characterized as essentially a conservative, even fundamentalist, religion.

From the original church organized with six members in 1830, the Church of Jesus Christ of Latter-Day Saints has increased in size and influence to become recognized as a major religion. According to non-Mormon sociologist Rodney Stark, Mormonism "stand[s] on the threshold of becoming the first major faith to appear on earth since the Prophet Mohammed rode out of the desert."[1] While Stark's 1984 prediction that the LDS Church would expand to 280 million members by 2080 is considered extremely optimistic, the church's growth in the last decades of the twentieth and first decades of the twenty-first century has been impressive. Today, the Church of Jesus Christ of Latter-Day Saints has a worldwide membership of fifteen million and is the fourth largest denomination in the United States.[2]

BASIC TEACHINGS OF MORMONISM

Mormonism fits clearly within the Jewish and Christian tradition. It is patterned after, as well as an extension of, primitive Christianity. Thus, claiming to be a restoration of the original church of Jesus Christ, Mormons accept as axiomatic such central Catholic and Protestant doctrines as the Trinity (although Mormons interpret the Trinity differently than do Catholics and Protestants); the virgin birth; the passion, crucifixion, and resurrection of Christ; the essential principles and ordinances of faith, repentance, baptism, and the gift of the Holy Ghost; the necessity of living a godly life; the efficacy of grace and sanctification; and the reality of the Second Coming of Christ, the resurrection, the millennium, and the final day of judgment. As summarized in an official statement on Christ:

> Jesus suffered and was crucified for the sins of the world, giving each of God's children the gift of repentance and forgiveness. Only by His mercy and grace can anyone be saved. His subsequent resurrection prepared the way for every person to overcome physical death as well. These events are called the Atonement. In short, Jesus Christ

saves us from sin and death. For that, he is very literally our
Savior and Redeemer. In the future Jesus Christ will return
to reign on earth in peace for a thousand years. Jesus Christ
is the Son of God, and He will be our Lord forever.[3]

There are, however, distinctive ways in which Latter-Day Saints understand some of these teachings. For example, they see the members of
the Godhead as separate and distinct divine beings rather than as different manifestations of one being; they see God and Christ as having
glorified and perfected physical bodies (as opposed to being simply
spiritual entities); they believe in a universal resurrection; and they
place an emphasis on works as well as grace as necessary for salvation
(i.e., by grace Christ makes salvation possible, but individuals must
choose to accept that gift of grace through obedience to his commandments to make it efficacious on their behalf).

As mentioned earlier, for Mormons the necessity for a restoration
resulted from the falling away of the church Christ established
during his ministry. Following the crucifixion of Christ and the
martyrdom of the apostles, the authority to preach the Gospel and
administer the ordinances was lost. Without priesthood authority
or divine direction, many false ideas, distorted doctrines, and myths
crept into the church, significantly altering the Gospel as it was
taught by Christ and his apostles. While Catholic leaders sought to
centralize and stabilize the church over the centuries and Protestant
leaders to reform it, what was needed was a restoration of the original
authority, doctrines, and ordinances. Thus, the necessity of the First
Vision, the calling of Joseph Smith as a prophet, and the return of
John the Baptist and the chief apostles to restore the priesthood.
This last act, which Richard Bushman calls "the most crucial act
of the restoration,"[4] was essential because it provided a transfer of
priesthood authority by ancient prophets who had actually held it
during Christ's earthly mission.

Continuing Revelation, New Scripture, and the Open Canon

A central principle of Mormonism is the belief in continuing
revelation—that God's revelation did not end with the Bible
but continues as long as humans need spiritual knowledge and
direction—that is, until Christ returns to reign on the earth to
personally guide and preside over his church. Thus, in addition to

the Bible, Latter-Day Saints hold as sacred scripture the Book of Mormon, the Doctrine and Covenants (a series of revelations to Joseph Smith and other latter-day prophets), and the Pearl of Great Price. The last named contains the Book of Moses (an expansion on Genesis), the Book of Abraham (claimed to be the translation by Joseph Smith of an Abrahamic text found on an Egyptian scroll purchased by Smith in 1835), and Joseph Smith's personal account of the founding visions of Mormonism. Latter-Day Saints believe that revelation to the presiding authorities of the church, especially the prophet, is an ongoing necessity in providing spiritual guidance both to the church and to the world. According to Mormon theologian James E. Faulconer, because Mormons believe in continuing revelation and therefore have an open canon, they cannot be said to have a systematic theology.[5]

Cosmology and the Nature of Divine and Mortal Beings

Perhaps Mormonism's most radical departure from traditional Christianity (as well as from non-Christian religious traditions) has to do with its view of cosmology and the nature of God, angels, and humans. Together these beliefs constitute "a new story of creation and the destiny of humankind."[6] The central tenets of this new understanding include the following:

- God did not create the world *ex nihilo* but rather organized it out of eternally existing matter.

- We have a Mother as well as a Father in heaven. As the hymn Mormons sing argues:

   In the heaven are parents single?
   No, the thought makes reason stare.
   Truth is reason, truth eternal,
   Tells me I've a mother there.[7]

- We are literally the spiritual offspring of these divine parents, who know each of us personally and intimately and have created a plan to bring us back to their presence. As one Mormon scholar has described it, our Heavenly Mother and Father have designed a process for our spiritual growth to help us "evolve to ever higher degrees of faith, love, and glory—which is, after all, our Heavenly parents' and our Savior's most treasured work and, precisely because it leads to our becoming like them, both our and their greatest glory."[8]

- Heavenly Father and Mother have created and peopled millions of worlds like the one on which we live.

- "Intelligence," the essence out of which preexistent human spirits (the souls of mortals) were organized, is, like matter, co-eternal with God. Thus, as a revelation to Joseph Smith asserted, "Man was also in the beginning with God. Intelligence, or the light of truth, was not created or made, neither can be" (Doctrine and Covenants 93:29). Or, as Richard Bushman summarizes, "Human beings [meaning their eternal essence] are not the creations of God because he did not create their inner essence. They are radically free intelligences, as eternal as God himself."[9]

- God himself was once a man who became exalted through righteousness in the same process by which human dwellers on earth can become glorified beings. As the couplet known to all Mormons states, "As man is, God once was, and as God is, man may become." Rather than seeing such a statement as blasphemous, Mormons see it as the most hopeful message that humans can hear because it encompasses the potential for unlimited spiritual growth and glorification.

- Related to this concept is the idea that God's greatest and most loving act of generosity and benevolence, made possible through the atonement of Christ, is his desire that all mortal beings become "heirs of God, and joint-heirs with Christ" (Romans 8:17), thus inheriting the totality of godly knowledge, power, and glory. In the words of a revelation from Christ to Joseph Smith, "He that receiveth me receiveth my Father; And he that receiveth my Father receiveth my Father's kingdom; therefore all that my Father hath shall be given unto him" (Doctrine and Covenants 84:37–38). In other words, nothing of godly power or glory will be withheld from those who prove worthy to receive them.

The Plan of Salvation

For Mormons, all of this fits into a grand design for humanity, one that stretches from the preexistence to mortality to the end of time to the final judgment and into the eternities. Called "the Plan of Salvation" or "the Plan of Happiness," it encompasses every stage and every aspect of the moral and spiritual journey on which all of God's children must travel.

The Latter-Day Saints' Plan of Salvation includes a radically different view of heaven and hell from that of most other Christian denominations. Mormons believe that after death our spirits go not to heaven or hell but rather to temporary places, paradise for those who have been righteous and spirit prison for unrepentant sinners. This was the place Christ visited following his crucifixion. As he said to the thief who believed in him, "Today shalt thou be with me in paradise" (Luke 23:43), and, as Peter explained, it was also at this time that Christ visited and preached to those who were in spirit prison (1 Peter 3:18–19).

Hell, therefore, is not a place where the wicked literally burn forever, but rather a temporary state of mental, emotional, and spiritual anguish for unrepented sins of both commission and omission. Those who willfully reject Christ's suffering for their sins must bear the burden of those sins themselves (see Doctrine and Covenants 19:16–17). Mormons contend that other Christians mistake the spirit prison for their concept of hell.

Following the Second Coming of Jesus Christ, Mormons, like some other Christians, believe in the millennium, that thousand-year epoch of peace on earth during which Satan will be bound and have no power over people (Doctrine and Covenants 45:55; Revelation 20:1–3). During this period, the wicked will remain in spirit prison, while those who have been righteous and beneficiaries of "the first resurrection" will enjoy a long season of peace and constructive spiritual engagement and growth. At the end of the millennium, Satan "shall be loosed for a little season" (Revelation 20:7) and with his cohorts will fight one last battle against Christ and his righteous disciples, after which Satan and his followers will be cast into outer darkness (see Matthew 25:30 and Doctrine and Covenants 88:111–115). These we are told are the "sons of perdition," for whom, the Book of Mormon prophet Mosiah said, it "is as though there was no redemption made" (Mosiah 16:5).[10] The ultimate fate of these outcasts is unknown to everyone except God and Christ (see Doctrine and Covenants 76:43–46).

Instead of a single heaven, following Paul's metaphor of kinds or degrees of resurrected bodies, Mormons speak of three heavens or kingdoms: the telestial, the terrestrial, and the celestial. The glory or light of the first is like that of the stars; the second, that of the moon; and the third, that of the sun. In this conception of heaven, even the greatest of sinners (murderers, "liars, and sorcerers, and adulterers" [Doctrine and Covenants 76:103]) will ultimately have place in a kingdom, even though one of significantly diminished glory.

Latter-Day Saints teach that one of the privileges of attaining the celestial kingdom is eternal marriage. Worthy Latter-Day Saints who are married in a Mormon temple are married or "sealed" "for time and all eternity," not just until death. Also promised is that faithful couples will have an eternal relationship with their children and other earthly relatives. The Mormon slogan "Families are forever" is grounded in this fundamental teaching.

The ultimate outcome of the Plan of Salvation is that those who attain the celestial kingdom will have the power, like Heavenly Father and Mother, to create worlds of their own over which they, in the manner the divine parents now do, will reign as supreme beings over their own spirit children. Those who choose not to seek such an exalted state will, by the exercise of their agency, choose lesser states of glorification and exaltation. Mormons see eternity as a state during which all who choose to do so will continue learning, growing, and increasing in wisdom, love, and glory.

MAJOR SECTS AND THEIR DISTINCTIONS

There are various offshoots of the Latter-Day Saint or Restoration movement. Mormon scholar Claudia Bushman estimates, "About 130 other groups, mostly small, have broken off from the main body of Latter-Day Saints."[11] The most notable of these groups is the Community of Christ, formerly known as the Reorganized Church of Jesus Christ of Latter Day Saints, and the most notorious is the Fundamentalist Church of Jesus Christ of Latter-Day Saints (FLDS). While retaining many aspects of original Mormonism, the Community of Christ is more closely aligned with mainstream Protestantism than is the present Church of Jesus Christ of Latter-Day Saints. In 2011, it had approximately 250,000 members worldwide. The FLDS Church has continued the practice of polygamy begun during Smith's time but abandoned by the LDS Church at the end of the nineteenth century. In 2011, FLDS prophet Warren Jeffs was found guilty and sentenced to prison in Texas for taking underage girls as polygamous wives.

TRADITIONS OF SPIRITUAL GUIDANCE IN MORMONISM

Latter-Day Saints have many avenues for seeking spiritual guidance and a deeply entrenched tradition of using multiple avenues in times of spiritual need. As pointed out earlier, Mormon theology begins in the preexistence where the gift of agency, a fundamental law of existence, was the inheritance of all of God's spirit children. Thus, the idea of self-determination and self-responsibility governs LDS religious and social life. In this regard, agency is both the most exciting and the most frightening realization, because it gives humans the capacity for making a life that they truly choose. A Mormon axiom is "Men are that they might have joy" (2 Nephi 2:27) with the corollary that all are free as well to choose misery.

Mormons also believe in various spheres of both responsibility and inspiration or revelation. All individuals are responsible for seeking for and then abiding by the spiritual guidance they receive for those choices and decisions that lie within their individual stewardships. As the hymn Mormons sing states:

> Know this, that every man is free
> To choose his life and what he'll be.
> For this eternal truth is given,
> God will force no man to heaven.
> He'll call, persuade, direct aright,
> Bless with wisdom, love, and light;
> In nameless ways be good and kind,
> But never force the human mind.[12]

Much of Mormon theology and religious practice focuses on self-actualization, self-reliance, and self-responsibility. When asked how he governed the Mormon people, Joseph Smith remarked that the key was teaching them to follow correct principles and letting them govern themselves.[13] Mormon scholar Terryl Givens speaks of continuing revelation both to prophets as well as ordinary members as "the collapse of sacred distance," wherein each individual is privileged to have a direct communication with and relationship to deity.[14]

The Light or Spirit of Christ

Related to agency is the belief that every person born into mortality has a divine essence called the light or the spirit of Christ. This is a spiritual endowment distinct from the Holy Ghost, which is a special gift bestowed on those who are baptized. "The Light of Christ refers to the spiritual power that emanates from God ... and enlightens every man, woman, and child."[15] Mormons believe that, as John 8:12 declares, Christ is "the light and life of the world." As a revelation to Joseph Smith declares, his light is

> the same light that quickeneth your understandings; which light proceedeth forth from the presence of God to fill the immensity of space—the light which is in all things, which giveth life to all things, which is the law by which all things are governed, even the power of God who sitteth upon his throne, who is in the bosom of eternity, who is in the midst of all things. (Doctrine and Covenants 88:11–13)

This light also consists of the "intellectual light of our inward and spiritual organs, by which we reason, discern, judge, compare, comprehend, and remember the subjects within our reach."[16]

This light, which we might also call our conscience (although Mormons think of it as more expansive than that), allows us to make clear and intelligent choices between good and evil, which in turn makes us responsible for our moral choices. The spiritual light that is in us is therefore related to the light that is in Christ, and our light has the potential through our faithfulness to "grow brighter and brighter until the perfect day" (Doctrine and Covenants 50:24), meaning that we, too, have the potential to become "beings of light," or as Paul declares, "Ye are all the children of light, and the children of the day: we are not of the night, nor of darkness" (1 Thessalonians 5:5). Or, as Jesus said, "Believe in the light that ye may be the children of light" (John 12:36).[17]

The Holy Ghost

As with traditional Christians, Mormons see the Holy Ghost as a member of the Godhead (although unlike Catholics and Protestants they see the Holy Ghost as a separate divine personage rather than a manifestation of the same being). For Latter-Day Saints, the special role of the Holy Ghost is threefold: (1) to bear spiritual witness of the Father and the Son (2 Nephi 31:18); (2) to be a revelator of "the truth of all things" (Moroni 10:5); and (3) as Christ promised his disciples when he left them, to be a comforter (John 14:26, 15:26). According to Mormon doctrine, "We can receive a sure testimony [i.e., a certain spiritual witness] of Heavenly Father and Jesus Christ only by the power of the Holy Ghost. His communication to our spirit carries far more certainty than any communication we can receive through our natural senses."[18]

As Mormons strive to stay on the path that leads to eternal life, they believe that the Holy Ghost can guide them in making important decisions and also warn them of impending physical and moral danger. Through the Holy Ghost, Latter-Day Saints believe they can receive additional gifts of the spirit for their own benefit and for the benefit of others (see Doctrine and Covenants 46:9–11), including spiritual guidance.

Ecclesiastical Leaders

Mormons look to their leaders—local, regional, and general—for guidance, particularly the prophet or president of the church, his counselors (who together constitute the First Presidency of the Church), and the Quorum of the Twelve Apostles, who as a body are charged with guiding the church. A Mormon maxim is "Follow the prophet," with its variation "Follow the brethren" meant to emphasize the special role of these "prophets, seers and revelators" in guiding individuals as well as the church itself. Mormons attend, listen to on radio broadcasts, and watch on television or over the Internet addresses by general authorities and other officers of the church at semiannual conferences broadcast worldwide. These conference addresses are later published, and members are encouraged to read them for guidance. It is at present an established practice that such spiritual addresses are also assigned as guides to speakers in weekly worship services throughout the church, thus expanding the possibilities of their being a source for guidance.

Spiritual Guidance through Others

Spiritual guidance extends to other spheres as well. For example, parents have the responsibility to seek for and receive guidance for the welfare of their children. It is not uncommon for Latter-Day Saint children who face an important decision or who are departing for a church mission or college to ask their father for a "father's blessing" as a guide and comfort. Leaders of priesthood, women's, and youth organizations are entitled to guidance in their respective callings; bishops, stake presidents, mission presidents, and other ecclesiastical leaders have responsibility for guidance within their respective jurisdictions. Thus, a bishop (head of a local congregation) seeks for spiritual guidance in ministering to his flock in general and to each individual in it, and each member of his congregation can approach him for guidance regarding his or her spiritual welfare and important personal and professional decisions. One individual cannot get guidance for another unless that person has a spiritually hierarchical relationship to that individual. In other words, one bishop cannot get guidance either for another bishop or for the other bishop's congregants. The First Presidency and the Quorum of the Twelve Apostles have the responsibility for spiritual guidance for the entire body of the church but not for individual members at each descending level of authority. This does not mean, however, that general authorities cannot receive guidance for individual members.

Patriarchal Blessings

As with the children of ancient prophets, all members of the church are entitled to a special "patriarchal blessing," and patriarchs are called within stakes or regions of the church to provide such blessings. Patriarchal blessings are special revelations unique to each individual and include (1) the declaration of the tribe of Israel to which the recipient belongs (Mormons believe that everyone on earth belongs to or can be adopted by baptism into one of the twelve tribes); (2) particular aspects of the person's spiritual gifts, callings, and even destiny; and (3) principles of guidance for the person's life. Members of the church are encouraged to read their patriarchal blessings often but especially at times when they are in need of spiritual comfort or guidance. The particular promises enumerated in such a blessing are contingent on living a righteous life as well as following the admonitions included in the blessing itself.

Other Blessings

Any member of the church may request a special blessing at any time from an ecclesiastical leader or from a priesthood leader assigned to them as a "home teacher" (special ministers assigned to each family and single adult in the congregation who make monthly visits to the home to ensure that any physical or spiritual needs are met). In advance of receiving such a blessing, the person usually explains the need and perhaps makes special requests for what the blessing might include. In preparation for such a blessing and at other times when seeking spiritual guidance though other avenues described above, Latter-Day Saints often fast to prepare themselves to be spiritually in tune and receptive to whatever guidance the blessing may hold.

Sacred Texts and Inspirational Literature, Music, and Art

In addition to their own sacred texts, Latter-Day Saints believe that there is inspiration and guidance in the sacred texts of other religious traditions. As the Book of Mormon states, "The Lord doth grant unto all nations, of their own nation and tongue, to teach his word, yea, in wisdom, all that he seeth fit that they should have" (Alma 29:8). While in general Latter-Day Saints don't typically turn to such texts for guidance, some do.

Mormons also believe that guidance and inspiration may lie in the best extra-scriptural sources, especially sacred music and inspirational literature. A revelation to Joseph Smith admonished, "And as all have not faith, seek ye diligently and teach one another words of wisdom; yea, seek ye out of the best books words of wisdom; seek learning, even by study and also by faith" (Doctrine and Covenants 88:118). Another LDS scripture states, "The song of the righteous is a prayer unto me" (Doctrine and Covenants 25:12). And one of the foundational Articles of Faith, following Paul, states, "If there is anything virtuous, lovely, or of good report or praiseworthy, we seek after these things" (Philippians 4:8; Articles of Faith 13).

Temples and Other Sacred Spaces

Mormons consider temples as sanctuaries to which they can go to find repose from the world. Many temple-worthy Latter-Day Saints go to the temple seeking inspiration and guidance for personal matters. Since the temple ceremony itself, called "the endowment ceremony," requires engaged participation in a symbolic journey from the preexistence to the next life, ending in a room representing the highest degree of exaltation or glory called the "celestial room" (symbolizing for Latter-Day Saints the place where God dwells),

Latter-Day Saints typically find a quiet spot within this room in which they can pray and meditate as they seek guidance. Latter-Day Saints typically do not find their local chapel similarly suitable for seeking guidance, but they may seek for guidance in garden areas surrounding temples or at historic Mormon sites, such as the "Sacred Grove" in western New York where Joseph Smith had his first vision or the first Latter-Day Saint temple in Kirtland, Ohio. As with believers of other faiths, Latter-Day Saints may seek for guidance in nature, especially on mountaintops, at the seashore, or other areas where they feel close to God.

LATTER-DAY SAINT SPIRITUAL PRACTICES

The Latter-Day Saint tradition is decidedly in the "low-church" tradition, especially in the nature of its liturgy. Latter-Day Saint worship services are simple in their organization, structure, and content. Typically, there is an opening hymn and opening prayer, after which there may be announcements, which are followed by a "sacrament hymn," the "blessing on the bread and water" (since the early days of the church when enemies apparently tried to poison the wine used in LDS sacrament services, water has been used to symbolize the blood of Christ), and the "passing of the sacrament" to the congregation, usually by the "deacons," twelve- to thirteen-year-old boys (who may be assisted by older boys and adults when there are insufficient numbers of deacons). Following the sacrament, the service normally consists of a youth speaker, an adult speaker, an "intermediate congregational hymn," and a concluding speaker. The service ends with a closing hymn and closing prayer. Following the sacrament or worship service, congregants attend Sunday school classes and then, in the third hour, separate meetings of priesthood (men) and Relief Society (women), young men, young women, and primary (children ages three to eleven). Children three and younger go to the nursery.

In addition to Sunday services, other traditional Latter-Day Saint spiritual practices include daily individual and, often, family prayer and scripture reading, prayers of thanksgiving at meals, and on Monday evenings, "Family Home Evening," a time for families to gather for religious instruction, family-centered entertainment, and "family councils," in which family members discuss practical and other matters.

Other spiritual practices include a monthly twenty-four-hour fast on the first Sunday of each month, during which the usual worship service becomes what Mormons refer to as "Fast and Testimony Meeting," an open service wherein anyone in the congregation can stand and bear "personal testimony" about his faith, God's blessings in her life, unusual spiritual experiences, and a witness or testimony of the divinity of Jesus Christ, the inspired calling of the current LDS prophet, and an affirmation that the LDS Church is "the true church." Testimonies often include examples of how an individual sought and received spiritual guidance through one or more of the sources mentioned above. Such personal expressions are often emotional in nature. Latter-Day Saints contribute "fast offerings" (the equivalent amount or more of what they would have spent on the meals they have forgone in fasting) to the church to be used for the poor and needy. Faithful Latter-Day Saints also tithe and contribute to other causes, including the church's Humanitarian Aid Fund, which funds usually go to help relieve suffering (of both members and nonmembers) resulting from natural disasters such as earthquakes, hurricanes, and tsunami.

An additional spiritual practice for qualified ("worthy") Latter-Day Saints centers on the temple, where attendees participate in proxy ordinances (baptism, confirmation, "washings and anointings," and even marriages) for deceased persons. Often referred to as "temple work," such spiritual practices represent a concrete manifestation of Latter-Day Saint belief that every mortal, from Adam and Eve to the end of the world, will have access to the "saving ordinances" of the Gospel.

Other practices are related to the principle that everyone can participate in the life of the spiritual and practical work of the church. As a church with both a lay leadership and a belief in the spiritual development of each individual, almost all members are given an opportunity to participate in the administrative, social, spiritual, and educational life of the church. Referred to as "callings," these range from heavy administrative and pastoral positions (such as bishop or Relief Society president) to less taxing callings (such as local missionary, primary teacher, scout master, music director, or nursery leader). Recently, members have also been responsible for basic janitorial work in LDS meetinghouses, with various groups taking turns cleaning the building and grounds on Saturdays in preparation for Sunday services. All of this points to a religious practice that is communal, involved, and active, and that has a mix of the practical and the spiritual.

Latter-Day Saints make commitments to follow various religious, personal health, and social rules and regulations, including the following:

- Abstaining from alcohol, tobacco, coffee, tea, and drugs
- Practicing premarital chastity and postmarital fidelity
- Being honest in their dealings with others
- Paying tithes and offerings
- Being good citizens
- Meeting financial obligations (including spousal and child support in the case of divorce)

LATTER-DAY SAINT UNDERSTANDING OF SPIRITUAL DEVELOPMENT

Latter-Day Saints believe in what is called the Plan of Salvation, a divinely inspired system of spiritual, emotional, mental, and physical growth and development that one could call evolutionary—from preexistent "intelligence," out of which individuals were created or formed by deity into individual spirit personalities, to birth into a moral probationary period in which they have the opportunity and choice to evolve spiritually through a process of sanctification to ultimate exaltation with the potential to become deities themselves, inheriting all of the characteristics and endowments of godhood as glorified, celestial beings.

Mormons believe, as articulated in the Book of Moses, that God's primary objective is "to bring to pass the immortality and eternal life of man" (1:2) and God's greatest wish is to bestow on his righteous children all of the rights, powers, and privileges he possesses. Thus, all humans born into mortality have within them the seeds of godhood. As one modern scripture puts it, "That which is of God is light; and he that receiveth light, and continueth in God, receiveth more light; and that light groweth brighter and brighter until the perfect day" (Doctrine and Covenants 51:24).

Models for such spiritual growth and righteousness include past and present prophets, patriarchs, other spiritual luminaries, and ordinary people, both male and female, of spiritual and moral courage and integrity. The ultimate model of course is Jesus Christ, who, as Paul says "was in all points tempted like as we are, yet without sin" (Hebrews 4:15). Latter-Day Saints believe that they take upon themselves the name of Christ at baptism and covenant to remember his sacrifice and keep his commandments. They also believe that they renew those covenants each Sunday when they partake of the sacrament. Emulating Christ in all ways is the greatest goal and the greatest challenge for Latter-Day Saints.

In an age in which there is a tendency to blame human behavior on others (including the devil), institutions, circumstance, bad luck, and other factors, it is refreshing to find a religion that teaches people to take responsibility for their own behavior and, when that behavior violates God's commandments or their own ethical standards, or injures others, to take steps to correct their behavior and make amends to others whom they may have harmed. Because Latter-Day Saints believe their behavior has both mortal and eternal consequences, practitioners can appeal to their sense of self-responsibility, even reminding them of their covenants and commitments. The downside of this ethic is that Latter-Day Saints may have a greater tendency to blame themselves in ways that are not emotionally or spiritually healthy and they may take on too great a burden in striving for perfection.

MORMON SPIRITUAL GUIDES

Unlike most churches, Latter-Day Saints have a lay ministry. There is no formal course of study or theological training that prepares or qualifies a man (all priesthood holders and ecclesiastical leaders are male) for the ministry. Mormons believe, as their fifth Article of Faith states, "that a man must be called of God, by prophecy, and by the laying on of hands by those who are in authority, to preach the Gospel and administer in the ordinances thereof." In some ways, the entire lived religious experience is considered training for the ministry. One consequence of a lay ministry is that those called to such positions generally lack truly systematic training in scripture, doctrine, and, perhaps especially, counseling skills. That is, most ecclesiastical LDS leaders are less likely than the clergy of other denominations to be experienced in addressing more complex problems such as divorce, family relationships, sexual orientation, or various kinds of addictive behaviors. However, ecclesiastical leaders can refer members to LDS Family Services, which provides fee-based counseling for individuals, couples, unwed mothers, adoptive parents, and others. The church also has a free addiction-recovery program in most stakes. Thus, priesthood leaders have access to professional or quasi-professional services for a variety of support programs.

An additional shortcoming of a lay ministry is that missionaries and ecclesiastical leaders are unlikely to have much understanding of the traditions, doctrines, and spiritual practices of other religions. Perhaps to compensate somewhat for this, in the past several decades the church has placed a new emphasis on interfaith work, especially in large cities, and frequently participates in interfaith activities.

COMMON SPIRITUAL ISSUES FOR LATTER-DAY SAINTS

Since each individual is ultimately responsible for seeking for and abiding by the spiritual guidance he or she receives through prayer, scripture study, special blessings, and other avenues, one of the potential points of conflict is between one's own inspiration or revelation and that of ecclesiastical leaders or of the church itself. For example, during the last century, some Latter-Day Saints felt that the church's official teaching of withholding the priesthood from males of black African descent was in conflict with teachings in both the Christian scriptures and the Book of Mormon. Some broke with the church over this issue, while others who held the same conviction simply coexisted with the conflict. Therefore one potential point of conflict for Latter-Day Saints is the tension between individual conscience and institutional loyalty.

Since Mormons strive to live by high moral and religious standards, it is not unusual to find problems related to perfectionism. The counseling center at Brigham Young University reports that perfectionism is one of the most prominent and persistent problems for Latter-Day Saint students.[19] Professional counselors report similar problems among the Latter-Day Saint population in general.

A related issue centering on high standards, unrealistic expectations, the pull for conformity, and the quest for perfection is hypocrisy. Although the principle of forgiveness of sins is central to Latter-Day Saint belief, in practice it is sometimes difficult for people to forgive themselves when they fall short of the church's, others', and their own expectations. This can lead to discrepancy between inner and outer spirituality. Some Latter-Day Saints may blame themselves and simply withdraw from expectations that they feel they can't meet. Others may have a tendency to mask their real feelings and failures, which can lead to inauthenticity and therefore emotional and spiritual dissonance.

OFFERING SPIRITUAL GUIDANCE TO LATTER-DAY SAINTS

In counseling Latter-Day Saints, one of the most effective approaches is directing them to seek guidance or confirmation of personal inspiration through one or more of the avenues of spiritual guidance described in this chapter. Since Latter-Day Saints believe they are ultimately responsible for their own spiritual and moral choices, the best counsel one can give is to encourage them to draw upon their own inner spiritual resources while at the same time seeking for guidance and confirmation through prayer, meditation, scripture study, inspirational literature and music, and consultation with friends, family members, and ecclesiastical leaders. For mental and emotional guidance, they should also be encouraged to seek the best medical and psychological counseling guidance available, consistent with their own spiritual values. In other words, giving guidance to members of any faith tradition begins with honoring the values of that tradition.

Since Mormons tend to be resourceful and self-reliant, validating their personal strengths and encouraging self-responsibility can be an effective way of supporting them. One can also inquire as to which of the avenues of spiritual guidance they generally pursue and with which they are most confortable. Since perfectionism can be a problem for some Mormons, helping them be less self-judgmental and more self-forgiving can lead to a more balanced attitude toward mistakes and transgressions.

Since Latter-Day Saints consider themselves Christian in the deepest meaning of that word,[20] they can be sensitive regarding the accusation from other Christians that they are non-Christian. They can also be sensitive to suggestions that they are "weird" or have "weird beliefs." Latter-Day Saints who have been to the temple wear special undergarments (called simply "garments") with embroidered symbols to remind them of temple covenants relating to faithfulness, chastity, and consecration. Denigrating remarks about "funny underwear" can be experienced as sacrilegious by Latter-Day Saints. Many Latter-Day Saints may wear such garments in hospitals and other care facilities.

By and large, Latter-Day Saints are optimistic, happy, and healthy people. They are also highly cooperative and tend to be good citizens. As Richard Bushman says, Mormons have "inveterate confidence" and tend to "read existence as a divine comedy with a happy ending in sight. Their resolve is not easily broken."[21] Mormons also tend to be "tribal," having a deep identification with and an ultimate commitment to Mormon religion and culture. They are proud of their pioneer heritage and in the United States celebrate the arrival of their forebears into the Salt Lake Valley every July 24.

Mormons are also highly patriotic, with disproportionate numbers serving in local, state, and national public offices. Although the church itself attempts to be politically neutral, there is a strong identification with the Republican Party among Mormons living in the United States, especially in the Intermountain region. Mormons place a significant emphasis on education and tend to have a high educational level. Perhaps surprisingly, faithfulness tends not to decrease with educational attainment. Latter-Day Saints tend to rise to prominence in other professional areas as well, especially business, medicine, and education.

In short, Latter-Day Saints tend to have high moral standards, have a positive outlook on life, consider themselves literal and figurative children of God,[22] have a strong identity with and loyalty to family and church, and have a wide repertoire of channels for seeking spiritual guidance. Although they can be skeptical of other faith traditions and suspicious of secular authority and institutions, most Mormons are friendly, kind, and compassionate, following principles of behavior that are emphasized in their religious upbringing and religious experience.

NOTES

1. "The Rise of a New World Faith," *Review of Religious Research* 26, no. 1: 18–27.

2. Chad Phares, "Church Now Fourth Largest in United States," *News from the Church*, April 10, 2005. The source for this statistic is *Yearbook of American and Canadian Churches* (http://www.yearbookofchurches.org).

3. "Jesus Christ, Our Savior," Church of Jesus Christ of Latter-Day Saints, http://mormon.org/jesus-christ.

4. Richard Lyman Bushman, *Mormonism: A Very Short Introduction* (Oxford: Oxford University Press, 2008), 51.

5. See James Faulconer, "Why a Mormon Won't Drink Coffee but Might Have a Coke: The Atheological Character of the Church of Jesus Christ of Latter-Day Saints," *Element* 2, no. 2 (Fall 2006): 21–37.

6. R. Bushman, *Mormonism*, 71.

7. Eliza R. Snow, "Oh My Father," *Hymns of the Church of Jesus Christ of Latter-Day Saints* (Salt Lake City: Church of Jesus Christ of Latter-Day Saints, 1985), 292–93.

8. Robert A. Rees, "'The Cost of Discipleship': Dimensions of a Mature Mormon Faith" (unpublished manuscript).

9. R. Bushman, *Mormonism*, 73.

10. According to Joseph Smith, "All sins shall be forgiven, except the sin against the Holy Ghost; for Jesus will save all except the sons of perdition. What must a man do to commit the unpardonable sin? He must receive the Holy Ghost, have the heavens opened unto him, and know God, and then sin against him. After a man has sinned against the Holy Ghost, there is no repentance for him. He has got to say that the sun does not shine while he sees it; he has got to deny Jesus Christ when the heavens have been opened unto him, and to deny the plan of salvation with his eyes open to the truth of it" ("The King Follett Sermon," *Ensign*, May 1971, 13).

11. Claudia L. Bushman, *Contemporary Mormonism: Latter-Day Saints in Modern America* (Westport, CT: Praeger, 2006), xi.

12. Anonymous composer; published in the first LDS hymnal in 1835. *Hymns of the Church of Jesus Christ of Latter-Day Saints*, 240.

13. John Taylor, one of Smith's closest associates and later one of the prophets called to lead the church, reported, "Concerning government: Some years ago, in Nauvoo, a gentleman in my hearing, a member of the [Illinois] Legislature, asked Joseph Smith how it was that he was enabled to govern so many people, and to preserve such perfect order; remarking at the same time that it was impossible for them to do it anywhere else. Mr. Smith remarked that it was very easy to do that. 'How?' responded the gentleman; 'to us it is very difficult.' Mr. Smith replied, 'I teach them correct principles, and they govern themselves'" (*Millennial Star*, November 15, 1851; https://archive.org/details/millennialstar8546eng).

14. Terryl Givens, *People of Paradox: A History of Mormon Culture* (Oxford: Oxford University Press, 2007), xiv.

15. "Light of Christ," *Encyclopedia of Mormonism*, http://eom.byu.edu/index.php/Light_of_Christ.

16. See B. H. Roberts, *Seventy's Course in Theology*, 5 vols. (Salt Lake City, 1907–12); vol. 3 on the doctrine of deity, and vol. 5 on divine immanence.

17. For insight into this subject from the Book of Mormon, see my "Children of Light: How the Nephites Sustained Two Centuries of Peace," in *Third Nephi: An Incomparable Scripture*, eds. Andrew C. Skinner and Gaye Strathearn (Provo, UT: Maxwell Center, Brigham Young University, 2011).

18. "Holy Ghost," Church of Jesus Christ of Latter-Day Saints, www.lds.org/topics/holy-ghost.

19. Private conversation between various counselors and the author in 2009.

20. As one Book of Mormon prophet exclaimed, "We talk of Christ, we rejoice in Christ, we preach of Christ, we prophesy of Christ, and we write according to our prophecies, that our children may know to what source they may look for a remission of their sins" (2 Nephi 25:26).

21. R. Bushman, *Mormonism*, 80.

22. A favorite Latter-Day Saint hymn is "I Am a Child of God," by Naomi W. Randall, with the following verse reflective of how they see themselves: "I am a child of God / and he has sent me here, / Has given me an earthly home, / With parents kind and dear. / Lead me, guide me, walk beside me, / Help me find the way. / Teach me all that I must do / Live with him some day." *Hymns of the Church of Jesus Christ of the Latter-Day Saints*, 301.

RESOURCES

The best source for material on the Church of Jesus Christ of Latter-Day Saints (Mormons) is the Church's official website: www.lds.org. Especially relevant information can be found under Resources / Welfare / LDS Family Services.

Bergin, Allen E. *Eternal Values and Personal Growth: A Guide on Your Journey to Spiritual, Emotional, and Social Wellness.* Provo, Utah: Brigham Young University Press, 2002

Richards, P. Scott, and Allen. E. Bergin, eds. *Handbook of Psychotherapy and Religious Diversity.* 2nd ed. Washington, DC: American Psychological Association, 2014.

Swedin, Eric G. *Healing Souls: Psychotherapy in the Latter-day Saint Community.* Urbana, IL: University of Illinois Press, 2003.

INTERFAITH, HUMANIST, AND ECLECTIC TRADITIONS

Rev. Cathleen Cox, MAT, MDiv, is a Unitarian Universalist minister and interfaith spiritual director. Her ministry encompasses both a private practice serving individuals and life partners and an outreach ministry exploring best practices for spiritually grounded growth and development in congregations, religious communities, and service-oriented organizations nationwide. Her passion is companioning others in the creation of joyful, meaning-centered lives and work that offer our best gifts in service to the world. Her community ministry is affiliated with the Unitarian Universalist Church of Berkeley. Contact her at www.revcat.net.

Spiritual Guidance in Unitarian Universalism

Rev. Cathleen Cox, MAT, MDiv

AN OVERVIEW OF UNITARIAN UNIVERSALISM

In 1961, the two most liberal denominations in the "mainstream" Protestant world—the Unitarians and the Universalists—merged, forming the Unitarian Universalist Association.

One of the speakers at the merger ceremony made the bold proclamation that "a new world faith ... is coming to birth in our time. It is taking its place beside the Big-Three religious groups on this continent, the Catholics, Protestants and Jews."[1] Today, in light of a more globally conscious religious pluralism, Hinduism, Buddhism, Islam, and the earth-centered traditions would no doubt also be added to that catalog; however, the essential meaning would remain the same.

Unitarian Universalism was breaking free of its liberal Protestant moorings, born of and nurtured by the "Radical Reformation" wing of the Protestant Reformation and declaring itself a new equal as a "world religion," no longer subsumed under the liberal Protestant label that both denominations had embraced since their emergence during or after the Protestant Reformation (Unitarianism in the 1560s and Universalism in the 1750s). Since that day in 1961, Unitarian Universalism has sought, with varying degrees of success, to fulfill that promise. It is still trying.

Perhaps the genius—and the curse—of Unitarian Universalism, as well as its precursor denominations (the Unitarians and the

Universalists), has been just this capacity to stand on the cutting edge, embracing change as new theological, cultural, and ethical understandings emerge out of new theological, psycho-spiritual, and cultural understandings.

The great historian of Unitarianism Earl Morse Wilbur declared that the *sine qua non* of Unitarianism through the ages has consistently been its commitment to "freedom, reason, and tolerance."[2] These moral and intellectual values have driven the quest for individual and collective evolution within Unitarianism especially and still drive the spiritual, intellectual, ethical, social, and institutional development of the Unitarian Universalist Association today.

Certainly throughout their history, the progenitors of these two faiths have prided themselves on their capacity to step away from the truisms of the day to scan the horizon unflinchingly and to work for the changes they see needed and called for in the world. Unitarian and Universalist spiritual or religious leaders and the communities they serve have enacted the archetypal "hero's journey," as mythologist Joseph Campbell famously outlined it.

Living often as outliers on the unfolding edge of Western religious consciousness, they have repeatedly set out, leaving behind the safety of conventional religious and social thought, limits, and norms, journeying into unknown territory and descending into the depths of our individual and collective experience, there undergoing trials of censure, ridicule, isolation, persecution, and at times martyrdom.

All this Unitarians and Universalists have undertaken throughout their history in order to bring back into the world the transformative gift of the hero's journey: new understandings; new, more just, and life-giving social constructs; renewed and more meaningful individual and community lives.

This capacity has been their genius and their gift, because it has enabled Unitarians and Universalists proudly to claim the label of freethinkers not bound by creed and dogma, who repeatedly have proclaimed a transforming vision that moved society forward in its religious imagination, its intellectual depth and range, its moral development, its engaged social conscience, and the expansion of civil rights. These are large claims, and they are justified by history.

At the same time, this very capacity for reinvention has also resulted in the denomination's being socially marginalized, religiously persecuted, and, at times, lacking a clear sense of identity. It has driven away many who were wearied by more change than they could absorb and accept.

In a tragic and ironic twist of fate, the one individual who could lay stronger claim than any other to being the founder of modern-day Unitarianism, Transylvanian Francis David, died imprisoned in 1579 because he refused to accept that there would be "no more innovations" in Unitarianism.

TRADITIONS OF SPIRITUAL GUIDANCE IN UNITARIAN UNIVERSALISM

Receiving individual spiritual guidance is only now becoming a meaningful part of Unitarian Universalism and, even then, only for a minority of its members.

Traditionally, spiritual guidance has been offered to the congregation as a whole, primarily through sermons and worship services. However, even here, worship in UU congregations for the past seventy-five years has been most widely seen as having the purpose of uniting, uplifting, educating, inspiring, and challenging the congregation to action, rather than as offering specifically "spiritual" guidance.

"Freedom of the pulpit," which is central to the UU tradition, means that a minister or lay leader speaks for himself or herself out of personal experience and personal conviction.

Thus, worship celebrants offering spiritual guidance, especially if it arises out of a specific theological stance in the directive or authoritative way that would be expected in many traditions, is not generally looked on kindly by most UUs today. It would not be too much to say that it is not tolerated.

Some congregations have, in fact, moved away from using the words *worship service* to describe their weekly gatherings. Most still do use this term, but the question of who or what is being worshipped is an uncomfortable one mostly left unexplored.

At present, however, the pendulum appears to be swinging in the other direction as more of the younger generation of congregants are explicitly expressing spiritual hunger, and many are now seeking out individual spiritual guidance. This resurgence of explicit and expressed spiritual yearning is creating tensions as some UU congregants express their need for spiritual sustenance through worship and the language and style of worship are changing.

Pastoral care, which is a strong part of the UU tradition, generally focuses on support through difficult life passages. No doubt this situation of discomfort with explicit spiritual guidance or corporate spiritual experience results in large part from the highly eclectic nature of present-day UU spiritual understandings, differing levels of interest in spiritual development, as well as differing theological starting points.

Another factor is the lingering effect of the "fellowship movement." During the 1940s and 1950s, a highly influential initiative of the American Unitarian Association directed the formation of hundreds of small lay-led Unitarian fellowships, especially in the West, which were encouraged to think of themselves as self-sufficient without clergy leadership.

The results have been a double-edged sword for Unitarian Universalism today. On the one hand, thousands more people had the opportunity to create and participate in Unitarian gatherings than might otherwise have been the case. On the other hand, the lack of trained clergy often resulted in both a spiritual "thinness" as well as an insularity that has made it difficult for many fellowships to welcome new leadership and to evolve with the times. A brand of humanism that is rigid and less than tolerant of theological diversity has characterized many such fellowships.

Today, most of these fellowships are either dwindling or transitioning to at least part-time professional leadership.

A wide range of comfort (or discomfort) with "spiritual fervor"— either one's own or anyone else's—has been present in the historical tension between the core cultural and religious stances of the two denominations, both since the eighteenth century, when they eyed each other a bit warily, and since their merger in 1961.

The merger almost fell apart over whether to refer in the "Principles and Purposes" to "the" Jewish and Christian teachings or "our" Jewish and Christian teachings. (The current version of the "Principles and Purposes" uses neither.[3]) The pervasive humanist ethos of the 1960s may have softened or obscured this tension during the period of merger, but the underlying fault lines continued and in the present have reemerged.

The Unitarians, often referred to during the era of the American Revolution, and sometimes since, as the "Boston Brahmins," were at the center of the intellectual/political/ethical/egalitarian creative foment of the Age of Enlightenment, out of which this nation was born, or emerged. Unitarian Universalism still attracts, for the most part, people who greatly enjoy the intellectual life, who are or value being highly educated, and who staunchly believe they are responsible for forging their own destinies.

That iconoclast Ralph Waldo Emerson, who left the UU ministry after quarreling with his congregation over his refusal to continue serving communion, is one of a handful of preeminent theologians whose stance of individualism blended with civic responsibility—an important combination in the Unitarian tradition. Emerson's most widely known essay, after all, is *Self-Reliance.*

Emerson was a deeply spiritual man, as was his dear friend Henry David Thoreau. Yet, for each man, spirituality was an intensely private affair. For Emerson, Thoreau, and other transcendentalists, spirituality was to be experienced and practiced in private, and the sacred was mediated primarily through deep meditative encounters with nature. For them, Jesus was a valued teacher and companion.

Theodore Parker, another transcendentalist, averred in his groundbreaking sermon "The Transient and the Permanent in Christianity" that the truth of Christianity rests on its moral principles. He did not believe that Christianity needed Jesus.[4] The latter was too much for most of Parker's contemporary Unitarian clergy colleagues, who ceased pulpit exchanges with him and banned him from their ministerial gatherings. Parker showed up anyway. Such is the rebel spirit of Unitarianism!

However, the individualism of Unitarianism has a blind spot. Rev. Barbara Hamilton-Holway regularly lifts up in her Benediction what Unitarian Universalists are called to remember: "We are all connected, and we need each other more than we know." There is an upsurge of realization of that within Unitarian Universalism today. (That fierce individualist Thoreau, who held himself so apart from human society and who wrote, "The stupid you will have always with you,"[5] also dined regularly at Emerson's house and walked into Concord from Walden Pond every week to have his mother do his laundry.)

Universalists have from their inception been more comfortable with religious fervor. John Murray, the primary founder of Universalism in America, was known to be a passionate "bring the roof down" preacher who filled his services with a Pentecostal passion for being carried away by the Divine. Congregants rose and "testified" as they felt moved. The message of universal salvation and a God of Love was intoxicating.

About 1800, a young woman named Maria Cook was so carried away by Universalist fervor that she is said to have preached Universalism nonstop on New England street corners to large, fascinated crowds drawn by the "oddity" of a woman preacher. Finally arrested for vagrancy and bodily carried away to jail—perhaps our earliest example of civil disobedience through nonviolent noncooperation—Cook continued to preach Universalism in jail so vociferously "night and day" that her jailers eventually petitioned the local judge to release her, and she was once again bodily carried to the street corner from which she had been so unceremoniously removed, where, it was said, she continued to preach Universalism with "undiminished fervor."

American Universalism also has a mystical tradition. The ministry of John Murray, the first Universalist preacher in America and founder of the Universalist movement here, was catapulted into his ministry against his will by "the Universalist miracle."

As the story is recounted in *Universalism in American: A Documentary History of a Liberal Faith,* Murray came to the American colonies from England following the heartbreaking deaths of his wife and child, with no intention of continuing his Universalist ministry here.[6] His American ministry began when his ship made a stop at a New Jersey inlet where a local farmer, John Potter, who had read about Universalism and—in the true spirit of "if you build it, they will come"—had constructed a chapel for "the Universalist preacher who will come."

The excited Potter, upon learning that there was a Universalist preacher onboard ship, beseeched Murray to preach. Murray initially declined but finally promised, "If the wind does not change in three days, and the ship remains here, I will preach on Sunday."

The wind did not change, and Murray began a forty-year ministry together with the wife he married in the New World, Judith Sargent

Murray—said to be a fine preacher in her own right. Such has been the "God-drunk" spirit of Universalism, to use the phrasing of another wild-eyed mystic, Rumi.

SPIRITUAL PRACTICES IN UNITARIAN UNIVERSALISM

It would not be an exaggeration to say that the primary communal spiritual practice among present-day Unitarian Universalists is engaged social action and that the primary individual spiritual practice is spending time in nature.

Such spiritual practices as meditation, sharing in small "wisdom circles" (usually similar in structure to 12-step groups), journaling, art making, Tai Chi, and yoga are also well accepted.

Dreamwork, prayer, and other modes of direct encounter with "that transcending Mystery," as the Unitarian Universalist Association's seven principles name it, have also been garnering more general interest and acceptance in recent years.

Other "depth" spiritual practices such as active imagination or dialogue (work with the Jungian archetypes), enneagram work, inquiry practices, and various types of energy work such as meridian tapping (EFT) are also growing in popularity and offered by UU spiritual directors.

Small group spiritual direction programs such as Evensong and other adult religious education curricula of a specifically spiritual nature are also gaining in popularity. Rites of passage such as coming-of-age and croning ceremonies are now common in congregations.

Both the Covenant of Unitarian Universalist Pagans and the Unitarian Universalist Christian Fellowship have reintroduced rituals and rites of passage such as spiral dance and chanting into some congregations. Some UUs now seek out and pursue vision quests.

HOW SPIRITUAL DEVELOPMENT IS UNDERSTOOD IN UNITARIAN UNIVERSALISM

In Universalism, the "correction" for human sin is the "hell on earth" of direct suffering that individuals experience when they have hurt, oppressed, or exploited another person. Such actions require acts of atonement such as remorse and amends, and these acts are salvific in the sense that they restore peace of mind and a sense of reconnection with self, others, and the Divine.

To the claim—put forward by many for over two hundred years—that some people do not suffer such remorse and consequent self-correction, the Universalist reply is that every person has experienced the way in which doing good to others is far more rewarding than doing harm. There is no greater satisfaction and joy than feeling oneself to be open to receiving God's ever-abundant compassion and love, which, like sunshine, is ever streaming toward us behind any and all darkness and clouds. Thus, the spirituality of Universalism is all about opening to the presence of that love.

Because Universalists have traditionally seen human beings as inherently good, inherently disposed to become the best they are capable of becoming, the primary problem of spiritual development is how to remove whatever obstacles exist to experiencing God's love. When they do so, people will be moved to do good to others because this direct connection with God will inspire and move them to do so. Feeling loved by God, they will naturally express that love to others.

No longer isolated or separated from God's love, Universalists hold that we will be naturally moved to act from our best selves in our best interests and for the benefit of others.

Universalists moved more slowly and less distinctly toward a view of Jesus as a fully human "exemplar" of the best humans can be, but they were always clear that in the "brotherhood" of Jesus they had a mediator and spiritual teacher through whom they could experience the fullness of divine love.

Universalist theology is a strand of the spirituality of many, if not all, of the world's religions and wisdom traditions. This spiritual understanding is also core to the many 12-step programs that, growing out of Alcoholics Anonymous, are the center of many people's spiritual life and practice today.

Unitarians, by contrast, have traditionally seen human beings more as a *tabula rasa*, neither good nor bad, but capable of moral development. The Unitarian tradition often sees moral and spiritual development as synonymous. This development Unitarians call on themselves and others to accomplish.

Thus, spiritual development for Unitarians often involves greater ethical commitment and engaged social action within the context of inherent personal freedom of choice. This is not always easy to accomplish.

Rev. Thomas Starr King, who served both the Unitarians and the Universalists, and who has been credited with keeping California in the Union during the Civil War, is reported to have defined the theological difference between Unitarians and Universalists this way: "The Universalists believe God is too good to damn them. The Unitarians believe they are too good to be damned by God."

Historically, the Unitarians understood Jesus himself to have been theologically unitarian, seeing himself as fully human and God as one and indivisible. The Universalists understood Jesus to have been theologically universalist, experiencing God solely as love and acting as a mediator and exponent of that love on earth. These understandings persist among UUs, particularly UU Christians, who are more inclined to give the life of Jesus serious thought.

COMMON SPIRITUAL ISSUES FOR UNITARIAN UNIVERSALISTS

Perhaps the most common spiritual issue for Unitarian Universalists seeking spiritual guidance today is not knowing what to do with—or even how to make sense of—their spiritual yearnings. This universal element of our humanity has not always found a comfortable home within the interfaith world of Unitarian Universalism, particularly in the last hundred years. Yet, Unitarian Universalism, which has no creed, is, ironically enough, the only denomination named for two theological positions.

UUs have generally not been directly supported by other members in their congregations in explicit spiritual development efforts, because such matters are probably not often discussed, nor have they known how to approach their ministers with explicitly spiritual questions.

Some are not certain they would be welcomed in doing so, and unfortunately, they may not always be mistaken in their misgivings. Some UU clergy are still in discernment themselves about spiritual matters—and this is certainly not unique to UUs—but more prominently they are often so engaged with the manifestation of their values in the congregation, and beyond that the concrete leadership and management of congregations and community-oriented projects may take up almost all their time. Many UU congregations today are understaffed, and a great deal may fall on the minister.

Overall, the spirit of individualism remains strong within Unitarian Universalism and its many "supporters" who are not members. Currently, two-thirds of American adults who identify as UU are not members of a UU congregation.

The "Humanist Manifesto" of 1933 ushered in an era of religious humanism as central to many, if not most, UU congregations, especially in the West and Midwest, and led to a widespread trend away from theism, particularly Christian-oriented theism, within Unitarianism and Universalism.

The majority of UUs today are "come-outers" from other religions, and regretfully, many of these come from a religious background in which they experienced oppression and/or exploitation. Such individuals have been deeply wounded in their spiritual nature, and many have responded by taking spiritual questions off the table as a focus for their lives. Even the words *God* or *Jesus* are upsetting to some.

Unfortunately, the response of many UU leaders in recent decades, both clergy and laity, has been to steer clear of spiritual or theological conversations, not only out of sensitivity to those who have been hurt, but also out of a desire not to spark divisive conflict over differences of belief. This has had several regrettable results that create spiritual issues for Unitarian Universalists that they may bring into spiritual direction:

- Spiritual questioning or deepening is often missing in UU congregational life; UUs often lack facility with spiritual language even to name their concerns.

- A fear of conflict over religious beliefs and an absence of trust and skills in engaging differences constructively may have been fostered by the norms of UU culture, hampering openness about spiritual questions.

- As humanism is less the norm in UU congregations and the "language of reverence" has been returning, many UU Humanists feel as marginalized as many UU Christians did in the 1930s. Tensions between humanists and theists and/or mystics of many kinds, especially UU Christians or UU Pagans, create challenging questions of how or whether our unity can truly embrace such theological diversity, again creating tension around spiritual exploration for those feeling a yearning for it, including many humanists.

- UUs may need help forming a core understanding of a kind of spirituality that embraces nontheistic language.

- Many UUs are uncertain how to relate to authority in any area of their lives.

- The challenge of becoming truly multicultural and antiracist calls into question many UU congregational norms around keeping spirituality quiet and private, as such restrained spiritual expression is not the norm in many communities of color; this shift is creating tension for many UUs who want expanded, more "heart-centered," invitational and participatory worship or corporate spiritual experiences but also don't want anyone to be uncomfortable.

- Social justice work, a primary place where UUs come together, may lack a source for spiritual renewal, resulting in conflict and burnout.

- Engagement within and beyond the congregation may not be grounded in the golden rule of compassionate understanding for the unknown "other" that is at the core of all spiritual traditions, immortalized by Jesus as "Love your enemy."

- There has been a loss of explicit teaching of the very UU history that this chapter outlines, resulting in a loss of core identity for many UUs.

- Spiritual yearnings and questions about purpose, meaning, the nature of ultimate realty, death and dying, and what it means to live a spiritually grounded life may be approached tentatively, if at all.

- Problems of daily living within and beyond the congregation may not be engaged from the vantage point of any meaningful spiritual center that offers direction. UUs may not be aware that a spiritual lens can be applied to all life issues.

- Worship services may lack the passion and conviction that truly engages and meets the hungers of heart and soul; this may be hard to name.

- Of the four traditional spiritual paths (devotion, ecstasy, learning, and service), the paths of service and learning are well known to contemporary UUs. The paths of ecstasy and devotion are not.

And yet, as the eminent contemporary UU minister Robert Latham has said, "The role of religion in society is to offer a vision of the nature of reality with the promise that, if this vision is embraced, life will be transformed."[7] Unitarian Universalists have such a vision at the core of their faith tradition: *All really is one. Love really is the ground of our being.*

Is there a spiritual message more profoundly needed in our broken world? Unitarian Universalists sense the power and the truth of this unifying, transforming vision of the nature of reality that is their religious birthright. Their primary spiritual need is to be supported in claiming and proclaiming it.

NOTES

1. Donald Szantho Harrington, "Unitarian Universalism: Yesterday, Today and Tomorrow," a sermon preached on the occasion of the celebration of the consolidation of the American Unitarian Association and the Universalist Church of America, May 23, 1960, Symphony Hall, Boston.
2. Earl Morse Wilbur, *A History of Unitarianism: In Transylvania, England, and America,* vol. 2 (Boston: Beacon Press, 1945), p. 487.
3. The Principles of the Unitarian Universalist Association (as adopted in 1981):

    We, the member congregations of the Unitarian Universalist Association, covenant to affirm and promote:

    The inherent worth and dignity of every person;

    Justice, equity and compassion in human relations;

    Acceptance of one another and encouragement to spiritual growth in our congregations;

    A free and responsible search for truth and meaning;

    The right of conscience and the use of the democratic process within our congregations and in society at large;

    The goal of world community with peace, liberty and justice for all;

    Respect for the interdependent web of all existence of which we are a part.

    The living tradition which we share draws from many sources:

    Direct experience of that transcending mystery and wonder, affirmed in all cultures, which moves us to a renewal of the spirit and an openness to the forces which create and uphold life;

    Words and deeds of prophetic women and men which challenge us to confront powers and structures of evil with justice, compassion and the transforming powers of love;

    Wisdom from the world's religions which inspires us in our ethical and spiritual life;

Jewish and Christian teachings which call us to respond to God's love by loving our neighbors as ourselves;

Humanist teachings which counsel us to heed the guidance of reason and the results of science, and warn us against idolatries of the mind and spirit;

Spiritual teachings of earth-centered traditions which celebrate the sacred circle of life and instruct us to live in harmony with the rhythms of nature.

The Preamble to the Unitarian Universalist Statement of Principles and Purposes declares: "Grateful for the religious pluralism which enriches and ennobles our faith, we are inspired to deepen our understanding and expand our vision. As free congregations, we enter into this covenant, promising to one another our mutual trust and support."

4. Theodore Parker, "The Transient and Permanent in Christianity," sermon delivered at the ordination of Rev. Charles C. Shackford, Boston, May 19, 1841. Parker says, "Christianity does not rest on the infallible authority of the New Testament, it depends on this collection of books for the historical statement of its facts.... To me it seems as presumptuous, on the one hand, for the believer to claim this evidence for the truth of Christianity, as it is absurd, on the other hand, for the skeptic to demand such evidence to support these historical statements. I cannot see that it depends on the personal authority of Jesus... It is God that was manifested in the flesh by him, on whom rests the truth which Jesus brought to light and made clear and beautiful in his life; and if Christianity be true, it seems useless to look for any other authority to uphold it, as for someone to support Almighty God. So if it could be proved—as it cannot—in opposition to the greatest amount of historical evidence ever collected on any similar point, that the gospels were the fabrication of designing and artful men, that Jesus of Nazareth had never lived, still Christianity would stand firm, and fear no evil."

5. Henry David Thoreau, *The Journal of Henry David Thoreau*, vol. 13, December 1859 to July 1860 (originally published Boston: Houghton Mifflin, 1906; reprinted Layton, UT: Peregrine Smith Books, 1984), 145.

6. Ernest Cassara, ed., *Universalism in American: A Documentary History of a Liberal Faith* (Boston: Skinner House Books, 1997).

7. Robert Latham, "A Transforming Message for the Twenty-First Century," keynote address to the Pacific Central District Assembly, April 28, 2012.

Jonathan Figdor, MDiv, is the Humanist chaplain at Stanford University, where he organizes events and programs for both students and community members from the San Francisco Bay Area. Figdor and his work have been discussed in the *New York Times*, the *Washington Post*, the *Huffington Post*, and the *San Francisco Chronicle*. He received his BA with honors in philosophy from Vassar College and holds a master's degree in Humanism and interfaith dialogue from Harvard Divinity School. A transplanted New Yorker, he lives and works in the San Francisco Bay Area in California.

Guiding Humanists

Jonathan Figdor, MDiv

HUMANIST ROOTS IN THE ANCIENT WORLD

Humanism, while often seen as a purely modern, post-Enlightenment philosophy, actually traces its roots to ancient Greece, India, and China. The first philosopher in the West, the pre-Socratic Greek philosopher Thales of Miletus, in the sixth century BCE, rejected humanlike Gods, preferring naturalistic explanations of the world. Xenophanes of Colophon, in the fifth century BCE, rejected gods altogether and explained the world in terms of reason, not gods and superstition. Protagoras, an early agnostic, wrote, "Concerning the gods, I have no means of knowing whether they exist or not or of what sort they may be, because of the obscurity of the subject, and the brevity of human life."[1] He was later indicted for blasphemy and probably drowned while trying to cross the sea to Sicily to escape.[2] Democritus of Abdera, most famous for the idea that the universe is constructed of physical matter, or atoms, also hypothesized that people must have invented the gods. Diagoras of Melos exposed the Eleusinian mystery religion's secret rituals, acting as a skeptic and debunker in the grand tradition of Harry Houdini and James Randi. Diagoras was also persecuted for his beliefs, but, being a clever chap, he escaped. Epicurus, in 350 BCE, spoke of his "Four Herbs" to ameliorate the human fears: "There is nothing to fear from gods, / There is nothing to feel in death, / Good can be attained, / Evil can be endured."[3]

Socrates, while indicted as an atheist and ultimately put to death for the crime of blasphemy, wasn't an atheistic Humanist.

But he was a great doubter, and he did emphasize the importance of secular ethics. In the dialogue *Euthyphro*, Socrates rejected the commonsense definition of morality of the day ("morality is that which the gods love"), arguing that such a definition is circular and could not possibly serve as a definition of morality. Plato's student, Aristotle, can be seen as a proto-Humanist. Aristotle conceived of the ultimate purpose, or *telos*, of human life as *eudaimonia*, or the pursuit of human flourishing and excellence. Modern Humanists largely agree.[4]

Humanism can also trace its roots to India, specifically some of the writings of the founder of Buddhism, Siddhartha Gautama, as well as the Lokayata (also known as Carvaka) school of Indian philosophy. The Buddha refers to the idea of an eternal, permanent, persistent soul in the Pali canon as "a foolish doctrine."[5] The Buddha's statement rejects not only the possibility of an unchanging eternal soul, but also the notion of an unchanging eternal god. In 600 BCE, well before the invention of Christianity, the Lokayata school of Indian philosophy taught, along with modern Humanists, that (1) there is no heaven, no hell, no afterlife, and to assert that there is an afterlife without solid evidence is silly; (2) there is no body/soul dichotomy, we are our bodies, and when our bodies die, we die; (3) consciousness emerges as a natural phenomenon; and (4) the only way we have to access reality is through our senses, and our senses are imperfect (known in modern philosophy as "perspectival realism").

Finally, a third clear root of Humanism is found in ancient China, specifically in the Duke of Zhou, an important Confucian thinker. Zhou introduced the democratic concept of the "Mandate from Heaven" which made Chinese rulers' continued ruling authority dependent on the happiness and well-being of the people. Zhou was also highly skeptical of supernatural matters and famously said, "Heaven is not believable." Further, the most preeminent modern Confucian scholar Dr. Tu Wei Ming sees a strong connection between the Humanist concept of human dignity, the Humanist belief that humans are happiest when they help other humans, and the Confucian concept *ren*, often translated in short as "human-heartedness" or "generous compassion." Hsun Tzu, a later Confucian from the third century BCE, propounded a naturalistic interpretation of Confucianism. He specifically rejected the supernatural, writing:

When stars fall or trees make a [strange] noise, all
people in the state are afraid and ask, "Why?" I reply:
There is no need to ask why.... It is all right to marvel
at them, but wrong to fear them. For there has been no
age that has not had the experiences of eclipses of the
sun and moon, unseasonable rain or wind, or occasional
appearance of strange stars. If the ruler is enlightened
and the government peaceful, even if all of these things
happen at the same time, they would do no harm....
Human portents are the most to be feared. To plough
roughly so as to injure the crops, to hoe impurely ...
these are what is meant by human portents.[6]

HUMANISM IN AND AFTER THE ENLIGHTENMENT

While Humanism can trace its roots to the ancient past, Humanism
in its modern form is a product of the Enlightenment. The
Enlightenment, often called the "Age of Reason," was a rationalist
movement that promoted the use of science, logic, and philosophy
and rejected tradition, faith, and superstition. The French philosopher
Voltaire rejected the Bible as a source of knowledge, moral or otherwise,
and ruthlessly mocked the prevailing Christian theology of the day in
the wildly popular book *Candide*.

The Enlightenment also gave rise to the social contractarian school
of philosophy, popularized by Thomas Hobbes in *Leviathan*, Jean
Baptiste Rousseau in *Le Contract Sociale*, and John Locke in his *Second
Treatise on Government*. Social contractarian philosophy recast ethics
and morals as purely naturalistic and argued that human beings create
morality. They argue that the "state of nature" is so bad, so "nasty,
brutish, and short" that human beings voluntarily come together to
form tribes. In joining a tribe, the members agree to give up some
freedoms that exist in the state of nature (e.g., stealing, murdering)
in exchange for the collective protections and rights secured by the
tribe (e.g., the right to not be murdered or burglarized). The social
contractarian school of thought is the explicit source of the United
States Constitution and the legal system that we enjoy. Indeed, Thomas
Jefferson was a Deistic Humanist who edited the Christian scriptures,
removing all miracles and supernatural phenomena, and leaving only
what he saw as valuable: the moral teachings of Jesus of Nazareth. Ben

Franklin, George Washington, James Madison, and John Adams, who famously signed the Treaty of Tripoli, which states that "America is not in any sense founded on the Christian religion," were all Deists of a Humanistic bent. There are several definitions of Deism, but the most common one is the belief that God set the universe into motion and let it run according to its own laws. Additionally, Deists are often skeptical about the afterlife. Indeed, in their time, Deism was the farthest they could push the theological envelope toward atheism or Humanism and not invite violence.[7]

Existentialist Humanists included Jean Paul Sartre and Albert Camus. Sartre's essay "Existentialism and Humanism" argues against the idea that people have a God-given human nature, either sinful or otherwise. He writes:

> Atheistic existentialism, of which I am a representative, declares with greater consistency that if God does not exist there is at least one being whose existence comes before its essence.... That being is man.... What do we mean by saying that existence precedes essence? We mean that man first of all exists, encounters himself, surges up in the world—and defines himself afterwards.... Thus, there is no human nature, because there is no God to have a conception of it. Man simply is.... Man is nothing else but that which he makes of himself. That is the first principle of existentialism.[8]

Albert Camus's novel *The Plague* is often cited as one of the clearest explications of a Humanist view of ethics. In the story, a young journalist, Rambert, is trapped in Oran, Algeria, a town that has been overcome with a deadly plague. Rambert is angry at the world because he feels like he is a victim. He didn't live in the town, so why did he deserve to be stuck there? In contrast, Dr. Rieux, the Humanist character in the story, recognizes the truth of the situation: no one in the town deserved to be trapped there to suffer the plague. My colleague from the Humanist chaplaincy at Harvard, Greg M. Epstein, in his book *Good without God*, writes, "Obviously, Rambert misses the point. Unless the plague is some purposeful, vengeful work of God … the residents of Oran, screaming and dying all around him, are no less accidental victims than a tourist such as he. We are all accidental victims."[9] The knowledge that we are all potential victims of bad luck drives Humanists to the conclusion that without a God to pray to, we must help our fellow human beings, or in the words of the first African American president, Barack Obama, "Change will not come if we wait for some other person or some other time. We are the ones we've been waiting for. We are the change that we seek."[10]

One cannot talk about the history of Humanism without mentioning the development of psychology, beginning with Sigmund Freud and his explanation for why humans believe in God. In his book *The Future of an Illusion*, Freud writes:

> The gods retain their threefold task: they must exorcize the terrors of nature, they must reconcile men to the cruelty of Fate, particularly as it is shown in death, and they must compensate them for the sufferings and privations which a civilized life in common has imposed on them.... [People who do not believe in God] will, it is true, find themselves in a difficult situation. They will have to admit to themselves the full extent of their helplessness and their insignificance in the machinery of the universe; they can no longer be the centre of creation, no longer the object of tender care on the part of a beneficent Providence. They will be in the same position as a child who has left the parental house where he was so warm and comfortable. But surely infantilism is destined to be surmounted. Men cannot remain children for ever; they must in the end go out into "hostile life."[11]

Before Charles Darwin and his theory of evolution by survival of the fittest, atheists and Humanists had no solid answer for how life came to exist in such various and diverse forms. Darwin's own theory was so revolutionary, so transformative of humankind's understanding of nature, that he himself had trouble understanding how God could possibly have chosen the savage brutality of the evolutionary struggle in nature as the mechanism for the creation of the diversity of life. He wrote in *On the Origin of Species*:

> But I own that I cannot see ... evidence of design and beneficence on all sides of us. There seems to me too much misery in the world. I cannot persuade myself

that a beneficent and omnipotent God would have designedly created the Ichneumonidæ with the express intention of their feeding within the living bodies of caterpillars, or that a cat should play with mice.[12]

BASIC TEACHINGS OF TWENTY-FIRST-CENTURY HUMANISM

Let us begin with three definitions of Humanism, each of which highlights an important aspect of the Humanist philosophy. Humanism is (1) being good without god (popularized by the Humanist Community at Harvard); (2) using reason, science, technology, and compassion to solve problems (popularized by the Humanist Community at Stanford); (3) a progressive philosophy of life that, without supernaturalism, affirms our ability and responsibility to lead ethical lives of personal fulfillment that aspire to the greater good of humanity (the official American Humanist Association definition).

The first definition is extremely brief but usefully points our attention to the idea of being a good person without a belief in god. In addition, it focuses one's attention on the importance of ethics to the Humanist philosophy. This is essential, especially because nonbelievers are often falsely pilloried as immoral because of their nonbelief.[13] The second definition of Humanism focuses on Humanism's problem-solving dimension. Inspired by the idea that without a god to rely on, human beings have to support each other, Humanists leverage their natural affinity for reason, science, and technology to ameliorate human suffering and to spread the benefits of science and technology around the world.[14]

The third definition of Humanism, while perhaps overly wordy and too detailed for most conversations, both encapsulates the two previous definitions while adding some additional information. The third definition introduces the idea that Humanism is a *progressive* philosophy that aims for a better future for everyone, as opposed to a conservative vision that hearkens back to a bygone era when things were better. Instead, we know, in part from the research from Humanist philosophers and psychologists like Steven Pinker in *The Better Angels of Our Nature: How Violence Has Declined Over Time,* that we are truly lucky to have been born in the times we are in. We believe that not only will the future be better than the distant past, but it will be better than today. This third definition of Humanism also addresses the idea of personal fulfillment. Again, in this concept one can see traces of Aristotle's thought, particularly the importance of *eudaimonia* (human flourishing). Finally, this definition points to the fact that Humanism is not a purely hedonistic philosophy for selfish people, but a philosophy that values service to others and human solidarity as part of the good life.

Humanism is a way to look at the world and a set of values. It sees humans as a part of nature and nature as self-existing, not created. It sees human experience as the best source of both our understanding of the world and morality. Humanists believe that human beings can live ethical and meaningful lives regardless of the existence or nonexistence of God. A serious commitment to Humanism requires, above all else, an ethical commitment to treating all individuals as having inherent dignity and worth—focusing ethics on the human—and a naturalistic worldview, at barest minimum the outright rejection of supernaturalism.

Humanism also has an ecumenical nature. Instead of having dogmatic official positions like most religious organizations, Humanism employs the idea of an "overlapping consensus." Hence, while there is a great diversity of views among Humanists, we generally agree on the principles articulated in Humanist Manifesto III. I have reproduced that document in full, as it manages to define the Humanist perspective in clear and easily understandable language.

HUMANISM AND ITS ASPIRATIONS

Humanist Manifesto III, a successor to the Humanist Manifesto of 1933

Humanism is a progressive philosophy of life that, without supernaturalism, affirms our ability and responsibility to lead ethical lives of personal fulfillment that aspire to the greater good of humanity.

The lifestance of Humanism—guided by reason, inspired by compassion, and informed by experience—encourages us to live life well and fully. It evolved through the ages and continues to develop through the efforts of thoughtful people who recognize that values and ideals, however carefully wrought, are subject to change as our knowledge and understandings advance. Humanism is a progressive philosophy of life that, without supernaturalism, affirms our ability and responsibility to lead ethical lives of personal fulfillment that aspire to the greater good of humanity.

This document is part of an ongoing effort to manifest in clear and positive terms the conceptual boundaries of Humanism, not what we must believe but a consensus of what we do believe. It is in this sense that we affirm the following:

Knowledge of the world is derived by observation, experimentation, and rational analysis.

Humanists find that science is the best method for determining this knowledge as well as for solving problems and developing beneficial technologies. We also recognize the value of new departures in thought, the arts, and inner experience—each subject to analysis by critical intelligence.

Humans are an integral part of nature, the result of unguided evolutionary change. Humanists recognize nature as self-existing.

We accept our life as all and enough, distinguishing things as they are from things as we might wish or imagine them to be. We welcome the challenges of the future, and are drawn to and undaunted by the yet to be known.

Ethical values are derived from human need and interest as tested by experience.

Humanists ground values in human welfare shaped by human circumstances, interests, and concerns and extended to the global ecosystem and beyond. We are committed to treating each person as having inherent worth and dignity, and to making informed choices in a context of freedom consonant with responsibility.

Life's fulfillment emerges from individual participation in the service of humane ideals.

We aim for our fullest possible development and animate our lives with a deep sense of purpose, finding wonder and awe in the joys and beauties of human existence, its challenges and tragedies, and even in the inevitability and finality of death.

Humanists rely on the rich heritage of human culture and the lifestance of Humanism to provide comfort in times of want and encouragement in times of plenty.

Humans are social by nature and find meaning in relationships.

Humanists long for and strive toward a world of mutual care and concern, free of cruelty and its consequences, where differences are resolved cooperatively without resorting to violence. The joining of individuality with interdependence enriches our lives, encourages us to enrich the lives of others, and inspires hope of attaining peace, justice, and opportunity for all.

Working to benefit society maximizes individual happiness.

Progressive cultures have worked to free humanity from the brutalities of mere survival and to reduce suffering, improve society, and develop global community. We seek to minimize the inequities of circumstance and ability, and we support a just distribution of nature's resources and the fruits of human effort so that as many as possible can enjoy a good life.

Humanists are concerned for the well being of all, are committed to diversity, and respect those of differing yet humane views.

We work to uphold the equal enjoyment of human rights and civil liberties in an open, secular society and maintain it is a civic duty to participate in the democratic process and a planetary duty to protect nature's integrity, diversity, and beauty in a secure, sustainable manner.

Thus engaged in the flow of life, we aspire to this vision with the informed conviction that humanity has the ability to progress toward its highest ideals. The responsibility for our lives and the kind of world in which we live is ours and ours alone.[15]

TRADITONS OF SPIRITUAL GUIDANCE IN HUMANISM

Spiritual guidance is not necessarily a term embraced by many Humanists or other nonreligious people who are seeking the kind of counsel a spiritual guide can offer. However, Humanism does have chaplains, philosophical counselors, and celebrants who are recognized as companions for journey and facilitators for important moments and celebrations.

Philosophical Counselors

Though Humanism doesn't have a tradition of spiritual guidance, it does have a tradition of philosophical counseling, which is the rough equivalent of spiritual guidance for nonbelievers. The purpose of philosophical counseling is to help people address the problems and concerns that they're facing in a compassionate and reasonable manner. While Humanist chaplains are the only people recognized officially as counselors in this tradition, Humanist "laypeople" (or as we call them in Humanism, "people") also provide some "spiritual" guidance on an informal basis.

Humanists might be disinclined to speak to someone calling themselves a minister, a rabbi, an imam, or a reverend, since these titles send a message of religiosity that Humanists and other nonreligious clients may not wish to hear. As a result, spiritual guides who want to work with Humanists and other nonreligious people will have more success if they choose a secular title that isn't off-putting to Humanists, such as "philosophical counselor."

Humanist Celebrants

There are many forms of secular ceremonies, including the inauguration of the president of the United States, university commencements, courtroom ritual, parades, marches, and vigils. However, when it comes to honoring and celebrating important moments in life (such as weddings, funerals, and the birth of children), many nonreligious people are unaware that there are Humanist celebrants who can perform legal, official ceremonies for nonreligious people. The American Humanist Association's Humanist Society maintains a list of Humanist celebrants licensed to perform ceremonies in every state in the United States, as well as having referrals in most foreign countries, including England, Scotland, France, Germany, and throughout Scandinavia. Anyone interested in training to become a Humanist celebrant to provide wedding or funeral services for nonreligious people can apply for training from the Humanist Society (http://humanist-society.org).

Otherwise, please refer nonreligious people to that website to find a celebrant, after, of course, congratulating them on their plans to get married!

COMMON SPIRITUAL ISSUES FOR HUMANISTS

Some of the most common philosophical and theological issues Humanists will want to discuss include issues surrounding religion and their relationships with religious people; issues around dating, gender, and sexuality; and issues around making meaning in a world without god.

Religious Issues

One of the most common problems that Humanists face is trying to maintain relationships with religious friends and relatives, especially if those friends and relatives are religiously conservative. The pressure can come from two directions: either the religious friends or family members reject the Humanist for his or her irreligious beliefs, or the Humanist might begin to distance him- or herself from religious friends and family members. Additionally, some Humanists were raised in certain conservative religious traditions that emphasize concepts such as hell. Others grew up in traditions that exploited fear in the form of hell houses, for example, to intimidate children into belief and obedience. These Humanists, while they might intellectually know that a sky deity doesn't sit in the heavens, judging the wicked and punishing the good, might suffer from emotional or psychological distress from being indoctrinated to fear such concepts in their childhood. If this fear is sufficiently distressing, then, in addition to meeting with this person, encourage him or her to contact a psychologist with expertise in recovery from religious trauma or childhood trauma, and if possible, provide a referral.

Others might question their religious beliefs or may have given up most of their religious beliefs but call themselves "Christian Humanists" or "Deist Humanists." These sorts of people want to know if they have to reject all of their religious upbringing, traditions, stories, and values in order to become Humanists. This is a common stage in many people's de-conversion stories. Once they recognize that god wouldn't punish people who are authentically good with eternal judgment or punishment in the afterlife, they begin to think about how compatible their religion's beliefs are with Humanist values. Individuals raised in a liberal religious tradition will often see a significant overlap between Humanist values and their old religion's values. For example, Rev. Jim Wallis, the editor of *Sojourners,* sees clear similarities between the Humanist belief in the inherent dignity and worth of people and the Christian belief that we are all God's children and Jesus's social justice teachings in the Sermon on the Mount.

Humanists from the LGBTQ community face additional challenges, particularly from socially or religiously conservative relatives and friends who might regard homosexuality as "sinful," "morally wrong," or "disordered." One of the defining aspects of Humanism is the value it places on individual freedom. Quoting from Humanist Manifesto III: "We are committed to treating each person as having inherent worth and dignity, and to making informed choices in a context of freedom consonant with responsibility."[16] Treating someone with inherent dignity and worth means accepting them for who they are and for whom they love. From a Humanist perspective, gays, lesbians, bisexuals, transgendered people, and the entire queer community can and do engage in loving and fulfilling relationships. It is essential to support LGBTQ Humanists and their right to love whom they love. Reassure them that they are not sinners, that they aren't immoral, and that their love isn't disordered.

Issues of Meaning, Purpose, and Values

Some Humanists will struggle with the idea of finding meaning and purpose in life. They might point to the fact that our sun will eventually become a supernova and destroy the earth in the process or that the universe is destined to end in cosmic heat death. They may struggle with the fact that human life is so ephemeral, so fleeting, and that human beings as a species are even more fleeting still, in the grand context of the universe in which we live. However, Humanists should not despair. While it is true that we will all someday die, the fact that we do not live forever does not cheapen our lives and render them meaningless. Instead, the very fact that our lives are finite gives them more meaning. Though we will all die, and so, too, our planet, we can still find meaning and solace in our relationships with our fellow human beings. While our time may be brief in the grand scheme of the universe, our loves, our labors, and our lives have great meaning.

Social Atomization

We live in a time in which it isn't uncommon to receive and send more than two hundred email messages, phone calls, and text messages a day, not to mention all those Tweets, Facebook posts, and Snapchat pics. However, despite the 24/7 connectedness of contemporary life, many people feel like they're living in lonely bubbles. More than ever before, we travel out of state for education and work, often transplanting ourselves across the country into towns and cities where we have few, if any, personal connections. Further, as our work hours expand and we increasingly eat our lunches at our desks and our dinners in front of the television, sitting together to enjoy a meal and some company without being incessantly distracted by notifications from our smartphones is increasingly uncommon.

The solution here isn't to bemoan the advances of technology and hearken back to a simpler time before cell phones, the Internet, and the advantages of life in "the cloud." Instead, we might ask ourselves how we can use technological advances to bring us closer together. When used well, technology does a pretty good job of helping us connect. Social connection tools like Meetup.com and Facebook make it easier to plan and coordinate social events and to share them with others. This makes it easier to expand one's social network and meet more people with shared interests, beliefs, and causes.

However, just because technology can be used for good doesn't mean we have to let it invade our lives constantly. It is healthy to encourage Humanists who find themselves overwhelmed by the constancy of communication to set aside a few hours every day where they don't answer their phone or emails. Unplugging from the Internet for a few hours a day might help them feel refreshed and recharged, and thus more efficient when they return and reconnect. Many Humanists, myself included, recommend meditation as a particularly effective way of detaching from the chaos of being connected 24/7.[17]

Dating and Romance

As of this writing, there are more men than women in atheist and Humanist groups and organizations. While women like American

Humanist Association president Rebecca Hale are well represented in leadership in Humanist organizations, there remains a gender gap—approximately 60/40—between men and women. There are many explanations for the gender gap, but change is coming: the gender gap seems to be smaller among younger nonreligious people. As a result, the atheist and Humanist movement can sometimes suffer from men who seek to use atheist and Humanist groups to find dates, and perhaps, a future spouse, in much the same way that some religious people still use churches for dating opportunities. Unfortunately, this can result in some unwanted attention—often, but not exclusively, men flirting with women. If a Humanist woman comes to you to complain about the problem of men bestowing unwanted sexual attention on her at Humanist meetings, encourage her to speak to the community organizer to express her concerns. Tell her that the unwanted flirting or sexual harassment isn't her fault and that she shouldn't be made to feel uncomfortable among people who should be friends. (Of course, the gender of the person harassing or the person receiving the harassment is irrelevant. Nobody should be made to feel uncomfortable or harassed at a Humanist meeting.)

Sometimes Humanists may complain to you about the problems of finding a partner who is also atheist or Humanist, particularly if they're located in the South or Midwest. We've already pointed out some of the challenges involved in interreligious friendships and relationships, but it is important to clarify that Humanists completely and enthusiastically endorse relationships across religious lines. While such relationships certainly have their challenges, there are many examples of happy Humanists who are married to Christians, Jews, Muslims, or Buddhists. So, while it is reasonable to want a partner who shares your beliefs, it turns out that it's more important that your partner shares the same values. In assessing whether or not a relationship is worth pursuing, you should encourage Humanists to ask not "Are my beliefs compatible with their beliefs?" but instead "Are our values compatible?"

Finally, Humanists are generally quite liberal socially and tolerant and accepting of people involved in polyamorous or "kinky" lifestyles. Spiritual guides should reflect this same tolerance in order to discuss issues around dating and sexuality with Humanists. It is important to accept and support people for who they are and how they love—as long as their preferences involve *consenting adults*. In thinking through polyamorous relationships or when addressing sexual issues with which they are not familiar, guides should feel free to ask questions, as long as they are not judgmental questions. Guides who feel uncomfortable or unprepared to deal with these issues should probably refer clients to other guides who might be more comfortable addressing such topics. Building a network of fellow guides who have different specialties and experience is an important part of being a good guide.

SECULAR ETHICS OF HUMANISTS

There are many secular ethical traditions, but for our purposes, we will briefly consider seven major types of Humanist ethics:

1. *Consequentialism*: Moral decisions focus on consequences rather than rules, and actions with the least deleterious consequences are the best.

2. *Rule utilitarianism*: A type of consequentialism that formulates laws or moral rules based on a utilitarian calculus.[18]

3. *Social contractarianism*: Moral decisions are informed by the preferences and aversions of human beings; human beings form societies to protect their interests and preferences.

4. *Neo-Kantian deontology*: Moral decisions involve acting only if you would want all other people to act the same way you did in the same circumstance.

5. *Virtue ethics:* Moral decisions require finding a virtuous teacher and following the advice and emulating the behavior of that teacher (becoming "habituated"); moral decisions require acting to achieve *eudaimonia*, or "human flourishing."

6. *Care ethics*: Moral choices are determined by our relationships to other people and our caring for them; we have greater obligations to people with whom we are in close relationships than to strangers.

7. *Ethical intuitionism*: When most people see a human being suffering, they cannot help but sympathize with that suffering and will feel uncomfortable in the presence of someone in distress; ethics is as obvious as giving water to a man dying of thirst.

Drawing insights from these secular moral perspectives means that Humanist answers to ethical dilemmas will be interrogated by all of these legitimate moral perspectives. Humanist answers to moral problems must be attentive to the challenges raised by different schools of moral thought. However, Humanists might be troubled when they perceive serious conflicts between these various moral perspectives. For example, a care ethicist and a neo-Kantian will address moral issues extremely differently. In order to help a Humanist navigate the similarities and differences of the various moral perspectives, a spiritual guide will need to be familiar with at least the first six moral theories, as they are the most popular among Humanists.[19]

While the various secular ethical perspectives lead to different conclusions as to what one ought to do in a given circumstance, it is important to bear in mind that apparent contradictions between moral systems can be explained by their priorities. For example, the consequentialist perspectives are interested in making morality as apersonal as possible. It doesn't matter who the stranger drowning in shallow water is, you have a moral obligation to help your fellow human being. This insight, that people ought to matter to us regardless of whether we know them and have relationships with them, is important. People matter and our fundamental humanity unites us. On the other hand, care ethics rightly points out that relationships matter. A parent's obligations to his or her child are fundamentally different than that parent's obligations to strangers. The care ethicist rightly points out we would consider someone to be a bad parent if, upon seeing both his or her child and a stranger's child drowning fifty feet away, the parent chose to save the stranger's child. Relationships matter a great deal.

In thinking through these apparent conflicts between ethical theories, it is useful to remember the essay "Existentialism Is a Humanism," by the French existentialist philosopher Jean Paul Sartre. In the essay, Sartre asks us to consider a young man who is facing a choice: (1) to stay and take care of his ailing mother, who is completely dependent on him, or (2) to leave and fight with the French Resistance against the Nazis, trying to secure his and his mother's freedom. Sartre makes the point of saying that there isn't one right answer as to what the young man should do. On the other hand, he recognizes that whatever the young man chooses to do reveals something important about his character. The young man who chooses to stay with his mother reveals that he strongly values his relationship with his mother and his role as a caretaker. The young man who chooses to leave and fight in the Resistance reveals that he is committed to fight for his freedom and the freedom of his fellow citizens.

WORKING WITH HUMANIST AND NONRELIGIOUS CLIENTS: A SHORT LIST OF DO'S AND DON'TS

Things Not to Do

Offer to pray for them.

Be judgmental.

Quote the Bible, the Qur'an, the Bhagavad Gita, or any other religious text as if it were authoritative for Humanists or other nonreligious people.

Tell them God has a plan for them.

Try to convert them.

Try to get them to go to your church.

Try to argue with them about the truth of religious teachings or of the Bible, the Qur'an, the Bhagavad Gita, or any other religious text.

Things to Do

Sympathize with them.

Be empathetic.

Be a good listener.

Appeal to science.

Temporarily bracket your religious beliefs, and make an effort to view things from a secular perspective.

NOTES

1. Richard D. McKirahan, *Philosophy before Socrates: An Introduction with Texts and Commentary* (Indianapolis: Hackett, 1994), 364.
2. This theme of persecution for atheistic and nonreligious beliefs sadly permeates the history of atheism and Humanism.

3. "A Brief History of Humanism Thought: Classical Greece and Rome," Continuum for Humanist Education, accessed Dec. 1, 2013, http://cohe.humanistinstitute. org/intro-to-humanism/lesson-1-classical-greece-and-rome.

4. Humanists also endorse the concept of human excellence and flourishing but layer on top of Aristotle's somewhat teleological understanding of human development a view of human development informed by advances in biology, psychology, linguistics, cognitive science, and neuroscience.

5. Alagaddupama Sutta, Majjhima Nikaya 22 (M i.130).

6. Wing-Tsit Chan, *A Source Book in Chinese Philosophy* (Princeton, NJ: Princeton University Press, 1969), 116.

7. Many Deists feel comfortable in Humanist and atheist communities, where they find common ground over the view that god doesn't act in the world, granting prayers and punishing sinners. Deists and Humanists, while they completely disagree about the existence of god, find an enormous shared core of beliefs and values because the god that Deists believe in is so limited in scope that it might as well be a synonym for nature or naturalistic processes. Deists and Humanists agree that morality is a human creation and that without a god to intervene, we are the only ones who can help each other.

8. Jean-Paul Sartre, "Existentialism Is a Humanism (*L'existentialisme est un humanism*)," 1946.

9. Greg M. Epstein, *Good without God: What a Billion Nonreligous People Do Believe* (New York: William Morrow), 62.

10. "Barack Obama's Feb. 5 Speech," *New York Times,* February 5, 2008, www.nytimes. com/2008/02/05/us/politics/05text-obama.html?pagewanted=print&_r=0.

11. Sigmund Freud, "The Future of an Illusion," www.adolphus.nl/xcrpts/ xcfreudill.html.

12. *Wikipedia*, s.v. "Religious Views of Charles Darwin," last modified December 5, 2013, http://en.wikipedia.org/wiki/Religious_views_of_Charles_Darwin.

13. The two greatest philanthropists of our time, Bill Gates and Warren Gates, are both nonbelievers.

14. Great examples of organizations with a Humanist mission include the Bill and Melinda Gates Foundation; One Laptop, One Child; Doctors without Borders; the Leukemia and Lymphoma Society; and the Dana Farber Cancer Institute. These organizations promote the benefits of science and technology and do not mandate religious belief or disseminate religious propaganda.

15. "Humanism and Its Aspirations: Humanist Manifesto III," American Humanist Association, accessed Dec. 1, 2013, http://americanhumanist.org/Humanism/ Humanist_Manifesto_III. Used with the permission of the American Humanist Association, copyright 2003.

16. Ibid.

17. For more information about secular meditation, visit the website of the Secular Buddhist Association, http://secularbuddhism.org, or the Humanist Mindfulness Group on Facebook.
18. Utilitarian calculus refers to the idea of making ethical decisions based on what provides the best outcomes (utility) for the greatest number.
19. I have provided only very brief definitions, which need to be supplemented with additional reading; *Stanford Encyclopedia of Philosophy* (http://plato.stanford. edu) is an excellent online resource for people looking to learn about these philosophies.

Rev. Dr. Jim Lockard is active in the Centers for Spiritual Living organization as a member of the Growth and Development Commission and as the Disaster Relief Coordinator and is currently spiritual leader of the Center for Spiritual Living, Simi Valley, California. His most recent book, *Sacred Thinking: Awakening to Your Inner Power*, is now out in paperback. He received his bachelor of arts degree from the University of Maryland, College Park, and his master's degree from the University of Miami. He has served on the board of directors of the Orphan Foundation and on the board of advisors of the Foundation for Self-Esteem (Jack Canfield). Dr. Jim lives in Oak Park, California, with his wife and stepdaughter.

Spiritual Guidance in New Thought— the American Metaphysics

Rev. Dr. Jim Lockard

> There is a Power for good in the universe that is greater than you are, and you can use it.
>
> —*Ernest Holmes*[1]

The New Thought movement consists of a family of denominations, the oldest founded a bit over one hundred years ago, the youngest from the 1980s. Each of these denominations or "families" shares certain elements with others but incorporates its own unique slant.

New Thought should not be confused with "New Age," which is a term used for a Western spiritual movement of loose groups and diverse teachings. While there may be some overlap, New Thought is a group of spiritual denominations sharing a common philosophy.[2] New Thought is based exclusively on what might be termed "mental science."

New Thought is based on metaphysical principles that are ancient in lineage. Some essential ideas common to most New Thought philosophies are as follows:

- There is an essential Oneness of all things.
- God or Spirit[3] is infinite in its nature.
- Human beings are part of this Oneness, this infinity of all being.
- We human beings are creative by means of our thought.

- The laws of the universe are inviolable.
- Consciousness is the guiding force of all reality.

All of the New Thought denominations recognize the validity of science, including evolution. They see science as one means of proving the spiritual principles that have always been present in the universe and that ancient thinkers often stated. It is not unusual for discussions of quantum physics, string theory, and other current scientific topics to be held in New Thought services and classes.

A BRIEF HISTORY OF NEW THOUGHT

> In following the history of the New Thought we are
> therefore concerned with practical life. The intel-
> lectual movements of the new age do not explain
> its practical tendencies. We cannot account for the
> New Thought unless we learn the sources of the gos-
> pel of healing, without which the New Thought in
> its present forms would not have come into being.
>
> —*Horatio Dresser*[4]

New Thought arose in the late nineteenth century out of a variety of elements—American transcendentalism, spiritual healing, progressive Christianity, Christian Science, and a medical field that left many seeking other means of physical healing. There are Eastern influences as well, indirect at first, through the transcendentalists, particularly Ralph Waldo Emerson, and more direct in the mid-twentieth century as Buddhist and Hindu principles began to take hold on the American scene. New Thought people study all scriptures, philosophies, and theologies, as well as science, to determine what are the best and most powerful concepts, practices, and technologies to use in their lives.

The "father" of New Thought is generally considered to be a man named Phineas Parkhurst Quimby, a New England clockmaker who learned mesmerism (the forerunner of hypnotism) and noticed that he could diagnose illness and facilitate healings through suggestion. Quimby probably never heard the term *New Thought*, nor did he give any indication that he was interested in starting a spiritual or philosophical movement. His association with a young Mary Baker Eddy as a patient is the key link to later New Thought development.

The term *New Thought* is generally attributed to Julius Dresser and his son, Horatio, both of whom saw the work of Quimby as seminal in the formation of spiritual healing as a recognized methodology.

Each New Thought family has a founder, the most prominent being Charles and Myrtle Fillmore, who founded Unity, and Ernest Holmes, who founded Religious Science. Religious Science, also called the Science of Mind, encompasses four of the ten families of New Thought, including two that integrated in 2012, the International Centers for Spiritual Living and United Centers for Spiritual Living.[5]

THE TEN "FAMILIES" OF NEW THOUGHT AND THEIR FOUNDERS

Unity Worldwide Ministries	Charles and Myrtle Fillmore
Association of Unity Churches	Charles and Myrtle Fillmore
Science of Mind United Centers for Spiritual Living	Ernest S. Holmes
International Centers for Spiritual Living	Ernest S. Holmes
Agape International Ministries	Michael Bernard Beckwith
Affiliated New Thought Network	Harry Morgan Moses, Dominic A. Polifrone
Divine Science	Melinda Cramer, Nona Brooks, Fannie Brooks
Universal Foundation for Better Living	Johnnie Colemon
Hillside International Truth Center	Barbara King
Association for Global New Thought	Multiple founders

Several of the New Thought founders have in common a relationship with teacher Emma Curtis Hopkins, who was a former lieutenant of Mary Baker Eddy in the Christian Science Church. Hopkins left Christian Science and formed a seminary in Chicago, where she taught several of the New Thought founders. Ernest Holmes, of Religious Science, was not a formal student but had a number of personal sessions with her.

The New Thought movement grew quickly during the twentieth century. It has not grown as quickly over the last quarter century, which is due, in part, to the fact that many New Thought precepts—such as the focus on positive thinking, the idea of mind-body relationships, and the popularization of the concepts of manifesting and healing by such authors as Wayne Dyer and Deepak Chopra—have become more a part of the mainstream.

Since the inception of the earlier groups, there have been a number of associations of New Thought organizations, including the International New Thought Alliance (INTA) and the Association for Global New Thought (AGNT). New Thought adherents are notoriously independent, so all such associations and the organizations of the families are not all that organized. Free and independent thinking is prized in the movement. Even so, the associations have been effective in bringing New Thought principles to a larger audience. AGNT has facilitated a number of programs and events involving other spiritual, religious, and secular organizations on an international level. Two examples are the Synthesis Dialogues, featuring world religious leaders such as the Dalai Lama, and the Seasons for Peace and Nonviolence, coordinated initially with the United Nations and Harvard University and since expanded to an international scope.

As the movement has grown from its early days, it has become more cohesive in many respects. New Thought had the largest number of representatives at the most recent Parliament of the World's Religions in Melbourne, Australia, in 2009. New Thought groups are greatly expanding their world outreach through a variety of programs, ministries, and other activities.

BASIC TEACHINGS OF NEW THOUGHT

> The practice of the presence of God is the whole of
> Divine Science.   —*Malinda E. Cramer* [6]

The philosophy underlying all New Thought teachings is that God, or Spirit, is universal, infinite Intelligence; that all of creation is a part of or an aspect of this universal Mind; that all is One, and that human beings are creative by means of their thoughts, interacting with this One Mind. New Thought is a panentheistic philosophy ("God in everything and everything in God").

This philosophy is very similar to that of Christian Science. However, where Christian Science has strict dogmatic rules of belief, like restrictions on seeing doctors, in most cases New Thought has no such requirements of belief nor restrictions on behavior.

All of the New Thought organizations begin with these concepts and teach spiritual practices or technologies to bring each person into alignment with the greater Truth of his or her being. The largest groups are Unity and those groups that teach the Science of Mind. The major difference between the two is that Unity ministries tend to have more of a Christian perspective. In fact, Unity was originally called the Unity School of Christianity. Ernest Holmes, developer of the Science of Mind philosophy and the Religious Science movement, also considered himself a Christian and refers to Jesus more often than to any other individual in his book, *The Science of Mind* (1926, 1938). However, the descendants of Holmes (Centers for Spiritual Living and others) have become more accommodating of Eastern influences and have generally reduced their focus on the Christian perspective.

TRADITIONS OF SPIRITUAL GUIDANCE IN NEW THOUGHT

> We are unlimited beings. We have no ceiling. The capabilities and the talents and the gifts and the power that is within every single individual that is on this planet, is unlimited. —*Michael Bernard Beckwith*[7]

Spiritual guidance in New Thought is normally provided through ministers. Each denomination or "family" of New Thought has its own method of selecting and educating ministers. Normally there is a church or center headed by a minister or two or more co-ministers. Larger organizations often have staff and assistant ministers or lay ministers. In Religious Science, there are practitioners who are educated and organizations licensed to perform spiritual mind treatment or affirmative prayer for others, similar to Christian Science practitioners. Ministers are sometimes called pastors, spiritual directors, or spiritual leaders.

There are a variety of forms of ministry within each of the denominations, often including chaplaincies and "focus" ministries, in which ministers operate outside the confines of a church or center. These may include music ministries, social service sector ministries, and corporate spiritual support providers. There are also study groups that form in locations that are distant from a church or center. Some denominations offer prayer services via telephone and the Internet; both Unity and the Centers for Spiritual Living provide these resources.

The predominant form of ministry in New Thought today is in a church or center setting. These locally based organizations range from a few dozen members to many thousands, and it is these groups that are reaching out via the Internet and using social media to expand their congregations. New models are also emerging with a focus on spiritual education classes, either in person or online. In such "teaching centers" there is usually no Sunday service.

The essential focus of all spiritual guidance in New Thought is to show each person how to actualize in a fuller way his or her own spiritual identity. The recognition is that only the individual knows what is best for him or her, but in order to discover that truth, one has to get beyond the conditioning of many years that commonly causes a person to develop false ideas about the self and the world.

SPIRITUAL PRACTICES IN NEW THOUGHT

> Words are also seeds, and when dropped into the
> invisible spiritual substance, they grow and bring
> forth after their kind.   —*Charles Fillmore*[8]

The main spiritual practice in New Thought is prayer, usually referred to as affirmative prayer or spiritual mind treatment. Affirmative prayer assumes several qualities that make it different from more traditional forms of prayer.

First, affirmative prayer assumes the infinite nature of God in that there is no separation between the person praying and God. Second, there is an assumption that God is accessed from within the individual. Third, since God is infinite, God is unchanging, so the prayer is to change the mind of the one praying to a belief that is more receptive to the good that is being sought. New Thought believes that when a person has fully accepted the good at the subconscious level, the good will demonstrate or manifest itself according to the laws involved. Fourth, affirmative prayer seeks the consciousness of the thing or quality desired (e.g., peace, happiness), rather than the thing or quality itself. When you have the consciousness of something desired, it will tend to manifest in your life automatically.

Affirmative prayer is very different from traditional prayers of supplication to a distant deity or prayers of an intercessory nature. New Thought principles do not include the use of intercessors (e.g., saints) or objects. All healing is done in the mental realm. God is accessed within, and that connection is never diminished or broken; the realization of that connection with the divine is what allows a person to realize his or her good. As Ernest Holmes wrote, "Let the imagination lay hold of it, let the feeling respond to it, let the emotion tie up with it, and let the intellect and the will give it form."[9]

Meditation is also taught in most New Thought ministries. The type or types of meditation taught would be up to the individual minister. New Thought also teaches a variety of other practices such as tithing and spiritual service. New Thought denominations do not have dogma as such, so there are no strict rules about what practices each ministry teaches or uses. It is safe to say that nearly all teach meditation and affirmative prayer in some form.

Spiritual education is a core element of New Thought ministries. Formal or "accredited" classes in each denomination are supplemented by other classes, small groups, and book studies. Ministers see themselves as teachers, and much of a minister's time is spent developing, preparing, and teaching classes. New Thought adherents often claim that "we are a teaching, not a preaching philosophy."

The goal of spiritual education is to foster a deep spiritual realization within each student of his or her divine nature. New Thought teaches that each person will realize what is already true about him or her—that each of us already has within us everything that we need to live a happy and fulfilling life, and that we have access to an infinite Intelligence that provides all of our experience.

HOW SPIRITUAL DEVELOPMENT IS UNDERSTOOD IN NEW THOUGHT

> Spirit slumbers in nature, awakens in mind, and
> finally recognizes itself as Spirit in the transpersonal
> domains.   —*Ken Wilber*[10]

There are a variety of developmental models used explicitly and implicitly within the various New Thought traditions. These models may be unique to each individual ministry. Some ministries are more psychologically oriented, while others more esoterically oriented. It would be safe to say that spirituality is generally understood in New Thought as a developmental process.

The recognition of spiritual development is mirrored in the structure of classes and workshops used by most of the New Thought groups. These are designed to meet the student where he or she is in terms of spiritual development and move the student along a pathway of self-awareness and spiritual practice that ultimately leads to a fuller expression of the authentic potential of the student.

In the Centers for Spiritual Living class structure, for example, there are four levels of classes, from beginning metaphysical thought and practice through professional practitioner and ministerial education classes. The four levels take a minimum of seven years to complete.

During these programs, students also learn practices such as affirmative prayer, meditation, service, and more. Each teacher has some degree of freedom in what he or she teaches beyond the principles of each New Thought tradition, so there is a diversity of concepts and practices that emerge from these training processes.

Students progress through greater levels of self-awareness, and the level of commitment to their practices determines how much transformation takes place. Each student has his or her own goal or goals and some degree of freedom in pursuing topics of study. Again, this varies among the groups.

A unique aspect of New Thought philosophy is its use of Western psychology in conjunction with prayer and Eastern practices such as meditation to provide the spiritual student with a developmental pathway to self-realization. Such practice is illustrated in two distinct but intertwined levels of approach. One can be called "working with the Law," which refers to universal laws governing how our thoughts become beliefs and our beliefs affect our life experience. Here psychology is paramount, as the student learns to reframe many beliefs relating to his or her understanding of reality.

The student learns to change patterns of thought and to create new beliefs about him- or herself—such as moving from a belief about personal inferiority to one of personal empowerment. The result of such movement in belief is a new experience of life. This movement is accomplished at this early level of development through learning techniques such as affirmation (positive statements of a desired belief) and visualization (the use of imagination in a directed manner). These techniques are then incorporated into affirmative prayer or used to create affirmative statements as one goes through the day.

Affirmative prayer is essentially a group of affirmations that are visualized by the student to build a new set of beliefs in the subconscious mind. This process is called a change of consciousness. The successful student changes her mind (beliefs) about certain areas of life and has a different experience of that aspect of life from then on.

This change in consciousness can lead to healing in the physical, emotional, and mental areas of a student's life and result in healthier interactions with the world around her and a greater sense of the Truth of her being.

The student is taught to use these techniques to greater and greater effect over time. Often related practices such as meditation, tithing, conscious kindness, and service to others are taught and encouraged.

Over time, the student reprograms her mind, creating a mind-set and a worldview that is based on an empowered idea of herself and her relation to an Infinite Spirit. The underlying belief is always that Spirit, or God, is the only Source and that everyone and everything exists within the expression of Spirit. The student learns that by realigning her consciousness, her subconscious mind gives direction to the expression of Spirit, creating her experience of life.

The student is encouraged to monitor her experience of life as she goes through her day, noticing when she is feeling positive and when she is feeling negative, and to use this feedback to adjust her thinking to create and reinforce beliefs that lead to the positive experiences.

The student learns that her experience of life is dependent on her and her alone.

The second level of approach is what might be called "courting the Beloved," or seeking a closer relationship with Spirit. This approach is mystically based, meaning that one experiences a much deeper sense of the Divine through practices designed to take the student deeper into the experience of the mystical self.

New Thought philosophy teaches that everything is mystical, that is, everything is fully or wholly Spirit. Our experience as human beings is one of separation, as our experience of reality is based on the input of our senses. Our senses give us the experience of physical separation but do not detect the more subtle levels of energy that exist. These more subtle energies are connected to the One Source—God.

So, the mystical approach to New Thought is cultivated throughout the student's education in metaphysical principles. Often, the student must do the work with the Law to put himself into a psychological state where he can accept the ideas of Oneness and of his own mystical nature. Affirmative prayer is one technique that cultivates both approaches—working with the Law and courting the Beloved. However, meditation and contemplation, two more passive practices, really support the cultivation of the mystical self. Stillness and silence are the ground from which individuals realize the mystical. Whereas students often make significant changes in their relationship to the Law very quickly, demonstrating new conditions in their lives, the experiences associated with courting the Beloved are more elusive. It may take years or even decades of doing practices before a student recognizes the depth of his or her mystical nature.

These two approaches are intertwined in the New Thought educational approach. The various families of New Thought and the individual ministers and teachers within each family will, of course, have their own styles and may focus on various concepts and practices differently.

The objective for the New Thought adherent is to realize his divine nature and to incorporate that realization into the psyche so that his experience of life is enhanced and so that he develops the capacity to express himself naturally and easily from an empowered self-concept. This ideally translates to an adherent's more creative expression of his life that results in being of service to humanity.

There is a long tradition of recognizing developmental levels in religious practices. Often, ancient writers preserved certain teachings for "adepts," or people who had attained a certain level of understanding. This is evident in the Kabbalah, the Gnostic Gospels, and Hindu teachings, to name but a few. New Thought generally teaches that each person has the capacity to realize his or her spiritual nature right now but that there is a general process of growth through the practice of disciplines that are necessary for the deepening of awareness and realization.

COMMON SPIRITUAL ISSUES FOR PEOPLE OF NEW THOUGHT

Prosperity is a way of living and thinking, and not just money or things. Poverty is a way of living and thinking, and not just a lack of money or things.

—*Eric Butterworth*[11]

People in New Thought have the same issues as everyone else: how to live a happy and fulfilling life; how to overcome loss and adversity; how to heal physical, mental, and emotional issues; how to come to terms with the nature of the world and the universe beyond. What New Thought teachings offer is insight into these issues that includes the wisdom of the ages, modern science, and the development of each person's intuitive awareness. The central idea of Oneness is essential to helping people to develop as fully aware human beings. A recognition of Oneness can lead to the development of what is called a healing consciousness—the expectation of good in all forms.

There is also a focus on understanding the psychological principles relating to how the mind works in order to use thoughts and emotions to build beliefs. Individuals must understand the development of networks of beliefs in the subconscious if they are to make changes in their lives. All issues relate to psychology and the creation of new, more empowered beliefs that enable people to live more confidently and fully.

Following are some common issues that New Thought believers frequently encounter.

False Beliefs

A person may be struggling because he or she holds false beliefs that are holding him or her back. Such false beliefs might include that one is a failure, or useless, or inadequate. Limiting beliefs lead one to a limited experience of life. These messages create their own reality; they are self-fulfilling prophesies that can undermine a person's wholeness, progress, and success. A spiritual guide can help New Thought clients struggling with such false beliefs by helping them replace such beliefs with more truthful beliefs that recognize their intelligence and empowerment and affirm that they are the power in their own life. Spiritual guides can do this through the use of affirmative prayer, visualization exercises, spiritual education, and positive self-talk.

Poor Health

The New Thought movement originated at a time when physical healing was the dominant concern. People are still attracted to New Thought because of its practical approach to healing. If you are guiding a New Thought seeker who needs healing, you can help him or her by affirming the greater Truth: that there is no substance to illness and that a strong belief in health as the more natural order of things leads to a healing of the condition. This is best accomplished as part of an affirmative prayer.

Financial Insecurity

People are also attracted to New Thought because of its teaching of prosperity and manifestation: belief in yourself as a prosperous being in a prosperous universe has a positive effect on the condition of abundance in your life. If a client who follows New Thought teachings is struggling with financial matters, you can help him or her by affirming the idea that prosperity comes naturally and easily when he or she develops a consciousness of him- or herself as a prosperous person. One creates a vision of the desired result in the conscious mind and focuses on that vision, claiming it for him- or herself. Then one looks for opportunities in the world that relate to that vision. Again, the belief in New Thought is that you must first develop the consciousness of the thing or quality (peace, happiness) desired. That consciousness then leads to a demonstration of the thing or quality that you desire.

Relationships

How to be fully realized in relationship with Spirit, with yourself, and with others is a key focus in New Thought. The belief that all relationships with others are dependent on your relationship with self is a foundational tenet. That relationship with self is, in turn, based on your relationship with Spirit or God. Through the alignment of these relationships, a person lives a coherent life and has many positive and powerful relationships. Using affirmative prayer and affirmations is a powerful way to change the limiting beliefs.

World Peace

New Thought communities are very focused on peace as an idea and on bringing that idea into actualization. Such communities believe that peace, like all qualities, must first be realized within, that when you are at peace with yourself, you can also be at peace with others. New Thought also teaches that affirmative prayer and meditation can have a salutatory effect on the conditions in the world. So New Thought groups pray for peace and also engage in various outreach programs to encourage the manifestation of peace at every level of humanity.

WHAT ADVICE AND GUIDANCE DOES NEW THOUGHT OFFER?

> All causes are essentially mental, and whosoever
> comes into daily contact with a high order of think-
> ing must take on some of it.   —*Charles Fillmore*[12]

We are all One, and as Ernest Holmes said, "There is a power for good in this Universe greater than you, and you can use it."[13] This means that each of us already has what we need to successfully function in whatever situations we find ourselves. We must first recognize that all is One, then we must accept that whatever is showing up in our lives is the perfect result of the Laws of Mind (that our consciousness produces our experience of life), then we must use our minds to allow the best of ourselves in that moment to emerge and respond to life.

New Thought does not teach a doctrine of redemption, that is, it does not teach that we need to be "saved." Instead, we are "redeemed," or awakened, by coming to know what is eternally true, that each of us is fully spiritual and we have access to whatever we need within ourselves to realize joy, love, and success in our lives.

New Thought offers great hope for a fulfilling life by helping people recognize their own empowerment. In this regard, it is a highly practical spiritual approach to life. Your answers are within you, and spiritual guidance from another can, at best, point you within in such a way that you can more readily realize what is already there.

THINGS TO KEEP IN MIND WHEN GUIDING PEOPLE OF NEW THOUGHT

> There is Good for you and you ought to have it!
> —*Emma Curtis Hopkins*[14]

People in New Thought develop a profound sense of their own empowerment, which leads to a sense of personal responsibility. They also recognize that all is One, so they see the Divine in everyone and everything. This allows them effectively to heal their lives and to be a positive influence on others, while at the same time recognizing the essential integrity in each person. This perspective is developed through increased awareness and through spiritual practices like affirmative prayer and meditation. The goal is to develop yourself to the fullest realization of your true nature so that you are able to give your gifts in service to humanity and all of creation.

NOTES

1. Ernest Holmes, *Living the Science of Mind* (New York: DeVorss & Company, 1991), 18.

2. The number of New Thought denominations is now nine, as two of them integrated into a new organization in 2012.

3. The terms *God* and *Spirit* are the most common names used to refer to the infinite deity. Others include *Universal Intelligence, Universal Mind, Mind, Life,* and *Love.* I will use *God* in this article.

4. Horatio W. Dresser, *A History of the New Thought Movement* (New York: Thomas Y. Crowell, 1919; electronic edition by Cornerstone Publishing, 2001).

5. An excellent reference work to the history of New Thought is Charles S. Braden, *Spirits in Rebellion* (Dallas: Southern Methodist University Press, 1963).

6. Malinda E. Cramer, *Divine Science and Healing* (San Francisco: Home College of Divine Science, 1905), 16.

7. James K. Walker and Bob Waldrep, *The Truth Behind the Secret* (Eugene, OR: Harvest House, 2007), 119.

8. Charles Fillmore, *Prosperity* (Unity Village, MO: Unity Books, 1936), 64.

9. Ernest Holmes, "There Is a Power and You Can Use It," *Science of Mind Magazine,* June 1996, 19.

10. Ken Wilber, *A Brief History of Everything* (Boston: Shambala, 1996), 370.

11. Eric Butterworth, *Spiritual Economics* (Unity Village, MO: Unity Books, 1983), preface.

12. Fillmore, *Prosperity,* 23.

13. Ernest Holmes, *This Thing Called You* [1948] (New York: Jeremy P. Tarcher/Putnam, 2007), 179.

14. Emma Curtis Hopkins, *Scientific Christian Mental Practice* [1888] (New York: Cosimo, 18.

RESOURCES

Barker, Raymond Charles. *The Power of Decision: A Step-By-Step Program to Overcome Indecision and Live Without Failure Forever.* New York: Putnam, 1968.

Fillmore, Charles. *Prosperity* [1936]. Many editions available.

Holmes, Ernest. *The Science of Mind.* New York: Tarcher Putnam, 1938.

Hopkins, Emma Curtis. *High Mysticism.* Cornwall Bridge, CT: High Watch Fellowship, 1983.

Troward, Thomas. *The Edinburgh and Dore Lectures on Mental Science.* Camarillo, CA: DeVorss and Company, 1989.

Rev. John R. Mabry, PhD, is a writer and a United Church of Christ pastor. He is the director of the Interfaith Spiritual Direction Certificate Program at the Chaplaincy Institute in Berkeley, California. He is the author of several books on spiritual guidance and ministry, including *Faith Styles: Ways People Believe*, *Noticing the Divine: An Introduction to Interfaith Spiritual Guidance*, and *Faithful Generations: Effective Ministry across Generational Lines*.

Spiritual Guidance for Spiritual Eclectics

Rev. John R. Mabry, PhD

I am a Christian, but most of my spiritual direction clients are not. They, like most of my students, fall into a category that did not even exist fifty years ago. They are part of the fastest-growing religious demographic on the planet: Spiritual Eclectics.[1] Thirty-three percent of Americans today identify themselves as "spiritual but not religious,"[2] and while not all of these are Spiritual Eclectics, a good many would fit into this category.

Spiritual Eclectics are people who are serious about their spiritual paths who, in their pursuit of authentic spirituality, do not limit themselves to the practice of a single spiritual tradition. Instead, they draw from the wisdom, beliefs, and practices of many different spiritual, philosophical, and humanist traditions, weaving together a unique spirituality that is idiosyncratic, yet possesses an integrity that they cannot find in an "off the rack" religious tradition.

While there may indeed have been people who were spiritually eclectic sixty years ago in postwar America, few would have trumpeted the fact. This was an era when liberal Protestantism reigned supreme, and everyone was religious or tried to appear so. Religion was part of the "ideal suburban American life" that the Baby Boomers rebelled against in their youth.

This rebellion had a religious dimension to it. The children of the 1960s rejected every aspect of life that smacked of hypocrisy, the "show" of suburban religiosity included. Instead, the Boomers sought spiritual wisdom in uncommon places: Eastern religions, new philosophical movements, political ideologies, and what were previously thought of as "occult" sources.

Their approach to these new spiritual or philosophical ideas was different from that of previous generations. They embraced them even while keeping them at arm's length. Certainly, there were some that went "whole hog" into Eastern faiths or Spiritualism, but for the most part, Boomers had a "won't get fooled again" approach to religious traditions, no matter how groovy or exotic they appeared to be on the surface.

For such an idealistic generation, this skepticism proved healthy, and most avoided the gullibility that proved the downfall of some of their peers. Those who dove headfirst into Eastern traditions found that in their native contexts these traditions were just as patriarchal, sexist, abusive, and mired in "mindless tradition" as the religions of their youth.

Thus, as Baby Boomers grew into adulthood, they felt at liberty to take those beliefs or practices they found useful in a variety of faiths and simply leave the rest behind. From Eastern religions, they appropriated various forms of meditation, hatha yoga, and the chakra system. From Western religions, they kept the writings of the mystics, prayer, and angels. Also from the West, they turned to esotericism to provide discernment practices, such as tarot cards and spiritual wisdom through channeled sources. They held none of these dogmatically, but lightly, provisionally, weighing what worked and discarding what didn't.

This approach is not without historical precedent, of course. All religions appropriate elements of those traditions that came before them. All religions, when new, keep some of the elements of previous religions and discard others, usually in response to a cultural or spiritual crisis. But even new ideas usually crystallized into a new "dogma" or accepted teaching, an orthodoxy passed down from one generation to another.

Even specifically "eclectic" movements from the past eventually developed an orthodoxy. Consider, for instance, the Theosophical Society, which arose in the late nineteenth century, reaching its peak in the mid-war period of the 1920s. The Theosophical Society valued many of the same qualities that the Boomers did; they sought to select the best of the wisdom and practices of the world's religions and to simply leave aside the more dogmatic, exclusive, or problematic elements of them. They attempted to synthesize a "world" faith, drawn from the best that could be gleaned from both human and divine wisdom (*theosophy* means "the wisdom of God").

Before long, however, Theosophy articulated a belief system and created a new dogma that its adherents were expected to espouse. When Krishnamurti, the young man selected as the new "messiah" or world teacher by the movement, disavowed these teachings, the movement went into a tailspin from which it has never recovered.

The 1980s saw a new spiritual movement with much in common with the Theosophical project. The New Age movement valued many of the same ideas that the Theosophists did, but it did not articulate a specific set of beliefs. Thus, the New Age movement was a headless, amorphous movement, actually more a generational listing, a motion in a common direction, than it was a proper "movement."

Spiritual Eclecticism didn't end with the Boomers, of course. Generation X inherited the Boomer distrust of institutions, religious and otherwise, and amplified it to the tenth power. Their eclecticism is born of a refusal to bow to any authority and an innate opinion that all institutions are inherently evil. Unlike Boomers and Xers, the Millennial Generation's eclecticism is non-ideological. Many of them have had little or no exposure to religious traditions. Theirs is not a rejection so much as an understandable non-engagement with things unfamiliar. Millennials, overwhelmingly, are simply uninterested in religion or even spirituality. It's not that they consider these qualities corrupt, just irrelevant. The Millennials' eclecticism is less informed than that of Boomers or Xers, almost an eclecticism by default.[3]

The energy surrounding the New Age movement has dissipated since its early 1990s heyday, but its defining characteristics—and the Boomer Spiritual Eclectics who created it—are still very much alive and kicking. As they are entering later life, they are discovering another valuable practice from the Western tradition: spiritual direction. Boomer and, slowly, Xer Spiritual Eclectics are starting to come to us for spiritual guidance—whether one-on-one or in groups—in increasing numbers. Eclectics are also enrolling in spiritual direction training programs in order to become spiritual directors themselves.

PREVALENT BELIEFS OF SPIRITUAL ECLECTICS

Spiritual Eclectics may adorn their home altars with a staggering variety of divine images: Jesus might be cheek by jowl with Krishna, Shiva, Kali, Ganesha, or other Hindu deities; Tibetan *thangkas* may adorn the walls; statues of the Buddha or the Virgin Mary may be nearby. In Hindu fashion, Spiritual Eclectics are likely to see all of these as many faces of the One Being that is the universe. At heart, most Spiritual Eclectics tend to be pantheists: all things, all people, all deities are simply manifestations of the one animating force behind creation.

Typically, Spiritual Eclectics see little or no distinction between Creator and creation; they, too, are divine manifestations. Spiritual growth, for Spiritual Eclectics, is largely concerned with seeing through the illusion of separateness, uncovering the manipulative deceptions of the ego to experience and gain an increasing awareness of his or her oneness with all things.

Modeling their sense of purpose on the Mahayana Buddhist notion of the bodhisattva, Spiritual Eclectics find meaning in their lives through action on behalf of others, including the earth and its creatures. Spiritual Eclectics are likely to be activists or at least to be supportive of environmental and humanitarian causes, including those that seek justice and protection for animals. Spiritual Eclectics also see their purpose as being agents for political, environmental, and spiritual change. An important concept for Eclectics is "raising consciousness," educating and bringing awareness to important social and environmental needs, thereby advancing human beings morally and spiritually.

Spiritual Eclectics honor many sources of spiritual wisdom, including the scriptures and traditions of all the major world religions and many smaller faiths and individual spiritual teachers as well. They will also honor the works of poets, novelists, songwriters, and other artists, affording them equal esteem with more traditional sources. Above all, Spiritual Eclectics honor their own experiences, their own reason, and their own bodies as wisdom sources. Indeed, these are the sources that trump all others.

Just as they may honor a wide variety of deities, Spiritual Eclectics will likewise embrace a staggering array of spiritual practices. Yoga, meditation, prayer, divination, trance work, vision quests, shamanic journeying, rituals, and simply being in nature are all important spiritual practices for Eclectics.[4]

SPIRITUAL GROWTH FOR SPIRITUAL ECLECTICS

Spiritual growth schemas in New Age circles abound, and there are nearly as many models as there are Spiritual Eclectics. Nevertheless, the chakra system remains the hands-down favorite among Eclectics in some form or another.

Borrowed from Hindu and Buddhist teaching, the chakra (literally "wheel") system refers to a series of seven energy centers located in the body. As New Age teacher Anodea Judith writes,

> At the inner core of each one of us spin seven wheel-like energy centers called *chakras....* Chakras are organizing centers for the reception, assimilation, and transmission of life energies. Our chakras, as core centers, form the coordination network of our complicated mind/body system.... The body is a vehicle for consciousness. Chakras are the wheels of life that carry this vehicle about—through its trials, tribulations, and transformations.[5]

The seven chakras are aligned with the spine, each of them corresponding to a progressively more subtle and refined variety of spiritual energy as they ascend. Each variety of energy contributes to human wholeness, and conscious acquaintance with each variety—integrating its insights and powers into one's life—provides a systematic method for intentional spiritual growth.

A person usually works on awakening and integrating the gifts of each energy center, or wheel, in ascending order. One begins with Maladhara, the root chakra at the very base of the spine, related to survival and security issues. Next is Swadhisthana, near the genitals, governing sexuality and relationships. Third is Manipura, near the stomach, which concerns digestion, growth, and emotion. Fourth is Ahahata, located behind the heart, related to love, compassion, and devotion. Fifth is Vishuddha, at the throat, which is related to communication. Sixth is Ajna, the "third eye" chakra, located in the middle of the forehead, governing intuition, *gnosis*, and spiritual guidance. Finally there is Sahasrara, the "crown chakra" located at the top of the head, the point of unity with all things.

As a seeker pays conscious attention to each one, he or she appropriates the gifts of each in ascending order, leading to higher and higher states of awareness and consciousness. Thus, "raising consciousness" is a personal aspiration for many Spiritual Eclectics, as well as a goal to pursue in society at large.

The chakra system was popularized in the West through the writings of Theosophist C. W. Leadbeater, among others. Spiritually Eclectic writers ever since have pointed out correspondences between the Hindu and Buddhist system and other esoteric schemas. Most recently, Carolyn Myss's best-selling *Anatomy of the Spirit* illustrates correspondences between the seven chakras and the seven sacraments of the Christian tradition, mapping these to the seven levels of the *sephirot* in the Jewish Kabbalah.[6]

GUIDING SPIRITUAL ECLECTICS

Spiritual guides who work with Spiritual Eclectics will find them joyful and eager participants, at least at first. Their spiritual enthusiasm is infectious. This is in part due to the effervescent idealism that Boomers naturally bring to all that they do. Xer Eclectics will be more circumspect and hesitant, but no less earnest in their endeavors.

Spiritual Eclectics have a great advantage in their embracing of spiritual diversity. They are open to wisdom, regardless of its source. They are tolerant of many faith traditions,[7] and they are spiritually generous, slow to judge unfamiliar sources and traditions, and indeed are often curious. Spiritual Eclectics are often extroverted about their spiritual paths, eager to talk about it to anyone who will listen, and are unabashedly hungry for spiritual experience and knowledge. Partly because of this, they are often delightful clients for spiritual guides. If guides can "go along for the ride," they will rarely be bored and often surprised and challenged by clients who are Spiritual Eclectics.

Spiritual Eclectics also have some unique spiritual needs of which guides should be aware and tend to carefully. Spiritual Eclectics (especially in their Boomer manifestation) tend to be idealistic, wanting to raise the consciousness of the world, to work for global change, and to create programs or movements that will change the course of history. While these goals are noble, they are rarely realistic, and Eclectics can experience disappointment and depression when their ideas and plans don't succeed as they had hoped. Spiritual guides can help keep Spiritual Eclectics grounded in the here and now and help them focus their efforts on achievable goals that are still in line with their sense of mission and meaning. Helping Spirtual Eclectics discern the best use of their time and energy can be invaluable to them.

Spiritual Eclectics often have a difficult time because of their lack of groundedness in a particular tradition. One of the gifts of tradition is a long history of spiritual disciplines and practices, along with a family of ancestors who have walked this path before. These saints and mystics have left writings showing where the pitfalls and dangers are regarding serious spiritual practice, offering advice and often a "road map" around the difficult spots. Spiritual Eclectics, because they usually pick "a little of this, a little of that" from a variety of spiritual traditions, often don't go deeply enough into a tradition to avail themselves of these important sources of guidance. Also, when the going gets tough with an Eclectic's spiritual practice, the great temptation for a Spiritual Eclectic is to simply discard the difficult practice and move on to some novel practice, at least until that also becomes "difficult."

Because Spiritual Eclectics often do not have experienced mentors within a specific tradition guiding them, when they run up against these obstacles in their practice, they simply abandon the path instead of working through the obstacles. This results in a widely variegated, but all-too-often shallow practice that ranges widely but rarely goes deep. Spiritual Eclectics may become discouraged to find that every time they pick up a new practice, they eventually run headlong into the same difficulty. Spiritual guides can assist Eclectics by assuring them that this is to be expected and that spiritual difficulties are normal and necessary gateways to greater spiritual awareness. Spiritual guides can be invaluable mentors to Eclectics, supporting them in the absence of mentors from specific traditions, helping them to work through difficulties in spiritual practice, breaking through to new levels of consciousness and insight.

Spiritual guides can help Eclectics be more disciplined in their spiritual practices, holding them accountable for discipline in their practice, inquiring what is "coming up" for them as they practice, and suggesting practices that will be of help in a client's present circumstances. Spiritual Eclectics will resent an authoritarian approach, but as trust builds, clients will appreciate guidance that is offered, as long as they may freely reject such guidance.

Because of the lack of connection with a particular tradition, Spiritual Eclectics often find themselves without spiritual community. This is a painful situation for many Eclectics, who can't understand why it is so hard to find other like-minded folks with whom to meet. Spiritual guides can help their Eclectic clients by pointing out that there is no such thing as a perfect-fit community. It is a hard truth but can be liberating for Eclectics to hear it: if you are looking for a community that is a perfect fit, where everyone believes exactly as you do, you will have a very lonely spiritual journey.

Instead, spiritual guides can help guide Eclectics to find a "good enough" community. This will be a community that does not believe exactly what your client believes but will not be so far askew as to compromise his or her sense of integrity. It will be a community filled with flawed, sometimes hurtful human beings (because those are the only kind there are).

Spiritual Eclectics can often find community in movements such as New Thought churches (Unity, Church of Religious Science), which tend to be metaphysically oriented and nondogmatic. Eclectics may also find a home in liberal congregations of specific traditions— liberal Christian denominations (such as the United Church of Christ), Jewish denominations (such as the Reform, Reconstructionist, or Renewal communities), Zen centers, Sufi groups, and many others provide welcoming homes to many Spiritual Eclectics.

Spiritual guides can help Eclectics discern the reliability of spiritual sources of wisdom, since an "all-comers" approach to spiritual wisdom leads to sources of wildly varying quality. Are channeled teachings from a guy from Oregon really on par with the centuries-old, tried-and-proven insights of the Upanishads? There is a dangerous gullibility factor among many Spiritual Eclectics, and professional spiritual guides can remind clients that a critical approach to all spiritual sources is valuable and necessary.

Finally, Spiritual Eclectics have an Achilles' heel that any spiritual guide encounters before long: a spiritual perfectionism, born of the idealism so rampant among Baby Boomers. Eclectic clients often have an idea in their imaginations of how the spiritual life should look, and they become anxious, depressed, and discouraged when their own spiritual lives don't measure up to this ideal.

Spiritual guides can help clients by reminding them that "perfection" actually exists nowhere in the created universe, except in the human imagination. It is a fictional notion that we have used chiefly as a stick to beat ourselves up ever since Plato extolled it to the ancient Greeks. Spiritual guides will serve their Eclectic clients well by helping them stay grounded in the here and now of everyday life, reminding them that spirituality is not "out there" somewhere, but right here in the messy flesh and bone.

Spiritual Eclecticism is a spectacular spiritual phenomenon showing no signs of slowing down. Since Spiritual Eclectics often do not have spiritual communities in the traditional sense, professional spiritual guides can offer an invaluable service, as they can provide them with assistance that traditionally has come through community, such as spiritual mentorship, guidance, and accountability. Spiritual Eclectics make charming and exciting clients, and as long as the spiritual guide can keep up with their roaming, journeying with them will often mean covering a large swath of spiritual geography. For those who enjoy travel, this is a blessing indeed.

NOTES

1. The term *spiritual eclectic* was coined by Jurgen Schwing, a colleague at the Chaplaincy Institute in Berkeley, California, and trainer of chaplains at Kaiser, Walnut Creek.
2. George H. Gallup Jr., "Americans' Spiritual Searches Turn Inward" (February 11, 2003), http://www.gallup.com/poll/7759/americans-spiritual-searches-turn-inward.aspx
3. For more on generational spirituality, see John R. Mabry, *Faithful Generations: Effective Ministry across Generational Lines* (Harrisburg, PA: Morehouse, 2013).
4. For a more complete look at Spiritual Eclectic beliefs, see "Spiritual Eclectics," chap. 2 in John R. Mabry, *Faith Styles: Ways People Believe* (Harrisburg, PA: Morehouse, 2006).
5. Anodea Judith, *Wheels of Life*, 2nd ed. (Woodbury, MN: Llewellyn, 1999), 4.
6. Carolyn Myss, *Anatomy of the Spirit* (New York: Three Rivers Press, 1996).
7. The only exception to this is a common "allergy" to Christianity, due in part to unfortunate experiences of spiritual neglect, abuse, and hypocrisy on the part of some in the Christian community.

Inspiration

Finding God Beyond Religion: A Guide for Skeptics, Agnostics & Unorthodox Believers Inside & Outside the Church
By Tom Stella; Foreword by The Rev. Canon Marianne Wells Borg
Reinterprets traditional religious teachings central to the Christian faith for people who have outgrown the beliefs and devotional practices that once made sense to them.
6 x 9, 160 pp, Quality PB, 978-1-59473-485-4 **$16.99**

Fully Awake and Truly Alive: Spiritual Practices to Nurture Your Soul
By Rev. Jane E. Vennard; Foreword by Rami Shapiro
Illustrates the joys and frustrations of spiritual practice, offers insights from various religious traditions and provides exercises and meditations to help us become more fully alive.
6 x 9, 208 pp, Quality PB, 978-1-59473-473-1 **$16.99**

How Did I Get to Be 70 When I'm 35 Inside?: Spiritual Surprises of Later Life *By Linda Douty*
Encourages you to focus on the inner changes of aging to help you greet your later years as the grand adventure they can be. 6 x 9, 208 pp, Quality PB, 978-1-59473-297-3 **$16.99**

Journeys of Simplicity: Traveling Light with Thomas Merton, Bashō, Edward Abbey, Annie Dillard & Others *By Philip Harnden*
Invites you to consider a more graceful way of traveling through life. PB includes journal pages to help you get started on your own spiritual journey.
5 x 7¼, 144 pp, Quality PB, 978-1-59473-181-5 **$12.99**
5 x 7¼, 128 pp, HC, 978-1-893361-76-8 **$16.95**

Perennial Wisdom for the Spiritually Independent
Sacred Teachings—Annotated & Explained
Annotation by Rami Shapiro; Foreword by Richard Rohr
Weaves sacred texts and teachings from the world's major religions into a coherent exploration of the five core questions at the heart of every religion's search.
5½ x 8½, 336 pp, Quality PB Original, 978-1-59473-515-8 **$16.99**

Saving Civility: 52 Ways to Tame Rude, Crude & Attitude for a Polite Planet
By Sara Hacala
Provides fifty-two practical ways you can reverse the course of incivility and make the world a more enriching, pleasant place to live.
6 x 9, 240 pp, Quality PB, 978-1-59473-314-7 **$16.99**

Spiritually Healthy Divorce: Navigating Disruption with Insight & Hope
By Carolyne Call
A spiritual map to help you move through the twists and turns of divorce.
6 x 9, 224 pp, Quality PB, 978-1-59473-288-1 **$16.99**

Who Is My God? 2nd Edition
An Innovative Guide to Finding Your Spiritual Identity
By the Editors at SkyLight Paths
Provides the Spiritual Identity Self-Test™ to uncover the components of your unique spirituality. 6 x 9, 160 pp, Quality PB, 978-1-59473-014-6 **$15.99**

Or phone, fax, mail or e-mail to: SKYLIGHT PATHS Publishing
Sunset Farm Offices, Route 4 • P.O. Box 237 • Woodstock, Vermont 05091
Tel: (802) 457-4000 • Fax: (802) 457-4004 • www.skylightpaths.com
Credit card orders: (800) 962-4544 (8:30AM–5:30PM EST Monday–Friday)
Generous discounts on quantity orders. SATISFACTION GUARANTEED. Prices subject to change.

Judaism / Christianity / Islam / Interfaith

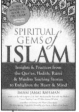

Spiritual Gems of Islam: Insights & Practices from the Qur'an, Hadith, Rumi & Muslim Teaching Stories to Enlighten the Heart & Mind
By Imam Jamal Rahman
Invites you—no matter what your practice may be—to access the treasure chest of Islamic spirituality and use its wealth in your own journey.
6 x 9, 256 pp, Quality PB, 978-1-59473-430-4 **$16.99**

All Politics Is Religious: Speaking Faith to the Media, Policy Makers and Community   *By Rabbi Dennis S. Ross; Foreword by Rev. Barry W. Lynn*
Provides ideas and strategies for expressing a clear, forceful and progressive religious point of view that is all too often overlooked and under-represented in public discourse.   6 x 9, 192 pp, Quality PB, 978-1-59473-374-1 **$18.99**

Religion Gone Astray: What We Found at the Heart of Interfaith
By Pastor Don Mackenzie, Rabbi Ted Falcon and Imam Jamal Rahman
Welcome to the deeper dimensions of interfaith dialogue—exploring that which divides us personally, spiritually and institutionally.
6 x 9, 192 pp, Quality PB, 978-1-59473-317-8 **$16.99**

Getting to the Heart of Interfaith: The Eye-Opening, Hope-Filled Friendship of a Pastor, a Rabbi & an Imam   *By Pastor Don Mackenzie, Rabbi Ted Falcon and Imam Jamal Rahman*
6 x 9, 192 pp, Quality PB, 978-1-59473-263-8 **$16.99**

Hearing the Call across Traditions: Readings on Faith and Service
Edited by Adam Davis; Foreword by Eboo Patel
6 x 9, 352 pp, Quality PB, 978-1-59473-303-1 **$18.99**

How to Do Good & Avoid Evil: A Global Ethic from the Sources of Judaism
By Hans Küng and Rabbi Walter Homolka; Translated by Rev. Dr. John Bowden
6 x 9, 224 pp, HC, 978-1-59473-255-3 **$19.99**

Blessed Relief: What Christians Can Learn from Buddhists about Suffering
By Gordon Peerman   6 x 9, 208 pp, Quality PB, 978-1-59473-252-2 **$16.99**

Christians & Jews—Faith to Faith: Tragic History, Promising Present, Fragile Future   *By Rabbi James Rudin*
6 x 9, 288 pp, HC, 978-1-58023-432-0 **$24.99***   Quality PB, 978-1-58023-717-8 **$18.99***

Christians & Jews in Dialogue: Learning in the Presence of the Other   *By Mary C. Boys and Sara S. Lee; Foreword by Dorothy C. Bass*   6 x 9, 240 pp, Quality PB, 978-1-59473-254-6 **$18.99**

InterActive Faith: The Essential Interreligious Community-Building Handbook
Edited by Rev. Bud Heckman with Rori Picker Neiss; Foreword by Rev. Dirk Ficca
6 x 9, 304 pp, Quality PB, 978-1-59473-273-7 **$16.99**; HC, 978-1-59473-237-9 **$29.99**

The Jewish Approach to God: A Brief Introduction for Christians
By Rabbi Neil Gillman, PhD 5½ x 8½, 192 pp, Quality PB, 978-1-58023-190-9 **$16.95***

The Jewish Approach to Repairing the World (*Tikkun Olam*): A Brief Introduction for Christians *By Rabbi Elliot N. Dorff, PhD, with Rev. Cory Willson*
5½ x 8½, 256 pp, Quality PB, 978-1-58023-349-1 **$16.99***

The Jewish Connection to Israel, the Promised Land: A Brief Introduction for Christians *By Rabbi Eugene Korn, PhD* 5½ x 8½, 192 pp, Quality PB, 978-1-58023-318-7 **$14.99***

Jewish Holidays: A Brief Introduction for Christians *By Rabbi Kerry M. Olitzky and Rabbi Daniel Judson* 5½ x 8½, 176 pp, Quality PB, 978-1-58023-302-6 **$16.99***

Jewish Ritual: A Brief Introduction for Christians
By Rabbi Kerry M. Olitzky and Rabbi Daniel Judson 5½ x 8½, 144 pp, Quality PB, 978-1-58023-210-4 **$14.99***

Jewish Spirituality: A Brief Introduction for Christians *By Rabbi Lawrence Kushner*
5½ x 8½, 112 pp, Quality PB, 978-1-58023-150-3 **$12.95***

* A book from Jewish Lights, SkyLight Paths' sister imprint

Professional Spiritual & Pastoral Care Resources

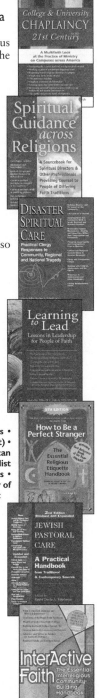

College & University Chaplaincy in the 21st Century
A Multifaith Look at the Practice of Ministry on Campuses across America
Edited by The Rev. Dr. Lucy Forster-Smith
Examines experiences and perspectives that arise at the intersection of religious practice, distinct campus culture, student counseling, and the challenges of the secular context of today's college or university campus.
6 x 9, 368pp, HC, 978-1-59473-516-5 **$40.00**

Spiritual Guidance across Religions: A Sourcebook for Spiritual Directors and Other Professionals Providing Counsel to People of Differing Faith Traditions   *Edited by Rabbi Stephen B. Roberts, MBA, MHL, BCJC*
This comprehensive professional resource offers valuable information for providing spiritual guidance to people from a wide variety of faith traditions. Covers the world's major faith traditions as well as interfaith, blended and independent approaches to spirituality.
6 x 9, 480 pp, HC, 978-1-59473-312-3 **$50.00**

Disaster Spiritual Care
Practical Clergy Responses to Community, Regional and National Tragedy
Edited by Rabbi Stephen B. Roberts, BCJC, and Rev. Willard W.C. Ashley, Sr., DMin, DH
The definitive guidebook for counseling not only the victims of disaster but also the clergy and caregivers who are called to service in the wake of crisis.
6 x 9, 384 pp, HC, 978-1-59473-240-9 **$50.00**

Learning to Lead: Lessons in Leadership for People of Faith
Edited by Rev. Williard W.C. Ashley Sr., MDiv, DMin, DH
In this multifaith, cross-cultural and comprehensive resource for both clergy and lay persons, contributors who are experts in the field explore how to engage spiritual leaders and teach them how to bring healing, faith, justice and support to communities and congregations.
6 x 9, 384 pp, HC, 978-1-59473-432-8 **$40.00**

How to Be a Perfect Stranger, 5th Edition
The Essential Religious Etiquette Handbook
Edited by Stuart M. Matlins and Arthur J. Magida
The indispensable guidebook to help the well-meaning guest when visiting other people's religious ceremonies. Covers: **African American Methodist Churches • Assemblies of God • Bahá'í Faith • Baptist • Buddhist • Christian Church (Disciples of Christ) • Christian Science (Church of Christ, Scientist) • Churches of Christ • Episcopalian and Anglican • Hindu • Islam • Jehovah's Witnesses • Jewish • Lutheran • Mennonite/Amish • Methodist • Mormon (Church of Jesus Christ of Latter-day Saints) • Native American/First Nations • Orthodox Churches • Pentecostal Church of God • Presbyterian • Quaker (Religious Society of Friends) • Reformed Church in America/Canada • Roman Catholic • Seventh-day Adventist • Sikh • Unitarian Universalist • United Church of Canada • United Church of Christ**
6 x 9, 432 pp, Quality PB, 978-1-59473-294-2 **$19.99**

"The things Miss Manners forgot to tell us about religion."
—*Los Angeles Times*

The Perfect Stranger's Guide to Funerals and Grieving Practices
A Guide to Etiquette in Other People's Religious Ceremonies
Edited by Stuart M. Matlins   6 x 9, 240 pp, Quality PB, 978-1-893361-20-1 **$16.95**

Jewish Pastoral Care, 2nd Edition: A Practical Handbook from Traditional & Contemporary Sources   *Edited by Rabbi Dayle A. Friedman, MSW, MAJCS, BCC*
6 x 9, 528 pp, Quality PB, 978-1-58023-427-6 **$30.00**
(A book from Jewish Lights, SkyLight Paths' sister imprint)

Caresharing: A Reciprocal Approach to Caregiving and Care Receiving in the Complexities of Aging, Illness or Disability   *By Marty Richards*
6 x 9, 256 pp, Quality PB, 978-1-59473-286-7 **$16.99**; HC, 978-1-59473-247-8 **$24.99**

InterActive Faith: The Essential Interreligious Community-Building Handbook
Edited by Rev. Bud Heckman with Rori Picker Neiss
6 x 9, 304 pp, Quality PB, 978-1-59473-273-7 **$16.99**; HC, 978-1-59473-237-9 **$29.99**